Borges's Poe

Borges's Poe

The Influence and Reinvention of Edgar Allan Poe in Spanish America

EMRON ESPLIN

THE UNIVERSITY OF GEORGIA PRESS *Athens*

© 2016 by the University of Georgia Press
Athens, Georgia 30602
www.ugapress.org
All rights reserved
Set in Sabon MT Pro and Whitney by Graphic Composition, Inc.
Printed and bound by Sheridan
The paper in this book meets the guidelines for
permanence and durability of the Committee on
Production Guidelines for Book Longevity of the
Council on Library Resources.

Most University of Georgia Press titles are
available from popular e-book vendors.

Printed in the United States of America
20 19 18 17 16 C 5 4 3 2 1

Library of Congress Cataloging-in-Publication Data

Esplin, Emron.
    Borges's Poe : the influence and reinvention of Edgar
Allan Poe in Spanish America / Emron Esplin.
        pages cm — (The New Southern Studies)
    Includes bibliographical references and index.
    ISBN 978-0-8203-4905-3 (hardcover : alk. paper) —
ISBN 978-0-8203-4904-6 (e-book) 1. Poe, Edgar Allan,
1809–1849—Criticism and interpretation—History—
20th century. 2. Borges, Jorge Luis, 1899–1986—Criticism
and interpretation. 3. Poe, Edgar Allan, 1809–1849—
Influence. 4. Poe, Edgar Allan, 1809–1849—Appreciation—
Latin America. I. Title.
    PS2637.3.E75 2016
    818'.309—dc23   2015023633

tered version of "Reading and Re-Reading: Jorge Luis Borges's Literary Criticism on Edgar Allan Poe," first published in *Comparative American Studies* 8, issue 4 (2010), makes up my second chapter; it is republished here with permission from Maney Publishing by way of the Copyright Clearance Center, Inc. I have received, from the Knopf Doubleday Publishing Group, permission to quote from Herbert Weinstock's reviews and rejection slips held in the Alfred A. Knopf Inc. Records at the Ransom Center at the University of Texas at Austin. Finally, the Estate of Julio Cortázar has granted me permission to cite an unpublished essay by Cortázar on Roger Caillois that is held at the Benson Latin American Collection at the University of Texas at Austin and an unpublished letter from Cortázar to Borges that is held at the Albert and Shirley Small Special Collections Library at the University of Virginia—Julio Cortázar (copyright © 2014 by the Estate of Julio Cortázar).

Many friends and colleagues have offered me constructive criticism on this project. I would like to thank my former writing group at KSU—Katarina Gephardt and Larrie Dudenhoeffer—for helping me revise three of my chapters. Thanks to John Alba Cutler for listening to my thoughts and for offering me new ones. Thanks to Brian Russell Roberts for his help with the book proposal process and for several useful ideas, especially with the epilogue. Thanks to Ashley Nadeau and Sean Ash Gordon for inviting me to present on a panel with them about Poe and empire at the 2012 American Studies Association meeting. Special thanks to Caroline Egan, Margarida Vale de Gato, and Scott Peeples for organizing with me, over the past several years, various seminars on Poe for the American Comparative Literature Association's annual meeting since these seminars have continually provided quality feedback on my work with Poe and Borges. Thanks to Bill Rice (my former chair at KSU), Sarah Robbins, Lois Davis Vines, and Stephen Rachman for writing letters of support at one time or another that helped me obtain the grants and awards that funded my research. Thanks to Richie Essenburg and Todd Frary, who served as my graduate research assistants at KSU during the first years of this project. Thanks, also, to Enid Zafran for the help with the index.

Finally, I would like to thank my family for their support while I wrote this book. Thanks to my parents, DaLon and Lisa Esplin, for teaching me how to work and for always encouraging my studies. Thanks to Marlene for her patience, for her intelligence, and for her consistent willingness to talk with me about this and other projects, and thanks to Moses, Anya, Ansel, and Edith for making our home both louder and more rewarding than any book project.

A Note on Translation

Throughout *Borges's Poe*, I offer citations of Spanish-language works in Spanish and provide translations of these citations in the text. The vast majority of Borges's fiction and poetry has been translated into English, but only a fraction of his literary criticism has been published in English translation. For Borges's works, I offer my own translations when the particular pieces have not previously been translated into English, and I cite published English translations when they are available. For the works of other Spanish-language writers and critics, I provide my own translations unless otherwise cited.

Borges's Poe

Introduction

Reciprocal Influence

No other U.S. writer has enjoyed the same level of influence on and affinity
with Spanish American letters for such a lengthy time period as Edgar Allan Poe. From early and anonymous rewritings/translations of three of his
works in a biweekly Peruvian newspaper, *El instructor peruano*, in 1847,
when Poe was still alive, to the influence of his detective stories on current
crime fiction in Buenos Aires and Mexico City, Poe has maintained both a
long-standing and widespread reputation throughout the region. Adored by
the *modernistas* at the turn of the twentieth century, respected by the writers
of the so-called Latin American Boom, and praised by contemporary or post-
Boom authors, Poe's presence in Spanish America has been constant from the
middle of the nineteenth century onward. His image and his import, however,
shifted during the twentieth century, and this shift is clearly connected to the
work of three writers from the Río de la Plata region of South America—
Uruguayan Horacio Quiroga and Argentines Jorge Luis Borges and Julio
Cortázar. *Borges's Poe* focuses on the second author in this trio and argues
that Borges, through a sustained and complex literary relationship with Poe's
works, served as the primary catalyst that changed Poe's image throughout
Spanish America from a poet-prophet to a timeless fiction writer. This book
also posits that literary influence runs both ways, since Poe's writings visibly
affected Borges the poet, story writer, essayist, and thinker while Borges's
analyses and translations of Poe's work and his responses to Poe's texts in his
own fiction forever changed how readers of Poe return to his literary corpus.

During his long life, Borges engaged Poe on almost every possible level in
both his private and professional lives and became a full rewriter of Poe in
the various manners described by translation studies theorist André Lefevere,
who claims that translators "have the power to construct the image of one
literature for consumption by the readers of another. They share this power
with literary historians, anthologizers, and critics. [. . .] Translators, critics,
historians, and anthologizers all rewrite texts under similar constraints at
the same historical moment. They are image makers, exerting the power of
subversion under the guise of objectivity" (6–7). Borges rewrote or re-created

1

Poe from each of these vantage points. He translated two of Poe's famous short stories—"The Facts in the Case of M. Valdemar" and "The Purloined Letter"—with his friend and occasional writing partner Adolfo Bioy Casares, and he published these translations in several well-known anthologies that he edited with Bioy Casares and other colleagues. He examined Poe in the literary history he cowrote with Esther Zemborain de Torres, *Introducción a la literatura norteamericana* [*An Introduction to American Literature*], and as a literary critic, he approached Poe in scores of articles, prologues, introductions, interviews, and dialogues. Finally, Borges directly and indirectly conversed with Poe's work in his own fiction and poetry throughout the twentieth century.

Borges began his literary career in the 1920s as a radical poet and a talented literary critic who challenged the aesthetics of the dominant literary movement of the time: Spanish American *modernismo*. Launched by the 1888 publication of *Azul* by Rubén Darío, *modernismo* was primarily a poetic movement concerned with beauty and art for art's sake. Although Darío was Nicaraguan, he spent a significant amount of time in Buenos Aires, and some of *modernismo*'s most important writers hailed from the Río de la Plata region, including Borges's fellow Argentine Leopoldo Lugones. When Borges returned to Buenos Aires in 1921 after a seven-year stay in Europe with his family, the young poet entered a literary climate saturated with thirty years of *modernista* literature, and he almost immediately challenged the norm by attempting to create an Argentine branch of the avant-garde poetic movement he had joined in Spain called *ultraismo*. Young Borges was particularly critical of Lugones, and although Borges's zeal for *ultraismo* soon faded, his disagreements with Lugones and the *modernistas* in general remained visible until much later in his career.[1]

The *modernistas* revered Poe as a poet-prophet, and as John Eugene Englekirk demonstrates in his seminal text on Poe's literary relationship with the Spanish-speaking world from the late nineteenth century to the early 1930s—*Edgar Allan Poe in Hispanic Literature*—this poet-prophet from the north was one of the primary influences on *modernismo*. Englekirk avers that "[i]n Spanish America Poe's fame as a poet has [. . .] long since outdistanced his renown as a writer of tales" (97), and he claims that "[a]lmost all of the followers of Modernism were directly or indirectly influenced by Poe" (146). Englekirk even suggests that Poe's work will never again wield as much influence in the region as it did with the *modernistas:* "[I]nspiration from Poe is by no means a thing of the past. But we must not expect to encounter any such palpable evidence of his influence as has been the case in our study of the Modernistas" (466). Englekirk's study slightly predates Borges's first attempts at fiction, and he only mentions Borges once, calling him a poet who radically departs from the aesthetics of *modernismo* (466). What Englekirk could not have foretold, however, was that this young poet would eventually transform Poe's reputation in the Río de la Plata region and throughout Spanish-speaking America by completely redefining Poe in his literary criticism as a story writer rather than a poet, by liberally translating and widely disseminating two of Poe's tales, and by responding to Poe in some of his most important short fiction.

Borges was not the first writer in the region to seriously and repeatedly approach Poe's fiction rather than his poetry. That distinction belongs to Horacio Quiroga, who published multiple Poe-like stories and openly claimed Poe as one of his revered literary models. The first rule in Quiroga's "Decálogo del perfecto cuentista," which he published in the pages of the Buenos Aires literary journal *Babel* in 1927, demands, "Cree en un maestro—Poe, Maupassant, Kipling, Chejov—como en Dios mismo" ["Believe in a master—Poe, Maupassant, Kipling, Chekhov—as in God himself"], and his fifth rule closely resembles Poe's own ideas on effect: "No empieces a escribir sin saber desde la primera palabra adónde vas. En un cuento bien logrado, las tres primeras líneas tienen casi la importancia de las tres últimas" ["Do not begin to write without knowing from the first word where you are going. In a well done story, the first three lines are almost as important as the last three"] (86–87).[2] Quiroga's fiction, with its horror, naturalism, and regional color, often deviates from *modernismo*'s aesthetics, but his career coincided with *modernismo* rather than challenging the movement. Indeed, Quiroga had a long-lasting relationship with *modernismo*. His first major publication, a short collection of poems titled *Los arrecifes de coral*, was a *modernista* endeavor, several of his close friends were well-known *modernista* writers, and he first discovered the jungle that came to dominate his life and his writing while traveling as Lugones's photographer.[3] As Englekirk argues, Quiroga was one of the most important fiction writers of both the Río de la Plata region and Spanish-speaking America by the early 1930s, and his fiction "inspired and guided" several of the "younger prose writers" in the region (368). However, Quiroga's work did not change the way his friends and contemporaries read Poe and understood his image.[4] Poe remained for the *modernistas* the melancholy bard with the tragic biography. Borges's literary criticism, his Poe translations, and his fiction first delicately and then blatantly challenged Poe's place as a poet and as a muse for the *modernistas* by emphasizing Poe's favoring of reason over inspiration and by focusing almost exclusively on Poe's prose while either ignoring or disparaging his poetry.

Borges's Poe carves out a unique space at the intersection between U.S. literary studies, Latin American literary studies, the specializations of Poe studies and Borges scholarship within the aforementioned traditions, and the field of comparative literature—a space that allows both Borges and Poe to function as literary protagonists whose work reciprocally influences one another. Poe scholars have long acknowledged the debt that Poe's current global and domestic reputations owe to his nineteenth- and twentieth-century advocates in France, but the field usually downplays the influence that subsequent writers from other literary and linguistic traditions have on Poe in favor of recounting the influence Poe has on the writers of these traditions. This tendency merely repeats at the microcosmic level the favoritism that U.S. (and British) texts often receive in comparative scholarship published in English, and it has created a negative effect among many scholars of Latin American literatures who see attempts at comparative literary scholarship in the Americas (whether performed by Americanists who define American literature as U.S. literature or by scholars who have embraced the transnational turn in American Studies) as academic imperialism, a disciplinary invasion in which English departments occupy the territory of Latin American literature.[5] Ironically, Poe studies as typically practiced in Spanish also fetishizes Poe as influence rather than confronting what Spanish American writers have done with/to Poe.

Over the past thirty years, however, several literary critics in various traditions have juxtaposed Borges's and Poe's oeuvres in a more even-handed manner that emphasizes the stature of each writer rather than treating Poe as source and Borges as receptacle.[6] The most notable work in this field of Borges/Poe scholarship includes Maurice J. Bennett's article "The Detective Fiction of Poe and Borges," which offers one of the earliest comparative readings of Borges's famous story "La muerte y la brújula" ["Death and the Compass"] alongside Poe's Dupin trilogy, and John T. Irwin's interdisciplinary tour de force, *The Mystery to a Solution: Poe, Borges, and the Analytic Detective Story*, which examines everything from chess theory to Greek mythology and from psychoanalysis to advanced mathematics to reveal Borges's centennial doubling of the Dupin tales with his own trio of detective stories. Most Borges/Poe scholarship, including the work of Bennett and Irwin, focuses primarily on the fiction of each author while only occasionally referring to their critical writings, and the vast majority of these publications revolve around the detective genre itself while leaving other themes and issues from each writer's fiction and their literary criticism in general on the periphery of the conversation.[7] Furthermore, works that couple Borges and Poe typically avoid specific discussions of either author's particular American context. Much Borges/Poe scholarship—especially the scholarship available in English—reads Borges as a world writer reacting to Poe as both a precursor and a literary peer while deemphasizing the cultural context in which Borges interprets Poe.

Borges's Poe avoids the paternalistic approach of some Poe studies scholarship, in both English and Spanish, and the imperialistic specter of some comparative American literary studies by emphasizing Borges's role in the Borges/

Poe relationship. This book engages and expands the conversations in current Borges/Poe scholarship by exploring the connections between Borges's and Poe's literary criticism, by analyzing Borges's Poe translations and his success anthologizing those translations, and by examining several of each writer's nondetective stories. This study also approaches archival materials that have received little to no coverage in other Borges/Poe scholarship, including the handwritten notes Borges made in his personal copies of various editions of Poe's works. Finally, *Borges's Poe* emphasizes the spatial and temporal context in which Borges interprets Poe—the Río de la Plata region from the 1920s through the 1980s—because Borges's influence on Poe's reputation occurs in and is most significant for this specific time and space. Although Borges first read Poe in English rather than Spanish or French, he offered his interpretations of Poe (particularly the readings he provided before 1961, when his reception of the Formentor Prize in France launched him onto the global stage) to *porteño*, national, and regional audiences in Buenos Aires's largest daily newspapers, *La Nación* and *La Prensa*, and in important weeklies such as *El Hogar*; and he delivered similar thoughts to a broader Spanish American audience in the literary magazine *Sur*.[8] In short, Borges's recasting of Poe is both local and transnational. His literary criticism, translations, and fiction alter Poe's image at national (Argentina), regional (Río de la Plata), and hemispheric (from Mesoamerica to the Southern Cone) levels, and to understand this shift in Poe's reputation, *Borges's Poe* highlights Borges's place as a national and regional writer who eventually becomes a global figure rather than simply juxtaposing Borges and Poe as two icons in the canon of world literature.

Borges, Poe, the Souths, and Southernness

Borges's Poe also refocuses inter-American or hemispheric American literary studies and the New Southern Studies by concentrating specifically on the direct literary relationship between Borges and Poe. Over the past two decades, the majority of monographs in these fields have offered analyses of shared histories or similar traumatic experiences between writers of disparate national and literary traditions.[9] For example, several important titles that bring a hemispheric perspective to the New Southern Studies—including George Handley's and Deborah Cohn's first books, *Postslavery Literatures in the Americas* and *History and Memory in the Two Souths*, respectively, Cohn's and Jon Smith's coedited volume *Look Away!*, and more recent books like Elizabeth Christine Russ's *The Plantation in the Postslavery Imagination*— all ground their comparative readings of U.S. southern, Latin American, and Caribbean literatures on a shared history of slavery, the pervasiveness of the plantation system, and/or the common experiences of defeat, occupation, and poverty that, as C. Vann Woodward argues in *The Burden of Southern History*, separate the U.S. South from the U.S. North and connect the U.S. South to most other regions and peoples.[10] To be sure, tracing these shared experiences across geopolitical and linguistic borders justifies the comparisons these critics make between disparate authors and literary traditions and avoids the type of disciplinary cannibalism that some Latin Americanists fear from comparative literary studies in the Americas, but the ubiquity of this stance in recent hemispheric scholarship obfuscates the direct connections that exist between certain writers.

Adopting this type of approach could also work for a project on Borges and Poe since both writers identify as southern in one form or fashion; however, calling Poe and Borges "southerners" reveals the shifting nature of regional terminology when approaching the study of literature or history from a hemispheric vantage point, highlighting how markers of place and the cultural connotations that may accompany them are always relative to the position of the person passing judgment. Both Poe and Borges are and are not southern writers in the geographical and cultural senses of the term. Geographically, Poe was raised in Richmond, Virginia—the northeast corner of what is typically defined as the U.S. South, although the city's latitude is fairly central on a national map, but a northern city when viewed from a hemispheric viewpoint. Culturally, Poe is often identified as a southern writer. Indeed, some of Poe's biographers, both from inside and outside the United States, see his childhood in a U.S. southern town as a key to his future literary output. For example, Hervey Allen identifies Poe as a southerner and speculates that he must have spent significant time listening to the stories told by slaves in the home of his guardian, John Allan, or in the slave cabins on the plantation. These narratives, Allen suggests, created a fascination with death and burial that dominates much of Poe's fiction (49–50). Julio Cortázar, citing Allen as one of his primary sources, also calls Poe a southerner in his short Poe biography, claiming that "creció como sureño, pese a su nacimiento en Boston, y jamás dejó de serlo en espíritu" ["he grew up as a southerner, in spite of his birth in Boston, and he never stopped being one in spirit"] (22). However, as Allen notes, many readers and critics ignore Poe's southern youth (49). For these readers, Poe's birth in Boston, his five-year stint as a child in England, his adult life in the largest cities of the eastern U.S. seaboard, and/or the proclivities he reveals in his works trump his early years in Richmond, his brief studies at the University of Virginia, and his views on slavery and aristocracy. For example, Borges, dissenting with Baudelaire and others who read Poe as "accidental en América" ["accidental in America"] ("Una vindicación" 13), goes so far as to claim: "No solo americano sino *yankee*, es el terrible y humorístico Poe: ya en la continua precisión y practicidad de sus variados juegos con la tiniebla, con las escrituras secretas y con el verso, ya en las ráfagas de enorme charlatanería que recuerdan a Barnum" ["Not only American, but *Yankee*, is the terrible and humorous Poe: whether in the continual precision and practicality of his varied games with darkness, with secret writings, and with verse, or whether in the bursts of enormous charlatanism that recall Barnum"] (13–14). Finally, neither Borges nor Cortázar mentions, probably because such commentary would seem obvious to them and to their readers in the Río de la Plata region, that Poe's southernness or lack thereof carries a completely different connotation than when the same marker is used to describe someone in Argentina.

Borges's southernness is equally problematic. Geographically, he lived in one of the southernmost metropoles in the Americas—Buenos Aires—but his personal and Argentina's national perspective do not include Buenos Aires (at least not the neighborhoods in which Borges lived) in what they call "*el sur*" [*the* South]. Culturally, Borges both wrote for and edited the prestigious literary journal *Sur*, and one of his most famous short stories—a tale that is often read autobiographically—carries the title "El sur" ["The South"].[11] Also, Borges's literary career began to blossom in the mid-1930s at the same time that Uruguayan artist Joaquín Torres García (recently returned to Montevideo after decades abroad) was calling, first to Uruguayans and then to other South Americans, for a southern school of art, claiming "*nuestro norte es el Sur*" ["*our north is the South*"] ("La escuela" 193, italics in original).[12] In contrast, although he consistently identified as Argentine—both in moments of pride and moments of shame—Borges always disconnected Argentina and himself from the so-called Latin America. He was an anglophile fascinated with British and U.S. histories and literatures, loved the English language, and occasionally lamented what he saw as his calling as a Spanish-language writer. Like Poe, he was and was not a southerner.

Apart from the contested southern identities of both Borges and Poe, comparing Borges's and Poe's souths also runs the risk of glossing over significant historical and political differences. Both authors are not only connected to *a* South but to a distinct *the* South—one that begins at the Mason-Dixon line and another that begins, according to Borges's character Juan Dahlmann, on the "otro lado de Rivadavia" ["other side of Avenida Rivadavia"] ("El sur" 525; "The South" 176) in Buenos Aires—and the histories of these two particular souths are not as similar as the histories of the U.S. South, the Caribbean, Mexico, and Brazil. Indeed, Argentina's history, with its frontier narrative of civilization versus barbarity, its policies that pushed indigenous peoples out of the civilized space rather than mixing with them, its relatively low number of slaves of African descent compared to its neighbor and rival Brazil, and its massive waves of European immigration, has much more in common with the history of the U.S. North and/or the history of the broader United States than it does with the history of the U.S. South.

In short, Borges's and Poe's southernness and the connections and/or disparities between the U.S. South, Argentina, and the broader United States lie outside the parameters and goals of this book, but that is not to say that *Borges's Poe* devalues inter-American scholarship that focuses on shared experience across borders. Rather, this book advocates for giving renewed attention to the literal/literary relationships between writers in the American hemisphere by analyzing Borges's and Poe's works and demonstrating how they impact each other through a complex literary relationship of two-way influence.[13] Instead of mapping out a shared or not-so-shared history between Poe's U.S. southern experience (or even Poe's U.S. experience) and Borges's life in Argentina, *Borges's Poe* explores the literary connection created between these two authors when Borges reads and incorporates Poe's work into his own, and it examines the impact of Borges's interpretations of Poe's literature and his reshaping of Poe's image within the national, regional, and hemispheric contexts of Argentina, the Río de la Plata region, and Spanish-speaking America.[14] My approach fits under what Gustavo Pérez Firmat once called the "*genetic*" method in his introduction to *Do the Americas Have a Common Literature?* (3), but it grants importance to the context behind Borges's and Poe's relationship, to the time and space in which Borges interpreted Poe, in a manner more similar to Pérez Firmat's descriptions of the "*generic*" and "*appositional*" modes (3–4, italics in original). In short, *Borges's Poe* is an influence study, but an influence study that emphasizes that literary influence is both multifaceted and contextual.

Borges, Bloom, and the Concept of Two-Way Influence

Borges, like Quiroga before him, discovered Poe's work at an early age and returned to Poe's texts often. Unlike Quiroga, however, Borges's literary relationship with Poe existed first outside of and then in spite of Spanish American *modernismo* and this movement's infatuation with Poe as tragic poet. In his "Autobiographical Notes," which Borges and Norman Thomas di Giovanni published in the *New Yorker* in 1970, Borges claims, "[i]f I were asked to name the chief event in my life, I should say my father's library" (42). Borges found Poe on the shelves of that library, and as a young boy, he first read Poe in English (42).[15] In two different dialogues with Osvaldo Ferrari, Borges suggests that he was purposefully morose as a youth because he wanted to be a Hamlet, a Poe, a Baudelaire, or a Byron ("La ética y la cultura" 268; "Sobre la personalidad y el Buda" 160). More important than this contrived attitude of youthful melancholy, Poe's influence reveals itself at various stages of Borges's writing and teaching careers, including Borges's penchant for detective fiction, his work as a literature teacher, and his preference for rereading rather than reading. Borges first called Poe the inventor of the detective genre in 1933 ("Leyes de la narración policial" 36–37; "Una sentencia del *Quijote*" 64), eight years before he published his first detective story—"El jardín de senderos que se bifurcan" ["The Garden of Forking Paths"]—nine years before he and Adolfo Bioy Casares released their collection of detective parodies, *Seis problemas para don Isidro Parodi* [*Six Problems for Isidro Parodi*], and a decade before translating "The Purloined Letter" as "La carta robada" with Bioy Casares for their anthology *Los mejores cuentos policiales*. Borges taught Poe as one of nine U.S. writers during his first teaching stint as "a teacher of English literature at the Asociación Argentina de Cultura Inglesa" ("Autobiographical" 85) in the mid-1940s after losing his municipal library post due to his criticism of Argentina's president Juan Perón, and he discussed Poe's life and his works in his and Zemborain de Torres's textbook-like *Introducción a la literatura norteamericana*. He spoke about Poe in various public settings throughout his career, including his well-known lectures collected in *Siete noches* [*Seven Nights*] and *Borges, oral*.[16] Finally, Borges claimed to have read and reread Poe up until the last years of his life.

Borges's early access and perennial returns to Poe cannot be overstated; however, any study on Borges and Poe must decide how best to tackle the complex concept of influence. The time-tried model of the influence study offers a one-way approach to influence by mapping the effects of an earlier writer or literary tradition on a later author or tradition. As previously mentioned, Pérez Firmat calls influence studies "*genetic*" and lists this approach as one of four methods for conducting inter-American literary research (3, italics in original). He moves beyond a simplistic understanding of influence by suggesting that a genetic critique not only uncovers literary or literal markers of influence but also analyzes these points of contact to elaborate on how later writers use the work of their forerunners for their own ends (3). However, Pérez Firmat's own terminology cuts against his definition since the biological baggage of the term "genetic" implies that a former writer passes literary traits down to a later author, regardless of the will of the second writer. The term itself suggests that the later writer relies on the former author to exist in the first place, that the influenced writer is his or her predecessor's offspring.

Pérez Firmat doubly responds to Harold Bloom's famous treatise *The Anxiety of Influence* by simultaneously arguing that later writers demonstrate agency in their usage of the works of former authors while labeling this same relationship in genetic terms that underline the concepts of literary parents and offspring that are essential to Bloom's theory. In a study solely on Poe, we could, and perhaps should, disregard Bloom's text since his well-known dislike for Poe—as seen in his scathing introductions to *Bloom's Modern Critical Views: Edgar Allan Poe* and *Bloom's Classic Critical Views: Edgar Allan Poe*—leaves few, if any, reasons for approaching Poe from a Bloomian perspective. In short, why use Poe's literature to question or sustain Bloom's theory when Bloom himself sees Poe as unworthy of serious study?[17] Further-more, Bloom's theory of influence—itself highly influential, especially during the 1970s and 1980s—appears to have run its course, and scholarship that grapples with Bloom's theory risks appearing passé. This debate, however, is crucial for *Borges's Poe* for three reasons. First, Bloom's theory on influ-ence, regardless of the fact that it has now fallen out of style, was the most prominent theorization of the concept during the twentieth century. Second, the concept of influence has still not recovered any of the positive connotation that it held before Bloom—it continues to connote competition, anxiety, and negative debt in the mind of most literary critics. Third (and most important), Bloom's entire theory is a misreading of Borges's thoughts on influence in "Kafka y sus precursores."

The Anxiety of Influence performs exactly what it claims to be theorizing. The later poet or theorist, Bloom, willfully misreads Borges's famous essay on influence, "Kafka y sus precursores" ["Kafka and His Precursors"], for his own ends and concludes with the Borgesian thought that John Milton's poetry demonstrates William Wordsworth's influence or that Walt Whitman's works reveal the influence of Hart Crane (154) only to openly state that the "*apophrades,*" or the last step in the process of influence in his model, is something different from Borges's idea "that artists *create* their precursors, as for instance the Kafka of Borges creates the Browning of Borges" (141, italics in original). Bloom begins the book with a nod to Borges in the first two sentences of the opening chapter: "Shelly speculated that poets of all ages contributed to one Great Poem perpetually in progress. Borges remarks that poets create their precursors" (19); he then offers a lengthy, six-step de-scription of influence as an oedipal struggle between later writers and their precursors that serves as a creative misreading and rewriting of Borges's con-ceptualization of influence; and he concludes that the last step of the process makes the precursors' work appear "as though the later poet himself had written" it (16). These last words sound very much like Borges's thoughts in the Kafka essay, but as I mentioned briefly above, Bloom openly sets out "to distinguish the phenomenon from the witty insight of Borges" (141) and, in doing so, performs the very apophrades he claims to be analyzing by making a statement in Borges's terms that now appear to be Bloom's. In short, Bloom's text *is* an example of the very concept he sets out to examine. One could argue that such an ontological performance actually strengthens his theory—that performing the theory while creating it helps to demonstrate its value—but Bloom's version of Borges's concept of influence appears much less radical and less attractive when read alongside Borges's Kafka essay.

The Anxiety of Influence, as its very title suggests, brings an anxiety to the concept of influence that Borges openly denounces in "Kafka y sus precur-sores." In this essay, Borges claims to see Kafka's influence in the works of at

C. Jared Loewenstein, the founding curator of the Jorge Luis Borges Collection, for talking with me in person, on the phone, and via email about the collection and about Borges the writer and the person. I need to thank Alexander Gilliam, Matthew Kelly, and the Raven Society at the University of Virginia for answering my questions and for sending me lesser-known materials about Poe's relationship with UVA. Finally, I would like to thank the Fundación Torres García and the Museo Torres García for the permission to use Torres García's *América invertida* on my book's cover.

I have researched and written this book while working at two outstanding institutions: Kennesaw State University (KSU) in Kennesaw, Georgia, and Brigham Young University (BYU) in Provo, Utah. Both institutions funded conference trips where I was able to present parts of this manuscript and receive valuable feedback. KSU also funded my research trips to Buenos Aires, Montevideo, UT Austin, and the University of Virginia through the following awards: a 2009–2010 College of Humanities and Social Sciences Faculty Seed Research Award, a 2010–2011 Center for Excellence in Teaching and Learning Incentive Funding Award for Research and Creative Activity, a 2011 Global Learning Award, and a 2013 College of Humanities and Social Sciences Summer Grant. Without this generous support, *Borges's Poe* would not exist. BYU provided course releases during my first three years on campus that allowed me to craft my book proposal and to finish, revise, and proof my manuscript. BYU also provided funding for the index and the artwork on the book's cover. Classrooms at both KSU and BYU have also been important venues in which I have been able to share my ideas on Borges and Poe with my students and receive their feedback.

I also need to thank the editors and staff at the University of Georgia Press for their support with this book. Special thanks to Jon Smith, one of the New Southern Studies series editors, for showing interest in my work over the years, for contacting me to discuss this book project, and for creating a larger space for inter-American scholarship through his work with Deborah Cohn and through the conferences he has organized around New World studies. Thanks, too, to Walter Biggins, senior acquisitions editor, for answering all my questions throughout this process. I would also like to thank the peer reviewers who offered me both support and valuable feedback in their responses to my book proposal and to the entire manuscript.

I have previously published two chapters from *Borges's Poe*, and I would like to thank the copyright holders for allowing me to republish that work here. Material from "Borges's Philosophy of Poe's Composition," copyright © 2013 by the Pennsylvania State University Press, appears here in my first chapter and in a few paragraphs of my introduction. This article was originally published in *Comparative Literature Studies* 50, issue 3 (2013), and it is used by permission of the Pennsylvania State University Press. A slightly al-

Acknowledgments

For me, this book has been a long but enjoyable adventure—a journey I could not have accomplished without the support of key mentors, friends, family, libraries, and institutions. I need to begin by going back to Michigan State University in the early 2000s and thanking Stephen Arch and María Mudrovcic, whose graduate courses on nineteenth-century U.S. literature and the work of Jorge Luis Borges, respectively, inspired me to write comparative work on Poe and Borges. With their guidance and the encouragement of another MSU professor, Stephen Rachman, I published my first article on Poe and Spanish America and decided that I would return to this topic after finishing my graduate work. A few years and my dissertation—on Faulkner and Fuentes rather than on Borges and Poe—later, I took my first trip to Buenos Aires to begin my research for a book on Poe and Spanish America. That book quickly morphed into a book on Poe and the Río de la Plata region after finding so much material in Buenos Aires. The project changed, again, to focus specifically on Poe and Borges after conducting another pair of research trips to libraries within the United States.

I owe special thanks to the following organizations, libraries, and librarians for their support with *Borges's Poe*. First, thanks to María Kodama and to the Fundación Internacional Jorge Luis Borges for allowing me to visit the Fundación on two occasions, for granting me permission to view Borges's marginalia in his personal copies of books by Poe and Hawthorne, and for sharing several stories with me about Borges's works and the latter years of his life. I would also like to thank the Biblioteca Nacional Argentina—especially Laura Rosato, Germán Álvarez, Juan Pablo Canala, and the other librarians in the Sala del Tesoro—for their continual support with this project, both in person during three research trips to the library and via email over the past several years. Thanks to the staffs of the Harry Ransom Center and the Nettie Lee Benson Latin American Collection, both at the University of Texas at Austin, for their help while I conducted research in the Ransom's collection of Borges materials and the Benson's collection of Cortázar materials. Thanks, too, to the wonderful librarians in the Albert and Shirley Small Special Collections Library at the University of Virginia for their support while I conducted research in their Jorge Luis Borges Collection. I would like to specifically thank

Contents

least six writers who predate Kafka—Zeno's paradox as described by Aristotle, a ninth-century Chinese fable by Han Yu, the works of Søren Kierkegaard, "Fears and Scruples" by Robert Browning, *Histoires désobligeantes* by Léon Bloy, and "Carcassonne" by Lord Dunsany ("Kafka" 107–09; "Kafka" 363–65). Borges solves this anachronistic conundrum by suggesting that Kafka influences these pieces by influencing Borges the reader, that a later writer *"crea* a sus precursores" [*"creates* his precursors"] (109; 365, emphasis in original) by affecting the minds of his or her readers so that when they read older texts, they take their previous readings of newer texts into the experience with them and thus find remnants or strains of the newer texts in the older writings.[18] He states that the writer's "labor modifica nuestra concepción del pasado, como ha de modificar el futuro" (109) ["work modifies our conception of the past, as it will modify the future"] (365).[19] This modification, however, is not competitive or self-aggrandizing: "En el vocabulario crítico, la palabra *precursor* es indispensable, pero habría que tratar de purificarla de toda connotación de polémica o de rivalidad" (109, Borges's italics) ["The word 'precursor' is indispensable to the vocabulary of criticism, but one must try to purify it from any connotation of polemic or rivalry"] (365). Borges's descriptions of the precursor-successor relationship disallow the very competition that undergirds Bloom's theory of influence, and although this contradiction remains unspoken in *The Anxiety of Influence*, Bloom openly admits as much when he returns to the subject of influence almost forty years later in *The Anatomy of Influence: Literature as a Way of Life*.[20] In this 2011 text, Bloom recalls Borges's Kafka essay and states: "Sadly, Borges idealized his account of literary influence by rejecting any idea of rivalry or competition in regard to precursors" (25). That Bloom laments the lack of struggle that Borges calls the key to the understanding of influence emphasizes his theory's divergence from Borges's and clarifies why I follow the latter in *Borges's Poe*. It makes little sense to couch a study on the relationship of influence between Poe and Borges as an oedipal struggle, not only because such an approach would place Poe's work within the rubric of a literary critic who flatly rejects him in favor of Emerson and Whitman, but also because Borges's critical and fictional writings demonstrate that his relationship with Poe is not one of rivalry.[21] Their affiliation is, instead, a complex relationship in which the former writer, Poe, clearly affects the latter writer, Borges, who, in turn, influences his precursor by altering his reputation and changing the way modern readers approach his work. In short, the Poe/Borges relationship exemplifies both the typical and the uncanny influence Borges describes in his Kafka essay.

If Borges did have an oedipal relationship with a group of writers, it was with the *modernistas*—particularly fellow Argentine Leopoldo Lugones. One could argue that Borges's involvement in *ultraismo*, his early critiques of Lugones, and his eventual praise for Lugones and the *modernistas* in his middle and old age—when they were no longer a literary threat to him—demonstrate Bloom's theory of influence. The *modernistas* revered Poe as a poet, and their hyperbolic sentiments were best captured in "Los raros" when Rubén Darío called Poe

> un sublime apasionado, un nervioso, uno de esos divinos semilocos necesarios para el progreso humano, lamentables cristos del arte, que por amor al eterno ideal tienen su calle de la amargura, sus espinas y su cruz. Nació con la adorable llama de la poesía, y ella le alimentaba al propio tiempo que era su martirio.

> [a passionate sublime being, a nervous man, one of those divine partially madmen necessary for human progress, lamentable Christs of art who for the love of an eternal ideal have their *via dolorosa*, their thorns, and their cross. He was born with the adorable flame of poetry, and she nurtured him at the same time that she was his martyrdom.] (267)

Borges overtly challenges the *modernistas*' portrayal of Poe as poet-prophet by praising Poe as a writer of fiction. His reinterpretation of Poe recalls Irwin's discussion of Jacques Derrida's move to "one up" Jacques Lacan by offering a different reading of Poe's "The Purloined Letter" (*Mystery* 3–5). Just as Derrida seeks to show the problems with psychoanalysis by contradicting Lacan's interpretation of "The Purloined Letter" from his famous 1956 reading of the story, perhaps Borges renames Poe to reveal an inherent problem at the origins of *modernismo*—that the movement has misidentified its own icon. That Borges may have used Poe as a way to challenge *modernismo* is not unlikely; however, unlike Derrida, whom Irwin claims "is motivated less by an interest in Poe or 'The Purloined Letter' than by a desire to score points off Lacan" (4), Borges was already invested in Poe long before his debates with the *modernistas* even began. Borges's early access to Poe in English suggests that his literary relationship with Poe exists before, and possibly outside, his competitive relationship with the *modernistas*. In any case, Borges's relationship with Poe lacks both the aggressive edge that remains visible in his relationship with the *modernistas* and the oedipal angst necessary for a Bloomian interpretation of influence.

In *Borges's Poe*, I argue that influence runs both ways rather than following the trickle-down theory of influence inherent in Pérez Firmat's use of the label "genetic" to describe influence studies or the model of oedipal struggle as described in Bloom's theory. *Borges's Poe* reveals that Poe's literature influences Borges the young reader and Borges the author, not only in Borges's detective fiction where Poe's influence has been repeatedly highlighted by other scholars and by Borges himself, but also in more surprising places, like his cerebral short story "El Aleph." Borges, in turn, influences both Poe's reputation and Poe's fiction itself. Borges reframes Poe's image through his own literary criticism and his Poe translations, and he changes how Poe's readers return to Poe's stories through his own short fiction. Borges's Kafka essay is particularly relevant in the latter case. The final paragraph of "Kafka y sus precursores" creates a radical, early type of reader-response criticism that illuminates the way Borges's fiction affects Poe's. After describing the six sources he identifies as Kafka precursors, Borges claims:

> Si no me equivoco, las heterogéneas piezas que he enumerado se parecen a Kafka; si no me equivoco, no todas se parecen entre sí. Este último hecho es el más significativo. En cada uno de esos textos está la idiosincrasia de Kafka, en grado mayor o menor, pero si Kafka no hubiera escrito, no la percibiríamos; vale decir, no existiría. El poema "Fears and Scruples" de Robert Browning profetiza la obra de Kafka, pero nuestra lectura de Kafka afina y desvía sensiblemente nuestra lectura del poema. Browning no lo leía como ahora nosotros lo leemos. [. . .] El hecho es que cada escritor *crea* a sus precursores. Su labor modifica nuestra concepción del pasado, como ha de modificar el futuro. (109)

> [If I am not mistaken, the heterogeneous pieces I have listed resemble Kafka; if I am not mistaken, not all of them resemble each other. This last fact is what is most significant. Kafka's idiosyncracy is present in each of these writings, to a greater or lesser degree, but if Kafka had not written, we would not perceive it; that is to say, it would not exist. The poem "Fears and Scruples" by Robert Browning prophesies the work of Kafka, but our reading of Kafka noticeably refines and diverts our reading of the poem. Browning did not read it as we read it now. [. . .] The fact is that each writer *creates* his precursors. His work modifies our conception of the past, as it will modify the future.] (365)

According to Borges, the successor creates the precursor in two ways, or the reader feels the presence of the later writer in the work of the former author on two levels. On the first level, the reader experiences an odd, anachronistic sensation that the work they are reading was written by an author who postdates the publication of the text. In the context of *Borges's Poe*, passages from Poe's "Loss of Breath" seem Borgesian to the Poe reader who is familiar with Borges's "Funes el memorioso." On the second level, the reader returns to a work she has read before and sees it with new eyes because she has been affected by a piece or a body of work she has read by a more contemporary writer. For example, Poe readers reinterpret the revenge plots from "Metzengerstein" and "The Black Cat" if they reread those stories after having read Borges's "El Aleph." Level two goes beyond feeling that a text resembles the work of a later writer, changing the rereading of a piece even if that text does not produce the anachronistic feeling created in level one. For example, "The Black Cat" does not feel Borgesian, even if the Poe reader is familiar with "El Aleph"; instead, this reader questions the possibility of a just revenge that "The Black Cat" offers after seeing revenge fail in Borges's tale. In short, the concept of two-way influence that I follow in *Borges's Poe* reiterates the importance of Poe's influence on Borges, but more importantly, it reveals (1) how Borges takes Poe's influence, along with the influence of scores of other writers in a number of languages, and tweaks it for his own ends and (2) how Borges's texts alter our understanding of works we have read and reread by Poe.

I have organized *Borges's Poe* into three sections, with each part focusing on a distinct role Borges played in shifting Poe's reputation in the American hemisphere. The first section, "Renaming Poe: Jorge Luis Borges's Literary Criticism on Edgar Allan Poe," examines how Borges reshaped Poe's image through a decades-long return to Poe and his work in both oral and written literary criticism. Borges referred to Poe in solo-authored articles, essays, and prologues over 130 times between his first written reference to Poe in 1923 and his last approaches to Poe in 1986, the year of Borges's death. He also mentioned Poe in several of his collaborative works of literary criticism and in scores of interviews and dialogues in both Spanish and English. The sheer number of references and their continual appearance during more than sixty years of Borges's writing career demonstrate both Poe's lasting influence on Borges as a writer and thinker and Borges's profound influence on how Poe is read and interpreted in the Río de la Plata region and across Spanish America during the twentieth century and into the twenty-first. This section expands Borges/Poe scholarship by engaging Borges's literary criticism rather than focusing solely on the fiction (or, more particularly, the detective fiction) of each writer. It challenges the paternalistic approach of some Poe scholarship by examining Borges's position as a Poe reader and interpreter—his role as a critical lens that altered Poe's poetic reputation in Spanish America and, ultimately, recast Poe as a timeless fiction writer. Finally, this section reminds inter-American and New Southern Studies scholars that, along with the shared histories, experiences, or trauma that can bring the works of two writers into the same critical conversation, individual authors often transverse borders by reading, responding to, and re-creating one another.[22]

Chapter 1, "Borges's Philosophy of Poe's Composition," reveals how Borges perennially interprets Poe's most famous analytic essay, "The Philosophy of Composition," as detective fiction in order to downplay Poe's role as a poet and increase his visibility as the inventor of the detective genre. This chapter reads "The Philosophy of Composition" as a theory for writing fiction, and it engages Borges's 1935 article—"La génesis de 'El cuervo' de Poe"—to demonstrate how Poe's Dupin trilogy enacts his theory far better than the theoretical essay itself. Borges shows his attraction to Poe's desire to disclose the workings of the writer's mind by making a handwritten note in his 1927 Johnson edition of *The Works of Edgar Allan Poe*—"elaborate and vacillating crudities of thought"—a direct quote from Poe's essay. Poe never actually provides this promised glimpse into the creative-analytic mind in his theoretical texts, but Borges finds a satisfactory depiction of this mental process in Poe's creation of the original analytic detective—C. Auguste Dupin. This thought process is particularly visible in "The Murders in the Rue Morgue," in which Dupin's thought sequences while solving the original locked-room conundrum and while reading the narrator's mind in the story's analytical introduction are more "elaborate and vacillating" than the simplistic trail of ideas Poe offers to connect his need to repeat the word "Nevermore" and his arrival at the raven as the speaker of the refrain. The chapter also examines Borges's descriptions of his own writing process to show how he consistently performs intellectual tricks espoused by Poe—for example, the hiding of an object in plain sight—while professing that the muse, rather than the intellect, serves as his creative spark. Finally, this chapter shows how Borges openly reframed Poe in 1949 by criticizing his poetry and praising his fiction, and it argues that Borges's campaign to alter Poe's image found resonance with other literary critics in Argentina during the 1940s and began to shift Poe's long-standing reputation throughout the Río de la Plata region.

"Reading and Rereading," the book's second chapter, approaches Borges's preference for rereading over initial reading, and it highlights Poe as one of the authors whom Borges reread from his childhood until his death. The chapter focuses on what could be called Borges's secondary Poe criticism—the scores of book reviews, prologues for other writers' books, and articles on authors other than Poe—in which Borges mentions Poe. In almost every case, Borges describes Poe as either the inventor of the detective genre or as the creator of *Pym*. In the first instance, he continually frames his discussions of twentieth-century detective fiction via Poe and invites his audience to reread Poe, either literally or via memory, each time they read a contemporary detective novel. Borges's insistence on Poe as creator of the genre led to a printed dispute in the 1940s between Borges and Roger Caillois, Borges's eventual French advocate in the 1950s and the person most responsible for Borges's winning of the Formentor Prize in 1961, the prize that cast him onto an international stage, opened his work up for extensive translation into English, and moved Borges from a member of the regional literati to a global literary icon. This chapter examines several rejection slips for proposed translations of Borges's fiction into English from the Knopf publishing house in the 1940s and 1950s, and it argues that Caillois's decision not to seek revenge on Borges, not to take upon himself the role of Dupin or Red Scharlach, has a remarkable impact on Borges's career, bringing his work to French- and English-speaking audiences and launching him onto the world literary scene. The final section of the chapter examines Borges's unlikely fascination with Poe's *The Narra-*

tive of Arthur Gordon Pym and suggests that Borges embraces this novel, even though he almost universally prefers short fiction to novels and continually critiques Poe for the type of overbearing prose that *Pym* contains, because he reads the later chapters as their own story—a detective story. Borges claims that while this novel has a primary plotline, the adventures and hardships Pym faces at sea, it also contains a secondary plot, a mystery around the vilification of whiteness. Borges reads and rereads *Pym*'s later chapters as a detective narrative in which the reader solves this hidden mystery. Through this reading, Borges reiterates the same message that he sends with each of his reviews, prologues, and articles on detective fiction: Poe remains important, not due to his poetry, but because he created the most widespread genre of fiction the world has ever seen.

This monograph's second section, "Translating Poe: Jorge Luis Borges's Edgar Allan Poe Translations," sits in the middle of the book and serves as a bridge between Borges's literary criticism and his fiction. This section fills a gap in Borges/Poe scholarship and a void in current inter-American literary criticism by interrogating translation as theory and as practice and by revealing the image-altering work that Borges performs on Poe when he translates Poe's fiction. Apart from a few select pages in Efraín Kristal's *Invisible Work: Borges and Translation*, Borges/Poe critics and translation studies scholars have said precious little about Borges's translations of Poe's prose. This silence is symptomatic of a current blind spot in hemispheric literary studies and American Studies scholarship in general after the transnational turn in the field. Scholars are trained to read texts in multiple languages, and Borges, a true polyglot, read from several literary traditions in their source languages. However, the majority of Borges's Spanish-speaking readers (and, on the macro level, the majority of any readership in any particular language in the Americas) access Poe—or any other foreign-language writer—via translation. This section sheds light on a process that often remains in the shadows of academic discourse or is simply taken for granted.

Chapter 3, "Theory, Practice, and *Pym*," analyzes Borges's theory of translation, his role in the current field of translation studies, and how he begins to put his translation theory into practice in his translations of two fragments from *Pym*, Poe's only published novel. Borges honed his theory of translation in a trio of essays he published on the subject from 1926 through 1936. In each essay, he prefers literary or creative translations over literal translations, and he openly challenges the concept of fidelity. Borges further complicates the idea of fidelity in his masterful "Pierre Menard, autor del Quijote" ["Pierre Menard, Author of the *Quixote*"] and completely deflates the concept in his 1943 article on William Beckford's *Vathek*. Borges's translations of two fragments from *Pym*, the first published in his famous essay "El arte narrativo y la magia" ["Narrative Art and Magic"] and the second published in both of

Borges's coauthored anthologies on fantastical creatures, are quite conservative compared to his longer Poe translations. They hint, however, at Borges's willingness to streamline a text in translation and at his ability to make a significant change in a text by only shifting one word. In the first fragment, Borges reduces, by nearly half, the word count from Poe's description of the multiveined water that Pym and his companions discover on an island in the Antarctic while maintaining the passage's sense of awe and possible magic. In the second piece, Borges offers a nearly literal translation of Pym's description of the carcass of a white animal he finds in the water, but his specific diction subtly casts the passage in terms of detective fiction. This translation, like Borges's rereadings of *Pym* examined in chapter 2, underscores Poe's position as creator of the detective genre.

"Facts and an Envelope," the book's fourth chapter, examines Borges's translations of "The Facts in the Case of M. Valdemar" and "The Purloined Letter" alongside Poe's source texts and two other significant Argentine translations. This pair of translations clearly demonstrates how Borges's translation practice usually follows his theory. In both cases, he liberally translates Poe's works, streamlining the prose and altering significant plot details at will. His translation of "Valdemar" stresses the believability of mesmerism's temporary power over death, and his translation of "The Purloined Letter" deemphasizes the source text's focus on the object hidden in plain sight to highlight the intellectual duel between Dupin and the minister. In the translations of both "Valdemar" and "The Purloined Letter," Borges makes significant changes to the story's plotlines, which create new Poe stories that are Borges's as much as they are Poe's. Chapter 4 also reminds us that what is at stake in Borges's Poe translations, like his literary criticism on Poe, is the triangulated relationship between Borges, Poe, and the *modernistas*, not just the direct relationship between Borges and Poe. In short, Borges's Poe translations recast Poe as a fiction writer and strip him of his sacred garb as the *modernistas*' poet-prophet.

The third section of *Borges's Poe*, "Rewriting Poe: Jorge Luis Borges's Poe-Influenced and Poe-Influencing Short Fiction," reiterates the multifaceted nature of the literary influence between Borges and Poe by offering two chapters of comparative analysis that revolve around three Poe tales—"Loss of Breath," "Metzengerstein," and "The Black Cat"—and two Borges stories, "Funes el memorioso" ["Funes, His Memory"] and "El Aleph," that have not been juxtaposed in previous Borges/Poe criticism. This section, once again, moves the conversation about Poe and Borges beyond the detective genre, which has received so much coverage in Borges/Poe scholarship; emphasizes the reciprocal nature of the influence between the two writers rather than casting Poe as singular influence and Borges as passive receptor; and offers the type of paired readings that have been lacking in recent inter-American and

New Southern Studies scholarship—readings based on the literary relationship between Borges and Poe rather than on the historical or regional connections between the two spaces from which both authors wrote.

Chapter 5, "Buried Connections," unearths significant links between Poe's lesser-known tale "Loss of Breath" and Borges's famous stories "Funes el memorioso" and "El Aleph." Borges buries the most important connections between these stories three times over. First, his texts talk back to passages in Poe's story that Poe deleted before republishing "Loss of Breath" for the third time in 1846. Second, Borges only alludes to Poe's story indirectly in his literary criticism. And third, Borges hides this veiled allusion within a postscript to a republished prologue. "Buried Connections" demonstrates how particular descriptions of Ireneo Funes's amazing memory and specific items in the list of what Borges's narrator sees in the infinite Aleph spring directly from Poe's narrator's account of the sensations he suffered while being hanged. This account is not well known to most Borges readers nor to typical Poe readers since Poe cut the hanging scene from the 1846 version of "Loss of Breath," which is the canonized version of the text. When Borges readers do stumble across this text, however, Poe's narrator's account of hanging feels, following the first manner Borges describes in the Kafka essay, uncannily Borgesian and recalls both Funes's memory and Borges's narrator's view of the Aleph. Proving that this connection is influence rather than coincidence, however, requires some digging, and chapter 5 provides this evidence by examining some of Borges's lesser-known critical texts—a prologue and its footnotes and an interview from the early 1980s—and by referring to the Poe books in Borges's libraries. Disinterring the buried connections between "Loss of Breath" and "Funes"/"El Aleph" reemphasizes the depth and breadth of Borges's knowledge of Poe's literary canon, and it increases the stature of Poe's early satire by revealing how it serves as a secret source for Borges's descriptions of infinity in two of his more cerebral tales.

The sixth and final chapter of *Borges's Poe*, "Supernatural Revenge," reads Borges's "El Aleph" alongside Poe's "Metzengerstein" and "The Black Cat" as fantastic revenge stories in which the supernatural happenings within each tale mask each story's revenge plot. Chapter 6 begins by theorizing the fantastic, a subject on which Borges offered several lectures, and by differentiating this literary mode from the magical real and other types of supernatural fiction. "The Black Cat," "Metzengerstein," and "El Aleph" all qualify as fantastic tales, and this chapter reveals how the supernatural events in each story—for example, the appearance of the demonic stallion in "Metzengerstein," the imprint of a gigantic cat on the only remaining wall of the narrator's fire-ravaged home in "The Black Cat," and Borges's narrator's simultaneous view of everything in the universe from every possible angle while gazing inside the minuscule Aleph in Carlos Argentino Daneri's basement—

obfuscate the driving theme behind each tale: revenge. The side-by-side reading of these three stories exposes three hidden revenge plots and demonstrates how Borges's tale flips the gratification of revenge provided by Poe on its head. In the second manner that Borges describes in the Kafka essay, the backfiring of Borges's narrator's revenge on Daneri changes how the Poe reader interprets Poe's revenge plots and leaves the reader critical of the idea that revenge can bring satisfaction.

Borges's recasting of Poe's image via his literary criticism, translations, and fiction not only alters the *modernistas'* image of Poe, but it also creates the atmosphere for the total revamping of Poe's reputation via Julio Cortázar's massive translation project in the 1950s. *Borges's Poe* scrutinizes and proves one of the primary tenets of inter-American literary studies, the idea that various literary traditions in the Americas should be read alongside one another regardless of the linguistic, political, or geographical borders that might divide them. This book also invites inter-Americanists and scholars in the New Southern Studies to return to the concept of direct (although reciprocal) influence between writers while simultaneously paying attention to the specific contexts in which one writer reinterprets another. The book also requires Borges/Poe scholars to reevaluate the relationship between the two writers as a long-running, intricate association that goes far beyond an affinity for detective fiction. Finally, *Borges's Poe* reframes the concept of literary influence as a multidimensional dialogue rather than a genetic discourse or a parricidal conflict. Poe affects one of Argentina's most essential authors, one of the Southern Hemisphere's most unique literary voices, and one of the world's most important writers of the twentieth century via direct literary influence, and Borges reshapes how a vast portion of the world understands the image and interprets the literature of one of the United States' most vital authors by renaming, translating, and rewriting Poe.

PART 1

Renaming Poe

Jorge Luis Borges's Literary Criticism on Edgar Allan Poe

CHAPTER 1

Borges's Philosophy of Poe's Composition

In his effort to rename and reframe Poe, Borges repeatedly granted two particular accolades to his precursor—he argued that contemporary literature could not exist without the works of Poe and Walt Whitman, and he described Poe in biblical fashion as the writer who "engendró a Baudelaire, que engendró a Mallarmé" ["begat Baudelaire, who begat Mallarmé"] ("La eternidad" 51).[1] Borges's coupling of Poe to Whitman and his discussion of Poe's influence on the French literary tradition all mirror comments made by the *modernistas* and Borges's other Spanish American predecessors. For example, in his prologue to Juan Antonio Pérez Bonalde's famous 1887 translation of "The Raven" as "El cuervo," Colombian scholar Santiago Pérez Triana claims that the influence of Poe's poetry on literature in English is even greater than that of his compatriots (qtd. in Rojas 157) while Cuban literary critic Enrique Piñeyro praises Poe as the best U.S. poet besides Whitman in 1888 (566), the year typically marked as the beginning of *modernismo* with the publication of Rubén Darío's *Azul*. The *modernistas'* knowledge of Poe's influence on Baudelaire and the French symbolists is well documented by Englekirk, and Darío, in "Los raros," suggests that "[c]ada día se afirma con mayor brillo la gloria ya sin sombras de Edgar Poe, desde su prestigiosa introducción por Baudelaire, coronada luego por el espíritu trascendentalmente comprensivo y seductor de Stéphane Mallarmé" ["[e]very day the glory, now without shadows, of Edgar Poe is affirmed with greater brilliance, from his prestigious introduction by Baudelaire, crowned soon after by the transcendentally understanding and seducing spirit of Stéphane Mallarmé"] (250).

The primary difference between Borges's praise for Poe and that of the *modernistas* lies where Borges places the impact of Poe's influence. For Borges, Poe's poetic theory, not his poetry, gives birth to the French symbolists, and his fiction, not his verse, makes him timeless ("Edgar Allan Poe" 1). Indeed, he tells Osvaldo Ferrari "que Poe dibujó, dejó su imagen en los cuentos. O podríamos decir también que proyectó póstumamente una gran sombra; una sombra luminosa habría que decir" ["that Poe drew, left his image in his stories. Or we could also say that he posthumously projected a great shadow; a shining shadow we would have to say"] ("Sobre Edgar" 191). For Darío and the *modernistas*, Poe's poetry creates a glory without shadow, while for

Borges, Poe's fiction creates a great shadow that glows. The principal text that Borges returns to over and over to distinguish between Poe's poetic theory and his actual poetry and to lay the groundwork for his eventual claim that Poe was a major fiction writer and a minor poet is Poe's famous interpretation of how he wrote "The Raven": "The Philosophy of Composition."

In this chapter, I analyze several of Borges's critical approaches to Poe while outlining the regional context in which Borges offered these interpretations and examining the impact of his analysis, aspects that are lacking in most Borges/Poe scholarship. I read Poe's "The Philosophy of Composition" as a theory for writing fiction, and I engage Borges's first interpretation of Poe's famous essay—a 1935 newspaper article entitled "La génesis de 'El cuervo' de Poe"—to demonstrate how Poe's Dupin trilogy enacts his theory far better than the theoretical essay itself. I examine Borges's descriptions of his own writing process to show how he consistently performs intellectual tricks espoused by Poe—for example, the hiding of an object in plain sight—while overtly professing that the muse rather than the intellect serves as his creative spark. Finally, I reveal how Borges's literary criticism both alters Poe's Spanish American image from poet-prophet to masterful story writer and constructs a predecessor for Borges's own short fiction.

"The Philosophy of Composition" and/as Detective Fiction

Borges takes up Poe's "The Philosophy of Composition" early and often, returning to the essay several times between his 1927 article "Indagación de la palabra" and his 1985 and 1986 prologues to two collections of Poe's tales translated into Spanish.[2] To date, however, only one scholarly article— Santiago Rodríguez Guerrero-Strachan's "Idea de Edgar A. Poe en la obra crítica de Jorge Luis Borges"—offers extended analysis of Borges's readings of "The Philosophy of Composition," and his article does not engage Borges's 1935 article "La génesis de 'El cuervo' de Poe," which serves as Borges's primary piece of criticism about Poe's famous essay. "The Philosophy of Composition" invites Borges's attempt to shift the focus on Poe away from his poetry and toward his fiction since Poe begins the article in which he supposedly reveals the "*modus operandi*" behind his most famous poem—"The Raven"— by theorizing the concept of plot: "Nothing is more clear than that every plot, worth the name, must be elaborated to its *dénouement* before any thing be attempted with the pen" (163).[3] The fact that the essay opens with a discussion of plot, the essay's focus on effect, and the narrative aspects of "The Raven" itself all suggest that Poe's poetic theory is really (or, at least, alternately) a theory for writing fiction, regardless of Poe's efforts to cast "The Philosophy of Composition" as a poetic theory by analyzing a poem rather than a short story, by describing beauty as "the sole legitimate province of the poem," and by suggesting that "[m]elancholy is thus the most legitimate of all poetical tones" (164). Indeed, Poe's discussion of effect recalls his interpretations of fiction rather than poetry in his own literary criticism. For example, in his second review of Hawthorne's stories, he claims that "the prose tale" is only slightly inferior to "a rhymed poem, not to exceed in length what might be perused in an hour," and that a quality writer of tales, after "conceiv[ing], with deliberate care, a certain unique or single *effect* to be wrought out, [. . .] then invents such incidents—he then combines such events as may best aid him in establishing this preconceived effect" ("Nathaniel" 197–98). "The Raven" certainly has a plot and a *dénouement*, and it does create the effect of melancholy that Poe argues for in "The Philosophy of Composition." However, these facts point to the narrative or story-like quality of this poem rather than creating a theory of poetry.[4] Borges notes that "Poe aplicó a sus cuentos la misma técnica que a sus versos; juzgó que todo debe redactarse en función de la última línea" (*Introducción* 20) ["Poe applied to his tales the same technique that he used in his verse; he believed that everything should be written with the last line in mind"] (*An Introduction* 23), and Borges, too, applied Poe's so-called poetic theory to prose, suggesting that Poe's argument that long poetry does not exist "es trasladable a la prosa" ["is transferable to prose"] ("La última" 207).[5]

Borges both subtly and blatantly supports his claim that Poe is not a poet but a master fiction writer throughout the various summaries and analyses he offers of "The Philosophy of Composition." He provides his most in-depth reading of Poe's essay in "La génesis de 'El cuervo' de Poe." Much later in his career, Borges devotes several paragraphs to "The Philosophy of Composition" in both *Introducción a la literatura norteamericana* and "El cuento policial," and while each of these pieces more explicitly praises Poe's fiction over his poetry, Borges summarizes more than analyzes Poe's essay in these later works. In "La génesis de 'El cuervo' de Poe," Borges does not conspicuously state that Poe's fiction trumps his poetry. Instead, he pulls a trick from Poe's tale "The Purloined Letter" and leaves several clues hidden in plain sight that allow the reader familiar with Borges's later commentary on Poe to see that Borges subtly develops and states his argument about the superiority of Poe's fiction over his poetry as early as 1935.

Borges published "La génesis de 'El cuervo' de Poe" in the pages of the Buenos Aires daily *La Prensa* in August 1935, just months after publishing his first collection of fiction, *Historia universal de la infamia*. After a short summary of the essay, Borges notes that literary critics typically reject Poe's description of how he purportedly wrote "The Raven," claiming that some scholars dismiss the essay as a ploy on Poe's part to cash in on the fame of the poem while others reject it out of fear "que el misterio central de la creación poética hubiera sido profanado por Poe" ["that the central mystery of poetic creation had been desecrated by Poe"] (2).[6] Borges suggests that a "más inteligente y letal" ["more intelligent and lethal"] critic than the group to which he alludes "pudo haber denunciado en aquellas hojas una vindicación romántica de los procedimientos ordinarios del clasicismo, un anatema de lo más inspirado contra la inspiración" ["could have denounced in those pages a romantic vindication of the ordinary procedures of classicism, an anathema against inspiration from the most inspired"] (2).[7] Borges leaves these critiques behind, stating, "Se adivinará que no comparto esas opiniones" ["It will be guessed that I do not share those opinions"] (2), and he claims to believe Poe's theory, at least to a point: "Yo—ingenuamente acaso—creo en las explicaciones de Poe. Descontada alguna posible ráfaga de charlatanería, pienso que el proceso mental aducido por él ha de corresponder, más o menos, al proceso verdadero de la creación. Yo estoy seguro de que así procede la inteligencia: por arrepentimientos, por obstáculos, por eliminaciones" ["Perhaps naïvely, I believe Poe's explanations. Apart from a possible burst of charlatanism, I think that the mental process alleged by him corresponds, more or less, with the true process of creation. I am sure that intelligence proceeds thus: by contradictions, by obstacles, by eliminations"] (2). Borges's suggestion that Poe's essay comes close to describing how the poetic process truly functions demonstrates Borges's own penchant for reason, and by accepting Poe's analytic account of how he supposedly creates a poem, Borges reads against the iconic Poe of the *modernistas*, the tragic and melancholic poet-prophet, and subtly begins to cast Poe as a predecessor for the ratiocinative fiction he will publish over the next decade and a half.

Borges accepts Poe's overarching analytic method and agrees that an artist can pinpoint some of the moments of poetic creation. He does, however, argue that Poe had to simplify a complex thought process and that "The Philosophy of Composition" only provides its reader with a summarized version of that process: "La complejidad de las operaciones descritas no me incomoda; sospecho que la efectiva elaboración tiene que haber sido aún más compleja, y mucho más caótica y vacilante. En mi entender, Poe se redujo a suministrar un esquema lógico, ideal, de los muchos y perplejos caminos de la creación" ["The complexity of the described operations does not bother me; I suspect that the real elaboration had to have been even more complex, and much more chaotic and vacillating. In my opinion, Poe limited himself to supplying a logical, ideal schematic of the many and perplexing paths of creation"] (2). Borges's words mirror Poe's own when the latter suggests that "[m]ost writers—poets in especial—[. . .] would positively shudder at letting the public take a peep behind the scenes, at the elaborate and vacillating crudities of thought [. . .] which, in ninety-nine cases out of the hundred, constitute the properties of the literary *historio*" ("Philosophy of Composition" 163). Poe's description of this complexity fascinates Borges, not only in "La génesis de 'El cuervo' de Poe" but in his lifelong reading of Poe, as his marginalia in his editions of Poe's works demonstrate. In Borges's personal copy of R. Brimley Johnson's 1927 edition of *The Works of Edgar Allan Poe: The Poems and Three Essays on Poetry, Narrative of Arthur Gordon Pym, Miscellanies*, he notes the following on the inside of the text's back cover: "elaborate and vacillating crudities of thought—p. 192" ("Notations in *The Works of Edgar Allan Poe: The Poems*").[8] The small size of Borges's script suggests that Borges made this particular note after writing "La génesis de 'El cuervo' de Poe"—probably in the 1940s or 1950s—since both Borges's widow and literary heiress, María Kodama (Personal Interview), and the founding curator of the Borges Collection at the Small Special Collections Library at the University of Virginia, C. Jared Loewenstein (Personal Interview), affirm that Borges's handwriting decreased significantly in size between the 1920s and the 1950s as Borges neared blindness in 1955.[9] However, this text also contains a note in Borges's medium script that cites a short passage from *Pym*, demonstrating that Borges owned this edition as early as the 1920s and most certainly by 1935, when he penned his first article on Poe's "The Philosophy of Composition." Either way, this note shows that Poe's portrayal of the poet's mental process stood out to Borges long after he first analyzed it in the pages of *La Prensa*.

Notwithstanding this fascination, Borges does not fully accept Poe's theory because Poe's mathematical description of how he wrote "The Raven" denies even the slightest possibility of inspiration and ignores the reality that the artist's preferences or past experiences function as variables rather than constants in this poetic calculus. Once Poe has logically decided on the need to repeat the word "nevermore" throughout his poem, he is left with the problem of how to justify the use of this refrain. He solves the conundrum thus: "I did not fail to perceive, in short, that the difficulty lay in the reconciliation of this monotony with the exercise of reason on the part of the creature repeating the word. Here, then, immediately arose the idea of a *non*-reasoning creature capable of speech; and, very naturally, a parrot, in the first instance, suggested itself, but was superseded forthwith by a Raven, as equally capable of speech, and infinitely more in keeping with the intended *tone*" (165). Poe's explanation suggests that his solution to this dilemma is not only a logical answer but *the* logical answer, that thinking the problem through analytically creates a chain of thoughts with only one possible resolution—a speaker without reason requires an animal, parrots are known to mimic human speech, ravens are also known to mimic human speech and are far more melancholy than parrots, a raven will be the speaker of the refrain. Poe's explanation shows little internal debate or wrestling between options—the thought of a creature without reason "immediately arose," the idea of a parrot "very naturally" appeared but was "superseded forthwith by a Raven" (165). This explanation shows a line of thought, but it is much more direct and clean than the "elaborate and vacillating crudities" (163) of the poet's mental state that Poe claims he will reveal to the public. In short, Poe casts the problem of justifying the repetition of "nevermore" as a mathematical equation, and as the analytic poet, he offers the only possible solution.

Borges astutely demonstrates that Poe's explanation becomes a part of the theory Poe seeks to craft in the essay rather than a recounting of his mental process. He states, "En los eslabones examinados, la conclusión que el escritor deriva de cada premisa es, desde luego, lógica; pero no es la única necesaria" ["in the examined links, the conclusion that the writer derives from each premise is, of course, logical; but it is not the only necessary one"] ("La génesis" 2). Borges then offers another possible solution, arguing that if Poe needed an irrational speaker to repeat "nevermore," he could have chosen "un lunático, resolución que hubiera transformado el poema" ["a lunatic, a resolution that would have transformed the poem"] (2). Borges's suggestion of an idiot as the speaker of the refrain not only shows that Poe could have arrived at a different final solution but that each step in the thought process allows for different outcomes, an idea that Borges later toys with in his infinite portrayal of time in his own "El jardín de senderos que se bifurcan" ["The Garden of Forking Paths"].[10] Poe's first step to justify the repetition of "nevermore" is to claim that the speaker must be irrational, and to meet this requirement, in the second step, he opts for the animal over the human even though humanity offers several options for beings with little or no reason—the child, the lunatic, the drunk.[11] Borges's comment reveals that the poem's portrayal of a talking raven rather than a ranting lunatic is the result of a decision—it represents a choice made by Poe rather than an inevitable outcome.[12] One could argue that the poet's ability to choose is a part of the creative process that Poe claims to be unveiling to the public in "The Philosophy of Composition," but Poe's descriptions of the process suggest that each "correct" step or link has only one "correct" answer and that by following the chain the poet arrives at the only possible outcome.

Poe's descriptions of his creative process as one of intellect rather than inspiration mirror the deductive process he displays in his Dupin trilogy, with the poet thinking in the same terms as Poe's analytic detective—C. Auguste Dupin. In Poe's inaugural detective story, "The Murders in the Rue Morgue," Dupin suggests that "there is but one mode of reasoning" that can solve the locked-room conundrum which the story presents and that "that mode *must* lead us to a definite decision" (551). Upon surveying the scene, Dupin determines that the murderers must have escaped the house from the bedroom where the murder took place or from the adjoining room. Then, step by step, he eliminates the doors and the chimneys from both rooms and the windows from the adjoining room as possible escape routes. After a thorough examination of one of the bedroom's windows, Dupin recounts, "[t]he conclusion was plain, and again narrowed in the field of my investigations. The assassins *must* have escaped through the other window" (552). Dupin's deductive logic foreshadows Poe's description of his mind's workings while composing "The Raven." However, Poe does a more complete job describing Dupin's thought process about the escape route than he does describing his own arrival at the raven as speaker. Dupin considers, investigates, and then rejects the house's other rooms, the multiple doors, the chimneys, and the first window along his path to finding the window with the broken nail while Poe considers and eliminates only one option—a parrot—before arriving at the raven as the solution to his repetition conundrum.

Poe's portrayal of Dupin's analytic/creative mind rather than his portrayal of his own mind in "The Philosophy of Composition" begins to reveal "the elaborate and vacillating crudities of thought" (163) that interest Borges. However, Poe's repeated use of "must" in his description of Dupin's analytic method suggests that Dupin's narrative is also controlled, ordered, and limited. Poe uses the word "must" twenty times in "The Murders in the Rue Morgue." Typically, the word comes from Dupin's lips—or, more precisely, from the narrator's recounting of Dupin's words. Dupin speaks the word sixteen times total and ten times in only the few paragraphs in which he discovers that the window was the murderer's means of escape and thus solves the locked-room conundrum. The word receives Poe's emphasis via italics seven times—all within Dupin's examination of the murderer's means of escape—leaving the narrator and the reader with the feeling that Dupin never makes a wrong turn. His logic always works, and his solution *must* be correct. However, Dupin, like Poe, gives the story's narrator only a summary of his thought process, for as Borges suggests about Poe's descriptions of how he wrote "The Raven," "[s]in duda, el proceso completo era irrecuperable, además de tedioso" ["[d]oubtless, the complete process was irretrievable, as well as tedious"] ("La génesis" 2).

Borges is satisfied with this type of order and control when it appears in detective fiction. In fact, he often praises order as one of the detective genre's saving graces: "En esta época nuestra, tan caótica, hay algo que, humildemente, ha mantenido las virtudes clásicas: el cuento policial. [. . .] Yo diría, para defender la novela policial, que no necesita defensa, leída con cierto desdén ahora, está salvando el orden en una época de desorden. Esto es una prueba que debemos agradecerle y es meritorio" ("El cuento policial" 239–40) ["In this chaotic era of ours, one thing has humbly maintained the classic virtues: the detective story. [. . .] I would say in defense of the detective novel that it needs no defense; though now read with a certain disdain, it is safeguarding order in an era of disorder. That is a feat for which we should be grateful"] ("The Detective Story" 499).[13] In a pair of articles, Borges even speaks of detective fiction's order as one of the genre's three "musas glaciales" ["glacial muses"] ("Leyes" 38; "Los laberintos" 128), a strange phrase that suggests a fusion between intellect and inspiration, a cold and calculating type of muse. However, Borges is not satisfied with Poe's simplistic ordering of chaos in "The Philosophy of Composition," not because Poe offers a very ordered summary of his thought process but because Poe refuses to discuss the gaps or spaces in that process. Borges suggests that this mental exercise requires either inspiration or experience to move from the necessity for an irrational speaker to a parrot and then to a raven rather than to a lunatic or a drunk. Borges argues that in Poe's essay "[c]ada eslabón es válido, pero entre eslabón y eslabón queda su partícula de tiniebla o de inspiración incoercible. Lo diré de otro modo: Poe declara los diversos momentos del proceso poético, pero entre cada uno y el subsiguiente queda—infinitesimal—el de la invención. Queda otro arcano general: el de las preferencias" ["each link is valid, but between link and link a particle of darkness remains, or of irrepressible inspiration. I will say it another way: Poe declares the diverse moments of the poetic process, but between each subsequent step the infinitesimal moment of invention remains. Another general secret remains: the secret of preferences"] (2). For Borges, then, Poe's step-by-step explanation of how he decided to have a raven speak his gloomy refrain is logical, but he could have arrived at another conclusion. Poe could have chosen a different route, but in these moments or gaps of thought between irrational being to parrot to raven, Poe's own experiences, preferences, and/or the muse that he denies exists prod him from one point to the next until he arrives at *a* solution rather than *the* solution.

Poe does show the gap or void that Borges sees as essential to the writer's thought process, but once again, he does so in his detective fiction rather than in "The Philosophy of Composition." In the opening pages of "The Murders in the Rue Morgue," the narrator seeks to reveal Dupin's acumen through a brief example in which the Frenchman finishes the narrator's thoughts for him, or, in effect, reads the narrator's mind. When the narrator asks for "the method—if method there is—by which you have been enabled to fathom my soul in this matter," Dupin replies, "that you may comprehend all clearly, we will first retrace the course of your meditations [. . .] [t]he larger links of the chain run thus—Chantilly, Orion, Dr. Nichol, Epicurus, Stereotomy, the street stones, the fruiterer" (534–35). Dupin's reference to the "larger links" supports Borges's claim that any attempt to reveal the human thought process provides a summarized or tidied version of the chaotic or vacillating activities of the brain, and his detailed explanation of how he moves from one step to the next also reveals experience, revelation, and even guessing. Almost every mental leap Dupin makes, from the moment he observes the narrator mutter "stereotomy" to the moment in which he vocalizes the narrator's thoughts on

Chantilly, relies on personal conversations he has had with the narrator. His experience fills in the spaces or serves as the informing muse between each link, guiding him from one step to the next. Dupin's confident step-by-step explanation of his thought process makes the movement between links or steps appear infallible, but his reference to Epicurus—in which he ponders "how singularly, yet with how little notice, the vague *guesses* of that noble Greek had met with confirmation in the late nebular cosmogony" (536, my emphasis)—reminds the reader that Dupin, too, offers *informed* guesses that end up being correct. When interpreted with Borges's critique of "The Philosophy of Composition" in mind, "The Murders in the Rue Morgue" both prefigures and exemplifies the analytic thought process that Poe attempts to elucidate in his famous essay, since the story suggests that something other than intelligence exists between each link in the poet's or analyst's chain of thought while the essay ignores this possibility.

Borges summarizes his partial acceptance of Poe's poetic theory in the penultimate paragraph of "La génesis de 'El cuervo' de Poe" as follows: "¿Qué conclusiones autorizan los hechos anteriores? Juzgo que las siguientes: primero, la validez del método analítico ejercido por Poe; segundo, la posibilidad de recuperar y fijar los diversos momentos de la creación; tercero, la imposibilidad de reducir el acto poético a un puro esquema lógico, ya que las preferencias del escritor son irreducibles" ["What conclusions do these facts authorize? I suggest the following: first, the validity of the analytic method exercised by Poe; second, the possibility of recovering and pinpointing the diverse moments of creation; third, the impossibility of reducing the poetic act to a purely logical outline since the preferences of the writer are irreducible"] (2). Borges's disagreement with Poe lies not in Poe's attempt to logically explain the poetic process but in his suggestion that the *entire* process— including the poet's "irreducible" predilections—lacks even a hint of magic. Borges applauds Poe for using logic to analyze creativity, but he baulks at Poe's suggestion that all creativity can be reduced to a logical rubric.

The very pattern of Borges's summary subtly reiterates his point by alluding once again to Poe's ratiocinative Dupin. Borges's brief question and the answers that follow recall the summary Dupin offers of his analytic work in the final pages of "The Mystery of Marie Rogêt": "Let us sum up now the meagre yet certain fruits of our long analysis. We have attained the idea either of a fatal accident under the roof of Madame Deluc, or of a murder perpetrated, in the thicket at the Barrière du Roule, by a lover, or at least by an intimate and secret associate of the deceased" (768).[14] By alluding to Poe's master of rational thought in the summary of his verdict on Poe's poetic theory, Borges again hints that Poe himself, in his fiction rather than in his theory, has already depicted analytic thought as a mixture of intellect and inspiration rather than as a process of reason alone. Dupin embodies this coupling of

creativity and acumen since Poe portrays him as both poet and mathematician in the final story of the trilogy—"The Purloined Letter." Dupin's narrative of how he found the queen's letter hidden by Minister D—— in plain
sight suggests that *real* analysis, not the algebraic kind that Dupin critiques
and that the prefect and his men perfect, requires both reason and creativity.
The minister, who is also both mathematician and poet, reasons that the prefect and his men will turn his person and his premises into a mathematical
grid and relentlessly search every inch until they find the letter. However, his
decision to place the letter, turned inside out, in the open where anyone can
see it is a stroke of creative genius based on his previous experience and proclivities. Dupin suggests that D—— "would be driven, as a matter of course,
to *simplicity*, if not deliberately induced to it as a matter of choice" (989), but
the minister's specific enactment of simplicity (the literal refolding and placement of the letter) and Dupin's ability to guess the minister's action before
actually entering the minister's quarters demonstrate that both men connect
the links of the logical chains of thought that they construct through inspiration or informed guessing that reveals their own preferences. In short, Borges
insinuates that Poe's theory in "The Philosophy of Composition," a theory
that Poe describes in logical terms similar to those that he uses to portray the
thought process of his rational detective, does not allow for the very inspiration that distinguishes Dupin from the prefect, the police, and the Parisian
algebraists.

Borges and the Writing Process

Borges's partial belief in Poe's poetic theory could be read as less of a threat
to the *modernistas*' image of Poe than I suggested in the introduction, especially since Borges maintains that inspiration plays a role in the process.
Still, his admission that Poe can even begin to explain the poetic process via
reason—his compromise in treating Poe as romantic classicist and Plato
as classical romanticist, that poetry is both intellect- and muse-inspired—
contradicts Rubén Darío's and the *modernistas*' portrayals of Poe as an "Ariel
hecho hombre" ["Ariel made man"] ("Los raros" 262). Darío, for one, did not
ignore Poe's attempts to replace the muse with the intellect, but he read Poe's
proclivities for science, mathematics, and even analysis as the poet's primary
weaknesses, claiming in "Los raros" that "La ciencia impide al poeta [Poe]
penetrar y tender las alas en la atmósfera de las verdades ideales. Su necesidad
de análisis, la condición algebraica de su fantasía, hácele producir tristísimos
efectos cuando nos arrastra al borde de lo desconocido. La especulación fi-
losófica nubló en él la fe, que debiera poseer como todo poeta verdadero"
["Science impedes the poet [Poe] from penetrating and spreading his wings in
the atmosphere of ideal truths. His need for analysis, the algebraic condition

of his fantasy, makes him produce dismal effects when he drags us to the brink of the unknown. Philosophic speculation clouded in him the faith that every true poet should possess"] (269). Darío's juxtaposition of Poe's "philosophic speculation" with his lack of "faith" attempts to refute in religious language Poe's argument for the intellect over the muse in "The Philosophy of Composition," and his critique of Poe's need for analysis also reiterates the *modernistas'* acceptance of Poe as poet.[15] The "dismal effects" that Darío claims Poe creates appear in Poe's fiction and in his literary criticism, not in his poetry. Darío can criticize Poe but still maintain that Poe is one of "los raros" ["the rare ones"] because he aims his critique only at Poe the fiction writer and the creator of "The Philosophy of Composition"—at the Poe that Poe himself often criticized, the Poe who had to write prose for money.[16]

Darío's critique of this Poe is less a critique of Poe as writer than it is of Poe as a symbol of the United States. Darío claims that Poe was "un fenómeno literario y mental, germinado espontáneamente en una tierra ingrata" ["a literary and mental phenomenon, spontaneously germinated in an ungrateful land"] (251), and he continues, "[n]acido en un país de vida práctica y material, la influencia del medio obra en él al contrario. De un país de cálculo brota imaginación tan estupenda" ["[b]orn in a country of practical and material life, the influence of the environment works in him to the contrary. From a country of calculation sprouts such a stupendous imagination"] (262).[17] By couching his critique of Poe in language that mirrors his critique of the United States, Darío suggests that Poe's supposed flaws—his scientifically, mathematically, and analytically driven prose—should either be forgiven or forgotten because they are the products of his national environment. In contrast, his primary strength, his melancholy poetry, is all the more miraculous because it flourishes in spite of his birth in an unappreciative nation of calculation and practicality and regardless of his need to dedicate significant amounts of time to writing prose in order to earn a living.

Unlike Darío, Borges recognizes the massive influence Poe's efforts to intellectualize poetry in "The Philosophy of Composition" have had on world literature even if the theory itself contains flaws. Indeed, Borges repeatedly claims that Poe's poetic influence—particularly on the French tradition—grows from his theory rather than his actual poetry. However, Borges's repeated recognition of the influence of Poe's theory as expressed in "The Philosophy of Composition" does not mask his growing mistrust in both the theory and the essay itself in his later approaches to Poe's piece. After the partial belief Borges demonstrates in Poe's account of his mental process in "La génesis de 'El cuervo' de Poe," Borges's references to Poe's essay become increasingly skeptical. In *Introducción a la literatura norteamericana*, Borges claims that Poe "explica de qué modo escribió su famoso poema *el cuervo* y analiza, o finge analizar, las diversas etapas de su labor" (18) ["explains how he wrote his famous poem 'The Raven' and analyzes, or pretends to analyze, the various steps in its composition"] (21); in "El cuento policial," he states that Poe's argument for poetry as an exercise of the intellect "es falaz" ["is fallacious"] (233); and in one of his many dialogues with Osvaldo Ferrari, he suggests that Poe either "se equivocaba" ["made a mistake"] when describing poetry as an exercise of the intellect or that he might have written "The Philosophy of Composition" as "una broma" ["a joke"] ("Silvina" 89).[18]

Borges often refers to the tensions between Poe's poetic theory and the theory of the muse when describing his own writing process, and he typically favors the muse. For example, in his prologue to *El informe de Brodie*, he states, "[e]l ejercicio de las letras es misterioso; lo que opinamos es efímero y opto por la tesis platónica de la Musa y no por la de Poe, que razonó, o fingió razonar, que la escritura de un poema es una operación de la inteligencia" (457) ["[t]he craft is mysterious; our opinions are ephemeral, and I prefer Plato's theory of the Muse to that of Poe, who argued, or pretended to argue, that the writing of a poem is an operation of intelligence"] ("Foreword," *Brodie's Report* 346). Borges also describes his writing process as an experience of inspiration in several lectures that he offered throughout his later career. In a lecture entitled "La Poesía" that Borges offered at the Coliseo theater in Buenos Aires in 1977, he claimed,

> Cuando yo escribo algo, tengo la sensación de que ese algo preexiste. Parto de un concepto general; sé más o menos el principio y el fin, y luego voy descubriendo las partes intermedias; pero no tengo la sensación de inventarlas, no tengo la sensación de que dependan de mi arbitrio; las cosas son así. Son así, pero están escondidas y mi deber de poeta es encontrarlas.

> [When I write something, I have the sensation that that something already exists. I begin with a general concept; I know more or less the beginning and the end, and then I go about discovering the intermediate parts; but I do not have the sensation that I invent them, I do not have the sensation that they depend on my will; things are this way. They are this way, but they are hidden, and my duty as a poet is to find them.] (305)[19]

This description of the creative process appears far more similar to the *modernistas'* sentiments on poetry as inspiration than to Poe's thoughts on poetry as intellectual exercise or even to Borges's compromise between inspiration and intellect in his reading of "The Philosophy of Composition" in "La génesis de 'El cuervo' de Poe." In "La poesía," Borges completely derationalizes the writing process by describing the work he goes through to fill in the spaces between the inspired beginning and the inspired ending of a piece as a function of what appears to be an archetypal memory rather than individual intelligence. Instead of inventing the lines, he recalls them, and these recollections have nothing to do with his own will or judgment—they simply exist.[20]

Borges made similar statements in a question-and-answer series at UCLA in 1976 entitled "Borges on Borges" and in one of his radio broadcasts with Osvaldo Ferrari in Buenos Aires in 1984: "Cómo nace y se hace un texto de Borges."[21] In each of these conversations, Borges calls the process a passive one, claims that inspiration *gives* him the key parts of his texts, and suggests that he does all he can to avoid ruining the work through his own intrusion. He appears to adopt the view of writing espoused by the *modernistas* whom he so ardently opposed in his youth. However, both dialogues also show that the muse only speaks momentarily to Borges and that he has to do the rest. At times he describes this work in passive terms—"tengo que descubrir, mediante mis muy limitados medios, qué sucede entre el principio y el fin" ["I have to discover, through my very limited means, what happens between the beginning and the end"] (Borges and Ferrari, "Cómo nace" 62)—but he also admits that both intervention and invention take place: "I have to imagine the setting[,] I have to invent the characters, and so on" ("Borges on Borges" 13). These descriptions support Plato more than Poe, but they do begin to suggest that human intellect participates in this inspired process. Borges's focus on the beginnings and endings of a text in these conversations also recalls the emphasis Poe places on effect and the need to know the end of a poem or a story before putting pen to paper in "The Philosophy of Composition." While Borges and Poe disagree about whether the poet receives or concocts the effect and the dénouement, they agree that the writer must work to connect the two.

Borges's tendency to revise and rerevise his texts several years after their original publications also suggests that he saw the intellect as a part of the muse-driven creation process. Even though Borges depends on the muse to begin the writing process, his own ratiocinative mind eventually enters the picture, and these interruptions can take place during the actual creation process or years later when reviewing his already published work for republication in books, new editions, and/or his ever-growing series of *Obras completas*. One could argue that the revisions themselves are new moments of inspiration. However, in "Borges on Borges" and "Cómo nace y se hace un texto de Borges," Borges claims to see the writing process, after the initial moment of insight, as a drawn-out attempt to portray the original epiphany without ruining it rather than as a process of continual inspiration. While he was alive, so were his texts, and the number of changes he made to them demonstrates sustained thought on a given text's subject matter.

Borges offered these descriptions of his writing process during the last decade of his life, after he had become a global literary icon and while he was writing more poetry than prose. More important for our discussion of

Borges's complex literary relationship with Poe, he made these statements twenty-five to thirty-five years after publishing what is considered his last detective story: "Abenjacán el Bojarí, muerto en su laberinto" ["Ibn-Ḥakam al-Bokhari, Murdered in His Labyrinth"] in 1951. While Borges also gave lectures on detective fiction late in his career, including "El cuento policial" in 1978, in which he dedicates more words to Poe than in any other piece he ever wrote, his depictions of his own writing process in these later years reveal a visible shift from a description of that same process that he provided in the 1950s when he was still immersed in detective fiction.

In a short piece published in the Buenos Aires daily *Clarín* in May 1955, Borges told Lizardo Zia:

> Escribo porque no puedo no escribir, sin ese peculiar sentimiento de desventura que engendran la cobardía y la deslealtad. Me creo mejor razonador, mejor inventor que otros escritores; sé que casi todos escriben mejor que yo, que a casi todos les asiste una espontánea y negligente facilidad que me está vedada y que no lograré ni por la meditación ni por el trabajo ni por la indiferencia ni por el magnífico azar. Escribo, sin embargo, porque para mí no hay otro destino.

> [I write because I cannot not write without that peculiar sentiment of misfortune that cowardice and disloyalty breed. I consider myself a better reasoner, a better inventor than other writers; I know that most writers write better than I do, that most of them are assisted by a spontaneous and careless ease that is forbidden to me and that I will not achieve, not by meditation, nor by work, nor by indifference, nor by the magnificence of chance. I write, however, because for me there is no other destiny.] (Zia 9)[22]

In this piece, Borges casts himself in terms very similar to those used by Poe in "The Philosophy of Composition." Other writers might tap into some sort of muse or "spontaneous" inspiration, but Borges sees himself as a reasoner—as a Dupin or a Poe—whose skills lie in the very concept of invention that is central to Poe's theory but lacking or passive in Borges's later descriptions of his own writing process. In short, Borges the poet of the 1970s and 1980s describes his creative process in the poetic terms of the muse while Borges the detective writer of the 1940s and 1950s portrays this same process as one of reason and intellect.

Perhaps Borges's most even-handed appraisal of his writing process appears in his prologue to *La rosa profunda*, in which he suggests that both Poe and the classicists properly describe the creative process but that they might explain different moments within that process. He states, "La doctrina romántica de una Musa que inspira a los poetas fue la que profesaron los clásicos; la doctrina clásica del poema como una operación de la inteligencia fue enunciada por un romántico, Poe, hacia 1846. [. . .] [E]s evidente que ambas doctrinas tienen su parte de verdad, salvo que corresponden a distintas etapas del proceso" (97) ["The Romantic notion of a Muse who inspires poets was advanced by classical writers; the classical idea of the poem as a function of the intelligence was put forward by a Romantic, Poe, around 1846. [. . .] [I]t is obvious that both doctrines are partially true, unless they correspond to distinct stages in the process"] (343). For most of the prologue, however, Borges favors the muse and practically ignores the compromise that he has set up between inspiration and intellect—that is, until he begins to describe his blindness. He concludes the piece lamenting that blindness takes too central a role in *La rosa profunda:* "Al recorrer las pruebas de este libro, advierto con algún desagrado que la ceguera ocupa un lugar plañidero que no ocupa en mi vida. La ceguera es una clausura, pero también es una liberación, una soledad propicia a las invenciones, una llave y un álgebra" (98) ["Going over the proofs of this book, I notice with some distaste that blindness plays a mournful role, which it does not play in my life. Blindness is a confinement, but it is also a liberation, a solitude propitious to invention, a key and an algebra"] (345). Borges's description of his literal lack of vision functions simultaneously to describe his literary vision. While his blindness closes him off from the world, it creates a solitude that allows his mind to invent, and these inventions help him fill the space between the inspired beginnings and endings of a new literary work given to him by the muse.

Borges's final suggestion that blindness is both a key and an algebra recalls several significant elements in Poe's Dupin tales—the locked-room conundrum in "The Murders in the Rue Morgue" that requires the key of Dupin's intellect to unlock the mystery; the algebra in "The Purloined Letter," which Dupin suggests provides only half the ingredients necessary for true analysis; the blindness of both the king and the prefect of police in front of the letter hidden in plain sight in "The Purloined Letter"; and the feigned blindness of green spectacle–clad Dupin in Minister D——'s chamber, also in "The Purloined Letter."[23] This somewhat veiled allusion to Poe serves as a clue left in plain sight that, once discovered, allows us to connect Borges's concluding thoughts on blindness back to his earlier claim in the prologue that both the classicists and Poe captured part of the creative process in their disparate descriptions. This connection demonstrates that while Borges openly argues for inspiration, he covertly suggests that his own writing process is similar to the compromise between mind and muse that he first put forth in his analysis of Poe's creative process in "La génesis de 'El cuervo' de Poe."

Borges had already played Poe's game of hiding clues in plain sight while analyzing Poe's work in his 1936 piece "Las *Kenningar*," almost four decades before his prologue to *La rosa profunda* and only a year after playing this trick in "La génesis de 'El cuervo' de Poe."[24] In this text, Borges describes his fascination with the ancient and circular literary trope of the kenning and its usage in Icelandic poetry. In a list of over a hundred examples that he provides for his readers, Borges gives four kennings for "el cuervo" or "the raven": "gaviota del odio," "gaviota de las heridas," "caballo de la bruja," and "primo del cuervo" ["gull of hate," "gull of wounds," "horse of the witch," and "cousin of the raven"] (372). For this last kenning, he provides the following footnote: "*Definitum in definitione ingredi non debet* es la segunda regla menor de la definición. Risueñas infracciones como esta (y aquella venidera de *dragón de la espada: la espada*) recuerdan el artificio de aquel personaje de Poe que en trance de ocultar una carta a la curiosidad policial, la exhibe como al desgaire en un tarjetero" ["*A thing defined ought not to enter into a definition* is the second minor rule of the definition. Laughable infractions like this (and the upcoming one of *dragon of the sword: the sword*) recall the trickery of that character of Poe who, in the critical moment of hiding a letter from the police's curiosity, exhibits it carelessly in a cardholder"] (372 n.1).

Borges's reference to Minister D——'s ingenious hiding of the queen's letter out in the open for everyone to see is certainly relevant in his description of how certain kennings break the rule of not including the noun being described by the kenning itself. However, Borges practices his own artifice on the reader of "Las *Kenningar*," since the specific noun in question is "el cuervo"—the Spanish title of Poe's most popular poem in Spanish America, the key text in the *modernistas'* reception and proliferation of Poe as poet-prophet. Borges's allusion to "The Purloined Letter" and his glossing over "The Raven" serve as a type of reverse kenning that buries or hides the poem's visible title behind the unstated title of the story rather than suggesting the title through circumlocution the way a kenning typically does. Borges's reference to "The Purloined Letter" in his footnote to the phrase "primo del cuervo" also allows us to read both "el cuervo" and "primo del cuervo" as visible yet hidden titles to Poe texts rather than simply as a noun and its rule-breaking kenning. Indeed, the pair no longer breaks the rule of using the noun in its own definition since the short story "The Purloined Letter," rather than "The Raven" itself, steps in as the cousin to the poem. In this case, the kenning ceases to function as a kenning since it no longer describes the noun/title "The Raven" but instead describes something related to but distinct from "The Raven": "The Purloined Letter."

Borges's treatment of "el cuervo" and "primo del cuervo" serves as an early and complex plain-sight clue to Borges's favoring of Poe's fiction over his poetry. The noun "el cuervo" sits in open view and brings Poe's poem to mind, but it is merely a ruse that justifies Borges's reference to "primo del cuervo" or "The Purloined Letter." In "Las *Kenningar*," Borges subtly continues to supplant Poe's poetry with his fiction by glossing over the poem that the *modernistas* see as Poe's masterwork with a footnote that refers to Poe's detective fiction and by performing the entire stunt via one of Poe's preferred fictional methods of hiding an object in plain sight. Borges's emphasis on "The Purloined Letter" and his hiding or purloining of "The Raven" also cast Poe as a precursor to the detective fiction Borges writes during the next fifteen years of his career.

Borges had already started using this strategy of subtly praising Poe's fiction over his poetry by leaving hidden clues in plain sight in the conclusion of his analysis of "The Philosophy of Composition" in "La génesis de 'El cuervo' de Poe." Borges concludes this article—a piece that, as we have already seen, creates a hidden conversation with Poe's Dupin trilogy—by stating that "[e]l valor del análisis de Poe es considerable: afirmar la inteligencia lúcida y torpe y negar la insensata inspiración no es cosa baladí. Sin embargo, que no se alarmen con exceso los nebulosos *amateurs* del misterio: el problema central de la creación está por resolver" ["[t]he value of Poe's analysis is considerable: declaring intelligence lucid and clumsy and denying foolish inspiration is not a paltry thing. However, the nebulous *amateurs* of the mystery should not alarm themselves in excess: the central problem of creation is yet to be solved"] (2). Borges's use of the terminology of detective fiction to describe the creative process as "the central problem" or "mystery" that still has no solution transforms "The Philosophy of Composition" from a poetic theory into a detective story. Borges's continual focus on reason in this article and his concluding references to mysteries and solutions demonstrate that he sees fiction—particularly detective fiction—as Poe's strength even though Borges does not directly reference Poe's fiction even once in "La génesis de 'El cuervo' de Poe." Poe's "The Philosophy of Composition" serves as a springboard by which Borges enters the contemporary conversation about Poe as poet in both the Río de la Plata region and Spanish America, and it is the tool Borges uses to conceal various clues that will eventually shatter Poe's poetic image and replace it with a new version of Poe that emphasizes his invention of the detective genre and his fiction in general—a Poe who serves as a precursor to Borges's fiction rather than as the muse for the *modernistas*.

Renaming Poe

In 1949, fourteen years after Borges hinted at the supremacy of Poe's fiction over his verse in "La génesis de 'El cuervo' de Poe," he explicitly places Poe's fiction in a position of prominence over his poetry in a short piece entitled "Edgar Allan Poe," published in the Buenos Aires daily La Nación, in commemoration of the centennial of Poe's death. It is important to note that during this same interval between Borges's two primary newspaper articles on Poe he also published his most important collections of short fiction: *El jardín de senderos que se bifurcan* (1941), *Ficciones* (1944)—which includes a republishing of *El jardín de senderos que se bifurcan* and a collection of new stories under the title *Artificios*—and *El Aleph* (1949). Borges's willingness to more overtly praise Poe's fiction in 1949 than he did as a young poet and critic in 1935 reflects his own growing reputation as a fiction writer.

Borges begins "Edgar Allan Poe" by commenting on Poe's neurosis in a manner very similar to that which Charles Baudelaire, the French symbolists, Darío, and the Spanish American *modernistas* had adopted in their discussions of Poe. He states: "Detrás de Poe (como detrás de Swift, de Carlyle, de Almafuerte) hay una neurosis. Interpretar su obra en función de esa anomalía puede ser abusivo o legítimo. Es abusivo cuando se alega la neurosis para invalidar o negar la obra; es legítimo cuando se busca en la neurosis un medio para entender su génesis" ["Behind Poe (as behind Swift, Carlyle, Almafuerte) there is a neurosis. Interpreting his work based on that anomaly can be outrageous or legitimate. It is outrageous when the neurosis is put forth to invalidate or reject the work; it is legitimate when one searches for a means to understand the genesis of the work in the neurosis"] (1). Borges's statement appears to relegitimize, in the literary atmosphere of the Río de la Plata region that had finally begun to challenge this interpretation of Poe's biography, the emphasis Baudelaire and his followers had previously placed on Poe's manias, addictions, and so-called decadence and the sympathetic reading of Poe's alcoholism offered by Darío. While, as Englekirk suggests, Darío recognized in Poe's bouts with drinking a kindred spirit seeking to drown away sorrows (179–80), Borges's fellow Argentine, Carlos Obligado, had vehemently argued against such romanticized interpretations of Poe's tragic biography in the early 1930s when he published his now-famous translations of Poe's poems.[25] In the prologue to *Los poemas de Edgar Poe*, Obligado scoffs at "¡[l]a leyenda de Edgar Poe: su fantástica cuanto perdurable reputación de degenerado y de alcoholista!" ["[t]he legend of Edgar Poe: his fantastic yet lasting reputation as a degenerate and an alcoholic!"], blaming the "floración venenosa" ["poisonous blooming"] of Poe's negative reputation on "una sola semilla" ["one single seed"]: Rufus Griswold, who continually defamed Poe in print after Poe's untimely death (19–20).[26]

Although Obligado suggests that Poe "[m]urió, literalmente, de miseria" ["[d]ied, literally, of misery"] (19), he never argues that Poe's misery serves as his muse. Borges, in contrast, returns to Poe's miserable existence at the end of "Edgar Allan Poe" to claim that Poe's adversity makes his work possible: "Shakespeare ha escrito que son dulces los empleos de la adversidad; sin la neurosis, el alcohol, la pobreza, la soledad irreparable, no existiría la obra de Poe" ["Shakespeare has written that the uses of adversity are sweet; without neurosis, alcohol, poverty, and irreparable solitude, Poe's work would not exist"] (1). Borges's treatment of Poe's problems recalls Darío's lamentations for the fallen poet-prophet and serves to further romanticize Poe's image.[27] Indeed, Borges's claim that "cabría decir que Poe sacrificó la vida a la obra, el destino mortal al destino póstumo" ["it could be said that Poe sacrificed his life to his work, his mortal destiny to his posthumous destiny"] (1) appears to mirror Darío's own claim that Poe "[n]ació con la adorable llama de la poesía, y ella le alimentaba al propio tiempo que era su martirio" ["was born with the adorable flame of poetry, and she nurtured him at the same time that she was his martyrdom"] ("Los raros" 267). The juxtaposition of these two claims about Poe's death, however, demonstrates how Borges's interpretation of Poe breaks from that of the *modernistas*. Darío claims that "poetry" was the key to both Poe's life and death while Borges states that Poe sacrifices his life to his "work." As the remainder of "Edgar Allan Poe" demonstrates, this work, in Borges's eyes, is prose rather than poetry.

In sharp contrast with both his *modernista* predecessors and his contemporary Obligado, Borges argues that Poe's poetry is less important than his image as a poet: "Harto más firme y duradera que las poesías de Poe es la figura de Poe como poeta, legada a la imaginación de los hombres" ["Much steadier and more enduring than Poe's poems is the figure of Poe as poet, passed on to men's imaginations"] (1).[28] And this image, he suggests, is completely disconnected from any of Poe's poems, which, with few exceptions, Borges calls "mera trivialidad, sensiblería, mal gusto, débiles remedos de Thomas Moore" ["pure triviality, sentimentality, poor taste, weak imitations of Thomas Moore"] (1).[29] Instead, Poe's poetic image grows directly from the theory Poe puts forth in "The Philosophy of Composition." Borges states, "Nuestra imagen de Poe, la de un artífice que premedita y ejecuta su obra con lenta lucidez, al margen del favor popular, procede menos de las piezas de Poe que de la doctrina que enuncia en el ensayo *The philosophy of composition*. De esa doctrina, no de *Dreamland* o de *Israfel*, se derivan Mallarmé y Paul Valéry" ["Our image of Poe, the image of the author who premeditates and executes his work with slow lucidity, at the margins of popular favor, derives less from Poe's pieces than from the doctrine that he enunciates in the essay 'The Philosophy of Composition.' From that doctrine, not from 'Dreamland' or from 'Israfel,' stem Mallarmé and Paul Valéry"] (1).

After this scathing appraisal of Poe's poetry and this reminder of the far-reaching influence of "The Philosophy of Composition," Borges renames Poe as a master of short fiction: "Poe se creía poeta, sólo poeta, pero las circunstancias lo llevaron a escribir cuentos, y esos cuentos a cuya escritura se resignó y que debió encarar como tareas ocasionales son su inmortalidad" ["Poe believed himself a poet, a poet only, but his circumstances made him write stories, and these stories that he resigned himself to write and which he faced as occasional tasks are his immortality"] (1). This statement, regardless of the romantic and neurotic biography Borges uses to introduce it, shatters the Poe of Borges's *modernista* predecessors, the poet-prophet, and replaces him with a timeless craftsman of fiction. Following the terminology of detective fiction that Borges has so often returned to when discussing Poe, Borges's claim serves as the final solution to the mystery of Poe's identity—a solution that confirms the numerous but furtive clues Borges had left behind in his readings of "The Philosophy of Composition"—and simultaneously delegitimizes the *modernistas'* interpretation of Poe as a mistake, a trick, or a false solution.

To emphasize his break with the *modernistas'* image of Poe, Borges concludes "Edgar Allan Poe" by arguing that it is ridiculous to read Poe as somehow deracinated from the United States, as Baudelaire, the French symbolists, Darío, and the Spanish American *modernistas* typically do. He states, "La verdad es que Poe hubiera padecido en cualquier país. Nadie, por lo demás, admira a Baudelaire contra Francia o a Coleridge contra Inglaterra" ["The truth is that Poe would have suffered in any country. No one, moreover, admires Baudelaire against France or Coleridge against England"] (1). In short, Borges reintroduces the *modernistas'* Poe—the tragic, neurotic poet-prophet—only to supplant him, and although Borges's Poe is every bit as anxious as the *modernistas'* Poe, his anxiety—coupled with necessity— serves as the creative force for his tales of obsession, terror, ratiocination, and revenge rather than as a melancholy muse for the poems that Poe preferred and that his *modernista* admirers adored. By openly renaming Poe, Borges also "creates a precursor" for his own fantastic tales and detective stories and further legitimizes the fictional bent his own literary career takes from 1935 to 1949, fourteen of his most prolific years as a writer. With the publication of *Historia universal de la infamia*, 1935 was a year of genesis in which Borges began to change his own reputation. The publication of *El Aleph* in 1949, while certainly not the end of Borges's career as a fiction writer, serves, perhaps, as the zenith for Borges the author of fiction since Borges the poet and literary critic once again moves to the forefront by the 1960s and remains there until his death. Tellingly, Borges frames his fourteen most prolific years of fiction writing with two articles on Poe in which he reframes Poe the poet into Poe the fictional mastermind.

Even before Borges's reassessment of Poe in his 1949 article, at least one other literary critic in the Río de la Plata region had also shifted his emphasis away from Poe's poetry and toward his fiction. Santiago A. Ferrari states at the beginning of his 1946 *Edgar Allan Poe: Genio narrador* that "[a]l llamar a Poe *genio* narrador estamos diciendo desde la portada que le estudiamos ante todo como cuentista. [. . .] Y le llamamos *genio* no sólo por su valor, sino también por su temperamento: Poe tiene el genio, el alma del contador de cuentos, y esto es lo que queremos significar con el título" ["[b]y calling Poe a brilliant *narrator*, we are saying from the very beginning that we study him, above all else, as a short-story writer. [. . .] And we call him *genius* not only for his importance but also for his temperament. Poe has the temperament, the soul of a storyteller, and this is what we want the title to signify"] (7, italics in original). In his title and throughout his text, Ferrari plays with the multiple meanings of the word "genio" in Spanish. With the cognate "genius" so easily accessible in English, Ferrari's multiple meanings can easily be lost in English translation. The primary definitions of "genio" concern condition or temperament, while its secondary definitions refer to brilliance or genius, and each time Ferrari uses the term in his opening remarks, he does so with double meaning ("Genio"). His text's subtitle can be translated as *Brilliant Narrator*, *Genius Narrator*, or *Narrative Genius*, but his discussion of the title reveals that Ferrari also has *Narrative Temperament* in mind.

Ferrari analyzes the majority of Poe's stories, but he begins his analysis with a chapter on Poe's poetry in which he suggests that "'El cuervo' no es una oda ni es una elegía, es un cuento en verso, es un relato con todas las características que dan interés a los relatos: expectación, misterio, sorpresa, diálogo, hechos" ["'The Raven' is not an ode nor an elegy, it is a story in verse, it is a tale with all the characteristics that make tales interesting: anticipation, mystery, surprise, dialogue, actions"] (27) and that all of Poe's most well-known poems "son relatos o fragmentos de un relato" ["are tales or fragments of a tale"] (28). He concludes this chapter by stating that "[p]orque siendo un cuentista hasta la última fibra de su ser, forzosamente había de inclinarse cada vez más a la prosa cuando tenía una verdadera idea poética; y cuando se quedaba con el verso, muchas veces le faltaba la idea adecuada" ["[b]ecause being a story writer to the last fiber of his being, necessarily he had to become more and more inclined to prose when he had a truly poetic idea; and when he stuck with verse, many times he lacked the appropriate idea"] (29).

This judgment is a far cry from the *modernistas'* praise of Poe as poet. Santiago Ferrari's sentiments about Poe as a story writer who merely tried to create poetry do not correspond with the majority opinion on Poe in the Río de la Plata region in the 1940s, but neither do they emerge out of nowhere. Instead, Ferrari's thoughts on Poe are an early outcome of Borges's attempts to redefine Poe in his literary criticism and in his own fiction. Ferrari claims to have been studying Poe seriously since 1930 (7), and although Borges did not blatantly reclassify Poe as a fiction writer until 1949, we have already seen that he had been subtly suggesting as much since at least 1935. However, Borges's 1935 "La génesis de 'El cuervo' de Poe" was not his first commentary on Poe, nor was his 1949 "Edgar Allan Poe" his first attempt to differentiate between Poe's poems and his poetic theory. In the version of "El otro Whitman" that Borges published in his 1932 collection *Discusión*, he claims that Poe's "buena teoría" ["good theory"] rather than "su deficiente práctica" ["his deficient practice"] was what had served as such an immense influence on the French poetic tradition (208).[30] In a 1937 review of Edward Shanks's book on Poe, which Borges published in the pages of the Buenos Aires weekly *El Hogar*,

Borges claims that "Muy poco sobrevive de su verso; 'El cuervo', 'Las campa-nas' y 'Annabel Lee' han sido relegadas al submundo (sin duda menos infer-nal que molesto) de la declamación" ["Very little of his verse survives; 'The Raven,' 'The Bells,' and 'Annabel Lee' have been relegated to the underworld (without a doubt less infernal than bothersome) of oral delivery"] ("*Edgar Allan Poe*, de Edward Shanks" 332). Moreover,

> Queda su teoría poética, harto superior a su práctica. Quedan nueve o diez cuentos indiscutibles: "El escarabajo de oro", "El doble asesinato de la Rue Morgue", "El tonel de amontillado", "El pozo y el péndulo", "El caso del señor Valdemar", "La carta robada", el "Descenso al Maelström", el "Manuscrito encontrado en una botella", "Hop-Frog". Queda el ambiente peculiar de esas narraciones, inconfundible como un rostro o una música. Queda el *Retrato de Arthur Gordon Pym*. Queda la invención del género policial. Queda M. Paul Valéry. Todo ello basta para la justificación de su gloria, pese a las redundancias y languideces que sufre cada página. (333)

> [His poetic theory remains, much superior to his practice. Nine or ten indisput-able stories remain: "The Gold-Bug," "The Murders in the Rue Morgue," "The Cask of Amontillado," "The Pit and the Pendulum," "The Facts in the Case of M. Valdemar," "The Purloined Letter," "A Descent into the Maelström," "MS Found in a Bottle," "Hop-Frog." The peculiar ambiance of these narrations remains, unmistakable like a face or a song. *The Narrative of Arthur Gordon Pym* remains. The invention of the detective genre remains. M. Paul Valéry re-mains. All of this is enough to justify his glory, regardless of the redundancies and languishing suffered on each page.][31]

This passage not only shows how Borges's rankings of Poe's accomplish-ments favor the latter's prose over his poetry, but it also distinguishes Borges's interpretation of Poe from that of someone like Bloom. Borges and Bloom find similar weaknesses in Poe's work, but for Bloom these issues make Poe unreadable while for Borges the genius and the influence of Poe's pages trump the surface-level problems of his writing style.

Borges published both "El otro Whitman" and his review of Shanks's book after *modernismo*'s apogee but still during Poe's reign as poet-prophet in the Río de la Plata region. Indeed, both of these articles appeared during a decade-long translation frenzy of Poe's poetry in Buenos Aires that produced two of the most important translations of Poe's poetry ever into the Spanish language and another volume of translations that remains well respected in the region: Francisco Soto y Calvo's 1927 collection *Joyario de Poe*, which Englekirk notes as the first translation of Poe's complete poems in Spanish America (55); Carlos Obligado's aforementioned *Los poemas de Edgar Poe:*

Traducción, prólogo y notas from 1932; and Alberto L. Von Schauenberg's 1937 *Edgar Poe: Traducción de sus poemas*.[32]

The extensive bibliography that accompanies Englekirk's text demonstrates the influence Poe still exercised as a poet in Spanish America in the early 1930s, while Rafael Heliodoro Valle's "Fichas para la Bibliografía de Poe en Hispanoamérica" shows that this enthusiasm extends at least until 1949. Heliodoro Valle's bibliography contains more Spanish American translations of and critical pieces about Poe's fiction than Englekirk's, but he still claims that "[e]studiar a Poe sigue siendo preocupación de quienes se interesan por el destino de la Poesía" ["[s]tudying Poe continues to be the preoccupation of those who are interested in the destiny of Poetry"] (199). However, the very publication of Santiago Ferrari's text in 1946 suggests that Borges's thoughts on Poe were spreading, that other critics in the region were beginning to see Poe as something other than a poet.

Hensley C. Woodbridge's "Poe in Spanish America: A Bibliographical Supplement" in the second volume of the *Poe Newsletter* in 1969 cites almost an equal number of articles about and translations of Poe's fiction as his poetry, thus demonstrating a significant change in Poe's reputation throughout Spanish America. "The International Poe Bibliography," published by *Poe Studies* from 1969 into the twenty-first century, and edited collections such as Lois Davis Vines's 1999 *Poe Abroad: Influence, Reputation, Affinities* reveal even more clearly that Poe's standing in both the Río de la Plata region and Spanish America in general shifted from poet to fiction writer in the last quarter of the twentieth century and that this reputation has persisted into the first decade of the twenty-first. Most tellingly, the 2008–2009 rerelease of Julio Cortázar's translation of Poe's tales with introductions from Carlos Fuentes and Mario Vargas Llosa and commentary for each story from a different post-Boom fiction writer from either Spain or Spanish America shows that the Poe of today's Spanish-speaking world is Borges's Poe rather than the Poe of the *modernistas*.[33]

Borges's work alone did not cause this shift in Poe's reputation in Spanish America from poet to fiction writer, but he was the earliest, most insistent, and most successful catalyst for this change, and his influence on Poe's reputation in the Río de la Plata region and throughout Spanish America only continued to increase as Borges himself moved from national to regional to global literary icon. Unlike Baudelaire, Borges was not a Poe advocate as much as he was a writer whose criticism and fiction often responded to Poe. He effectively replaced the melancholy, tragic poet the *modernistas* adored with a creative reasoner and story writer by preferring the theory Poe declares in "The Philosophy of Composition" over the very poetry Poe claims to unpack through this theory, by reading the entire essay in terms of detective fiction, and by openly calling Poe a poor poet and a brilliant story writer. This reimagining of Poe rewrites Spanish American literary history, situating Poe as a predecessor to the fantastic, analytic, and cerebral fiction of the mid- to late 1900s, the literature that boosts Borges to world fame, rather than as a precursor to the *modernista* poetry that marked Spanish America's turn of the century.

CHAPTER 2

Reading and Rereading

Apart from his repeated analyses of "The Philosophy of Composition" and his open renaming of Poe, Borges also reveals in his literary criticism, lectures, and interviews that he was familiar with the breadth of Poe's literary canon from his poems to his stories and from his only published novel to his essays. In the third of seven lectures that Borges offered at the Coliseo theater in Buenos Aires between June and August 1980—"La poesía"—his discussion of Poe's fear of mirrors demonstrates his broad reading of Poe's literary corpus:

> [S]iempre he sentido el terror de los espejos. Creo que Poe lo sintió también. Hay un trabajo suyo, uno de los menos conocidos, sobre el decorado de las habitaciones. Una de las condiciones que pone es que los espejos estén situados de modo que una persona sentada no se refleje. Esto nos informa de su temor de verse en el espejo. Lo vemos en su cuento "William Wilson" sobre el doble y en el cuento de *Arthur Gordon Pym*.

> [I have always felt the terror of mirrors. I believe that Poe felt it too. There is a work of his, one of the lesser-known works, about the decoration of rooms. One of the conditions that he sets is that the mirrors be situated in a manner that a seated person is not reflected. This apprises us of his fear of seeing himself in the mirror. We see this in his story about the double "William Wilson" and in the story of *Arthur Gordon Pym*.] (311)

In this lecture, Borges demonstrates again, although this time in the covert fashion of his "La génesis de 'El cuervo' de Poe" rather than in the open manner of "Edgar Allan Poe," his favoritism for Poe's prose over his poetry since he titles the lecture "La poesía" but only mentions Poe's prose works. Borges recalls the terror caused by mirrors in two of Poe's most famous pieces— "William Wilson" and the *Narrative of Arthur Gordon Pym*—but more impressively, at almost eighty-one years old, he remembers how Poe situates mirrors in his far lesser-known essay "Philosophy of Furniture." The specificity of this recollection, especially for someone who read as widely as Borges did, suggests that Borges either had a remarkable memory like his title character in "Funes el memorioso" ["Funes, His Memory"] or that he often returned to Poe's works.

Borges's own writings and lectures suggest the latter. In his short story

"Utopía de un hombre que está cansado" ["A Weary Man's Utopia"], a man in the future tells the narrator/time traveler "no importa leer sino releer" (68) ["it is not the reading that matters, but the rereading"] (462),[1] and in his lecture "El libro," Borges claims: "Yo he tratado más de releer que de leer, creo que releer es más importante que leer, salvo que para releer se necesita haber leído" ["I have tried more to reread than to read, I believe that rereading is more important than reading, except that to reread one needs to have read"] (204).[2] On several occasions, Borges named the authors to whose work he most often returned. In his "Autobiographical Notes" with Norman Thomas di Giovanni, he states, "I have always been a reader and rereader of short stories. Stevenson, Kipling, James, Conrad, Poe, Chesterton, the tales of Lane's 'Arabian Nights,' and certain stories by Hawthorne have been habits of mine since I can remember" (78), and in "El taller del escritor"—an article Borges published in the Buenos Aires daily *La Prensa*—he claims: "No leo; releo [. . .] Releo a Poe" ["I do not read; I reread [. . .] I reread Poe"] (353).

Borges offers his most lengthy analyses of Poe's texts and Poe's life in a limited number of articles, prologues, lectures, and dialogues dedicated specifically to Poe, which we have already examined in the previous chapter. However, the vast majority of his references to Poe appear in articles on subjects other than Poe, book reviews, and prologues for other authors' texts. Reviews and prologues might not carry the scholarly weight (or length) of an academic article, interview, or lecture, but their close connection to the texts they review or precede makes them at least as influential on the reading public (rather than on the literati and/or academics) as longer and/or more formal types of literary criticism. Indeed, Borges even set out to reclaim the prologue as genre in "Prólogo de prólogos," stating, "[e]l prólogo, cuando son propicios los astros, no es una forma subalterna de brindis; es una especie lateral de la crítica" ["[t]he prologue, when the stars are propitious, is not a subaltern form of praise; it is a lateral form of criticism"] (14).

Borges's references to Poe in articles not focused on Poe, reviews, and prologues demonstrate that Borges not only rereads Poe on a personal level but that he also causes, or at least invites, his audience to reread Poe either literally or through memory every time he alludes to Poe's work. Furthermore, Borges's Poe references frame his audience's understanding of the subject at hand, the book being reviewed, or the text being prefaced via Poe. These references also ask the audience to reshape their own image of Poe away from that of poet toward that of fiction writer since almost all these references to Poe allude to his fiction rather than to his poetry. Borges's invitations cover a wide variety of Poe's stories, but they most often refer to his connection to the analytic detective genre or to Poe's only novel: *The Narrative of Arthur Gordon Pym of Nantucket*.

Poe in Borges's Reviews of Contemporary Detective Fiction

Borges most often referred to Poe and the detective genre in the pages of the Buenos Aires weekly *El Hogar* and the influential literary magazine *Sur* in the 1930s and 1940s. In these pieces, he consistently names Poe as the inventor of the genre, and he frames his readings of contemporary detective writers through Poe.[3] For example, Borges begins his discussion of G. K. Chesterton's detective novels as follows in "Modos de G. K. Chesterton," published in *Sur* a month after Chesterton's death:

> Edgar Allan Poe escribió cuentos de puro horror fantástico o de pura *bizarrerie*; Edgar Allan Poe fue inventor del cuento policial. Ello no es menos indudable que el hecho de que no combinó jamás los dos géneros. Nunca invocó el socorro del sedentario caballero francés Augusto Dupin (de la rue Dunot) para determinar el crimen preciso del Hombre de las Multitudes o para elucidar el *modus operandi* del simulacro que fulminó a los cortesanos de Próspero, y aun a ese mismo dignatario, durante la famosa epidemia de la Muerte Roja. Chesterton, en las diversas narraciones que integran la quíntuple Saga del Padre Brown y las de Gabriel Gale el poeta y las del Hombre Que Sabía Demasiado, ejecuta, siempre, ese *tour de force*.

> [Edgar Allan Poe wrote stories of pure fantastic horror and of pure *bizarrerie*; Edgar Allan Poe was the inventor of detective fiction. This is no less unquestionable than the fact that he never combined the two genres. He never invoked the support of the sedentary French gentleman Auguste Dupin (of the rue Dunot) to determine the precise crime of the Man of the Crowd or to elucidate the *modus operandi* of the simulacrum that struck dead the members of Prospero's court, and even this dignitary himself, during the famous epidemic of the Red Death. Chesterton, in the diverse narrations that make up the quintuple Saga of Father Brown and those of Gabriel Gale the poet and those of the Man Who Knew Too Much, executes, always, this *tour de force*.] (20)

Borges continues the article by praising Chesterton's ability to mix the natural with the supernatural while always providing a realistic and satisfactory solution to each story's crime or problem, but these compliments are couched in and remind the reader of the pattern set by Poe. What impresses Borges about Chesterton is that Chesterton successfully fuses two of Poe's genres that Poe never attempted to mix himself and that he does so without breaking one of the cardinal rules that Poe sets in "The Murders in the Rue Morgue," when Dupin begins to reveal how he solved the original locked-room conundrum with these thoughts on the supernatural: "It is not too much to say that neither of us believe in præternatural events. Madame and Mademoiselle

L'Espanaye were not destroyed by spirits. The doers of the deed were material, and escaped materially" (551). Unlike Poe, Chesterton allows his characters to consider supernatural solutions—something that Dupin eliminates immediately—but like Poe, Chesterton always provides a rational rather than a magical solution for every crime; his criminals, too, are of flesh and blood. Borges's praise for Chesterton shows how the latter complicates and enriches Poe's analytic detective model, but it does so in a way that respects Poe and casts him as the cornerstone upon which all detective fiction is built.

Borges also frames his accolades for the work of Ellery Queen around Poe. In a review published in *El Hogar*—"*Half-Way House*, de Ellery Queen"—he again names "The Murders in the Rue Morgue" as the genre's genesis and claims that Queen offers a significant "desviación, o un pequeño progreso" ["deviation, or a bit of progress"] in the genre's history (264). Borges suggests that "Ellery Queen juega con lo sobrenatural, como Chesterton, pero de un modo lícito: [. . .] Queen propone, como los otros, una explicación nada interesante, deja entrever (al fin) una solución hermosísima, de la que se enamora el lector, la refuta y descubre una tercera, que es la correcta: siempre menos extraña que la segunda, pero del todo imprevisible y satisfactoria" ["Ellery Queen plays with the supernatural, like Chesterton, but in an allowable way: [. . .] Queen proposes, like the others, a boring explanation; he allows the reader to glimpse (at the end) a beautiful solution that the reader falls in love with; he refutes it and discovers a third, which is the correct one: always less strange than the second, but completely unforeseeable and satisfactory"] (264). Borges's praise for Queen's detective fiction and his approval of Chesterton's work suggest that both writers improve upon Poe's detective fiction by bringing the supernatural into the text, but the progression reiterates Poe's model rather than obliterating it since both writers eventually disprove their supernatural resolutions in favor of ingenious yet plausible solutions.

In short, Chesterton and Queen accomplish in their detective fiction what Borges suggests the best supernatural writers, including Poe, achieve: the portrayal but eventual denial of the supernatural. In a review of "*The Haunted Omnibus*, de Alexander Laing" for *El Hogar*, Borges states that "los mejores cuentos sobrenaturales [. . .] son obra de escritores que negaban lo sobrenatural. La razón es clara. El escritor escéptico es aquel que organiza mejor los efectos mágicos" ["the best supernatural stories [. . .] are the work of writers who denied the supernatural. The reason is clear. The skeptical writer is the one who best organizes the magical effects"] (365).[4] Poe's usage of the supernatural almost always follows this pattern of denial. At times—for example, "Some Words with a Mummy," "Ligeia," or "The Angel of the Odd"—Poe drops subtle hints that the strangest events in the stories are substance induced, and in other stories, particularly "The Black Cat," Poe's narrator goes out of his way to use reason to trump the supernatural as he attempts to find a meaning in the figure of the hanging cat that appears on the only remaining wall of his fire-ravaged house (853). Borges sees in both Queen and Chesterton a fusion of Poe's disparate strengths—his ability to tell a believable supernatural tale and his creation of the analytic detective story whose protagonist uses his mental acumen to provide real solutions to difficult, or even "unnatural," crimes. Chesterton's and Queen's detective fictions, at least according to Borges's interpretations, do not reject Poe but "out-Poe" Poe by successfully developing the effects of the supernatural tale *and* the detective story in one piece, without letting either effect destroy the other—something that Poe never attempted.[5] Borges applauds Queen's and Chesterton's work for improving the detective genre by introducing supernatural elements; however, he enjoys their detective fiction precisely because it maintains Dupin's realist rules within its final solutions.

Borges's insistence on Poe as the inventor of the detective genre even leads to a controversy between himself and Roger Caillois—the very man who is credited with later introducing Borges's writings to the French-speaking world. Borges begins "Roger Caillois: *Le roman policier*"—his review of Caillois's book on detective fiction in the April 1942 issue of *Sur*—by claiming that the literary sections of Caillois's text are "muy valedero" ["very valid"] while the sociological and historical parts of the book are "muy *unconvincing*" (248). He ends the piece with a compliment: "Muchas páginas he leído (y escrito) sobre el género policial. Ninguna me parece tan justa como éstas de Caillois" ["Many pages have I read (and written) about the detective genre. None of them appear as right to me as these by Caillois"] (251), but the critique he offers in the body of the essay catches Caillois's attention and elicits a response. Borges criticizes Caillois for attempting to set "los espías anónimos de Fouché, el horror de la idea de polizontes disfrazados y ubicuos" ["Fouché's anonymous spies, the horror of the idea of disguised and ubiquitous police agents"] as the "circunstancia concreta" ["concrete circumstance"] that gave rise to the detective genre (248). "Verosímilmente," he claims, "la prehistoria del género policial está en los hábitos mentales y en los irrecuperables *Erlebnisse* de Edgar Allan Poe, su inventor; no en la aversión que produjeron, hacia 1799, los *agents provocateurs* de Fouché" ["Realistically, the prehistory of the detective genre is in the mental habits and in the irrecoverable *Erlebnisse* of Edgar Allan Poe, its inventor, not in the aversion that Fouché's *agents provocateurs* produced around 1799"] (249).

The same number of *Sur* includes Caillois's response, "Rectificación a una nota de Jorge Luis Borges," in which Caillois argues that he knows Poe invented the detective genre and that his discussion of Fouché's police agents was an attempt to show, not the origin of the genre, but the milieu of paranoia about the police that allowed for the detective genre's unprecedented success (71). Caillois appears to quickly thank Borges for the bits of praise his article offers, but the majority of the piece takes a defensive stance against Borges's review, and it concludes with this caustic bit of sarcasm: "Pero qué agradable es tan extraño modo de concebir la crítica, que obliga al autor sorprendido a formarse una buena opinión de sí mismo al verificar que en su propio texto estaba bien dicho lo que creía haber dicho, en vez de las tonterías que (para procurarle esta satisfacción de amor propio) su benévolo examinador había simulado descubrir" ["But how pleasant is this strange manner of conceiving criticism that obligates the author, surprised to form a good opinion of himself on verifying that in his own text it was well said what he believed he had said, instead of the stupidities that (seeking to find this satisfaction of self-love) his benevolent examiner had pretended to discover"] (72).[6] In the following number of *Sur*, Borges ends the debate with a short response entitled "Observación final." He does not react to Caillois's counterattack by taking a personal shot at Caillois. Instead, he calls the Frenchman's logic about history's influence on events flawed and argues that "[e]l género policial tiene un siglo, el género policial es un ejercicio de las literaturas de idioma ingles ¿por qué indagar su causalidad, su prehistoria, en una circunstancia francesa?" ["[t]he detective genre is a century old, the detective genre is a tradition of the literatures of the English language. Why investigate its origin, its prehistory, in a French circumstance?"] (252).

Borges's stance—his favoring of a literary genesis over a historical birth of the detective genre and his preference for English over the French language—should come as no surprise to scholars familiar with his work and his biography. However, the fact that he draws such a negative response from Caillois in the early 1940s is shocking considering Caillois's later championing of Borges in France from the 1950s onward. As Evelina Zoltowaska states in her article for *La Nación*—"La literatura argentina en París"—Caillois inaugurated a new series of South American titles in French—"La Croix du Sud"—with a French translation of Borges's *Ficciones* in 1952 (6). María Esther Vázquez also notes that Caillois first introduces Borges's literature to the French ("El encuentro" 1), and other writers recognize Caillois's involvement in making Borges's work and Latin American literature in general available to France and to the world. For example, in an untitled and unpublished essay that Julio Cortázar wrote about Caillois and the dichotomous relationship between European and Latin American understandings of the fantastic, Cortázar notes Caillois's preference for Borges's fiction and suggests that Borges's works "deben su acceso a la lengua francesa con todo lo que eso significó para el conjunto de la literatura latinoamericano" ["owe their introduction to the French language with all that that meant for Latin American literature as a whole"] to Caillois (5).[7]

Borges also recognized that he owed much of his world fame to Caillois. In

"Sobre Edgar Allan Poe," one of the last dialogues between Borges and Osvaldo Ferrari before Borges's death in 1986, Borges and Ferrari state:

> J.L.B.: Muchas cosas comienzan con Poe . . . Ahora, yo tuve una polémica con Roger Caillois, a quien debo tanto; ya que se olvidó de esa polémica y votó por mí para el premio de editores Formentor, y publicó un libro mío en francés. Y a esa publicación yo le debo, bueno, mi fama. Yo se la debo en gran medida a esa publicación que hizo Roger Caillois de unos cuentos míos al francés.
>
> O.F.: *Y también en gran medida al premio Formentor.*
>
> J.L.B.: Sí, indudablemente.

> [J.L.B.: Many things begin with Poe . . . Now, I had a polemic with Roger Caillois, to whom I owe so much; since he forgot about that polemic and voted for me for the Formentor Prize and published a book of mine in French. And to that publication I owe, well, my fame. I owe it in great part to the publication that Roger Caillois made of some of my stories in French.
>
> O.F.: *And also in great part to the Formentor Prize.*
>
> J.L.B.: Yes, undoubtedly.] (191)[8]

The controversy Borges mentions to Ferrari is the very debate he and Caillois had over Poe and the birth of the detective genre in the pages of *Sur* in 1942. Borges's reinterpretation of Poe via his own detective fiction, which Irwin so masterfully analyzes in *The Mystery to a Solution*, finds an unlikely advocate in the author of *Le roman policier*, who, unlike Dupin, takes no revenge on his literary "enemy" and, instead, introduces Borges's fiction to a large audience in France and acts as the primary force behind the campaign in support of Borges's 1961 co-reception of the Formentor Prize along with Samuel Beckett. Receiving the Formentor Prize appears to be the tipping point that pushes Borges from a writer who was well known in the Spanish-speaking world to a globetrotter who toured the universities of the United States and the U.K. as an invited guest from the 1960s through the 1980s.

This award not only brings more fame to Borges in France; it also opens doors for him in the English-speaking literary market that had remained closed up to this date. On May 3, 1961, both *La Nación* and *La Prensa* published small pieces announcing that Borges had won the Formentor Prize entitled "Recompensó un jurado literario a J. L. Borges" and "Obtuvo un premio literario el escritor Jorge Luis Borges," respectively. In the latter article, Borges notes that up to that point the most success his work had found outside of the Spanish-speaking world had been in Germany, he affirms his debt to Caillois for publishing his literature in French, and he laments that his work had found little success in English: "Eso es lamentable, si se tiene en cuenta que una cuarta parte de mi sangre es inglesa" ["That is lamentable, if one considers that a quarter of my blood is English"].

This lack of dissemination in English ends shortly after Borges receives the Formentor Prize with New Directions' publication of Borges's *Labyrinths: Selected Stories and Other Writings*, edited by Donald A. Yates and James E. Irby in 1962, and Grove's publication of a Borges story collection carrying the Spanish title *Ficciones*, edited by Anthony Kerrigan, also in 1962.[9] Before these collections went to press, no volume of Borges's fiction had been published in English; a few of his stories had been translated into English, but they had always appeared in journals or in book collections with the work of other writers. This lack of publication in English was not due to a lack of willing advocates and translators. The rejection slips from the editorial department of Alfred A. Knopf reveal that Harriet de Onís attempted to publish an English version of Borges's *El Aleph* as early as 1949 (the same year the original Spanish version was published in Buenos Aires); a collection entitled *Death and the Compass* in 1952; and a collection of seventeen of Borges's short stories, including "La muerte y la brújula," "El jardín de senderos que se bifurcan," and "El Aleph" in 1957. Knopf's rejection slips also show Yates's attempt to publish a collection entitled *La muerte y la brújula* in 1955.[10]

Editor Herbert Weinstock rejected each of these possible editions. He ends his rejection sheet of de Onís's 1957 proposed collection, claiming: "If we are in the mood to publish a very distinguished collection of seventeen short stories of a very special, peculiar, and remarkable sort, the selection indicated by Harriet de Onís [. . .] is extremely well considered and arranged. [. . .] I am inclined to feel that we ought to undertake this book, but I'd want to make clear that I think we'd be doing it on the basis of quality—with the profits very doubtful" (2). Each of Weinstock's rejection slips demonstrates an increasing amount of respect for Borges, but Weinstock could not overcome, even by 1957, the feeling that Borges's stories would not sell in English. In the 1949 rejection, he claims that the stories contained in *El Aleph* "are utterly untranslatable, at least into anything that could be expected to sell more than 750 copies in the United States. That they are remarkable is beyond argument, but their peculiar variety of remarkableness seems to me to legislate against them as $50-a-pound caviar to the general [public] (including me)" (2). In the 1952 rejection, he states that the recent publication of an English translation of "Emma Zunz" in *Partisan Review* "does nothing to alter my judgment that these stories are commercially untranslatable" (2); and in the 1955 rejection, he notes that Borges's "stories are very remarkable in the most arcane of possible ways—and a translated volume of them would have some enthusiastis [*sic*] and almost no sale" (2). Weinstock never denied the quality of Borges's stories, but each individual rejection slip, his shift in wording from "utterly untranslatable" to "commercially untranslatable," and his suggestion that

Knopf "ought to" publish a Borges collection in English even though it would not make much money, all show that Weinstock's fear that Borges could not cut a profit for Knopf effectively barred Borges's literature from the U.S. literary marketplace and from a broader English-speaking audience in the 1950s.

Borges's reception of the Formentor Prize seems to calm this fear, not with Knopf, but with the editors at New Directions. In his introduction to *Labyrinths*, Irby discusses Borges's previous absence from the English-language literary market but suggests that linguistic and national prejudice (or, more specifically, a francophile bias in the United States that can now be overlooked due to Borges's reception of the Formentor) had kept Borges a stranger in his home hemisphere:

> Borges's somewhat belated recognition as a major writer of our time has come more from Europe than from his native America. The 1961 Formentor Prize, which he shared with Samuel Beckett, is the most recent token of that recognition. [. . .] Not being French has undoubtedly also relegated Borges to comparative obscurity in the English-speaking countries, where it is rare that a Hispanic writer is ever accorded any major importance at all. Perhaps this selection of his writings will help correct that oversight[.] (xxii–xxiii)

In short, Caillois's decision to promote Borges's literature in French, regardless of his previous dispute with Borges over Poe and the detective genre, brings Borges fame in France and provides the necessary clout in the publication industry for Borges's work to break into the realm of Poe's native tongue—Borges's coveted field of the English language.[11] Borges's insistence to Caillois that Poe was the inventor of the detective genre—a part of Borges's dissemination of his version of Poe as a fiction writer rather than a poet—could have threatened the spreading of Borges's own literature if Caillois had allowed himself to follow Poe's and Borges's characters' models of getting even.[12] Instead, Caillois rejects Dupin's and Red Scharlach's move to one-up their adversaries and leaves the memory of his dispute with Borges over Poe in the past. By breaking away from Poe's Dupin, Caillois facilitates the spreading of Borges's literature (Scharlach included) and Borges's persona, and, perhaps ironically, assists in the dissemination of Borges's version of Poe.

Along with his repeated assertions that Poe was the inventor of the detective genre, Borges also used Poe to frame his own rules for detective fiction. In both his 1933 "Leyes de la narración policial" and his 1935 revision of this article for *Sur* as "Los laberintos policiales y Chesterton," Borges cites "The Mystery of Marie Rogêt" as one of "los primeros ejemplares del género" ("Los laberintos" 126–27) ["the earliest examples of the genre"] ("The Labyrinths" 112) and notes that the tale "se limita a la discusión y a la resolución abstracta de un crimen, [. . .] a muchos leguas del suceso" (127) ["is limited to the discussion and abstract resolution of a crime, [. . .] far from the event"] (112).[13] He then suggests that "[l]as cotidianas vías de la investigación policial—los rastros digitales, la tortura y la delación—parecerían solecismos ahí. Se objetará lo convencional de ese veto, pero esa convención, en ese lugar, es irreprochable: no propende a eludir dificultades, sino a imponerlas" (127) ["[t]he everyday methods of police investigation—fingerprints, torture, accusation—would seem like solecisms there. One might object to the conventionality of this rejection, but the convention here is irreproachable: it does not attempt to avoid difficulties, but rather to impose them"] (112–13).

With the strictness of Poe's model in mind, Borges then sets forth six rules for detective fiction:

> A) *Un límite discrecional de seis personajes.* [. . .] B) *Declaración de todos los términos del problema.* [. . .] C) *Avara economía en los medios.* [. . .] D) *Primacía del cómo sobre el quién.* [. . .] E) *El pudor de la muerte.* [. . .] F) *Necesidad y maravilla en la solución.* (127–28)

> [A.) *A discretional limit of six characters.* [. . .] B.) *The declaration of all the terms of the problem.* [. . .] C.) *An avaricious economy of means.* [. . .] D.) *The priority of how over who.* [. . .] E.) *A reticence concerning death.* [. . .] F.) *A solution that is both necessary and marvelous.*] (113–14)[14]

Each of these rules creates a rubric from elements Poe invented in one or more of his Dupin tales. In his explanation for rule A, Borges suggests that detective films consistently pull the cheap trick of trying to fool their audiences with too many suspects (127; 113). Such is not the case with the Dupin trilogy. In the first two Dupin stories, the number of suspects is limited, and in "The Purloined Letter" the culprit, Minister D——, is known from the start. If we include the narrator, the prefect, Dupin himself, and all the suspects for the crimes in each story—Le Bon and the orangutan in "The Murders in the Rue Morgue"; Beauvais, Madame Deluc, or the shady naval officer in "The Mystery of Marie Rogêt"; and Minister D—— in "The Purloined Letter"— we never arrive at more than six primary characters per story, and several of the supposed suspects—Le Bon, Beauvais, and Madame Deluc—are suspects only in the eyes of the Parisian newspapers, not in the eyes of Dupin.

As a part of rule B—the declaration of all the problem's terms—Borges criticizes Conan Doyle's tendency to rely on knowledge only known to Holmes as a minor infraction of the rule, but he holds a more serious critique for detective stories that reveal the criminal as a complete stranger (127–28; 113). The orangutan murderer in "The Murders in the Rue Morgue" could appear to be this unknown "culpable, terriblemente desenmascarado a última hora" (127–28) ["guilty party, horribly unmasked at the last moment"] (113) whom Borges criticizes, but instead, the ape functions as a minor infraction since Dupin has kept his suspicions and newfound knowledge—that is, his interpretation of the witnesses' inability to understand the second voice's language and, later, the animal's hair and the sailor's knot that he finds at the crime scene—as secrets from both the reader and the narrator until he has already set up the encounter between himself and the sailor. A better connection to the Dupin trilogy for this rule lies in Borges's favorite Dupin story, "The Purloined Letter." Borges notes his particular affinity for the plainness or simplicity of this mystery in his 1883 copy of Ingram's third edition of *The Works of Edgar Allan Poe (I): Memoir-Tales* with the following notations on the book's last inside page: "Perhaps the mystery is little too 'plain': 495" and "A little too self-evident: 495" ("Notations in *The Works of Edgar Allan Poe (I)*").[15] The tale overtly places the crime—criminal, victim, and stolen object—within the reader's view from the start. Indeed, it would be difficult to more openly declare a story's problem than Poe does in this tale whose solution also rests in plain sight.

In his explanation about rule C and the economy of means, Borges claims to enjoy the revelation that two characters within a detective story are one and the same as long as the author does not use "una barba disponible o una voz italiana" (128) ["a false beard or an Italian accent"] (113) to make the change. While none of Poe's creations in the Dupin tales plays multiple character roles, Poe is certainly economic with the characters he does create. "The Purloined Letter," again, provides us with the best example since Dupin and Minister D—— are not the same character but share the same *character*—they are both poets and mathematicians, both creative analysts—with the primary exception being the minister's willingness to challenge the sociopolitical hierarchy and Dupin's desire to uphold it.

Rule D, the precedence of how over whom, most clearly hearkens back to Poe and the Dupin tales. The revelation that Mary Rogers died of a botched abortion rather than as a murder victim before Poe published the third installment of "The Mystery of Marie Rogêt" disallowed Poe from offering a murderer in this tale, and the story remains a prime example of a "how-done-it" even if the term *whodunit* now serves as a one-word moniker for the genre. In "The Murders in the Rue Morgue," Dupin finds the orangutan, but his fascination lies much less in the actual animal than it does in how the orangutan entered and escaped from the locked room. Dupin's analysis of the premises and his eventual discovery of the faulty nail drive the narrative, and the story gives birth to a conundrum that countless writers have repeated, regardless, or perhaps in spite of, the identity of the culprit in the tale. Finally, "The Purloined Letter" values *how* over *whom* since the entire story revolves around Dupin's ability to solve what remains an insoluble problem for the prefect—the location of the letter—while the prefect and the narrator present the minister as unquestionably guilty of the crime.

The gruesome descriptions of the corpses of Madame and Mademoiselle

L'Espanaye could put "The Murders in the Rue Morgue" at odds with Borges's rule E concerning reserve or discretion about death. Unlike Poe's macabre stories, however, this tale does not focus on the death of the characters. The reader only sees the descriptions of the cadavers via the newspapers and Dupin's analytic retelling of the events that must have taken place. In short, the actual murders do not even happen within the narrative time of the story itself, and "The Murders in the Rue Morgue" remains as hygienic as Borges demands. "The Mystery of Marie Rogêt" follows a similar pattern since Marie's death takes place outside the narrative structure itself and is relayed to the reader via the narrator's and Dupin's reading of the newspaper accounts. This story moves even further away from death by avoiding it in the story's title, which revolves around the mystery, not the murder, of Marie Rogêt.[16] "The Purloined Letter," of course, shuns death altogether since the crime committed is one of larceny and blackmail rather than murder.

My analysis of Borges's praise for Chesterton's and Queen's detective fiction reveals the weight Borges places on his final rule—that the solution be both necessary and marvelous. For the latter half of this rule, Borges does not require that detective writers delve into the supernatural. In fact, he argues that the author must surprise or awe the reader "sin apelar a lo sobrenatural, claro está, cuyo manejo en este género de ficciones es una languidez y una felonía" (128) ["without, of course, resorting to the supernatural, whose use in this genre of fiction is slothful and felonious"] (114). The supernatural can be present in the story itself, but the solution must be of this world while still being singular. "The Mystery of Marie Rogêt" falls short on this requirement since Dupin offers no final solution, but his suggestion that Marie has either suffered "a fatal accident under the roof of Madame Deluc" or been murdered in "the thicket at the Barrière du Roule, by a lover, or at least by an intimate and secret associate" (768) does avoid the paranormal.[17] In "The Murders in the Rue Morgue" and "The Purloined Letter," the final solution appears as *the* solution, and the resolutions in both stories never approach the supernatural. In the latter story, Dupin notes that the circumstances required the "*simplicity*" of the minister's ploy and suggests that the only way D——could hide the letter from the prefect was not to hide it at all (989–90), while in the former Dupin deduces that only an animal would speak a language that no witness could interpret and that only an animal could enact such apparently mindless violence (556–60). While Poe's razor-wielding orangutan might stretch the limits of the audience's willingness to suspend disbelief, Dupin's analysis of both the physical and the circumstantial evidence makes this solution necessary while keeping it within the realm of possibility.[18]

Borges concludes "Los laberintos policiales y Chesterton" by replacing the final paragraph from "Leyes de la narración policial" with two paragraphs of analysis of Chesterton's detective fiction. The deleted paragraph from the earlier article, however, is of special interest when considering Borges's judgments on Poe's fiction versus his poetry. He begins the paragraph stating: "No soy, por cierto, de los que misteriosamente desdeñan las tramas misteriosas. Creo, al contrario, que la organización y aclaración, siquiera mediocres, de un algebraico asesinato o de un doble robo, comportan más trabajo intelectual que la casera elaboración de sonetos perfectos" ["I am certainly not one of those who mysteriously scorns mystery plots. I believe, on the contrary, that the organization and explanation, even if mediocre, of an algebraic murder or of a double robbery entail more intellectual work than the homebound elaboration of perfect sonnets"] (39).[19] To return to the discussion of Borges's fluctuating appraisal of the muse versus the intellect that I examined in the previous chapter, Borges's claim that writing detective fiction requires more intelligence than creating sonnets resonates with his repeated assertion during the latter end of his career that he prefers Plato's theory of the muse over Poe's theory of poetry as an intellectual exercise since a muse-inspired sonnet would supposedly rely on inspiration rather than intelligence in the first place. At the same time, the idea that writing detective fiction requires more acumen than writing poetry also supports the earlier description of Borges's writing process that he gave to Lizardo Zia in the 1950s in which he called himself a "mejor razonador" ["better reasoner"] than his peers who received inspiration (9). Borges's conclusion to "Leyes de la narración policial" foreshadows his later praise for Poe's fiction over his poetry by describing detective fiction—the genre he repeatedly traces back to Poe—rather than poetry (the genre that Borges sees as Poe's failure even though Poe both claims to prefer and to demystify poetry, with his rational explanation in "The Philosophy of Composition") as *the* genre of reason.

Borges's repeated references to Poe as the inventor of the detective genre, his referrals to Poe in his reviews of contemporary detective literature, and his propagation of Poe-influenced rules for detective fiction create an atmosphere for rereading Poe. Even if Borges's readers do not literally return to Poe's detective stories after reading Borges's literary criticism, they interpret the literature that Borges is analyzing through a filter that casts Poe as an origin. In short, Borges's penchant for rereading Poe induces him to continually mention Poe in his own criticism of detective stories, which, in turn, spreads Borges's version of Poe—the father of detective fiction, the masterful storyteller—throughout both the Río de la Plata region and Spanish America and begins to permanently shift Poe's reputation.

Borges and *Pym*

Apart from Poe's detective fiction, Borges also prefers to reread Poe's only novel, *The Narrative of Arthur Gordon Pym*. In "El taller del escritor," he claims, "Releo a Poe. Yo diría que su obra capital son los capítulos finales del relato de *Arthur Gordon Pym*, esa pesadilla de la blancura, que profetiza el *Moby Dick* de Herman Melville" ["I reread Poe. I would say that his seminal works are the final chapters of the story of *Arthur Gordon Pym*, that nightmare of whiteness that prefigures Herman Melville's *Moby-Dick*"] (353).[20] Borges's preference for *Pym* is odd considering Poe's own penchant for short fiction when writing prose and Borges's consistent favoring of the short story over the novel in both his literary criticism and his own fiction. Borges, however, follows the same line of logic with *Pym* as novel that Poe follows in "The Philosophy of Composition" when he claims that "[w]hat we term a long poem is, in fact, merely a succession of brief ones" (164), since Borges does not praise Poe's novel but rather the final chapters of the novel. The last chapters of the novel function as a tale that captures Borges's attention due to the mysterious absence or hiding of the color white among the Tsalalians and the eventual revelation that their fear is connected to the mysterious, snow-white, and massive "shrouded human figure" who supposedly engulfs Pym and Dirk Peters in the novel's finale (197–98).

Borges, much earlier in his career, offers a similar reading of *Pym* in his essay "El arte narrativo y la magia" ["Narrative Art and Magic"] that both suggests that the novel is about the fear of whiteness and reiterates the fact that Borges interprets the novel in parts or sections rather than as a whole. He states, "El secreto argumento de esa novela es el temor y la vilificación de lo blanco. [. . .] Los argumentos de ese libro son dos: uno inmediato, de vicisitudes marítimas; otro infalible, sigiloso y creciente, que sólo se revela al final" (229) ["This novel's secret theme is the terror or vilification of whiteness. [. . .] This novel has two plots: the high-seas adventure is more immediate, while the other, inexorable and secretive, expands until revealed at the very end"] ("Narrative Art" 78).[21] Borges's marginalia suggest that he is well aware of the visibility of the primary plot of the novel since the only note he makes in his copy of *Pym* in the Johnson edition of *The Works of Edgar Allan Poe: The Poems and Three Essays on Poetry, Narrative of Arthur Gordon Pym, Miscellanies* is "My visions were of shipwreck & famine: 262"—an early statement from Pym himself in the novel's second chapter that foreshadows the primary theme of most of the text ("Notations in *The Works of Edgar Allan Poe: The Poems*").[22] By calling *Pym* a novel about the fear of whiteness, Borges describes the entire book only by its latter parts since the novel's primary theme—the portrayal of sufferings at sea and eventual shipwreck—remains visible throughout the piece while the fear of whiteness only appears in the book's final chapters. This synecdoche not only demonstrates how Borges breaks the novel into shorter pieces, but it also reveals Borges's real interest in *Pym*. Borges's fascination with *Pym* does not lie in the primary nor the secondary themes of the novel; he is not that interested in shipwreck nor in the concept of whiteness. Instead, the *mystery* surrounding this latter concept in the novel intrigues him.

Borges continues "El arte narrativo y la magia" by stating:

> *Nombrar un objeto*, dicen que dijo Mallarmé, *es suprimir las tres cuartas partes del goce del poema, que reside en la felicidad de ir adivinando; el sueño es sugerirlo*. Niego que el escrupuloso poeta haya redactado esa numérica frivolidad de *las tres cuartas partes*, pero la idea general le conviene [. . .] La sugirió, sin duda, el *Narrative of A. Gordon Pym*. El mismo impersonal color blanco ¿no es mallarmeano? (229)

> ["Naming an object," Mallarmé is said to have said, "is to suppress three-fourths of the joy of reading a poem, which resides in the pleasure of anticipation, as a dream lies in its suggestion." I refuse to believe that such a scrupulous writer would have composed the numerical frivolity of "three-fourths," but the general idea suits Mallarmé. [. . .] It was inspired, no doubt, by *The Narrative of Arthur Gordon Pym*. The impersonal color white itself—is it not utterly Mallarmé?] (78–79)

With this passage, Borges reveals that his penchant for *Pym* rests in the hidden secret of the final chapters, and he foreshadows the theory of influence that he will later elaborate in his Kafka essay by reading the whiteness that Poe refuses to speak as Mallarmé-like.[23]

Finally, in "Edgar Allan Poe"—Borges's 1949 article for *La Nación* that I examined at length in chapter 1—Borges again places emphasis on the final pages of *Pym*, which he calls "una sistemática pesadilla cuyo tema secreto es el color blanco" ["a systematic nightmare whose secret theme is the color white"] (1). Each of these references to *Pym* reads the novel not as an adventure tale but as a mystery or a piece of quasi-detective fiction. The novel itself provides an odd template in its final "note" that invites this very reading when an editorial voice, rather than the voice of Dupin or the voice of the trilogy's narrator, enters the narrative to suggest that the strange markings in the chasms on the island of Tsalal are connected to the narrative and to imply that the repeated shriek of "Tekeli-li!" by the islanders and the birds refers to either the color white itself or to the snow-white figure at the end of the novel (199–201).

By reading the last pages of *Pym* as detective fiction and by casting the last chapters as their own story that can be read in one sitting, Borges's proclivity for this novel no longer seems to contradict his preferences for short fiction over novels and analytic detective fiction over adventure stories. More importantly, Borges's reading and perennial rereading of *The Narrative of*

Arthur Gordon Pym, like his reading and rereading of the Dupin tales, once again reiterates his praise for Poe as fiction writer rather than poet. Whether Borges considers *Pym* a novel, or whether he sees the last chapters of *Pym* as a fascinating tale within a larger text, this nightmare of whiteness is prose, not poetry, and Borges's repeated interpretation of Poe's text continues to spread Poe's reputation as a writer of fiction and effectively casts Poe as a precursor to Borges's own detective stories.

Borges shares one of his last experiences with reading and rereading Poe in 1985, the year before his death, in his prologue to his favorite Dupin tale— "The Purloined Letter." In this prologue, he refers to Poe's detective fiction and to *Pym*, but his commentary about rereading focuses on Poe's story "The Pit and the Pendulum." Borges finishes the prologue, in language that is far more sentimental than any of his other Poe references, by claiming:

> He escrito en el principio de esta página dos altos nombres americanos, Whitman y Poe. El primero, como poeta, fue infinitamente superior al segundo; pero ahora Edgar Allan Poe está mucho más cerca de mí. Hace casi setenta años, sentado en el último peldaño de una escalera que ya no existe, leí *The Pit and the Pendulum*; he olvidado cuántas veces lo he releído o me lo he hecho leer; sé que no he llegado a la última y que regresaré a la cárcel cuadrangular que se estrecha y al abismo del fondo.

> [I have written at the beginning of this page two great American names, Whitman and Poe. The first, as a poet, was infinitely superior to the second; but now Edgar Allan Poe is much closer to me. Nearly seventy years ago, sitting on the last step of a stairway that no longer exists, I read "The Pit and the Pendulum"; I have forgotten how many times I have reread it or had it read to me; I know that I have not arrived at the last and that I will return to the four-sided prison that closes in and to the abyss of the pit.] (12–13)

This prologue reaffirms that Poe was a constant in Borges's reading life—he read Poe in his youth, he continued to reread Poe, and he will read Poe again.[24] The presence of Poe in Borges's past, present, and future, Borges's claim that he cannot recall the number of times he has read "The Pit and the Pendulum," and his suggestion that his last reading of the story has not yet arrived recall Borges's own obsession with the concepts of infinity and eternity throughout his essays and fiction. The two authors stand side-by-side between two facing mirrors that cast their joined images infinitely in both directions. If Borges's last reading of "The Pit and the Pendulum" did not take place in 1985, are we to understand that it happened in 1986? Or are we to infer that Borges continues rereading Poe into eternity? Whether Borges reads Poe in the afterlife or not, his previous rereadings of Poe continue to resonate long after his death. These rereadings become infinite as new readers of Borges also approach Borges's Poe. In short, Borges's literary criticism continues to spread Poe—his Poe, the inventor of the detective genre, the author of *Pym*, the fiction master who dreamed of being a poet but found immortality through prose—to both regional and global audiences.

PART 2

Translating Poe

Jorge Luis Borges's
Edgar Allan Poe Translations

CHAPTER 3

Theory, Practice, and *Pym*

Borges began translating only a few years after he started his lifelong work as a reader and rereader of texts and approximately a decade before he published his first piece of literary criticism. In 1910, two months before his eleventh birthday, Borges published a translation of Oscar Wilde's "The Happy Prince" as "El príncipe feliz" in the Buenos Aires newspaper *El País*. Just as he continued to read and reread throughout the twentieth century, Borges continued to translate until his death in 1986. Among the scores of translations he performed, Borges translated two fragments from Poe's *The Narrative of Arthur Gordon Pym of Nantucket* and, along with Adolfo Bioy Casares, two of Poe's famous short stories: "The Facts in the Case of M. Valdemar" and "The Purloined Letter." These translations have been highly influential on the reading public of Argentina and Spanish-speaking America, and they deserve an extended comparative analysis that goes beyond the cursory nods they often receive from both literary and translation critics, especially since the process of translation very visibly reveals the dual influence between Borges and Poe.[1] Each of Borges's Poe translations, with the exception of the first fragment from *Pym*, originally appeared in one of the popular anthologies Borges coedited with Bioy Casares, Silvina Ocampo, or Margarita Guerrero: *Antología de la literatura fantástica*, *Los mejores cuentos policiales*, *Manual de zoología fantástica*, and its extended version, *El libro de los seres imaginarios*. Borges originally offered the first *Pym* fragment as a citation in his essay "El arte narrativo y la magia," but the fragment also appears as a standalone piece in his and Bioy Casares's anthology *Cuentos breves y extraordinarios* and in *Manual de zoología fantástica / El libro de seres imaginarios*.

The ever-growing field of translation studies, which emerged as a separate discipline during the last quarter of the twentieth century, offers several models for interpreting translated literature. My comparative approach to Borges's Poe translations in this and in the following chapter builds on the frameworks provided by early scholars in this field such as James S. Holmes, who named and framed what he calls "descriptive translation studies" or "DTS" in the early 1970s (176), and Itamar Even-Zohar, whose work examines the role of translations in what he calls "literary polysystem[s]" (192–97). I follow Even-Zohar's invitation to "conceive of translated literature not only as an integral system within any literary polysystem, but as a most active system within it" (193) as I examine how Borges's Poe translations solidify the position of Poe's fiction in the literary system of Borges's target language/culture.

Since the rise of *modernismo* in the late nineteenth century, Poe translations have long held a central position in the literary polysystems of Argentina, the Río de la Plata region, and Spanish America in general. Andrea Castro reveals Poe's centrality to these systems when she claims that

> [l]os textos narrativos de Poe se leen junto a otros textos, sin discutir el estatus de traducción del uno con respecto a los otros. Poe es leído o bien como un autor hispanoamericano más—como un texto fuente que no ha atravesado un proceso de mediación interlingüística y de reescritura—, o bien como un escritor estadounidense, cuyo texto no ha sido afectado por la nueva lengua que lo hace posible.

> [Poe's narrative texts are read together with other texts without disputing the translated status of one with respect to the others. Poe is read either as another Spanish American author—as a source text that has not gone through a process of interlinguistic mediation and rewriting—or as a U.S. writer whose text has not been affected by the new language that makes it possible.] (98)

The lack of distinction between Poe's translated texts and works written in Spanish by Spanish American writers demonstrates Poe's central location in these literary polysystems.[2] The important position of Poe's translations in Argentina and the Río de la Plata region does not rest solely on Borges's work as a Poe translator since the *modernistas* originally provided Poe with this privileged status by claiming him as their poet-prophet, translating several of his works, and tapping into his aesthetics and themes in their own literature. However, the emphasis on Poe's narrative works that Castro mentions here does link back to Borges and a few other important Argentine translators of Poe's fiction.

Borges's choice to translate Poe's fiction rather than his poetry, especially considering the science fiction and analytic detective genres of the two full texts he translates, continues to challenge the *modernistas'* image of Poe that Borges began disputing in the early 1930s. In chapter 3, I analyze Borges's brief *Pym* translations side-by-side with the selections from Poe's novel, while in chapter 4, I examine Borges's translations of Poe's tales alongside Poe's source texts and various other Argentine translations to demonstrate how Borges's translations engrain Poe's fiction, not his poems, into the Argentine, Río de la Plata, and Spanish American literary traditions.[3] In each of his Poe translations, Borges liberally alters Poe's source texts. His creative rewritings of Poe's works both streamline and "domesticate"[4] Poe's prose in a manner that allows him to praise Poe as a fiction-writing genius even though he often criticizes Poe's language usage.[5] Borges's translations also change significant plot elements in Poe's works, and these alterations make the target text *his* as much as Poe's. The modifications Borges makes in his translations of Poe's texts allow him to supplant the *modernistas*' version of Poe by creating "new" Poe stories that emphasize what Borges sees as Poe's genius (his imagination) while simultaneously minimizing what he sees as Poe's primary weakness (his language).

Borges's Theory of Translation

Borges often wrote about translation, and his primary essays on the subject are now considered, along with Walter Benjamin's "The Task of the Translator," precursors to contemporary translation studies theory.[6] Borges offers his most radical thoughts on translation in two pieces from the late 1930s and early 1940s: first, his brilliant tale "Pierre Menard, autor del Quijote" ["Pierre Menard, Author of the *Quixote*"] in which the title character, a French poet of the early twentieth century, re-creates verbatim passages from Cervantes's *Don Quijote* that the story's narrator describes as "verbalmente idénticos, pero [. . .] casi infinitamente más rico[s]" (449) ["verbally identical, but [. . .] almost infinitely richer"] (94),[7] and second, his article on William Beckford's *Vathek*, in which he reverses the dependent and pejorative role often assigned to translations by claiming that with Beckford's novel, "[e]l original es infiel a la traducción" (133) ["[t]he original is unfaithful to the translation"] (239). In "Pierre Menard," Borges emphasizes the importance of context, of time and space, for any source text and any translation since the exact same words that peg Cervantes, according to the story's narrator, as a seventeenth-century Spaniard, shock the reader when written by a twentieth-century Frenchman (449, 94). The story suggests that for a translation to bring back or re-create the source text, with all its linguistic and historical meanings, the translator would have to rely on mimesis, and that even such mimesis falls short due to the inevitability of change. For, as Menard himself claims in a letter to the narrator, "[n]o en vano han transcurrido trescientos años, cargados de complejísimos hechos" (448) ["[n]ot for nothing have three hundred years elapsed, freighted with the most complex events"] (93). If read as a commentary on the act of translation, Menard's extreme example of "translating" *Don Quixote* liberates the translator from having to attempt fidelity to an "original" text by demonstrating how even a carbon copy of a source text (and in Menard's case, even a copy in the same language) simply cannot be faithful to that source text. Borges further debunks the concept of fidelity in "Sobre el 'Vathek' de William Beckford" ["On William Beckford's *Vathek*"] by completely divesting the original of its purported superiority over the translations that follow it. According to Borges's pithy comment about the original's infidelity, it makes just as much sense to require an original to be faithful to its translations as it does to oblige a translation to be faithful to an original.[8] In other words, neither idea makes much sense at all; both originals and translations, both source texts and target texts, should be read in their own right as texts in conversation with, but not subservient to, one another.

Borges had already mapped out these liberating ideas on translation in somewhat less radical language in a trio of essays he published on translation from 1926 through 1936: "Las dos maneras de traducir," "Las versiones homéricas" ["The Homeric Versions"], and "Los traductores de *Las 1001 noches*" ["The Translators of *The Thousand and One Nights*"].[9] He begins the first essay by openly disagreeing with the concept of untranslatability, stating: "Suele presuponerse que cualquier texto original es incorregible de puro bueno, y que los traductores son unos chapuceros irreparables, padres del frangollo y de la mentira. [. . .] En cuanto a mí, creo en las buenas traducciones de obras literarias (de las didácticas o especulativas, ni hablemos) y opino que hasta los versos son traducibles" ("Las dos maneras" 256) ["It is often presupposed that any original text is so purely good that it is not correctable, and that translators are an irreparable bunch of bunglers, fathers of cattle feed and lies. [. . .] As far as I am concerned, I believe in good translations of literary works (let us not even speak of didactic or speculative ones), and it is my opinion that even verses are translatable"] (Waisman 45).[10] Borges obviates the possible objection "but what about poetry?" by diving directly into the most probable doubt that any of his readers who privilege source texts as originals and distrust translations could raise—the supposed untranslatability of poetry. He supports his claim about poetry's translatability by referring to Juan Antonio Pérez Bonalde's "traducción ejemplar de 'El cuervo' de Poe" ["exemplary translation of Poe's 'The Raven'"] (256).[11] What follows is a beautiful, tightly woven paragraph of inter-American literary criticism in which Borges combats the objection that Pérez Bonalde's Spanish-language version of the poem can never mean the same thing to a Spanish speaker that Poe's English version means to an English speaker by agreeing with the notion but noting that a Chilean does not have the same experience reading Evaristo Carriego that an Argentine has although both readers approach Carriego in Spanish.[12] If Carriego's work means more to an Argentine than to a Chilean when the two readers approach the poem in the same language, then the shift from English to Spanish when Pérez Bonalde translates "The Raven" as "El cuervo"—the translation process itself—is not *the* element that decreases the poem's effect. Borges suggests that everything from the personas in Carriego's work to the "pormenores de paisaje" ["landscape details"] create a response that simply does not register for foreigners regardless of the foreigners' language (256). This gap, however, does not make a work untranslatable; it does not disallow the translator from creating a significant effect with a translation. Translation simply requires the open realization by the reader that the effect of the translated piece may not be the same as the effect of the source text just as the effect of a text changes when read in the same language but in different national and/or historical contexts.[13]

Borges then puts forward a binary to describe the two types of translations he alludes to in his essay's title. He states, "Universalmente, supongo que hay dos clases de traducciones. Una practica la literalidad, la otra la perífrasis. La primera corresponde a las mentalidades románticas, la segunda a las clásicas" ["Universally, I suppose that there are two types of translations. One practices literalness, the other periphrasis. The first corresponds with romantic mentalities, the second with classical mentalities"] (257–58).[14] Borges suggests that the Romantics' desire for literal translations rests in their admiration of the individual ego while the classicists' favoring of roundabout or loose translations grows out of a respect for "la obra de arte" ["the work of art"] rather than "el artista" ["the artist"], and he suggests that the Romantics' desire for fidelity in translation inherently makes the translator "un falsario" ["a liar"] (258). He ends this essay by offering both literal and literary "translations" (from Spanish into Spanish) of the opening lines of *Martín Fierro* and claiming that the literal version he provides is "ridícula y cachacienta" ["ridiculous and slow"] (259). The distinctions Borges draws between literal and nonliteral translations in this essay, his critique of his own literal translation of the opening lines of Argentina's national poem, his praise for Pérez Bonalde's translation of "The Raven"—a poem whose peculiar rhyme and meter scheme tie it so closely to its source language—and the fact that he begins the piece by claiming that quality translations are real possibilities all demonstrate Borges's proclivity for a literary, rather than literal, translation practice that frees the translator from the shackles of fidelity.

Borges reiterates his positive stance on translation in his next two essays on the subject, but he also complicates his position on literal versus nonliteral translations by salvaging some literal examples. He opens "Las versiones homéricas" with the provocative claim that "[n]ingún problema tan consustancial con las letras y con su modesto misterio como el que propone una traducción" (239) ["[n]o problem is as consubstantial to literature and its modest mystery as the one posed by translation"] ("The Homeric Versions" 69). Borges deflates the concept of the original's superiority by focusing squarely on the idea of translation. The "problem" he notes is not a problem in the negative sense but a conundrum or puzzle that needs to be engaged and demystified. He continues with an overt attack on the sanctimonious treatment of source texts: "Presuponer que toda recombinación de elementos es obligatoriamente inferior a su original, es presuponer que el borrador 9 es obligatoriamente inferior al borrador H—ya que no puede haber sino borradores. El concepto de *texto definitivo* no corresponde sino a la religión o al cansancio" (239, emphasis in original) ["To assume that every recombination of elements is necessarily inferior to its original form is to assume that draft nine is necessarily inferior to draft H—for there can only be drafts. The concept of the 'definitive text' corresponds only to religion or exhaustion"] (69). Borges levels the field between source texts and translations by calling both categories drafts, and he emphasizes the arbitrary nature of favoring one over the other by labeling one draft with a numeral and the other with a letter. While symbols in an alphabet and in a number system *can* be interpreted as superior or inferior to other symbols within their given system (e.g., "2 is greater than 1" or "A comes before B"), the same cannot be said for a comparison of symbols between the two systems. What grounds exist to claim that H is better than 9 or vice versa? While the example would work with any pairing of one letter and one number—for example, the number 2 and the letter E—Borges subtly reinforces the idea that the two symbols (and the translation and the source text they represent) are equals by juxtaposing 9 with H, the ninth symbol of the Spanish alphabet.[15] Even if Borges were to choose two symbols within the same system, two numerals or two letters, his usage of the word "drafts" would complicate the passing of judgment; while 1 comes before 2 (which, simultaneously means that 2 is more or greater than 1) and A comes before B, drafts are often read as cumulative so that the last draft is considered definitive. Without a code to distinguish whether the symbols in his comparison between drafts—translations and so-called originals—should be read with increasing or decreasing value as they move from beginning to end in an alphabet or from small to large in a number system, one simply cannot claim that any given letter/numeral is superior to any other. Borges's leveling of the field between source texts and translations does not mean that he reads all versions of all texts as equals. Bad translations (and bad originals) can and do exist, but a poor translation is not worse than its original simply because it is a translation.

In both "Las versiones homéricas" and "Los traductores de *Las 1001 noches*," Borges re-demonstrates his interest in the problem or conundrum of translation via his willingness to consider several types of translations of Homer and *The Thousand and One Nights*. In each piece, he returns to the binary he described in "Las dos maneras de traducir" by referencing the 1860s debate between Francis W. Newman and Matthew Arnold in which Newman defended literal translation while Arnold advocated periphrasis. While his continued refusal to categorically favor source texts over translations recalls his critique of the Romantics (who, like Newman, favor literal translations), in "Las dos maneras de traducir" Borges remains unwilling to openly disparage Newman or to overtly praise Arnold. Instead, he basks in the "hermosa discusión Newman-Arnold" ("Las versiones" 241, "Los traductores" 400) ["beautiful Newman-Arnold debate"] ("The Homeric Versions" 71) and claims that both the literal and nonliteral approach to translation are "menos importantes que el traductor y que sus hábitos literarios" ("Los traducto-res" 400) ["less important than the translator and his literary habits"] ("The Translators" 95).[16]

However, through the examples of translations that he offers in both es-says, Borges again reveals his proclivity for literary or creative translations over literal ones. He concludes "Las versiones homéricas" by examining six disparate translations of a specific passage in *The Odyssey* and then asking, "¿Cuál de esas muchas traducciones es fiel?" (243) ["Which of these many translations is faithful?"] (74), and then responding, "Repito que ninguna o que todas" (243) ["I repeat: none or all of them"] (74). This response, once again, delegitimizes the concept of fidelity, not by suggesting that if any translation is faithful to Homer's text then all translations inherently are, but by implying that fidelity is such a broad concept that any translation can be faithful to a source text in one form or another and/or that fidelity can be such a rigid concept that no translation, no matter how literal, could ever be faithful to the source text. Borges specifies that all of the Homer translations he cites could relate Homer's "imaginaciones" ["imaginations"] to Homer's contemporaries but not to current-day readers, and he claims that each of these translations "salvo los literales" ["except for the literal versions"] can be faithful to Homer's "propósitos" ["intentions"] (243, 74).[17] He then suggests that the least literal of the translations he approaches, Samuel Butler's, might be the most faithful of all: "No es imposible que la versión calmosa de But-ler sea la más fiel" (243) ["It is not impossible that Butler's unruffled version is the most faithful"] (74). Borges's playfulness throughout this concluding paragraph—his juxtaposition of "all" and "none" and his quirky usage of "it is not impossible" rather than "it is possible"—confirms that he is not willing to simply condemn Newman and literal translations on the whole, but it also reiterates his preference for nonliteral translations.

"Los traductores de *Las 1001 noches*" also demonstrates both Borges's attempted compromise between Newman and Arnold and his attraction to literary translations as stated in his essay on the translations of Homer, but this longer essay goes a step further by explicitly calling for domestication in translation practice. After examining several translations of *The Thousand and One Nights* in French, English, and German, Borges concludes his piece by disagreeing with the privileged position assigned to Enno Littmann's lit-eral translation of *The Nights* into German precisely because Littmann does not do what Borges thinks the best translators of this text accomplish—create a translation infused with and heavily influenced by their native liter-ary traditions (411–12, 108–09). He states, "Alemania posee una literatura fantástica—mejor dicho, *sólo* posee una literatura fantástica. Hay maravil-las en las *Noches* que me gustaría ver repensadas en alemán. [. . .] ¿Qué no haría un hombre, un Kafka, que organizara y acentuara esos juegos, que los rehiciera según la deformación alemana, según la *Unheimlichkeit* de Alemania?" (412) ["Germany possesses a literature of the fantastic—rather, it possesses *only* a literature of the fantastic. There are marvels in the *Nights* that I would like to see rethought in German. [. . .] What might a man—a Kafka—do if he organized and intensified this play, remade it in line with the Germanic distortion, the *unheimlichkeit* of Germany?"] (108–09). Borges's desire to see the German philosophical and literary traditions written into *The Thousand and One Nights* is a desire for domestication, and it ties back to his idea from "Las versiones homéricas" about the importance of any given translator's literary habits. His preferred translations of *The Nights*—J. C. Mardrus's French translation and Richard Burton's English translation—reveal the translators' literary influences, tastes, and biases and can be read as both products of and parts of the French and English literary traditions. In other words, these translations enter the literary polysystems of France and England, respectively, and wield significant literary influence in their own right as texts rather than as translations. For Borges, Littmann's translation cannot become a core part of Germany's literary polysystem because it does not tap into that system in the first place. Littmann's version is too honest, too literal, and the closeness of his translation leaves Borges lamenting the lost possibilities: "En Littmann, incapaz como Washington de mentir, no hay otra cosa que la probidad de Alemania. Es tan poco, es poquísimo. El comercio de las *Noches* y de Alemania debió producir algo más" (412) ["In Littmann, who like Washington cannot tell a lie, there is nothing but the probity of Germany. This is so little, so very little. The commerce between Germany and the *Nights* should have produced something more"] (108). This "something more" is the space where the translator can/should create rather than transcribe.

Translation for Borges is not a simple relationship between source text and translated text, between author and translator. For him, a quality translation reveals a complex web of influence that includes source and target languages, cultures, and, perhaps most importantly, literary traditions. While Borges's essays on translation challenge the traditional idea that a translation should show fidelity to its source text, they also call for a different type of fidelity—faithfulness to the literary tradition of the target system. This radical form of domestication produces new texts that rely equally on the source text and the target literary tradition to create something in the literary polysystem of the target culture that could not exist without the mixture of the two; the translation could not exist without the source text, but it also could not exist without the literary tradition into which the source text is being incorporated (and altered) via translation. In other words, ideal translations for Borges are not imports, nor are they homegrown. They are hybrids that both reveal and create influence from/in both literary systems, and the only types of translations that can accomplish this feat are creative rather than literal.

Borges repeatedly brings his thoughts on translation to fruition when he translates texts from various source languages into Spanish. While some of his translations are more creative than others—changing not only language but also significant details within a given story's plot and/or characterization—few of his translations can be called literal. In *Invisible Work*, Efraín Kristal lists five translation strategies he sees at work throughout Borges's translation corpus:

> (1) Borges's most common practice as a translator was to remove what he once called the "padding" of a work: words and passages that seem redundant, superfluous, or inconsequential. (2) He removed textual distractions. This stratagem involves cutting part of the content of a literary work that might distract attention from another aspect Borges would prefer to highlight. (3) Borges often added a major or minor nuance not in the original: changing a title, for instance. (4) Borges sometimes rewrote a work in the light of another, as when he inscribes a post-Nietzschean sensibility to his translation of Angelus Silesius. (5) He sometimes included a literal translation of a work in one of his own works. (87)

All these strategies, with the exception of approach 5, are creative or literary, and they perform a type of domestication on the source text.[18]

Now, let us bring the discussion back to Poe. I do not argue that Borges's Poe translations serve as a microcosm for his translation practice at large, but his Poe translations, as a group, do demonstrate each of Borges's overall translation tendencies as noted by Kristal. More importantly, Borges's domesticating, "unfaithful," and literary Poe translations change Poe's texts so that they fit within the larger narrative Borges creates around Poe's persona. From minor changes in syntax and word choice to major changes in plot structure and characterization, Borges's Poe translations emphasize his interpretation of Poe as fiction writer rather than poet and place this particular Poe firmly within the literary polysystems of Argentina and Spanish America.

Poe's Water, Poe's Animal: The *Pym* Fragments

Two of Borges's Poe translations are fragments from *The Narrative of Arthur Gordon Pym of Nantucket*—famous passages in which Pym describes the remarkable, divisible water that he and his shipmates encounter on an island near the South Pole and the carcass of a strange, white animal they pull out of the sea. Both of these translations are fairly conservative compared to the changes Borges makes in his translations of "Valdemar" and "The Purloined

Letter," but the translation of the first fragment is significant because it demonstrates Borges's tendency to streamline the source text, in this case a Poe text with an imaginative plotline that Borges praises but with a wordiness that reaffirms Borges's reservations about novels in general when compared to short fiction. His translation of the second fragment, contrastingly, barely reduces Poe's text at all, but it subtly reminds the reader of Poe's connections to detective fiction regardless of the adventure genre in which *Pym* is typically bracketed.

Pym finishes his journal entry for January 19 with this lengthy description of the water that he and his companions encounter while accompanying a group of natives to their island village:

> *On account of the singular character of the water*, we refused to taste it, supposing it to be polluted; *and it was not until some time afterward we came to understand that such was the appearance of the streams throughout the whole group*. I am at a loss to give a distinct idea of the nature of this liquid, and cannot do so without many words. Although it flowed with rapidity in all declivities *where common water would do so*, yet never, except when falling in a cascade, had it the customary appearance of "limpidity." *It was, nevertheless, in point of fact, as perfectly limpid as any limestone water in existence, the difference being only in appearance. At first sight, and especially* in cases where little declivity was found, it bore resemblance, as regards consistency, to a thick infusion of gum Arabic in common water. But this was only the least remarkable of its extraordinary qualities. It was "not" colourless, nor was it of any one uniform colour—presenting to the eye, as it flowed, every possible shade of purple, like the hues of a changeable silk. *This variation in shade was produced in a manner which excited as profound astonishment in the minds of our party as the mirror had done in the case of Too-wit*. Upon collecting a basinful, and allowing it to settle thoroughly, we perceived that the whole mass of liquid was made up of a number of distinct veins, each of a distinct hue; that these veins did not commingle; *and that their cohesion was perfect in regard to their own particles among themselves, and imperfect in regard to the neighboring veins*. Upon passing the blade of a knife athwart the veins, the water closed over it immediately, *as with us*, and also, in withdrawing it, all traces of the passage of the knife were instantly obliterated. If, however, the blade was passed down accurately between the two veins, a perfect separation was effected, which the power of cohesion did not immediately rectify. (155, my emphasis)[19]

Borges translates the passage as follows:

> Primero nos negamos a probarla, suponiéndola corrompida. Ignoro cómo dar una idea justa de su naturaleza, y no lo conseguiré sin muchas palabras. A pesar de correr con rapidez por cualquier desnivel, nunca parecía límpida, salvo al

despeñarse en un salto. En casos de poco declive, era tan consistente como una infusión espesa de goma arábiga, hecha en agua común. Éste, sin embargo, era el menos singular de sus caracteres. No era incolora ni era de un color invariable, ya que su fluencia proponía a los ojos todos los matices del púrpura, como los tonos de una seda cambiante. Dejamos que se asentara en una vasija y comprobamos que la entera masa del líquido estaba separada en vetas distintas, cada una de tono individual, y que esas vetas no se mezclaban. Si se pasaba la hoja de un cuchillo a lo ancho de las vetas, el agua se cerraba inmediatamente, y al retirar la hoja desaparecería el rastro. En cambio, cuando la hoja era insertada con precisión entre dos de las vetas, ocurría una perfecta separación, que no se rectificaba en seguida. ("El arte" 229–30)[20]

Although Borges's Pym agrees with Poe's that it would be impossible to describe this water "sin muchas palabras" (229) or "without many words" (155), he uses significantly less words to do so. Borges reduces Poe's passage by almost half, from 338 words to 182. Shifting a text from one language to another will always cause a difference in word count, but this textual shrinkage is atypical of translation. As Antoine Berman notes in his essay "Translation and the Trials of the Foreign," "Every translation tends to be longer than the original" (290). Berman makes this claim at the beginning of his description of what he calls "expansion" (290), one of the twelve "deforming tendencies" (288) of translation that he examines in this piece. Borges's translation of this passage certainly demonstrates some of the tendencies described by Berman, including "rationalization" (288), but none of Berman's twelve tendencies adequately describes the way in which Borges overtly streamlines this text.[21] Berman does describe the tendency of "quantitative impoverishment," but this phrase refers to "lexical loss" when the target language has fewer signifiers for any given signified than the source language rather than to the complete elimination of sections of the source text (291–92).

Borges's translation of the divisible water passage in Pym clearly veers away from the translation norm of "expansion" due to Borges's decision to eliminate eight phrases or sentences from his translated version. To examine these erasures and to understand why Borges eliminated them, it is essential to recall the context in which Borges published and republished this piece. Each of the texts in which Borges's translation of this passage appears—"El arte narrativo y la magia," Cuentos breves y extraordinarios, and Manual de zoología fantástica / El libro de seres imaginarios—places this part of Pym in conversation with the supernatural. The translation, accordingly, emphasizes the magical or mysterious nature of Poe's purple-hued water. Of the eight deletions Borges makes in his translation, all marked in italics in the citation above, six of them eliminate verbal filling or surplus that matches the excessive style of the entire novel but does not add to the sense of awe created by the water, and one erases an allusion to an earlier scene in the novel. For example, Borges's deletion of the entire sentence, "[i]t was, nevertheless, in point of fact, as perfectly limpid as any limestone water in existence, the difference being only in appearance" (155), eliminates from his translation the assurance that the water, regardless of its appearance, is transparent, but this removal eradicates a particularly redundant sentence without decreasing the wonder caused by the water.[22] Similarly, Borges's elision of "and it was not until some time afterward we came to understand that such was the appearance of the streams throughout the whole group" (155) deprives Borges's audience of the knowledge that all of the waterways on this island contain the same magnificent water, but that information is not essential to the description of the water itself nor is it necessary for a passage that Borges isolates and basically casts as its own microstory. This isolation also justifies Borges's decision to eliminate the sentence that compares the sailors' reactions to the water with Too-wit's reaction to the mirror since the reader of the translation would not understand the allusion without returning to the novel itself. For the reader of Poe's novel, Too-wit's bewilderment upon seeing his own image in a pair of mirrors remains fresh since this scene takes place in the same chapter as the discovery of the water. Thus, the comparison, although a redundancy, emphasizes the awe felt by the sailors who contemplate this water by juxtaposing their bafflement with Too-wit's literal collapse in front of the mirrors. For Borges's reader, however, the allusion would either cause no effect, making it a superfluous part of the passage, or decrease the reader's astonishment with the water by literally taking him/her out of the text to hunt down the alluded scene in *Pym*.

Borges's decision to eliminate the remaining passage—"and that their cohesion was perfect in regard to their own particles among themselves, and imperfect in regard to the neighboring veins" (155)—is more puzzling. This clause could be seen as redundant since it simply elaborates on Pym's claim "that these veins did not comingle" (155). However, the clause makes up half of the description of the water's most surprising quality—its simultaneous homogeneity and heterogeneity. The water's purple appearance is certainly unique, but the consistency of the veins, not their color, makes the water magical, and Borges's elision decreases the emphasis Poe's narrator places on the oddity of this heterogeneous mixture of homogenous liquid strands that seems to cut against the purpose of the other elisions in this passage.

In short, Borges's translation of Poe's famous water passage from *Pym* demonstrates his willingness to drastically reduce the content of a source text in order to emphasize a particular message within that source text—in this case, the magic of the water. At the same time, this translation reveals that in his efforts to reduce Poe's redundancies, Borges also eliminates a specific clause that, while repetitive, could have added to the sense of awe that his leaner version of the text attempts to underscore. All the elisions in Borges's translation of this passage, including his deletion of the clause that provides further description of the water's veins, create a streamlined text that offers Poe's imagination to Borges's reader without his somewhat cumbersome— particularly in *Pym*—prose style. And, as we shall see shortly, the translation of this passage and Borges's usage of it in "El arte narrativo y la magia" allude to Poe as detective writer even though the passage itself does not openly converse with Poe's tales of ratiocination.

Borges's most literal Poe translation appears in both *Manual de zoología fantástica* and *El libro de los seres imaginarios* as "El animal soñado por Poe."[23] In this scene, which takes place in the same chapter as the amazing water, Pym describes a peculiar land animal that he and his companions discover dead in the water. He states:

> We also picked up a bush, full of red berries, like those of the hawthorn, and the carcass of a singular-looking land-animal. It was three feet in length, and but six inches in height, with four very short legs, the feet armed with long claws of a brilliant scarlet, and resembling coral in substance. The body was covered with a straight silky hair, perfectly white. The tail was peaked like that of a rat, and about a foot and a half long. The head resembled a cat's, with the exception of the ears—these were flapped like the ears of a dog. The *teeth* were of the same brilliant scarlet as the claws. (149–50)

Borges offers the following translation:

> Recogimos una rama con frutos rojos, como los del espino, y el cuerpo de un animal terrestre, de conformación singular. Tres pies de largo y seis pulgadas de alto tendría; las cuatro patas eran cortas y estaban guarnecidas de agudas garras de color escarlata, de una materia semejante al coral. El pelo era parejo y sedoso, perfectamente blanco. La cola era puntiaguda, como de rata, y tendría un pie y medio de longitud. La cabeza parecía de gato, con excepción de las orejas, que eran caídas, como las de un sabueso. Los *dientes* eran del mismo escarlata de las garras. ("El animal," *Manual* 24)

The passages are of almost the exact same length, and Borges rarely, and only in minor ways, plays with the syntax of Poe's English version. The animal's measurements, three feet long and six inches high, offer Borges the chance to domesticate the passage by shifting the measurements to the metric system, but he avoids the possibility and translates the creature's size as "[t]res pies de largo y seis pulgadas de alto" ["three feet in length and six inches in height"] (24). In two places, his translation slightly alters the source text. In Poe's piece, the animal's "body was covered with a straight silky hair" (149), while Borges's version drops the reference to the body in favor of "[e]l pelo era parejo y sedoso" ["the hair was even and silky"] (24), and while Poe's animal has "four very short legs" ending in "feet armed with long claws of a brilliant scarlet" (149), Borges's animal has "cuatro patas [. . .] cortas y [. . .] guarnecidas de agudas garras de color escarlata" ["four feet [. . .] short and [. . .] adorned with sharp claws of scarlet color"] (24).[24]

The only significant change Borges makes in this translation appears in his comparison of the strange animal to domestic cats and dogs. Poe's Pym avers that the animal's "head resembled a cat's, with the exception of the ears—these were flapped like the ears of a dog" (150) while Borges's Pym specifies the breed of the dog: "La cabeza parecía de gato, con excepción de las orejas, que eran caídas, como las de un sabueso" ["The head resembled that of a cat, with the exception of the ears, which were fallen, like those of a bloodhound"] (24).[25] On the surface level, Borges's choice of "sabueso" or "bloodhound" rather than "dog" simply emphasizes the droopy nature of the ears of the white animal since the ears of a bloodhound are extremely "flapped" or "caídas." However, "sabueso," like its literal translation in English, can also refer to a sleuth or detective.

Borges's nearly literal translation of this passage from Pym does little to alter Poe's language, but it furtively alludes to the detective genre that Poe inaugurated, which Borges consistently links back to him. When coupled with Borges's translation about the marvelous purple water, a translation that first appeared in the very section of "El arte narrativo y la magia" that I suggested in the previous chapter cast the last chapters of Pym as a standalone detective story, the subtle nod to detective fiction via the shift from "dog" to "sabueso" becomes an explicit signal. Remembering my previous analysis of Borges's portrayal of the late chapters of Pym, it will not be surprising to recall that the two Pym translations that Borges offers each form a part of what Borges sees as the novel's secret plotline, the fear of whiteness, which Borges casts as a mystery that needs to be solved. Borges's translation, publication, and various republications of these particular fragments not only allow him to alter the passages themselves (in both cases) and to create a more concise and direct Poe (in the first case), but they also provide him with another opportunity to portray Poe's longest, wordiest, and least-Borgesian piece of fiction as an example of, rather than an exception to, the detective genre that Borges sees as Poe's most important creation.

CHAPTER 4

Facts and an Envelope

Borges's translations of two of Poe's tales—"The Facts in the Case of M. Valdemar" and "The Purloined Letter"—provide a more extended opportunity to see Borges's translation strategies in action. The translation of "Valdemar" that Borges and Bioy Casares published in *Antología de la literatura fantástica*, which they coedited with Silvina Ocampo, demonstrates Borges's tendency to streamline Poe's source text while adding emphasis to one or more of the arguments put forth via Poe's plotline.[1] This domesticating practice consistently reduces and refines Poe's prose from the opening paragraph's approach to incredulity through Valdemar's nearly spontaneous putrefaction. Apart from altering the source text's style, Borges's translation choices also downplay or remove the vacillation between belief and disbelief visible in Poe's story, offering a tale that expects, rather than invites, the reader to willfully suspend her disbelief in mesmerism's ability to stall and/or penetrate death.[2]

To emphasize how Borges's specific translation decisions, rather than the translation process in general, make "La verdad sobre el caso de M. Valdemar" so different from "The Facts in the Case of M. Valdemar," I will juxtapose his translation, occasionally in the text proper and often in the notes, with two other important translations for late nineteenth-century to mid-twentieth-century Poe readers in the Río de la Plata region—Carlos Olivera's "Mr. Valdemar" and "El caso del señor Valdemar" in Armando Bazán's edition of Poe's *Obras completas*. Olivera published the former as part of his collection of Poe translations entitled *Novelas y cuentos* in 1884, and his version of "Valdemar" appears to be the first translation of the tale in the Río de la Plata region and perhaps the only version of the story from the region prior to Borges's translation in 1940.[3] Bazán published "El caso del señor Valdemar" in 1944 in the massive volume of Poe's works that he edited for the popular press Editorial Claridad, and this version dominated the regional literary market alongside Borges's rendition until the release of Julio Cortázar's Poe translations from the mid-1950s onward.[4] Each of these translations, in both style and content, follows a much more literal translation strategy than Borges's version. Indeed, Olivera's translation and the scathing commentary he provides about "traducciones libres" ["free translations"] in his introduction ("Al lector" i) set up a marked contrast with the theory of translation that Borges lays out in his essays on the subject and practices when he plays the part of translator.[5]

Borges begins the streamlining/domestication of "Valdemar" immediately by offering a much leaner first paragraph than Poe's source text. Poe's narrator opens the tale with this wordy exposition:

> Of course I shall not pretend to consider it any matter for wonder, that the extraordinary case of M. Valdemar has excited discussion. It would have been a miracle had it not—especially under the circumstances. Through the desire of all parties concerned, to keep the affair from the public, at least for the present, or until we had farther opportunities for investigation—through our endeavors to effect this—a garbled or exaggerated account made its way into society, and became the source of many unpleasant misrepresentations, and, very naturally, of a great deal of disbelief. (1233)

Borges's narrator, through both rationalization and explicit elision, cuts the introductory paragraph in half:

> No me sorprende que el caso extraordinario de M. Valdemar haya provocado discusión. Lo contrario hubiera sido un milagro, en tales circunstancias. Nuestra resolución de no divulgar el asunto hasta completar su examen ha dado lugar a rumores exagerados o fragmentarios y ha suscitado, naturalmente, mucha incredulidad.
>
> [It does not surprise me that the extraordinary case of M. Valdemar has provoked discussion. The contrary would have been a miracle, in such circumstances. Our resolution to not divulge the matter until completing its examination has given place to exaggerated or fragmented rumors and has caused, naturally, much incredulity.] (371)

Borges's translation of this paragraph serves as a miniature example for how he translates the remainder of the text. In the paragraph and throughout the translation, Borges alters Poe's syntax and decreases the wordiness of Poe's narrator's descriptions while delivering a similar, although at times slightly altered, message—in this opening paragraph, the idea that the attempts to hide Valdemar's experience from the public have led to rumors, exaggerations, and a general feeling of incredulity. The syntactical changes and the decreased verbosity Borges offers in his translation clearly alter Poe's style, which is significant because Borges continually claims to prefer Poe's imagination over his style. More importantly, however, these alterations allow Borges to approach what he sees as the story's key issue—believability versus incredulity—sooner and in a more direct fashion. Poe's source text, Olivera's translation, and Bazán's edition all arrive at the idea of disbelief by the end of their more extensive first paragraphs, but Borges's accelerated arrival at this concept foreshadows the ways in which his version of the story of Valdemar clarifies the ambiguity in Poe's source text. While Poe's, Olivera's, and Bazán's versions of this tale continually vacillate while describing Valdemar's incredible story, Borges's translation suggests that the occurrences in Valdemar's case are "facts," just as Poe's English title proposes.

Poe's tale initially casts Valdemar's strange case as factual in the story's title and in the paragraph that directly follows the narrator's wordy description of the confusion the case has caused. The narrator simply states: "It is now rendered necessary that I give the *facts*—as far as I comprehend them myself. They are, succinctly, these:" (1233). Olivera, Bazán's edition, and Borges all "give the facts" in nearly the same, fairly literal, translation: Olivera's narrator claims that "Se ha hecho necesario, pues, que yo relate *los hechos*" ["It has been made necessary, then, that I relate *the facts*"] (245); Bazán's suggests that "Es, por lo tanto, necesario que yo exponga los hechos" ["It is, therefore, necessary that I explain the facts"] (211); and Borges's states that "Es necesario, ahora, que yo exponga los *hechos*" ["It is necessary, now, that I explain the *facts*"] (371). These close translations, however, do not inherently repeat Poe's narrator's truth claim since "hechos" in Spanish also means "incidents" or "happenings," and the two latter options both make as much grammatical and contextual sense within each of the translations as the term "facts." Only Borges's translation clearly suggests that the "hechos" should be read as "facts" since only his title re-creates the claim of veracity embedded in the title of Poe's source text. While Olivera shortens Poe's title in favor of "Mr. Valdemar" and Bazán's edition offers "El caso del Señor Valdemar" ["The Case of Mister Valdemar"], Borges chooses "La verdad sobre el caso de M. Valdemar" ["The Truth about the Case of M. Valdemar"]—suggesting that the happenings the narrator describes are truthful, that the "hechos" are facts, not just incidents. Ironically, Borges's translation of the tale—the most literary of the three—most closely follows Poe's title, casting the bizarre events in the narrative as real even though Poe's source text and the other two translations quickly move away from such a bold assertion.

While Poe's title and his narrator's opening comments suggest that the narrative contains facts about Valdemar's experience, the narrator soon uses language—sometimes subtle, sometimes not—that wavers in confidence. In the tale's third paragraph, the narrator notes that no one had ever hypnotized a patient at the point of death. He then states:

> It remained to be seen, first, whether, in such condition, there existed in the patient any susceptibility to the magnetic influence; secondly, whether, if any existed, it was impaired or increased by the condition; thirdly, to what extent, or for how long a period, the encroachments of Death might be arrested by the process. There were other points to be ascertained, but these most excited my

curiosity—the last in especial, from the immensely important character of its consequences. (1233)

The third scenario is also the most important in my analysis since at this point Borges offers a minor change that turns Poe's conditional statement about the possibilities of arresting death into a moment that foreshadows the very event that takes place later in the story. Borges translates this third situation as follows: "tercero, hasta qué grado y por cuánto tiempo el hipnotismo podría detener el proceso de la muerte" ["third, to what degree *and* for how much time hypnotism could detain the process of death"] (371, my emphasis). Borges's verb remains conditional, but by replacing Poe's "or" with "y" ["and"], Borges delicately hints toward the narrator's ability, later in the story, to halt Valdemar's death for an extended period of time.[6] In short, Borges's translated title repeats the truth claim made in Poe's title, and the early paragraphs foreshadow the success the narrator will experience when he becomes the first mesmerist to put a dying person under his magnetic charm.

To better understand how Borges casts the incredible as credible in his translation of "Valdemar," we need to return again to the story's opening paragraph. The rampant disbelief in Valdemar's case that Poe's narrator describes in that paragraph grows out of the failure of the narrator and of the other witnesses at Valdemar's deathbed to keep the extraordinary narrative a secret from the public until they could better interpret what had happened: "through our endeavors to effect this—a garbled or exaggerated *account* made its way into society, and became the *source* of many unpleasant misrepresentations, and, very naturally, of a great deal of disbelief" (1233, my emphasis). Before the narrator ever decides to offer what he calls the real version of the narrative, too many details from the experience, regardless of how fragmented and/or hyperbolic they might be, had already reached the public sphere and had formed an "account" that served as the "source" for rumors and growing incredulity; the excess of voices and their secondhand nature, even though these voices exist outside and before the actual story itself, create confusion and skepticism, and the narrator has to place his version of events in competition with the "exaggerated" rendition already in the public's mind. In Borges's translation, on the other hand, rumors abound, but they do not coalesce into a competing narrative. The characters within the room appear to have been more successful at retaining ownership of the experience: "Nuestra resolución de no divulgar el asunto hasta completar su examen *ha dado* lugar a rumores exagerados o fragmentarios y *ha suscitado*, naturalmente, mucha incredulidad" ["Our resolution to not divulge the matter until completing its examination *has given* rise to exaggerated or fragmented rumors and *has caused*, naturally, much incredulity"] (371, my emphasis). Their very success at not letting the story out is what leads to the rumors but not, significantly, to a competing "account" of the events. While both the "rumors" in Borges's translation and the "account" that creates "unpleasant misrepresentations" in Poe's source text generate disbelief, Borges's narrator's version of the events has less of an obstacle to overcome to be read as *the* version of Valdemar's case than Poe's narrator's rendition.

Even within Valdemar's room itself, Borges streamlines the number of possible voices and reduces the layers of narration by occasionally collapsing Poe's narrator's first-person singular descriptions of events into first-person plural explanations of what is taking place. For example, Borges replaces Poe's narrator's claim that "[t]he only real indication, indeed, of the mesmeric influence, was now found in the vibratory movement of the tongue, whenever I addressed M. Valdemar a question" (1241) with "La única indicación del influjo magnético era el movimiento vibratorio de la lengua, cada vez que lo interrogábamos" ["The only indication of magnetic influence was the vibratory movement of the tongue, each time we questioned him"] (377).[7] This shift from singular to plural is particularly odd at this moment in the text since only two sentences later both Poe's and Borges's versions of the tale aver that Valdemar responds only to the narrator's voice and does not seem to hear anyone else. At other times, Borges simply writes the "narrator-I" out of a sentence. For example, Poe's narrator describes Valdemar's position after several months under hypnosis by referring back to his earlier descriptions: "All this time the sleep-walker remained *exactly* as I have described him" (1241). Borges, contrastingly, drops the narrator completely and offers the following: "Durante ese largo intervalo el estado del sonámbulo no cambió" ["During this long interval the state of the somnambulist did not change"] (378).[8]

The most fascinating simplification of the possible narratives born at Valdemar's deathbed takes place as the narrator describes how the narrative he is presenting to the public has been recorded. In Poe's source text, the narrator states that "Mr. L——l was so kind as to accede to my desire that he would take notes of all that occurred; and it is from his memoranda that what I now have to relate is, for the most part, either condensed or copied *verbatim*" (1236). In Borges's translation, the narrator claims that "El señor L. accedió a tomar notas de cuanto sucediera; este informe compendia, o transcribe literalmente, esas notas" ["Mr. L. agreed to take notes of what happened; this report summarizes, or transcribes literally, those notes"] (374). The story, then, is a transcription of the notes that L——l took during the ordeal, but only in Poe's version does the reader know who the transcriber/translator is. In Borges's version, the narrator suddenly disappears as the intermediary between the notes and the narrative even while his voice continues to tell the tale.[9]

Since Borges's translation often collapses the narrator's view into the experiences of others in the room, it is tempting to suggest that Borges erases the narrator from the text. Such an assertion, however, is inaccurate not only because the narrator remains as both the hypnotist (the character who speaks with Valdemar) and the narrator (the character who speaks to the reader) throughout Borges's translation, but also because Borges's text actually names the narrator. In Poe's source text, Valdemar sends a note to "My Dear P——," informing the narrator that the time for his experiment has arrived since Valdemar is about to die (1235). Borges begins Valdemar's note with "Mi querido Poe" ["My dear Poe"] (372), dragging the author of the source text into the translation as character/narrator.[10] So while Poe's narrator is both narrator (he tells the story from his perspective) and writer (he is the one who transcribes L——'s notes), Borges's narrator is an occasionally hidden narrator (his first-person singular narration can disappear and/or shift to plural) and a real writer (Poe). In short, Borges tackles the structure of confusion in Poe's first paragraph by suggesting that the narrator and his peers have virtually kept a lid on the experience, and he decreases the possible number of narratives by collapsing the narrator's and his colleagues' views into one voice. Both of these strategies challenge the source text's overriding feelings of doubt and prepare the rest of Borges's translation to offer a credible gloss on hypnotism's power over death and on Valdemar's eventual demise.

Borges goes even further to decrease the incredulity surrounding the narrator's version of events by significantly altering the escape valve that Poe's narrator provides for his readers. Just before Poe's narrator claims that Valdemar speaks from beyond death, he states: "I now feel that I have reached a point of this narrative at which every reader will be startled into positive disbelief. It is my business, however, simply to proceed" (1240). This statement, similar to moves that Poe offers in several of his stories which employ the supernatural, from "The Black Cat" to "Ligeia" to "The Angel of the Odd," allows the reader to continue reading without having to willfully suspend her disbelief.[11] As the narrator acknowledges the probable incredulity of his reader, Poe recognizes the likely state of doubt the reader of "The Facts in the Case of M. Valdemar" will experience in the remaining pages and invites her to continue the journey without having to swallow the extraordinary finale. The narrator in Borges's translation acknowledges that the remainder of the narrative will appear improbable, but he completely cuts the reader out of the equation, stating, "Ahora llego a la parte increíble de mi relato. Sin embargo, prosigo" ["Now I arrive at the incredible part of my account. Nevertheless, I proceed"] (376).[12] This elision casts the finale as more believable than the source text in two ways: first, it allows Borges to replace the idea of "disbelief"—a noun made even stronger in Poe's text since it is preceded by the adjective "positive"—with "incredible," an adjective that can mean "unbelievable" or "amazing," either of which could serve to describe the "part of [the] account" in question. Second, it erases the idea of a reader who could doubt the narrative, thus allowing Borges's narrator to quickly move on in his telling of this incredible happening without needing to offer an apology.

Borges's removal of the reader and of the escape valve designed to keep an incredulous audience engaged opposes the strategy he takes toward incredulity in his own tales "Funes el memorioso" and "El Aleph." In each of those stories, Borges's narrators, like the narrator of Poe's version of "Valdemar," make reference to their readers as they grapple with the inconceivable nature of the subject matters they broach. Borges's decision to avoid a reference to the reader in his translation of this particular passage in "Valdemar" serves as a prime example of how influence between the two authors runs both ways. Borges's translation alters Poe's story, casting the unbelievable conversation the narrator holds with Valdemar from beyond the veil of death as believable. At the same time, Poe's source text affects how Borges crafts his own narrators in both "Funes el memorioso" and "El Aleph"—the former published in 1942, two years after Borges translated "Valdemar," and the latter in 1945— since both narrators claim that they have arrived at an incredible point from which they cannot adequately express themselves to others.[13]

The first moment that the narrator fears will cause incredulity—Valdemar's verbal recognition that he is no longer sleeping but is actually dead— occurs in similar fashion in Poe's source text and in the three Río de la Plata translations, but after a few hours of contemplation, Borges's narrator describes the phenomenon in stronger language than Poe's narrator.[14] During the afternoon of the day when the dead Valdemar speaks to the narrator, the narrator claims: "It was evident that, so far, death (or what is usually termed death) had been arrested by the mesmeric process" (1241). Borges translates this passage as follows: "Era innegable que el proceso magnético había detenido la muerte: lo que en general se llama muerte" ["It was undeniable that the magnetic process had arrested death: what in general is called death"] (378). Borges's translation creates a bolder statement than Poe's source text by replacing "evident" with the stronger term "innegable" ["undeniable"] and by making the mesmeric process, rather than death, the subject of the subordinate clause. This shift simultaneously changes the sentence's syntax and places death at the end of the dependent clause rather than at the beginning, which allows Borges to move Poe's slight disclaimer "(or what is usually termed death)" to the very end of the sentence, after the narrator has already stated emphatically that hypnotism has stopped death. Borges's translation also erases the temporal limits of Poe's statement; Poe's use of "so far" in the source text emphasizes the short amount of time between Valdemar's statement (in the early hours of the morning) and the narrator's claim (which takes place sometime in the afternoon of the same day) while Borges's translation drops the temporal marker and thus makes a general proclamation concerning hypnotism's power over death.[15]

After claiming that mesmerism has halted death, both Poe's and Borges's versions of the story state that Valdemar remains in this odd state of arrested death for almost seven months until the narrator and his colleagues decide to attempt to wake him. In the source text, Poe uses the narrator's description of this decision both to reiterate the doubt the community feels concerning Valdemar and to foreshadow Valdemar's imminent destruction. He states: "It was on Friday last that we finally resolved to make the experiment of awakening, or attempting to awaken him; and it is the (perhaps) unfortunate result of this latter experiment which has given rise to so much discussion in private circles—to so much of what I cannot help thinking unwarranted popular feeling" (1241–42). Borges whittles this sentence down to its core and offers only "El viernes último resolvimos hacer lo posible para despertarlo" ["Last Friday we resolved to do what was possible to awaken him"] (378) for the independent clause before the semicolon break while omitting altogether the entire latter two-thirds of the sentence following that break.[16] This translation does not simply eliminate what Borges might see as repetitive information or excessive wording. Rather, it completely erases the concept of a failed experiment, or any experiment at all, from Borges's target text, avoiding the foreshadowing in the source text that hints toward the story's gruesome finale, and thus increasing the shock level of that final scene. The elision of the latter part of the sentence links back to Borges's translation of the story's opening paragraph. In that section, Borges streamlined Poe's source text to arrive sooner at the question of believability versus incredulity, and while maintaining the idea that rumors around Valdemar were rampant in the community, he eliminated the possibility of those rumors forming a competing narrative. In this section, Borges reiterates the stance he took previously by once again deleting the parts of the text that focus on the accounts of Valdemar's experience that exist outside the circle of individuals present at his deathbed, whether in "society" (1233) at large or "in private circles" (1242), thus strengthening the narrator's grip on the narrative and undergirding the target text's attempt to cast Valdemar's story as believable. Poe's narrator attempts to disregard the competing narratives by calling them "unwarranted" (1242), but by naming them, he reveals them as a threat to his rendition of the case. Borges's narrator, contrastingly, does not grant the rumors narrative status in the first place and fails to mention them in the second, effectively eliminating their ability to create incredulity in the "facts" that he claims to recount.

The final alteration of significance that Borges enacts in his translation of "Valdemar" occurs in the ultimate dialogue between the narrator and Valdemar just before the latter's body rots away. In Poe's source text, Valdemar pleads with the narrator: "For God's sake!—quick!—quick!—put me to sleep—or, quick!—waken me!—quick!—*I say to you that I am dead!*" (1242). Borges offers the following: "Por el amor de Dios, pronto—pronto—

hágame morir, o, pronto, despiérteme. *¡Le digo que estoy muerto!*" ["For the love of God, quick—quick—make me die, or, quick, waken me. *I tell you that I am dead!*"] (378).[17] While Poe's text previously foreshadowed how the failure of this hypnotic experiment had led to unjustified speculation about Valdemar's experience, Valdemar's plea in the source text momentarily hints that the experiment could continue indefinitely if the narrator could only put Valdemar back to sleep. In Borges's translation, Valdemar replaces sleep with death, disallowing a return to his hypnotic existence and showing death as an imminent threat—as one more fact, although horrific, in his strange case.

All the changes Borges makes throughout this translation accomplish the dual purposes of altering Poe's style (or, more specifically, of streamlining his prose) and emphasizing the believability of the narrative. Both purposes domesticate Poe's source text and his image to fit within Borges's particular agenda inside his target culture. His rationalization of the text via translation allows Borges to put forward a pithy version of Poe whose translated prose now resembles Borges's own; and his emphasis on the believability of Valdemar's narrative makes the piece fit comfortably in the anthology for which he and Bioy Casares had prepared it: *Antología de la literatura fantástica*. With "La verdad sobre el caso de M. Valdemar," Borges states as fact the opinion he has shared throughout his literary criticism on Poe—that Poe's fiction, not his poetry, make him timeless—and the enduring importance of his translation and this anthology in the Río de la Plata region over seventy years after their initial publication in Buenos Aires continues to reiterate Borges's assertion.

Enveloping "The Purloined Letter"

Borges's and Bioy Casares's translation of Poe's "The Purloined Letter" as "La carta robada" for their 1943 anthology *Los mejores cuentos policiales* follows a translation practice similar to the pattern revealed by juxtaposing their translation of "Valdemar" with Poe's source text. In "La carta robada," Borges once again alters Poe's style by streamlining and domesticating his prose throughout. More importantly, he offers several changes to the story's characters and plot. Kristal examines some of these changes in *Invisible Work* and concludes that Borges's alterations underscore the battle of wits between Dupin and the minister and deemphasize the idea of a solution resting on the surface (66). He also offers a fascinating interpretation of how Borges creates a new male character, a "functionary," who takes the place of the female victim (who is usually read as the queen of France) in Poe's source text (63–67). Much more remains to be said, however, about Borges's basic strategy of rationalization and elision in this story, about how Borges tones down Dupin's interest in a financial reward, and about how the elimination of various lengthy passages (even though some of them describe the intellectual duel between Minister D—— and Dupin) deemphasizes what is typically seen as the story's most ingenious element—the idea of an object hidden in plain sight. Finally, we must return to Borges's translation of "The Purloined Letter" to analyze how it fundamentally alters this puzzle, not only through the elisions and the lack of emphasis on the conundrum, but also by literally enveloping the letter itself.

When modifying Poe's style from "The Purloined Letter," Borges consistently delivers the gist of the source text while decreasing the wordiness of Poe's delivery. At times, he elides idioms or culture-specific information, and at other times he offers an equivalent phrase or concept in Spanish. One example of the former appears as the prefect of police explains to Dupin and to the story's narrator that he is convinced that the minister is not keeping the stolen letter in his hotel room. In Poe's version, he states: "I am not more sure that I breathe than I am that the letter is not at the Hotel" (981). Borges offers the following: "Estoy seguro de que la carta no está en la casa" ["I am sure that the letter is not in the house"] (30). The source text, which comes about as close to the usage of a double negative as allowed in English, leaves plenty of room for Borges to translate the odd expression into Spanish, a language that consistently utilizes double negatives. In other words, the prefect's strange English expression could have been maintained in Spanish through an equivalence or through a direct translation that would not need to be domesticated since the phrase's double negative already fits within the target language and culture, but Borges chooses to do neither and simply moves on with a direct statement about the prefect's confidence that the letter is not in the minister's room.[18] A contrasting example appears when Dupin explains to the narrator why he did not simply take the stolen letter from the minister's abode upon finding it hidden in plain sight. In Poe's source text, Dupin claims, "Had I made the wild attempt you suggest, I might never have left the Ministerial presence alive. The good people of Paris might have heard of me no more" (992). Borges's Dupin says, "El acto que usted me sugiere podía haberme costado la vida" ["The act that you suggest to me could have cost me my life"] (38).[19] Borges's translation streamlines the source text by cutting out the redundant sentence about the detective's relationship with the people of Paris, but it also domesticates the passage by offering a target-oriented equivalence of Poe's "might never have left the Ministerial presence alive" in the form of a well-known Spanish-language phrase.

Borges fills the pages of "La carta robada" with other domestications and equivalences while eliding passages from the source text throughout. His translation delivers the message of Poe's source text in a more direct fashion, but as the minor changes add up, they begin to tell a different story. Borges's translation of the tale's first paragraph demonstrates how repeated elisions and streamlining differentiate the storyline in "La carta robada" from that of "The Purloined Letter." The source text opens with the following lengthy paragraph:

> At Paris, just after dark one gusty evening in the autumn of 18—, I was enjoying the twofold luxury of meditation and a meerschaum, in company with my friend C. Auguste Dupin, in his little back library, or book-closet, *au troisième, No. 33, Rue Dunôt, Faubourg St. Germain.* For one hour at least we had maintained a profound silence; while each, to any casual observer, might have seemed intently and exclusively occupied with the curling eddies of smoke that oppressed the atmosphere of the chamber. For myself, however, I was mentally discussing certain topics which had formed matter for conversation between us at an earlier period of the evening; I mean the affair of the Rue Morgue, and the mystery attending the murder of Marie Rogêt. I looked upon it, therefore, as something of a coincidence, when the door of our apartment was thrown open and admitted our old acquaintance, Monsieur G——, the Prefect of the Parisian police. (974)

Borges hones the paragraph down by about a fourth and offers the following:

> En un desapacible anochecer del otoño de 18 . . . , me hallaba en París, gozando de la doble fruición de la meditación taciturna y del nebuloso tabaco, en compañía de mi amigo C. Auguste Dupin, en su biblioteca, *au troisième, No. 33, Rue Dunôt, Faubourg St.-Germain.* Hacía lo menos una hora que no pronunciábamos una palabra; parecíamos lánguidamente ocupados en los remolinos de humo que empañaban el aire. Yo, sin embargo, estaba recordando ciertos problemas que habíamos discutido esa tarde; hablo del doble asesinato de la Rue Morgue y de la desaparición de Marie Rogêt. Por eso me pareció una coincidencia que apareciera, en la puerta de la biblioteca, Monsieur G., prefecto de la policía de París. (25)

Borges alters the tone of the story's opening paragraph through both rationalization and small word changes. In Poe's text, the night is "gusty," but Borges's translation, perhaps foreshadowing the impending intrusion on the silent scene by the prefect of police, calls the evening "desapacible" ["inclement" or "nasty"]. Poe's narrator avoids the wind through "meditation" and a particular type of pipe in Dupin's small library while Borges's narrator enjoys "meditación taciturna" ["taciturn meditation"] and "nebuloso tabaco" ["nebulous tobacco"] in a "biblioteca" ["library"] rather than in a "little back library, or book-closet."[20] For the avid Poe reader, this small "book-closet" recalls the makeshift dormitory occupied by the whispering William Wilson in Poe's story of the same title. Borges's translation loses this intertextual reference, but it casts the primary space of narration for the story in both larger and quieter terms—a superior space for the development and display of Dupin's analytic mind. Borges's translation also emphasizes the superiority of

Dupin's intellect when compared to that of the narrator through the slight shift in how the narrator occupies his time before the arrival of the prefect. Poe's narrator "mentally discuss[es]" Dupin's former triumphs, but Borges's narrator only "remembers" them, using the verb "recordar." These changes are minor but real, and they set Dupin, the character Borges sees as the perfect armchair detective, apart from his friend and the prefect even more than Poe's source text, hinting toward one of the major shifts Borges creates in this translation—the focus on the battle of wits over the puzzle of the object hidden in plain sight.[21]

Borges's translation of this initial paragraph also reveals his familiarity with Charles Baudelaire's French translations of the Dupin trilogy even though Borges's translation of the allusions to the other two stories in the trilogy refuses to follow either Poe or Baudelaire. Borges often commented on Baudelaire's Poe translations, going as far as to call them "superior[es] al texto de Poe, ya que Baudelaire tenía un sentido estético más fino que Poe" ["superior to Poe's text, since Baudelaire had a more refined aesthetic sense than Poe"] (Borges and Ferrari, "Sobre los poetas" 177).[22] In the paragraph in question, Borges replaces what Poe's narrator calls "the affair of the Rue Morgue" with "doble asesinato de la Rue Morgue" ["double murder of the Rue Morgue"], and he prefers "la desaparición de Marie Rogêt" ["the disappearance of Marie Rogêt"] to Poe's "the mystery attending the murder of Marie Rogêt."[23] In both cases, Baudelaire's translations remain very close to Poe's source text: "l'affaire de la rue Morgue" ["the affair of the rue Morgue"] and "du mystère relatif à l'assassinat de Marie Roget" ["of the mystery relating to the murder of Marie Roget"]. In the latter example, Borges's translation is more true to the events depicted in "The Mystery of Marie Rogêt" and to the historical facts surrounding the death of Mary Rogers than either Poe or Baudelaire since Mary Roger's news story eventually revealed (and the fictional tale about Marie Rogêt finally hinted) that the young women in question died from an accident rather than murder. The first example also veers from the words that both Poe and Baudelaire offer in their versions of "The Purloined Letter." Borges's use of the concept of "double murder" in this example reveals, instead, the influence of Baudelaire's translation of "The Murders in the Rue Morgue" which he famously titled "Double Assassinat dans la rue Morgue." In both cases, Borges offers details from the other two stories in the Dupin trilogy ("Rue Morgue" and "Marie Rogêt") rather than directly translating either Poe's or Baudelaire's references to those earlier tales.

In Poe's "The Purloined Letter," Dupin appears to take the case for at least four reasons: (1) he is a supporter of the woman whose letter has been stolen (if read as the queen of France, Dupin also supports the sociopolitical hierarchy in which he lives); (2) he wants the 50,000 franc reward offered by the prefect; (3) he likes to show up the prefect and his men; and (4) he wants revenge on Minister D——. The two latter points are connected since they are both intellectual contests, one with a man whom Dupin considers inferior and one he considers his equal. In settling an old score with the minister, Dupin simultaneously reiterates his own superiority over the prefect, whom he has already outperformed in both "The Murders in the Rue Morgue" and "The Mystery of Marie Rogêt." The translation changes that Kristal analyzes show how Borges's rendition underscores reason number four, the intellectual duel between Dupin and D——, by significantly altering reason one. Borges also makes major changes in his text that deemphasize reasons two and three.

Throughout his corpus of articles and lectures on detective fiction, Borges consistently prefers Dupin, the "ingenioso autómata" ["ingenious automaton"] ("Ellery Queen" 231), to other detectives who work as paid professionals, and his translation of "The Purloined Letter" makes this preference clear. While Dupin accepts a check for 50,000 francs from the prefect in both Poe's source text and Borges's target text, Borges elides a lengthy dialogue between Dupin and the prefect that literally decreases the amount of space their discussion of money takes up in the text and casts Dupin's acceptance of the check as nonchalant. In both texts, the prefect returns to Dupin's home approximately a month after his original visit, and Dupin asks him about the letter and the amount of the reward. In Poe's story, the prefect responds: "Why, a very great deal—a *very* liberal reward—I don't like to say how much, precisely; but one thing I *will* say, that I wouldn't mind giving my individual check for fifty thousand francs to any one who could obtain me that letter. The fact is, it is becoming of more and more importance every day; and the reward has been lately doubled. If it were trebled, however, I could do no more than I have done" (982).[24] Borges eliminates the last two sentences completely, which is somewhat strange since the penultimate sentence contains an allusion to doubling that would subtly reinforce Borges's idea that the story is really about an intellectual battle between doubles, and he offers a fairly close translation of the first sentence although he depersonalizes the check so that the prefect offers to write "un cheque" ["a check"] (31) rather than "giving [his] individual check" (982) to whoever finds the letter. In Borges's version, Dupin immediately responds by taking out his checkbook and telling the prefect that he will hand him the letter after the prefect writes him the check (31). This direct approach shows an interest, but not an obsession, with the reward and reveals one of the most significant elisions, at least in terms of length, in the entire translation.

Borges eliminates the extensive dialogue between Dupin and the prefect that Poe provides in the source text before Dupin asks for the check. I cite Poe's story at length because this elision both downplays the role of money in the story and decreases the satisfaction Dupin takes in the duel with his less worthy opponent, Prefect G——, suggesting again that what is most important in the tale is the intellectual gamesmanship between Dupin and the minister. Between the prefect's lamentation that he could not find the letter even if the reward were tripled and Dupin's revelation that he already has the letter, the source text reads:

> "Why, yes," said Dupin, drawlingly, between the whiffs of his meerschaum, "I really—think, G——, you have not exerted yourself—to the utmost in this matter. You might—do a little more, I think, eh?" "How?—in what way?" "Why—puff, puff—you might—puff, puff—employ counsel in the matter, eh?—puff, puff, puff. Do you remember the story they tell of Abernethy?" "No; hang Abernethy!" "To be sure! hang him and welcome. But, once upon a time, a certain rich miser conceived the design of spunging upon this Abernethy for a medical opinion. Getting up, for this purpose, an ordinary conversation in a private company, he insinuated his case to the physician, as that of an imaginary individual. 'We will suppose,' said the miser 'that his symptoms are such and such; now, doctor, what would *you* have directed him to take?' 'Take!' said Abernethy, 'why, take *advice*, to be sure.'" "But," said the Prefect, a little discomposed, "*I* am *perfectly* willing to take advice, and to pay for it. I would *really* give fifty thousand francs to any one who could aid me in the matter." (982)[25]

Cutting this dialogue is consistent with Borges's attempts to tame Poe's verbosity; the elimination of this back-and-forth rids the story of the somewhat tedious puffing of Dupin's pipe and of the anecdote that might, at a glance, appear superfluous, but this translation decision accomplishes much more than a streamlining of the text. The elision demonstrates that Borges's version of Dupin does not waste his time mocking an unworthy opponent, thus erasing the competition between Dupin and Prefect G—— that Dupin had already won in the earlier stories of the trilogy.[26] Deleting this conversation also decreases the importance money plays in Dupin's scheme in two ways. In Poe's story, Dupin's sharing of the anecdote about Abernethy makes Dupin, like the doctor, appear unwilling to give advice for free. Eliminating Abernethy's story disallows the simple interpretation of Dupin as Abernethy and G—— as the wealthy miser. This revision also cuts out Dupin's apparent need for reassurance that the prefect will actually pay him. In Borges's rendition, the prefect says that he will pay 50,000 francs for the letter, and Dupin instantly accepts this offer, while in Poe's text he pauses until the prefect restates his willingness to pay for the letter. After this lengthy omission that downplays both the competition between Dupin and the prefect and the importance of monetary compensation, Borges's "La carta robada" is left with only one of the four reasons for Dupin to hunt down the letter—the chance to best his rival/double.

This rivalry, as Kristal suggests, becomes the key to Borges's version of the story to the point of overshadowing the tale's famous depiction of an object hidden in plain sight. For the competition to trump the conundrum, however, Borges does more than simply downplay the other motives behind Dupin's interest in the stolen letter; he deletes three of the primary passages from the source text that accentuate the idea that the mystery is self-evident.[27] The first elision in question takes place in the opening discussion between the prefect, Dupin, and the narrator as Dupin presses Prefect G—— about the paradoxical nature of a situation that is both "simple and odd" (975). In the source text, Dupin mentions simplicity or plainness four times in the four brief comments he makes to G—— during this part of the conversation, the second half of which reads as follows: "'Perhaps the mystery is a little *too* plain,' said Dupin. 'Oh, good heavens! who ever heard of such an idea?' 'A little *too* self-evident.' 'Ha! ha! ha!—ha! ha! ha!—ho! ho! ho!' roared our visiter, profoundly amused, 'oh, Dupin, you will be the death of me yet!'" (975). Borges ends the exchange with the literal translation "'Quizás el misterio es demasiado simple'—dijo Dupin" ["'Perhaps the mystery is too simple'—said Dupin"] (26) and then skips over Dupin's use of "self-evident" and the prefect's guffawing reply.[28] Deleting the latter half of this interchange removes the irksome onomatopoeia of the prefect's laughter and, once again, diminishes the portrayal of a contest between Dupin and the prefect, a competition that the latter implies by suggesting that Dupin will be his death. More importantly, by eliminating a possible redundancy in the source text, Borges also removes the emphasis that Poe places on the surface-level nature of this mystery. This deletion fits well within the overall translation strategy Borges adopts in "La carta robada," but the specific elision of Dupin's expression "A little *too* self-evident" is, itself, an "odd" choice since, as I mentioned in chapter 2, Borges made note of these very words in the back of his 1883 copy of Ingram's *The Works of Edgar Allan Poe (I): Memoir-Tales*. This note, written in María Kodama's hand sometime between 1975 and 1986, reveals that Borges the translator sacrifices the very phrase which later appeals to Borges the rereader during the last decade of his life.

Borges continues to cut this idea out of the text through two other lengthy deletions, which he separates from each other by including a translation of Dupin's brief description of a game played with names on a map. The first of this pair of elisions rids the story of another reference to the "mystery [. . .] being so *very* self-evident" (989), removes Dupin's comparison between inertia and momentum in both physical and intellectual realms, and leaves unasked Dupin's question to the narrator about whether he "notice[s] which of the street signs, over the shop-doors, are the most attractive of attention?" (989). The second elision erases Dupin's answer to his own question and a very clear description of the minister's strategy for hiding the letter where everyone could but no one will see it, "beneath the nose of the whole world" (989–90). Again, this appears to support Borges's strategy of replacing the conundrum with the intellectual competition between two rivals, but the final elision ends with this description from Dupin: "But the more I reflected upon the daring, dashing, and discriminating ingenuity of D——; upon the fact that the document must always have been *at hand*, if he intended to use it to good purpose; [. . .] the more satisfied I became that, to conceal this letter, the Minister had resorted to the comprehensive and sagacious expedient of not attempting to conceal it at all" (990). This last cut, too, diminishes the plain-sight puzzle, but it simultaneously eliminates one of the clearest passages that explains Dupin's understanding of D——. Dupin is able to outsmart the minister because he knows how the minister thinks, and he acts on that knowledge. He metaphorically reads the minster's mind by understanding his character so well. Borges's refusal to translate this passage demonstrates the difficulty of emphasizing the tale's battle of wits while minimizing the story's intellectual puzzle since the two themes are so intertwined in the source text. This elision also foreshadows how Borges's translation of "The Purloined Letter" attempts to conceal the letter in a different way than Poe's source text.

The final, and perhaps the most drastic, change that Borges makes when translating "The Purloined Letter" is to place the stolen letter in an envelope. In Poe's tale, Dupin describes the letter he discovers on his first visit to the minister's hotel in the following terms, contrasting it with the descriptions previously provided by the prefect: "Here the seal was large and black, with the D—— cipher; there it was small and red, with the ducal arms of the S—— family. Here, the address, to the Minister, was diminutive and feminine; there the superscription, to a certain royal personage, was markedly bold and decided; the size alone formed a point of correspondence" (991). Borges offers the following: "El sello no era ni pequeño ni rojo, ni ostentaba las armas de la familia S.: era grande y negro, con el membrete de los D. El sobre estaba dirigido al ministro, con diminuta letra de mujer; el de la carta original estaba dirigido a una persona de la casa reinante, con ostentosa letra de hombre; sólo coincidía el tamaño del sobre" ["The seal was not small nor red, nor did it boast of the arms of the S. family: it was large and black, with the letterhead of the D's. The envelope was addressed to the minister, with minute handwriting of a woman; that [envelope] of the original was addressed to a person of the reigning house, with ostentatious handwriting of a man; only the size of the envelope coincided"] (36–37).[29] While this passage shows, once again, the rationalization apparent in the majority of Borges's translations, what is most important here is the overt addition of an envelope to the story. Inserting an envelope into Minister D——'s card rack shifts the primary conundrum of the tale since the stolen letter is now covered rather than resting in plain sight. By saying "el de la original" in the sentence that refers back to the newly sighted envelope, Borges's Dupin also suggests that an envelope existed earlier in the story at the crime scene in which the minister stole the letter. This idea, however, is not consistent with the translation itself. In Poe's source text, the victim, while reading the letter, was surprised by the entrance of another person into the room and had "to place it, open as it was, upon a table" (977). Borges translates this passage as "dejarla, abierta como estaba, sobre una mesa" ["to leave it, open as it was, upon a table"] (27), eschewing the idea of an envelope that he introduces during Dupin's and the narrator's final conversation. In a strange twist of linguistic fate, the word "sobre" does appear in this translated passage, but not in its guise as an envelope since the term is a homonym in Spanish that means "upon" or "on top of" when used as a preposition rather than a noun. The passage in which Dupin introduces the envelope in Borges's translation, then, appears to create an inconsistency in Borges's rendition of the story since Borges's Dupin refers back to an envelope that never existed in either the source or the target texts while suggesting that he finds the stolen letter hidden in a different envelope.

To make matters even more confusing, Borges does not alter the plain-sight description of the letter in the next paragraph. As in Poe's text, Borges's Dupin examines "la carta" ["the letter"] (not an envelope) through tinted glasses while conversing with D, and like Poe's Dupin, Borges's detective also discovers that "los filos del papel parecían muy chafados. Tenían la apariencia de un papel rígido cuyos dobleces han sido invertidos" ["the edges of the paper seemed very creased. They had the appearance of a rigid paper whose folds have been inverted"] (37). This discovery allows him to surmise, again like Poe's Dupin, that "[l]a carta había sido dada vuelta como un guante, de adentro para fuera. Le habían puesto una nueva dirección y un nuevo sello" ["[t]he letter had been turned like a glove, from inside out. They had put a new address and a new seal on it"] (37). The translation of Dupin's explanation of the letter's appearance does not veer far from Poe's source text, but it appears to contradict the previous paragraph of the translation itself, suggesting that the existence of the envelopes may be nothing more than a misstep in the translation, for Dupin's glasses would need to be more than tinted for him to be able to see the creased edges of the letter and the doubling of the fold if the letter were really inside an envelope.

Reading the translation through to its conclusion, however, reveals that Borges's fairly literal translation of the crumpled edges of a sheet of paper turned inside out creates the inconsistency in "La carta robada," not the introduction of the envelope, since he refers to the envelope again in the narrator's parting question and since he elides a phrase from Dupin's response in the source text that he could have used to shift away from the envelope and back toward the refolded letter. In Poe's story, the narrator asks Dupin: "How? did you put anything particular in it" (993), with "it" referring back to Dupin's description of the facsimile of the letter he has left behind. Dupin responds "Why—it did not seem altogether right to leave the interior blank—that would have been insulting" (993) with "interior" referring to the inside of the refolded piece of paper Dupin leaves in place of the real letter. Borges translates this last exchange as follows: "'—¿Cómo? ¿Usted no dejó un sobre vacío?' '—No, eso hubiera sido injurioso'" ["'—How? You did not leave an empty envelope?' 'No, that would have been insulting'"] (38). The narrator's question reintroduces the notion that Minister D—— had enclosed the stolen letter in an envelope before placing it in his card rack, and Dupin's reply fails to refute this idea. Borges's decision to streamline Dupin's response of "it did not seem altogether right to leave the interior blank" down to only one word—"no"—confirms the existence of the envelope and proves that this newly introduced covering for the letter is an actual part of Borges's version of the story, not an error that other sections of the translation can explain away.

Borges's attempts to shift the emphasis of this story away from the idea of a mystery having a self-evident solution toward the competition between two intellectual rivals culminate in his burial of the letter inside an envelope. Hiding the letter this way, however, somewhat diminishes the rivalry by softening the portrayal of Minister D——'s audacity. It is simply not as daring to hide a letter in an envelope and leave that covering out in the open as it is to turn a letter inside out and leave the letter itself visible for all to see. Encasing the letter also fundamentally changes the story, which is famous for creating the conundrum of the object hidden in plain sight. In Poe's tale, the object itself rests in open view to anyone who enters the minister's room while in Borges's rendition the letter hides inside another object that is in plain view. In short, Borges's tendencies to streamline a source text and to shift the emphasis from one element within a story toward another are not insignificant translation preferences. These proclivities demonstrate Borges's penchant for literary rather than literal translations, and they make Poe's stories his own. In this case, Borges gives us a story whose title follows its source text literally but whose focus would be better captured by shifting the adjective that describes the letter. Poe gave the world "The Purloined Letter," and in his translation of that tale as "La carta robada," Borges really gave the world a covered or hidden letter—*una carta cubierta, escondida, oculta.*

Borges's work as a Poe translator is particularly important in his reshaping of Poe's image in Spanish America, not only because he literally transforms the Poe texts he translates according to his own desires, but also because of the broad and continual appeal of the anthologies in which he published these translations. To recall André Lefevere's discussion of the power rewriters wield, which I approached in my introduction, "Translators, critics, historians, and anthologizers all rewrite texts under similar constraints at the same historical moment. They are image makers, exerting the power of subversion under the guise of objectivity" (6–7).[30] Throughout his career, Borges rewrote Poe via each of these roles, but his role as Poe translator carries double weight since he also anthologized each of his Poe translations. The various anthologies in which Borges places his Poe translations provide him with a far-reaching (both in time and space) mechanism for delivering his version of Poe to readers in the Río de la Plata region and throughout Spanish-speaking America. *Antología de la literatura fantástica* and *Los mejores centos policiales* are two of the most well-known and republished literary anthologies in the Spanish language. The former places Poe among the early "maestros" ["masters"] (Bioy Casares, "Prólogo" 8) of the fantastic and delivers "Valdemar" to the Spanish-reading public over twenty times between the early 1940s and 2007, while the latter frames the entire detective genre as an outgrowth of Poe's Dupin tales (Borges and Casares, "Prólogo" 7–8) and redistributes "The Purloined Letter" as "La carta robada" a dozen times between 1943 and the turn of the millennium. Even the *Pym* fragments gain an extended afterlife since both of Borges's and Guerrero's texts on imaginary or fantastic beings, *Manual de zoología fantástica* and *El libro de los seres imaginarios*, have also seen several reprintings.

By translating Poe's fiction rather than his poetry in the early 1940s, Borges continued to challenge the poetics of the *modernistas* that he had questioned since the 1920s. Lefevere notes the importance of translations in struggles between competing poetics, and he explains that when newer writers attempt to challenge the poetics of a given literary tradition, they often do so by juxtaposing the works of the well-known authors in that tradition with translations that the new writers offer of famous authors from another tradition, foreign writers whose poetics match, or can be slightly transformed to match, the poetics of the up-and-coming group (129). In Borges's case, however, his own writings had already challenged the poetics of *modernismo* by the time he began to translate "Valdemar" and "The Purloined Letter." He confronts *modernismo* again, not by juxtaposing the translated work of an important but unknown foreigner against the *modernista* canon, but by choosing the foreign author most central to the existence of that canon and reframing that writer's image. Once again, his approach to Poe suggests that the *modernistas* have misread their own icon, have misunderstood their own muse. Borges's decision to offer domesticated and streamlined translations of Poe's fiction, translations that emphasize the features that Borges prefers within each piece while downplaying the elements in each source text that might compete with each new version's focus, further solidifies Poe's place in the Argentine and Spanish American literary polysystems. But this place is now held by a more succinct Poe, a spinner of tales that resemble Borges's stories of the 1940s more than they resemble Poe's source texts or the writings of Poe's contemporaries of the 1840s. This Poe appears and reappears for new generations of readers in Argentina's, the Río de la Plata region's, and Spanish America's literary landscape every few years as the anthologies Borges coedited continue to be republished and redistributed.

PART 3

Rewriting Poe

Jorge Luis Borges's Poe-Influenced and Poe-Influencing Short Fiction

CHAPTER 5

Buried Connections

Borges's fiction, like his literary criticism and his translations, demonstrates how he responds to, interprets, and modifies Poe for his own purposes. His fictional corpus solidifies the interpretation of Poe the story writer, rather than Poe the poet, which Borges offers as both a literary critic and a translator since Borges's own tales converse with several of Poe's stories while doing little to propagate Poe's verse.[1] Borges's stories spread Poe's principal invention (the detective genre), one of his primary modes (the fantastic), and several of his repeated themes (revenge, doubling, order/disorder, obsession, the will) to a broader audience while simultaneously altering Poe's image so that it is not simply the image of Poe as a fiction writer but Poe as a Borgesian author of fiction. Analyzing Borges's and Poe's short stories side-by-side both reiterates Poe's influence on Borges's work and, more importantly, reveals Borges's influence on Poe's reception in the very manners that Borges suggests later writers affect former authors in his Kafka essay. Borges's fiction creates Poe as a precursor by making the former writer's work read like the work of the later author (in this case, making certain Poe texts "feel" Borgesian) and by altering how a reader of the second writer reads the first writer (changing how Borges's readers interpret Poe's stories when they read or reread them).

In my analysis of Poe's and Borges's fictional works, I adopt a comparative approach that reads them alongside one another, noting the literal influence of Poe on Borges but emphasizing Borges's influence on Poe's works and his image. I also take an archival approach by paying attention to manuscript and edition changes in the texts when possible. Thomas Ollive Mabbott's two-volume scholarly edition of Poe's tales and sketches, along with the online archive maintained by the Edgar Allan Poe Society of Baltimore, make this an easy task with Poe's stories.[2] With Borges's texts, in contrast, this task is much more difficult since even the most recent "critical edition" of his *Obras completas* does not compare the various published versions of Borges's works, let alone grapple with the few Borges manuscripts that are currently available for scholarly study.[3] I cite the versions of his stories as published in Emecé's 2004–07 printing of the four-volume edition of his *Obras completas*, and when possible, as in the case with "El Aleph," I square the final published edition with the story's manuscript.[4]

To date, the most extensive analysis of Poe's and Borges's fiction appears in Irwin's *The Mystery to a Solution,* in which he convincingly demonstrates how Borges consciously responds to and rewrites Poe's Dupin trilogy with a trio of his own detective tales (37). Irwin offers an intricate reading of Poe and Borges that weaves his analysis of detective fiction through a labyrinth of which Borges himself would have been proud, but the only close readings he offers of Borges's and Poe's nondetective stories serve to illuminate his discussion of their detective tales. Indeed, the majority of Borges/Poe scholarship pays particular attention to the detective genre rather than exploring the other lines of influence that become visible when juxtaposing the fiction of both writers.

In the following chapters, I intentionally turn my focus away from the detective genre to show that the reciprocal influence between Borges and Poe runs beyond their shared interest in tales of ratiocination. With "Buried Connection," I uncover a hidden but significant link between the lengthier 1840 version of Poe's tale "Loss of Breath" and two of Borges's well-known fictional treatises on infinity and memory—"Funes el memorioso" ["Funes, His Memory"] and "El Aleph"—and argue that this connection reveals both the literal influence of Poe's fiction on Borges's work and the literary influence of Borges's fiction on Poe's story since, for the Borges reader, "Loss of Breath" feels Borgesian even if Poe's text serves as an influence for Borges's descriptions of the infinite in "Funes" and "El Aleph."[5]

Borges buries the most significant connections between Poe's "Loss of Breath" and Borges's own "Funes el memorioso" and "El Aleph" three times over. First, the textual links that connect "Loss of Breath" to Borges's pair of tales exist only in a section of the story that Poe excised before he republished the story for the third time in 1846. Second, Borges never mentioned "Loss of Breath" directly in all the articles in which he referenced Poe. Third, Borges doubly concealed his one indirect allusion to Poe's tale in a postscript to a republished prologue.[6] Borges's triple burial of the influence of "Loss of Breath" on "Funes el memorioso" and "El Aleph" seems only fitting since "Loss of Breath" itself reveals Poe's early and lingering obsession with the theme of live burial.[7] Analyzing the three stories side-by-side exhumes these interred connections, exposing both "Loss of Breath's" influence on Borges and "Funes el memorioso's" and "El Aleph's" influence on how contemporary readers understand Poe's story.

In November 1832 Poe published a short tale called "A Decided Loss" in *The Saturday Courier,* and he significantly expanded this story in 1833 in hopes of including it in his proposed Folio Club collection (Mabbott, "A Decided Loss" 51). The longer story carried the title "Loss of Breath," and Poe published it in *Southern Literary Messenger* in September 1835 and then republished it in his *Tales of the Grotesque and Arabesque* in 1840. Between 1840 and late 1845, Poe "cut [the story] down, reducing its bulk by nearly one third" before republishing it again in *Broadway Journal* in January 1846 (51), and this revision erases the previous versions' connections with Borges's "Funes el memorioso" and "El Aleph." Griswold published this leaner version of "Loss of Breath" in 1856 in volume 4 of Poe's *Works*, and this edition of the story has been republished numerous times in both scholarly and popular editions of Poe's work ever since.

Mabbott finds little value in any of these stories, suggesting that this group of revised tales "cannot be called a success" and noting that "[c]ritics have said little about any of the versions" (51). Indeed, Poe scholars and biographers commented very little on "Loss of Breath," in all of its varieties, before 1949. Arthur Hobson Quinn, for example, only mentions "A Decided Loss" once and "Loss of Breath" a handful of times in his *Edgar Allan Poe: A Critical Biography*—noting that the former demonstrates Poe's "early interest in the stage," since its narrator claims to memorize the contemporary melodramas *Metamora* and *Miantinimoh*, and suggesting that the "long description of the sensations of a man being hanged" that appears in the extended version of the story "is not badly done" (194). Marie Bonaparte offers the breakthrough reading of the tale in 1933 in *Edgar Poe: Étude psychanalytique*, which John Rodker translated as *The Life and Works of Edgar Allan Poe: A Psycho-Analytic Interpretation* in 1949. In this exhaustive text, Bonaparte dedicates an entire chapter to "Loss of Breath," reading Mr. Lack-o'Breath's inability to breathe as sexual impotence and connecting Poe directly to this narrator by arguing that "Loss of Breath" is a confession of impotence on Poe's part (373).[8] Her Freudian approach, particularly the direct connection she demands between Lack-o'Breath and Poe, often appears forced, but, as Scott Peeples argues, Bonaparte's reading "unlocked the story for future readers and commentators" (38). To name only two examples, Daniel Hoffman also equates "breath" and "potency" in his brief analysis of "Loss of Breath" as he examines marriage in several of Poe's tales in *Poe Poe Poe Poe Poe Poe Poe*, while Stuart and Susan Levine suggest that this story "mak[es] a sexual joke" rather than "revealing [Poe's] fears and inadequacies" as they place "Loss of Breath" among a group of stories they claim "show[s] 'multiple intention'" in *The Short Fiction of Edgar Allan Poe* (471).[9]

Borges's cerebral tales "El Aleph" and "Funes el memorioso" are, by far, more well-known in Borges's body of work than "Loss of Breath" is in Poe's fictional corpus.[10] Critics most often read the former story as a complex parody of Dante, as an autobiographical story about Borges's own failed relationships with women, or as a tale about language and its shortcomings. Emir Rodríguez Monegal, for example, reads "El Aleph" as "a parodic reduction" of Dante's *Divina Commedia* and suggests that Borges's "parody is so subtly achieved that many readers of Borges who also are devoted readers of Dante fail to recognize it" (*Jorge Luis Borges* 414). Humberto Núñez-Faraco interprets the story's portrayal of the relationship between Borges the narrator/ character and his ideal but already dead woman, Beatriz, as an autobiographical reference to Borges the writer's real relationship with Estela Canto, quoting Canto's *Borges a contraluz*, in which she claims that Borges compared himself to Dante and Canto to Beatriz (613).[11] One of Borges's recent biographers, Edwin Williamson, also connects the story to Borges's relationship with Canto (279–83), but he first suggests that "El Aleph" hearkens back to Borges's failed courtship with Norah Lange in the mid-1920s. He claims that the story "is not about the loss of love as such; it is a lament for the loss of what love might have afforded Borges" (278).

Other critics hone in on Borges's portrayal of the limits of language and/or literary creation in "El Aleph." Julio Rodríguez-Luis avers: "'The Aleph' is clearly about literary creation rather than about the existence of a magic window-compendium of the universe in a Buenos Aires basement" (39–40). The quandary faced by Borges-narrator as he tries to relate what he has seen in the Aleph—a simultaneous view of every object in the universe from every angle without confusion or layering—so pointedly foresees the poststructuralist concerns with language that dominated academic discourse in the latter half of the twentieth century that the story feels almost prophetic.[12] Borges-narrator's preoccupation about the difficulty of his task, the list-like paragraph of descriptions he provides, and the entire tale have been interpreted as everything from an exercise in existentialism (McBride 401) to a mystical experience about the impossibility of naming God (Canto 211–12). The story's very title, the object it names, and the infinite yet infinitesimal nature of the space or point that Borges the author calls an Aleph also open "El Aleph" to a variety of kabbalistic readings.[13]

Borges's biography and the limits of language also play central roles in several interpretations of "Funes el memorioso." In the prologue to *Artificios*, Borges claims that the story "es una larga metáfora del insomnio" (483) ["is one long metaphor for insomnia"] (129), which leads various critics to connect Funes's inability to forget with Borges's own purported difficulties with insomnia. Rodríguez Monegal, for example, reads Funes's physical crippling after being bucked off a horse as representative of Borges "be[ing] symbolically crippled by insomnia: riveted to his bed by a pitiless disease of the mind" (*Jorge Luis Borges* 276–77). He calls Borges's creation of Funes "a self-portrait, a view of himself as a man immobilized by memory and insomnia" (383). Beatriz Sarlo claims that the story "can be understood as a parable dealing with the possibilities and impossibilities of representation, because Funes experiences to the limit the problems of translating perception, experience, and memories of experience into discourse" (31), while David E. Johnson avers that "no Borgesian text more thoroughly and more overtly takes up the problem of language and conceptualization" than the story Borges crafts

about Ireneo Funes (25). The number of scholars who comment on the para-
lyzing effect of Funes's memory and/or the ways in which the story demonstrates language's inability to depict reality creates a list nearly as long as the
one Borges the narrator rattles off when describing what he saw in the Aleph,
but an occasional scholar takes the side of Funes, rather than the side of the
story's narrator, and interprets Funes's supermemory as a gift rather than a
curse.[14] Either way, "Funes el memorioso," like "El Aleph," sets out to portray
infinity via the finite system that is language.

On the surface level, all published versions of Poe's "Loss of Breath" contain a pair of coincidences that recall moments in either "Funes el memorioso"
or "El Aleph." First, both Lack-o'Breath and Funes suffer from ailments of
the lungs. Lack-o'Breath describes his new condition as "[his] own pulmonary incapacity" ("Loss," *Tales* 126) while the narrator of "Funes el Memorioso" ends his recollections about Ireneo Funes in anticlimactic fashion by
abruptly stating, "Ireneo Funes murió en 1889, de una congestión pulmonar"
(490) ["Ireneo Funes died in 1889 of pulmonary congestion"] (137). Second,
both Lack-o'Breath and Borges-narrator discover hidden letters revealing that
their love interests—Lack-o'Breath's new bride and Beatriz Viterbo—have
played them for fools. In Lack-o'Breath's case, he finds "a bundle of *billets-
doux* from Mr. Windenough to [his] wife" (126) while desperately looking
for his lost breath, and in Borges-narrator's case, he sees "cartas obscenas,
increíbles, precisas que Beatriz había dirigido a Carlos Argentino" (625) ["obscene, incredible, detailed letters that Beatriz had sent Carlos Argentino"]
(283). The relationships between these two men and these two women could
not be more different since Lack-o'Breath is married but appears to despise
his wife while Borges-narrator worships Beatriz from afar with little hope for
reciprocity. The revelations each narrator receives, however, mirror one another almost perfectly. Both Borges-narrator and Lack-o'Breath read rather
than hear their true standing with Beatriz and Mrs. Lack-o'Breath, and they
both discover the identity of their rivals. Finally, both narrators stumble upon
this knowledge without searching for it.

These explicit links reveal minor interplay between Poe's tale and Borges's
two stories, but the buried clues that further connect these pieces go far beyond this simple intertextuality. Poe's 1840 version of "Loss of Breath" in
Tales of the Grotesque and Arabesque, in particular, plays a significant and
previously unanalyzed role in establishing literary connections between Poe
and Borges since it both contains concepts that Borges tackles and passages
that he subtly re-creates—without explicitly acknowledging Poe—in his narrators' descriptions of Ireneo Funes's total memory and Carlos Argentino
Daneri's Aleph or visual portal to the entire universe. The premise behind all
the published versions of "Loss of Breath"—that a man, incapable of breath-
ing, remains alive only to endure countless other hardships that should also

take his life (e.g., a twisted neck, a fractured skull, dissection, and hanging)—is somewhat ridiculous, but it is no more incredible than the infinite capacity of Funes's memory or than the totality and simultaneity of the images revealed in the minuscule Aleph. In short, "Loss of Breath," "Funes el memorioso," and "El Aleph" all attempt to describe the indescribable.

In "Loss of Breath," Mr. Lack-o'Breath attempts to relate two experiences—his hanging and the preparations his body undergoes while awaiting burial—which should be indescribable because he has to lose his breath (die?) to be able to describe them. With the exception of "A Decided Loss," all versions of the story comment on the impossibility of such a narrative since, as Lack-o'Breath himself avers, "[t]o write upon such a theme it is necessary to have been hanged. Every author should confine himself to matters of experience" (134). This requirement places his account outside the realm of typical narrative possibility. At the same time, Lack-o'Breath's assertion that an author must write from experience, even though his particular experience is so outlandish that no reader could possibly approach it as though it were common ground, implies that his narrative will only be believed by one person—himself. The sensations of hanging for a person without breath, in the end, can only be understood by another victim of the gallows who happens to have already lost the ability to breathe. The same logic holds true for the breathless but cognizant body that waits to be interred. This lack of a common, although ridiculous, denominator emphasizes the impossibility of the story Lack-o'Breath tries to tell and places his narration in direct conversation with the narrators of "Funes el memorioso" and "El Aleph," who both face similar conundrums.

The narrator of "Funes el memorioso" begins his brief recollection of a young man with an infinite memory with an open confession: "Lo recuerdo (yo no tengo derecho a pronunciar ese verbo sagrado, solo un hombre en la tierra tuvo derecho y ese hombre ha muerto) con una oscura pasionaria en la mano, viéndola como nadie la ha visto, aunque la mirara desde el crepúsculo del día hasta el de la noche, toda una vida entera" (485) ["I recall him (though I have no right to speak that sacred verb—only one man on this earth did, and that man is dead) holding a dark passionflower in his hand, seeing it as it had never been seen, even had it been stared at from the first light of dawn till the last light of evening for an entire lifetime"] (131).[15] The project in which the narrator engages—the writing of a memoir for a collected volume of narratives about Ireneo Funes written by the many people who knew him—inherently fails from the start, not due to the narrator's supposed limits as an Argentine contributor rather than a Uruguayan, but due to the finite nature of the narrator's (and all the other contributors') memories.[16] Not only is language incapable of reproducing Funes's endless memory, but the narrator's imperfect memory cannot even replicate Funes's truncated oral descriptions of his memory's vastness. The narrator laments, "Arribo, ahora, al más difícil punto de mi relato. Éste (bueno es que ya lo sepa el lector) no tiene otro argumento que ese diálogo de hace ya medio siglo. No trataré de reproducir sus palabras, irrecuperables ahora. Prefiero resumir con veracidad las muchas cosas que me dijo Ireneo. El estilo indirecto es remoto y débil; yo sé que sacrifico la eficacia de mi relato" (487) ["I come now to the most difficult point in my story, a story whose only *raison d'être* (as my readers should be told from the outset) is that dialogue half a century ago. I will not attempt to reproduce the words of it, which are now forever irrecoverable. Instead, I will summarize, faithfully, the many things Ireneo told me. Indirect discourse is distant and weak; I know that I am sacrificing the effectiveness of my tale"] (134). The narrator simply cannot remember all that Funes told him, and he remains stuck in the quandary of attempting to re-create the gist of a conversation he cannot retell while realizing that the very dialogue itself was already an impossible attempt to bring the infiniteness of Funes's mind into a finite alphabet.

This same challenge reappears in "El Aleph." In language that echoes the narrator's words in "Funes el memorioso," Borges-narrator states, "Arribo, ahora, al inefable centro de mi relato; empieza, aquí, mi desesperación de escritor. Todo lenguaje es un alfabeto de símbolos cuyo ejercicio presupone un pasado que los interlocutores comparten; ¿cómo trasmitir a los otros el infinito Aleph, que mi temerosa memoria apenas abarca?" (624) ["I come now to the ineffable center of my tale; it is here that a writer's hopelessness begins. Every language is an alphabet of symbols the employment of which assumes a past shared by its interlocutors. How can one transmit to others the infinite Aleph, which my timorous memory can scarcely contain?"] (282). His experience with the Aleph traps Borges-narrator in a realm of triple impossibility. In the first instance, Borges-narrator's memory—like the memory of the narrator in "Funes el memorioso"—cannot maintain the infinite amount of knowledge he ingests while gazing into the Aleph, and so, unlike Ireneo Funes, Borges-narrator forgets the majority of what he has seen. In the second instance, Borges-narrator cannot truly share the vastness of his experience because his audience has never seen anything like the oxymoron that he attempts to narrate—infinity contained in an infinitesimal space. Finally, in the third instance, even if Borges-narrator could somehow keep infinity inscribed in his gray matter (if he could somehow turn himself into Ireneo Funes) and even if his audience had shared the same experience (if they had all been invited into Carlos Argentino Daneri's basement before his house was demolished), language as we know it would disallow the communication or re-creation of that experience because language is linear. Borges-narrator claims, "Lo que vieron mis ojos fue simultáneo: lo que transcribiré, sucesivo, porque el lenguaje lo es" (625) ["What my eyes saw was *simultaneous;* what

I shall write is *successive*, because language is successive"] (283). Language's sequential nature inherently denies the simultaneity of the Aleph and leaves Borges-narrator with an impossible experience to tell. In short, to understand what Borges-narrator has seen, what Ireneo Funes has thought, or what Lack-o'Breath has felt, an individual would have to have seen the Aleph, received an infallible memory, or hanged after already having no breath.[17]

Although Lack-o'Breath's claim about needing to be hanged in order to write about such an experience appears in the shorter versions of "Loss of Breath" that Poe published in 1846, that Griswold republished in 1856, and that editors continue to republish today, only the 1835 and 1840 versions of the text actually include the narrator's attempts to describe this indescribable event.[18] The twenty-six paragraphs of the story that Poe deleted between 1840 and 1846 provide vivid details of Lack-o'Breath's sensations both in the noose and in the small mortuary room where his body lies in preparation for the grave. These excised passages visibly alter the story's mood and shift the tale, at least momentarily, away from Lack-o'Breath's banter toward the horrific sensations of the gallows and the fears—both physical and philosophical—of death. Alexander Hammond argues that these deleted passages form "more or less an independent unit within the whole," which he titles "The Quick Among the Dead" and labels a "tale of terror" ("A Reconstruction" 29, 30).[19] This terrifying segment of the story, whether a tale on its own or a distinct discourse embedded within a larger burlesque, provides the reader with a more thoughtful approach to the indescribable in contrast to the remainder of the tale's jocular treatment of death and premature burial.[20] Most important, these omitted passages serve as an inspiration for Borges's descriptions of memory and infinity in "Funes el memorioso" and "El Aleph."

While scholars have examined both philosophical and literary influences on Borges's creation of Ireneo Funes from Friedrich Nietzsche to Mark Twain, no literary critic has connected Borges's tale to Poe.[21] Clancy W. Martin notes the narrator's allusion to "Nietzsche's famous character Zarathustra" (268)—"Pedro Leandro Ipuche ha escrito que Funes era un precursor de los superhombres, 'un Zarathustra cimarrón y vernáculo'" (Borges, "Funes," 485) ["Pedro Leandro Ipuche has written that Funes was a precursor of the race of supermen—'a maverick and vernacular Zarathustra'"] (131)—and examines the influence of Nietzsche's "On Truth and Lies in a Nonmoral Sense" on Borges's tale.[22] In similar fashion, René Lira connects Borges's portrayal of Funes's memory to Mark Twain's descriptions of Mr. Brown's memory in *Life on the Mississippi* (519–24). The examples the narrator of "Funes el memorioso" provides to describe Funes's prodigious memory, however, hearken all the way back to Mr. Lack-o'Breath's descriptions of the sensations of hanging in the longer versions of "Loss of Breath."

Lack-o'Breath begins his impossible narration with a simple claim that he "will endeavor to depict [his] sensations upon the gallows" (134). After describing the immense "pressure" that the noose causes for his veins, head, ears, and eyes (134), Lack-o'Breath calmly relates:

> Memory, which, of all other faculties, should have first taken its departure, seemed on the contrary to have been endowed with quadrupled power. Each incident of my past life flitted before me like a shadow. There was not a brick in the building where I was born—not a dog-leaf in the primer I had thumbed over when a child—not a tree in the forest where I hunted when a boy—not a street in the cities I had traversed when a man—that I did not at that time most palpably behold. I could repeat to myself entire lines, passages, chapters, books, from the studies of my earlier days; and while, I dare say, the crowd around me were blind with horror, or aghast with awe, I was alternately with Æschylus, a demi-god, or with Aristophanes, a frog. (135)

The instances that flash through Lack-o'Breath's mind initially appear more fleeting than Funes's memories since Lack-o'Breath describes them as shadowy while the narrator in "Funes" relates that Funes's recollections, and his present moments, were "casi intolerable de tan rico y tan nítido" (488) ["so rich, so clear, that [they were] almost unbearable"] (135). However, when Lack-o'Breath's mind moves from the memory of "incident[s]" to the memory of objects, he sees them "most palpably" (Poe, "Loss of Breath" 135), like Funes. His vision of every brick "in the building where [he] was born," every dog-eared page in the textbook of his childhood, and every "street in the cities" he walked as an adult (135) evokes Funes's total recall since Funes, too, sees wholes in parts: "cada hoja de cada árbol de cada monte" (489) ["every leaf of every tree in every patch of forest"] (136) or "todos los vástagos y racimos y frutos que comprende una parra" (488) ["every grape that had been pressed into the wine and all the stalks and tendrils of its vineyard"] (135). In each case, the vessel of his memory loses its ability to distinguish between significant and insignificant details and remembers, as the narrator in "Funes el memorioso" states, "las memorias más antiguas y más triviales" (488) ["his oldest and even his most trivial memories"] (135).

Funes's memory is certainly more exaggerated and more exhaustive than Lack-o'Breath's, especially since his ability remains with him from the time of his accident until his death while the enhanced power of Lack-o'Breath's "quadrupled" memory lasts only while being hanged (Poe, "Loss" 135). Yet Borges playfully repeats in his depiction of Funes's total recall some of the exact examples Poe creates to describe Lack-o'Breath's immense, though temporary, powers of memory, suggesting that Borges had Poe's text in mind while penning "Funes el memorioso." While Lack-o'Breath remembers each "dog-leaf" (135) in the text he read as a boy, the narrator of "Funes el memorioso" describes Funes's mental capacity by providing one example of how Funes perceives a dog and another about how he sees leaves. The narrator suggests that the generality of a word like "dog," which can be used to describe various breeds and types of an animal or to describe individuals within any given breed or type, frustrates Funes; however, language's attempt to provide one word for the same individual dog at different times of the day or seen from different angles aggravates him even more. The narrator states, "le molestaba que el perro de las tres y catorce (visto de perfil) tuviera el mismo nombre que el perro de las tres y cuarto (visto de frente)" (489) ["it irritated him that the 'dog' of three-fourteen in the afternoon, seen in profile, should be indicated by the same noun as the dog of three-fifteen, seen frontally"] (136). He also claims that Funes "no sólo recordaba cada hoja de cada árbol de cada monte, sino cada una de las veces que la había percibido o imaginado" (489) ["remembered not only every leaf on every tree in every patch of forest, but every time he had perceived or imagined that leaf"] (136), a hyperbolic extension of Lack-o'Breath's already preposterous claim to remember each "tree in the forest where I hunted when a boy" (135).[23]

At first glance, these illustrations could appear coincidental, but the fact that Borges provides these two specific examples—the dog and the leaves—out of an infinite number of possibilities he could have used to demonstrate Ireneo Funes's monumental powers of memory creates a link between the two texts that invites further investigation. Rather than coincidence, these examples of Funes's memory both play off of and greatly multiply the already impossible characteristics Lack-o'Breath's memory demonstrates while hanging. Funes's colossal memory simultaneously calls itself and Lack-o'Breath's short-lived mental powers into question. When read side-by-side, Funes's memory trivializes Lack-o'Breath's, not because its capacity dwarfs Lack-o'Breath's limited illumination, but because in exaggerating the concept of memory Borges's character emphasizes the absurdity of Lack-o'Breath's odd claims.

This type of exaggeration not only occurs with Funes's aforementioned recollection of all leaves on all trees in all forests versus Lack-o'Breath's recalling every tree in one specific forest, but it reappears in both characters' ability to memorize entire books. In this case, Borges seems to play a card that Poe had already played on himself. One of the slapstick moments in "Loss of Breath" takes place early in the story as Lack-o'Breath, to avoid his wife's possible suspicion about his new inability to breathe, instantly memorizes two long dramas in which the actors speak with guttural voices so that he can repeat them in her presence and feign a desire to become an actor. He nonchalantly states, "Being naturally quick, I committed to memory the entire tragedies of ——, and ——" (128).[24] During his hanging, this incredible ability with books returns, but multiplied both in quantity and in the amount of time between the initial reading and the memory of the texts, as Lack-o'Breath claims: "I could repeat to myself entire lines, passages, chapters, books, from the studies of my earlier days" (135). Borges takes Poe's amplification of an already hyperbolic idea and trumps it by showing Ireneo Funes memorizing a complex text at the very time he memorizes the language in which that text is written—Latin. The narrator of Borges's tale lends Funes a Latin thesaurus and "un volumen impar de la *Naturalis historia* de Plinio" (486–87) ["an odd-numbered volume of Pliny's *Naturalis historia*"] (133), annoyed by Funes's assumption that with a reference text and a copy of any book in Latin he can learn the language. Only a week later, Funes has mastered the language and greets the narrator in Latin by reciting one of Pliny's chapters, a chapter on memory (487; 134). Funes's instant learning of Latin and memorization of one of Pliny's volumes one-ups Lack-o'Breath's immediate mastery of what, for him, is a new guttural tongue and a pair of popular dramas, and although Borges does not have Funes or the narrator describe Funes's memories about any of the books that he has read throughout his life, those texts are surely there among Funes's recollections, which outnumber all the memories of "todos los hombres desde que el mundo es mundo" (488) ["*all mankind since the world began*"] (135).

Borges returns to the concept of seeing every page within a given book, and every page within every book, in "El Aleph." Borges-narrator includes the following description in the lengthy list of actions and objects he simultaneously views while gazing into the Aleph: "vi una quinta de Adrogué, un ejemplar de la primera versión inglesa de Plinio, la de Philemon Holland, vi a un tiempo cada letra de cada página (de chico, yo solía maravillarme de que las letras de un volumen cerrado no se mezclaran y perdieran en el decurso de la noche)" (625) ["I saw a country house in Adrogué, saw a copy of the first English translation of Pliny (Philemon Holland's), saw every letter of every page at once (as a boy, I would be astounded that the letters in a closed book didn't get all scrambled up overnight)" (283).[25] All published versions of "El Aleph"—the 1945 story published in *Sur*, the 1949 version published in Borges's collection *El Aleph*, and the 1952 version published and republished in the various versions of Borges's *Obras completas*—as well as the various renditions of this passage in Borges's original manuscript, openly connect the pages and letters viewed to the particular book Borges-narrator mentions. In other words, Borges-narrator sees "every letter of every page" of this particular text "at once" (283). However, Borges-narrator avers that his list is a weak attempt to describe "el inconcebible universo" (626) ["the inconceivable universe"] (284) that not only includes every single thing but every single thing simultaneously seen "desde todos los puntos del universo" (625) ["from every point in the cosmos"] (283). In essence, Borges-narrator sees all things in the universe from all viewpoints in the universe in the same way that Funes remembers all leaves from all trees from all forests (and everything else he has ever seen) from all angles. Borges-narrator's all-encompassing view not only includes every letter, word, and page of Philemon Holland's translation of Pliny but every symbol in every book ever written. His decision to name a translation of Pliny's encyclopedic text as the specific book whose pages and symbols he "reads" from all views at once also plays on the idea of totality since Pliny, with his encyclopedia, attempted to capture within the finite space of a multivolume book the entirety of the known universe of the first century. In Borges's manuscript of "El Aleph," the second of three versions of the lengthy list of what Borges-narrator sees in the Aleph includes Angelus Silesius's mystic *Cherubinischer Wandersmann*, rather than a volume of Pliny, as the exemplary text whose pages and letters Borges-narrator views ("Facsímil" 45).[26] In both cases, the text serves as a microcosm of the Aleph itself since both Pliny and Silesius attempt to contain something uncontainable within their texts—the known world in the case of Pliny and the complexities of panentheism in the case of Silesius.

Borges-narrator's view of all texts (although alluded to via one particular text), even more than Funes's complete memory of any text he reads, exponentially increases Lack-o'Breath's claim of remembering the books of his boyhood. The impossibility of Lack-o'Breath's assertion diminishes in the face of the indescribability of Funes's and Borges-narrator's experiences. Lack-o'Breath's lucidity while hanging, although uncanny, becomes comprehensible when compared to the colossal memory of Funes and the mindbending vision of Borges-narrator. For a Poe reader who has read Borges and then returns to these excised passages in "Loss of Breath," Funes's and Borges-narrator's experiences with infinity squared (infinity seen from infinite angles) make Lack-o'Breath's hyperbolic recollection of his own past palatable. The temptation for this rereader of Poe to forgo the suspension of disbelief dissipates since she has been asked to accept so much more in Borges's pair of tales.

The intertextuality between "Loss of Breath," "Funes," and "El Aleph" demonstrates how Borges plays with and exaggerates Poe's subtle hints at infinity, but the conclusion of Lack-o'Breath's thoughts while hanging shows an important difference, beyond magnitude, between Poe's depiction of memory and totality and Borges's approach to these concepts, particularly in "El Aleph." As "the crowd around [Lack-o'Breath] were blind with horror, or aghast with awe" while watching his theatrics in the noose, he "was *alternately* with Æschylus, a demi-god, or with Aristophanes, a frog" (135, emphasis added). Lack-o'Breath's experience remains sequential as he consecutively recalls his distinct readings of two ancient Greek playwrights while Borges-narrator's experience contemplating the Aleph creates a simultaneous view that makes him see everything from every angle at the exact same time "sin superposición y sin transparencia" (625) ["without superposition and without transparency"] (283).

Regardless of this difference between the successive nature of Lack-o'Breath's thoughts while hanging and the simultaneous nature of Borges-narrator's vision in the Aleph, the essential core of the concept Borges the author attempts to convey in "El Aleph"—the thought of infinity contained inside a finite, or even infinitesimal, space—also links back to an excised passage in "Loss of Breath." After Lack-o'Breath is taken down from the gallows, his body is placed in a small room to await burial. He states: "I was laid out in a chamber sufficiently small, and very much encumbered with furniture—yet to me it appeared of a size to contain the universe. I have never before or since, in body or in mind, suffered half so much agony as from that single idea. Strange! that the simple conception of abstract magnitude—of infinity—should have been accompanied with pain" (137–38). The small but cluttered room itself recalls Carlos Argentino Daneri's basement, the home of the Aleph, which Borges-narrator calls "apenas más ancho que la escalera, tenía mucho de pozo. [. . .] Unos cajones con botellas y unas bolsas de lona entorpecían un ángulo" (624) ["barely wider than the stairway, [it] was more like a well or cistern. [. . .] A few burlap bags and some crates full of bottles cluttered one corner"] (282). More significantly, Poe's chamber foretells the paradox Borges the author creates with the Aleph itself, whose physical properties Borges-narrator describes thus: "El diámetro del Aleph sería de dos o tres centímetros, pero el espacio cósmico estaba ahí, sin disminución de tamaño" (625) ["The Aleph was probably two or three centimeters in diameter, but universal space was contained inside it, with no diminution in size"] (283). Again, Borges takes a concept Poe offers in "Loss of Breath"—a small but cluttered room that somehow seems capable of holding the universe—and multiplies it. His Aleph is much smaller than the room Poe creates for Lack-o'Breath. At face value, this difference in size exaggerates the initial juxtaposition Poe offers between the small room and the cosmos; however, it makes no literal difference since infinity dwarfs both spaces, the room and the Aleph, equally. The real exaggeration rests in Borges-narrator's claim when compared to Lack-o'Breath's comparison. To Lack-o'Breath, the room "*appeared* of a size to contain the universe" (138, emphasis added) while Borges claims that the universe "estaba ahí" (625) ["was contained"] (283) within the Aleph. For Lack-o'Breath, the concept of contained or trapped infinity remains an idea while for Borges-narrator this paradox happens—he sees the infinite universe within a minuscule sphere.

In each tale, the thought and/or the reality of infinity create terror for the respective narrators. Lack-o'Breath's fear is instant, it expands to include "all objects" and "all *sentiments*" (138), and it finally shifts away from the spatial concept of infinity toward its chronological equivalent—eternity. Lack-o'Breath initially thinks that he is dead and fears that he will maintain a foggy mental capacity in a sort of ontological no-man's-land "forever, forever, and forever!" (139). He remains in this stupor until the sunlight reveals to him that he is not dead but that he is about to be buried alive; "the paraphernalia of the grave" (139) and "the actual terrors of the yawning tomb" (140), both finite in time and space, supplant his fears about infinity and eternity. In short, Lack-o'Breath's fear of the physical—live burial—trumps the terror of his philosophical musings from the previous night. Borges-narrator's terror, conversely, shifts from his initial, physical responses—tears and a feeling of vertigo—to the fear of permanent déjà vu (626; 284), to a lingering philosophical doubt in the reality of the Aleph. Borges-narrator's fallible, non-Funes-like memory eventually saves him from the feeling that he has already seen everything, but while his brain forgets the majority of the infinite images he saw in the Aleph, he cannot forget the concept, the idea that he saw everything in the entire universe simultaneously.

As the postscript of the story suggests, this idea continues to haunt Borges-narrator months after Carlos Argentino Daneri's house and the Aleph within its basement have been destroyed. For Borges-narrator, viewing infinity causes even more pain than Lack-o'Breath suggests, and "El Aleph" ends with Borges-narrator attempting but failing to refute what he has seen by calling Carlos Argentino Daneri's Aleph "falso" (627) ["*false*"] (285). Once again, Borges takes the seed of an impossible idea planted in Poe's story and brings it to fruition within his own tale, even though this process intensifies rather than solves the philosophical conundrum Poe suggests in the deleted passages of his lesser-known "Loss of Breath" concerning the overwhelming scale of the concept of infinity.

In previous scholarship that brings Poe's and Borges's works into conversation, the connections I have drawn between Poe's "Loss of Breath" and Borges's "Funes el memorioso" and "El Aleph" have never emerged. Perhaps these connections have remained hidden due to the fact that Borges never openly hints at them in any of his literary criticism, interviews, or collaborative works. Borges litters his literary criticism with both allusions to and direct references from several of Poe's detective stories, fantastic tales, and terror pieces, but he does not mention "Loss of Breath" even once. Yet I argue that the conversation I have unearthed by reading "Loss of Breath," "Funes el memorioso," and "El Aleph" side-by-side demonstrates Borges's knowledge of and reaction to "Loss of Breath" rather than coincidence or casual intertextuality.

The most direct manner to establish that Borges was familiar with the excised passages in "Loss of Breath" would be to refer to the Poe editions Borges owned that are now held by Argentina's National Library and by the

Fundación Internacional Jorge Luis Borges. However, none of the editions held by these two libraries contains the extended version of "Loss of Breath." Borges's copy of *The Centenary Poe: Tales, Poems, Criticism, Marginalia and Eureka* in the National Library does not contain any versions of this story, while the third edition copy of Ingram's *The Works of Edgar Allan Poe (II): Tales-Continued* and the copy of *The Complete Tales and Poems of Edgar Allan Poe* held at the Fundación both contain only the later, shorter version of "Loss of Breath"—a story for which Borges left no notes within the texts.

Laura Rosato and Germán Álvarez—archival librarians in the Sala del Tesoro in Argentina's National Library and the editors of *Borges, libros y lecturas*, a lengthy volume dedicated to the marginalia Borges left in the texts he donated to the library when he resigned in 1973—continue to receive notice from smaller libraries and private collectors about other books containing Borges's personal notes, and some of these books deal directly with Poe. For example, a private library informed Álvarez in August 2011 that they had recently found a copy of *Edgar Allan Poe*, by Edward Shanks, with Borges's marginal notes among their collection (Personal Interview).[27] The possibility exists, then, that a copy of *Tales of the Grotesque and Arabesque* with Borges's commentary could emerge from one of the many private libraries or collections to which Borges donated or lent books he had read, but even if this book never surfaces, digging deeper into Borges's published commentary on Poe proves that Borges read the extended version of "Loss of Breath."

As previously mentioned, Borges never refers to "Loss of Breath" in any of the articles, collaborative works, or interviews in which he approaches Poe. Apart from the textual connections I have made in my comparative analysis of "El Aleph," "Funes el memorioso," and "Loss of Breath," the evidence that Borges knew the longer version of "Loss of Breath" lies doubly buried in a postscript to a revision of a prologue for Ray Bradbury's *Crónicas marcianas* [*The Martian Chronicles*] that Borges published in *Prólogos, con un prólogo de prólogos* in 1975. Borges originally published a prologue for the Spanish translation of Bradbury's book in 1955 without referring to Poe, and the prologue he published in the 1974 republication of *Crónicas marcianas* also contains no Poe reference. Borges must have added the postscript, dated in 1974, specifically for his own book, *Prólogos*. The placement of the Poe reference Borges offers in this postscript buries alive Borges's knowledge of "Loss of Breath" since the allusion comes under/after a prologue, a genre that is already buried or peripheral in any author's written corpus.[28] Borges begins this short note by claiming: "Releo con imprevista admiración los *Relatos de lo grotesco y arabesco* (1840) de Poe, tan superiores en conjunto a cada uno de los textos que los componen" ["I reread with unexpected admiration the *Tales of the Grotesque and Arabesque* (1840) by Poe, so superior as a whole to each one of the texts that make up the collection"] (34). Even within the postscript, Borges veils the reference to "Loss of Breath" by referring to the larger collection by name without naming any of individual stories that make up the volumes. However, his claim that each story creates a superior whole to the inferior individual pieces within the text inherently reveals that Borges has reread the individual pieces themselves, including the lengthy version of "Loss of Breath" that contains Lack-o'Breath's impossible descriptions of hanging and preparing for burial. To judge the whole as superior to the parts, Borges must know the parts themselves.

Borges rereads "Loss of Breath" and the other stories in *Tales of the Grotesque and Arabesque* a full three decades after publishing "Funes el memorioso" and "El Aleph," but his use of "rereading" rather than "reading" to describe this literary encounter proves that he knew the tales long before he wrote this prologue. Indeed, in a question-and-answer series at a colloquium at the University of Maine at Orono in 1982, Borges claimed that *Tales of the Grotesque and Arabesque* were "the first stories of [Poe's] I read" (Yates 196), and since Borges states in various written pieces and interviews that he first read Poe as a child, Borges appears to have read the extended version of "Loss of Breath" for the first time in his youth, several years before he created Ireneo Funes's exhaustive memory and the all-encompassing yet minuscule Aleph in Carlos Argentino Daneri's basement. In short, digging through Borges's peripheral works validates the previously buried connections between "Loss of Breath," "Funes el Memorioso," and "El Aleph" that my side-by-side reading of the stories has unearthed and establishes the 1840 version of Poe's slapstick satire as an unlikely precursor to this pair of highbrow tales by Borges.

The influence between these stories, however, runs both ways, and while "Loss of Breath" serves as a creative springboard for Borges, it also *receives* influence via Borges in the two ways Borges posits that Kafka's works create Kafka's predecessors in "Kafka y sus precursores." While the casual Poe reader misses out on this influence because she reads the later, shorter version of "Loss of Breath" that is more readily available, the reader who tackles "Loss of Breath" as published in *Tales of the Grotesque and Arabesque* discovers in the now-excised passages the moments in which Lack-o'Breath describes the abilities of his memory while hanging and his fear of the idea of infinity. These passages now feel overwhelmingly Borgesian. The reverse effect—the Borges reader feeling that "Funes el memorioso" and "El Aleph" feel Poesque—does not occur for at least two reasons. First, most Borges readers are not familiar with the version of "Loss of Breath" published in *Tales of the Grotesque and Arabesque*, and second, even with a knowledge of this version of Poe's story, the primary concept within the excised "Loss of Breath" passages that influences "Funes el memorioso" and "El Aleph"—the idea of infinity and the mental anguish it can cause—does not define Poe's works the way it defines Borges's literary corpus. In Poe, this concept is exceptional to one section of one tale while the idea haunts Borges's work and is particularly visible in pieces such as "La biblioteca de Babel" ["The Library of Babel"], "La lotería en Babilonia" ["The Lottery in Babylon"], "Las ruinas circulares" ["The Circular Ruins"], "El jardín de senderos que se bifurcan" ["The Garden of Forking Paths"], and the two Borges stories I have analyzed in this chapter.[29] In his famous short essay "Borges y yo" ["Borges and I"], Borges even suggests that "los juegos con el tiempo y con lo infinito" (221) ["games with time and infinity"] (324) are now a part of his public persona.

Along with the Borgesian sensation created by the peculiar section of the 1840 edition of "Loss of Breath" for the Poe reader familiar with Borges, "Funes el memorioso" and "El Aleph" also change how that reader interprets Lack-o'Breath's attempts to describe the impossible. Lack-o'Breath's amazing memory while he is being hanged sounds exaggerated and somewhat ridiculous when it stands on its own, but it seems tame and even believable when juxtaposed with Funes's total recall. Likewise, the awe temporarily produced by Lack-o'Breath's contemplation of infinity but quickly supplanted by his fears of the physical threat of being buried alive regains its terror for the reader familiar with Borges-narrator's overwhelming sense of vertigo after contemplating the infinite.

In the end, "Loss of Breath" gains stature in my comparative analysis between the works of Poe and Borges because the story serves as a secret source for Borges's depictions of infinity in both "Funes el memorioso" and "El Aleph." At the same time, "Funes el memorioso" and "El Aleph" alter how contemporary readers interpret "Loss of Breath." Disinterring the buried connections between these stories also reiterates the depth and breadth of Borges's knowledge of Poe's literary canon. As I have already demonstrated in the opening section of chapter 2, Borges explicitly reveals having read the lesser-known essay "Philosophy of Furniture" in his lecture "La poesía," and as I have argued in this chapter, Borges covertly exposes his familiarity with the little-known version of Poe's already somewhat marginal tale "Loss of Breath." My comparative analysis of "Loss of Breath," "Funes el memorioso," and "El Aleph" reaffirms that even Poe's peripheral work had a visible influence on Borges's literature (that having read "Loss of Breath" influenced Borges's fiction), and it begins to demonstrate how Borges's literature has a literary influence on Poe's work by affecting how contemporary readers understand Poe, an argument that I will continue to cultivate in the next chapter as the discussion shifts from the impossibilities of infinity to the possibility/impossibility of revenge.

CHAPTER 6

Supernatural Revenge

To further unpack the complex literary relationship between Borges's and Poe's fiction, I return to Borges's "El Aleph" to reveal the conversation this tale creates about revenge and the supernatural when read alongside Poe's early narrative "Metzengerstein" and his famous short story "The Black Cat." Borges's approaches to revenge and to the supernatural in "El Aleph" are not direct responses to Poe since neither of these themes originates with Poe. Yet as Borges's literary criticism and marginalia suggest, Poe occupied a special place in Borges's memory, and Borges often returned to his thoughts on (and/or critiques of) Poe when writing his own stories. Borges's treatment of revenge via the mode of the fantastic in "El Aleph" demonstrates how his fiction, while both revealing and spreading Poe's influence, alters how we interpret Poe's stories about these same ideas.

In response to a question concerning his masterful revenge story, "Emma Zunz," in an interview with Richard Burgin, Borges claims the following: "I think there's something very mean about revenge, even a just revenge, no? Something futile about it. I dislike revenge. I think that the only possible revenge is forgetfulness, oblivion" (23). Borges's stated distaste for revenge draws a stark contrast when compared to Poe's tendencies to hold a grudge and to pick a literary fight.[1] As Kenneth Silverman suggests in *Edgar A. Poe: Mournful and Never-Ending Remembrance*, Poe had already stated the now-famous family motto of which his character Montresor painfully reminds Fortunato in "The Cask of Amontillado"—"*Nemo me impune lacessit*" (1260)—in a letter to his former employer William E. Burton, the owner of *Gentlemen's Magazine* (316). In June 1840 Poe wrote Burton that "[i]f by accident you have taken it into your head that I am to be insulted with impunity I can only assume that you are an ass" (*Letters* 1: 130). Silverman reads Poe's "Cask" as his attempt to avenge himself, not of Burton, but of a group of literary enemies who had raked him over the coals in the press in 1845–46 (316).[2] Similarly, Silverman points to a later correspondence from Poe to suggest that Poe's distance from the contemporary world of letters during the last three years of his life "had left him ornery" (404); Poe told Fredrick W. Thomas that "[b]y and bye I mean to come out of the bush, and then I have *some* old scores to settle. [. . .] The fact is, Thomas, living buried in the country makes a man savage—wolfish. I am just in the humor for a fight. You will be pleased to hear that I am in better health than I ever knew myself to be—full of energy and bent upon success" (*Letters* 2: 428).

This juxtaposition between Borges's and Poe's stated outlooks on revenge, however, does not erase the fact that Borges, like Poe, often sparred with his contemporaries in print and thus ran the risk of making literary and/or literal enemies on whom he could take revenge and vice versa. Borges's disagreement with Roger Caillois, which I examined in chapter 2, demonstrates that Borges also knew how to pick a literary fight. However, his assessment of Caillois's understanding of detective fiction is tame when compared to the mocking style of critique that Borges had previously adopted in "Leopoldo Lugones, *Romancero*" in 1926. Borges begins this review by calling the most popular Río de la Plata writer of the time period "[m]uy casi nadie" ["unimportant"] or, more literally, ["[v]ery almost nobody"] (105); he openly mocks Lugones's use of rhyme (106); and he concludes the piece by claiming that Lugones "ha querido hablar con voz propia y se la hemos escuchado en el *Romancero* y nos ha dicho su nadería. ¡Qué vergüenza para sus fieles, qué humillación!" ["has wanted to speak with his own voice and we have heard it in the *Romancero* and it has told us its trifles. How embarrassing for his believers, how humiliating!"] (108). Both his critique of Caillois and his mockery of Lugones set up what could have become long-lasting arguments between Borges and these writers, but in both cases, Borges softened his stance with time. As I suggested in chapter 2, Borges did not change his mind about the origins of the detective genre, the seed of the literary feud between himself and Caillois. He did, however, drop his critical references to Caillois in his reviews of detective fiction after May 1942, and by the 1980s, he appeared truly grateful that Caillois championed his literature regardless of their earlier disagreement. Similarly, Borges eventually demonstrated respect for Lugones in a book that he cowrote with Betina Edelberg in 1955 entitled *Leopoldo Lugones*, in various articles (e.g., "Sobre Lugones" published in *La Nación* in June 1974), and in several interviews in which he comes to terms with the earlier bard and storyteller (e.g., his discussion of Lugones with Miguel Enguídanos in "Now I Am More or Less Who I Am").

In his fiction, Borges portrays the theme of vengeance in a manner distinct from that typically adopted by Poe. In Poe's tales, revenge can be justified or unwarranted, appropriate or excessive, realistic or exaggerated, and while Poe scholars assign conflicting judgments on his characters'/narrators' disparate acts of vengeance, his stories depict revenge as a viable option for his literary creations.[3] In Borges's fiction, contrastingly, vengeance either fails completely or completely fails to satisfy. In this chapter, I concentrate my analysis on what I call Poe's and Borges's fantastic revenge tales—the aforementioned "Metzengerstein," "The Black Cat," and "El Aleph"—rather than on their more overt revenge stories (e.g., Poe's "The Cask of Amontillado" and "Hop-Frog" and Borges's "Emma Zunz") for four reasons. First, the former group of stories simultaneously allows for an examination of the supernatural—a key element in many of Poe's and Borges's works. Second, this approach also allows us to return to Borges's literary criticism on Poe and to analyze one of Borges's few available manuscripts, the manuscript of "El Aleph." Third, the revenge plots of "Metzengerstein," "The Black Cat," and "El Aleph" have received almost no coverage in previous Poe and Borges scholarship. And fourth, revealing how the supernatural plotlines of these three stories mask their revenge plots mirrors the unmasking of the reciprocal relationship of influence between Borges and Poe (a relationship that some Poe studies scholars cast as top-down from Poe to Borges) that my entire project performs. Reading "El Aleph" alongside "Metzengerstein" and "The Black Cat" demonstrates how Borges alters Poe's revenge motif and, in the second manner Borges describes in his Kafka essay, changes how his readers interpret revenge when they return to Poe's tales.

Theorizing the Supernatural

At a glance, Poe's "Metzengerstein" and "The Black Cat" are so dissimilar from Borges's cerebral story "El Aleph" that comparing the three narratives might appear unwise. Each tale, however, contains a revenge plot that is critical to the narrative's action but obfuscated by the horrific and/or supernatural elements within the story. Delineating a rubric for how to understand these supernatural happenings allows for the separation of the horror elements from the supernatural aspects of each story, produces a better understanding of the supernatural events themselves, and highlights the revenge theme in each piece. Poe's supernatural revenge stories emphasize the concept of a just revenge while Borges's supernatural revenge narrative trivializes vengeance. Read side-by-side, these stories demonstrate how Borges's revenge fiction both plays off of and alters Poe's.

Conducting this comparison requires a working understanding of the fantastic as a literary mode compared to other types of supernatural literature. Franco-Bulgarian literary critic and philosopher Tzvetan Todorov famously and rigorously theorized the fantastic in *Introduction à la littérature fantastique* [*The Fantastic: A Structural Approach to a Literary Genre*] in 1970, and since his text has created both avid followers and vehement opponents, most contemporary analyses of the fantastic approach Todorov's work in one manner or another. Todorov differentiates the fantastic from other types of literature that rely on the supernatural—particularly what he refers to as "the uncanny" and "the marvelous"—by focusing on a character's doubts when supernatural events take place in narratives that, from the beginning, occur "[i]n a world which is indeed our world, the one we know" (25).[4] According to Todorov, "The fantastic is that hesitation experienced by a person who knows only the laws of nature, confronting an apparently supernatural event" (25).[5] If/when the narrator or character satisfies their doubts and overcomes this hesitation—either by explaining away the supernatural event or by accepting a worldview that now allows for such events to take place—the fiction becomes either uncanny or marvelous, respectively (44). Todorov admits that this so-called genre "leads a life full of dangers, and may evaporate at any moment. It seems to be located on the frontier of two genres, the marvelous and the uncanny, rather than to be an autonomous genre" (41), and he allows for some slippage between the three by discussing the subgenres of "the fantastic-uncanny" and the "fantastic-marvelous" (44). The former hesitates for a long period within the text before offering a scientific or logical explanation that fits the supernatural event within the laws the character understands, while the latter finally overcomes the doubt by realizing that the supernatural events themselves are real even if they cannot be explained by the character's previous worldview (44–45).

Various critics follow Todorov's basic claims about the importance of hesitation in the construction of a fantastic narrative, but some claim that the fantastic can still exist even if the reader's hesitation ends before the story concludes. For example, in *Magical Realism and the Fantastic: Resolved Versus Unresolved Antinomy*, Amaryll Beatrice Chanady hones Todorov's analysis by arguing that the fantastic is "a mode" that appears in several genres rather than a genre or subgenre itself (1–2) and by describing what Todorov calls hesitation as "*antinomy*, or the simultaneous presence of two conflicting codes in the text" (12, italics in original). Chanady argues that "the fantastic creates a world which cannot be explained by any coherent code" (12), and she cites the difference between how the fantastic and the magical real deal with antinomy as one of the primary ways to distinguish between these two literary modes: "Whereas the antinomy appears to be resolved in magical realism, the contradictions between different conceptions of reality are placed in the foreground by the author of a fantastic text. In fact, the emphasis on conflicting world views which cannot be resolved according to the laws posited by the text itself is the most important distinguishing characteristic of the fantastic" (69).

Julio Rodríguez-Luis offers a complex interpretation of the fantastic that both converses with and occasionally veers away from Todorov's and Chanady's understandings of the concept in *The Contemporary Praxis of the Fantastic: Borges and Cortázar*. Rodríguez-Luis agrees with Todorov that the fantastic is a genre, but he does not see the genre as threatened in the way that Todorov does because he suggests that the "hesitation" created by the "existence [. . .] of a supernatural or impossible [. . .] element" in an otherwise "strictly realistic milieu" qualifies a text as fantastic regardless of whether or not this supernatural intrusion remains at the end of the text, is accepted as real, or is explained away (112). Like Chanady, Rodríguez-Luis allows for the type of text in which characters and readers finally accept the supernatural event as real even though it contradicts the code of reality they maintain (what Todorov calls the fantastic-marvelous), but unlike Chanady, Rodríguez-Luis also accepts as fantastic any fiction in which characters or narrators explain away the supernatural events according to the rational code of the text (what Todorov calls the fantastic-uncanny). As I examine Poe's and Borges's supernatural revenge tales, I follow Todorov's, Chanady's, and Rodríguez-Luis's claims that the fantastic requires a supernatural intrusion in an otherwise realistic narrative and a noticeable hesitation on the part of the character/narrator involved. However, my use of the fantastic is more like that of Rodríguez-Luis than that of Todorov or Chanady since I do not maintain that this hesitation must remain intact at the end of the tale in order for a story to qualify as fantastic. I read "Metzengerstein," "The Black Cat," and "El Aleph" as fantastic revenge stories even when—as in the case of "Metzengerstein"—the characters and/or narrative eventually explain away the story's supernatural events.

This understanding of the fantastic, however, does not completely match Borges's own and somewhat convoluted descriptions of the term. Years before Todorov's treatise, Borges and Adolfo Bioy Casares practiced and discussed the fantastic in ways that defy the later theorizations of the concept. Borges offered several lectures on the fantastic, and he used the term to describe his work and the work of others in various prologues and articles over the course of his career.[6] However, what, exactly, Borges meant by the term remains unclear since the methods, requirements, or techniques that he claimed create fantastic fiction sometimes shifted and, more importantly, because the very stories he called fantastic did not always meet the requirements he set out.

Borges made his only attempts to define the fantastic in a series of lectures he gave on the subject between 1949 and 1968 to audiences across the world from Montevideo, Uruguay, to Toronto, Canada, and from Tucumán, Argentina, to Gothenburg, Sweden.[7] In each of these discourses, Borges offered a list of elements, themes, or methods that he considers fantastic.[8] The themes increased in number while the newly added elements decreased in specificity between 1949 and the late 1960s. For example, in Borges's first lecture on the fantastic in Montevideo in 1949, he mentioned only four "procedimientos" ["methods"] of the fantastic: "la obra de arte [que] aparezca en la misma obra de arte" ["the work of art [that] appears within the same work of art"]; the contamination of reality by dreams, including the idea of time travel; "los dobles" ["doubles"]; and "la invisibilidad" ["invisibility"] (qtd. in Passos 4).[9] Three of these themes are extremely specific, and only the mixture of dream with reality actually allows for some play although Borges limits that play by offering time travel as a specific type of dream-reality mixture. According to this early list, a text in which a supernatural being—for example, a ghost or a monster—enters an otherwise realist narrative and causes doubt or hesitation for the characters/narrators would not be fantastic. In his later lectures, however, Borges tended to drop the method of self-referential art, keep the mixture of dream and reality, specify time travel as its own category, keep the theme of the double, and add more general themes such as "la magia [. . .] una suposición de leyes causales, de leyes causales que no parecen avenirse con la lógica" ["magic [. . .] a supposition of causal laws, of causal laws that do not appear to agree with logic"] ("La literatura fantástica," *Anales* 13), the appearance of supernatural beings in the everyday world, and the idea of transformation / metamorphosis / shape-shifting.[10] Even though Borges claims in his Montevideo lecture that "[l]os procedimientos de la literatura fantástica pueden reducirse, ciertamente, a unos pocos" ["[t]he methods of fantastic literature can certainly be reduced to very few"] (qtd. in Passos 4), his later and more open categories—for example, the entrance of laws that defy nature or the appearance of supernatural beings—certainly allow for an increased number of plotlines to be considered fantastic while more easily creating a conversation between his views on the fantastic and the rubrics offered by Rodríguez-Luis, Todorov, and Chanady.

The primary distinction between Borges's conceptualization of the fantastic in his lectures and Todorov's, Chanady's, and Rodríguez-Luis's understandings of the term lies in Borges's insistence on providing examples of stories that include supernatural themes versus these critics' focus on the effect these happenings have on a story's narrators, characters, and readers. In short, Borges *describes* the fantastic while these critics set out to *theorize* it—something that Borges purposefully avoids in his talks, claiming:

para que mi conferencia no peque de exceso de abstracción, voy a ilustrar cada uno de los medios de la literatura fantástica con ejemplos. Es decir, voy a contar cuentos, lo cual es sin duda, [. . .] más agradable para ustedes que asistir a una mera teoría de la literatura fantástica, una teoría a la cual no he llegado, por lo demás.

[so that my conference is not excessively abstract, I am going to illustrate each of the ways of fantastic literature with examples. That is to say, I am going to tell stories, which is, without a doubt, [. . .] more enjoyable for you all than being treated to a pure theory of fantastic literature, a theory that I have not arrived at yet anyway.] ("La literatura fantástica," *Anales* 12)

Even if Borges sees little value in a theory or rubric of the fantastic for the audience at his lectures, a schematic for understanding the fantastic becomes increasingly important when we attempt to understand why Borges labels certain stories fantastic—not in his lectures in which he connects each literary example with one of the specific categories that he sets forth, but in his articles and prologues where he often calls a given tale fantastic even though the specific story might not meet any of his own criteria. Examining the stories by Poe that Borges calls fantastic serves as a microcosm for Borges's convoluted use of the term throughout his literary criticism, emphasizes the two-way relationship of influence between Borges and Poe, and demonstrates the portability of a rubric for the fantastic based on narrator, character, and reader doubt.

In one of Borges's last pieces dealing with Poe, "Prólogo a Edgar Allan Poe, *Cuentos*," he makes the following statement concerning what he suggests are Poe's memorable fantastic tales: "De su literatura fantástica recordemos 'The Facts in the Case of Mr. Valdemar', 'A Descent into the Maelström', 'The Pit and the Pendulum', 'MS. Found in a Bottle' y 'The Man of the Crowd', todos de inaudita invención" ["From his fantastic literature let us remember 'The Facts in the Case of Mr. Valdemar,' 'A Descent into the Maelström,' 'The Pit and the Pendulum,' 'MS. Found in a Bottle,' and 'The Man of the Crowd,' all of unprecedented invention"] (647). Coming from Borges, this is certainly an odd list for at least two reasons. First, the stories that he lists do not visibly meet his own requirements, and second, he does not mention several of Poe's stories that clearly meet his criteria, even though he comments on these stories at other times in his literary criticism.

With the possible exception of "The Man of the Crowd," these five tales can only fit awkwardly within any of the four specific "procedimientos" of the fantastic that Borges offered in Montevideo: self-referential art, dream-contaminated reality (including time travel), the double, or invisibility. "The Man of the Crowd" is far more subtle than Poe's "William Wilson," but various literary critics read the story as a tale of doubling in which the narrator and the old man that he follows through the city streets are one and the same (P. Quinn 230; Mazurek 25–28). None of the tales include self-references. "MS. Found in a Bottle" and "The Man of the Crowd" both drop small hints that the narrators could be dreaming, but it would be a stretch to argue that in either story a dream has invaded reality, and none of the five stories contain time travel—the specific dream invasion Borges notes—unless, again, we stretch the concept to include the ancient boat in "MS. Found in a Bottle" or Valdemar's words from beyond the grave as evidence of traveling through time.[11] The only reference to invisibility in any of these texts would be the narrator's suggestion in "MS. Found in a Bottle" that the ship's strange passengers "*will not* see" him (141). Even Borges's later and more general categories such as the appearance of supernatural beings in the natural world or the existence of laws that go beyond logic cannot salvage all these tales as stories of the fantastic—although the former possibility could certainly fit the ancient men on the decrepit ship in "MS. Found in a Bottle" while the latter could apply to Valdemar's experience.

With so many Poe stories that do meet some of Borges's most specific descriptions of the fantastic—"Some Words with a Mummy" and "The Angel of the Odd" can both be read as dream-contaminated realities while "Ligeia," "Morella," "The Fall of the House of Usher," "A Tale of the Ragged Mountains," and "William Wilson" all approach the theme of doubling more directly than "The Man of the Crowd"—Borges's choice to call these five particular tales fantastic must rely on something completely different than the criteria he presents in his lectures on the subject.[12] Tellingly, the common thread that runs through "The Facts in the Case of M. Valdemar," "A Descent into the Maelström," "The Pit and the Pendulum," "MS. Found in a Bottle," and "The Man of the Crowd" is fear.[13] Borges never cites fear as an element of the fantastic in his lectures, but he does hint at this idea much earlier and much later in his career. For example, in his 1936 piece for *Sur*, "Modos de G. K. Chesterton," Borges claims that "Edgar Allan Poe escribió cuentos de puro horror fantástico o de pura *bizarrerie*" ["Edgar Allan Poe wrote stories of pure fantastic horror or of pure bizarrerie"] (20), and in his 1985 "Prólogo a Edgar Allan Poe, *La carta robada*," Borges again connects fear and the supernatural while describing Valdemar's tale: "en 'The Facts in the Case of M. Valdemar' el horror físico se agrega al horror de lo sobrenatural" ["in 'The Facts in the Case of M. Valdemar' the physical horror is added to the horror of the supernatural"] (12). This coupling of the fantastic with fear also matches the description Bioy Casares provides in the prologue he wrote for his, Borges's, and Silvina Ocampo's 1940 *Antología de la literatura fantástica*. While it is Bioy Casares, not Borges, who claims that the creation of an "ambiente" ["ambiance"] of terror was key to early writers of the fantastic such as Poe and Guy de Maupassant (8), Borges supports this reading, not simply by including Bioy Casares's prologue in the book, but also by translating "The Facts in the Case of M. Valdemar" with Bioy Casares and including this translation as the one Poe story to grace the anthology.[14]

In short, the juxtaposition of the methods of the fantastic that Borges describes in his lectures with the Poe stories he calls fantastic in "Prólogo a Edgar Allan Poe, *Cuentos*" creates confusion. In contrast, a rubric of the fantastic that relies on character / narrator / reader doubt when a supernatural event takes place in an otherwise realistic narration succinctly clarifies which of the Poe tales that Borges dubs fantastic actually match the concept. This rubric also distinguishes between doubt/hesitation and fear, and it demonstrates how the fantastic depends on the former emotion while the latter may exist within but does not create the fantastic. Out of the five Poe stories with horrific or terrifying elements that Borges calls fantastic in "Prólogo a Edgar

Allan Poe, *Cuentos*," only "MS. Found in a Bottle" provides a clear example of the fantastic while "The Man of the Crowd" can be read as fantastic if the reader picks up on the story's subtle reference to doubling.[15] In the latter story, the confusion the old man causes the narrator/flâneur can only be seen as supernatural if the reader follows Patrick Quinn's suggestion to read the man of the crowd as a future version of the narrator himself, but the story does not require this interpretation. The old wanderer confuses the narrator precisely because the latter cannot easily fit him within any of his predetermined human types. But, instead of introducing the supernatural into the story by labeling the man as nonhuman, the narrator humanizes the man of the crowd by calling him a criminal—a "genius of deep crime" (515). "MS. Found in a Bottle," in contrast, overtly depicts the supernatural in an otherwise natural enough tale of shipwreck. The narrator's ordeal aboard the rotting boat whose crew of ancient men ignores him qualifies as a supernatural experience more than any other moment in the list of Poe texts that Borges calls fantastic, and the narrator reacts to this event by consistently hovering between disbelief and confusion: "A feeling, for which I have no name, has taken possession of my soul. [. . .] Incomprehensible men! [. . .] Concealment is utter folly on my part, for the people *will not* see. [. . .] What [the ship] *is not*, I can easily perceive, what she *is*, I fear it is impossible to say" (141–42). While Mabbott identifies the legend of the Flying Dutchman as a source for Poe's tale ("MS. Found" 132), the narrator's lack of knowledge about this myth allows the doubt, hesitation, or antinomy to survive from the moment he enters the ship until the ship and its crew meet their demise. The narrator's fear as the ship "plung[es] madly within the grasp of the whirlpool" (146) coexists with his doubt about the boat and its crew, but it is the narrator's inability to understand this experience via the rational code of his everyday life rather than his fear of the ship sinking that makes "MS. Found in a Bottle" fantastic.

In what follows, I approach Poe's "Metzengerstein" and "The Black Cat" and Borges's "El Aleph" as fantastic texts. I analyze the hesitation that the characters and narrators of each tale demonstrate when confronted with the supernatural, and I differentiate between these emotions and the elements of fear that each story contains. By distinguishing how the supernatural functions within each of these stories, I uncover each tale's revenge plot and suggest that Poe's and Borges's opposing portrayals of vengeance are key to our understanding of these three stories and of the relationship of dual influence between Borges and Poe.

Fantastic Revenge

The theme of revenge that is so evident in Poe's later tales "The Cask of Amontillado" and "Hop-Frog" appears much earlier in his written corpus with his first published tale, "Metzengerstein," in early 1832. Critics have interpreted "Metzengerstein" disparately as a gothic parody or as a serious piece of horror fiction. Fred Lewis Pattee places "Metzengerstein" with Poe's proposed but never published collection "Tales of the Folio Club" and suggests that "Poe wrote the most of them in the hoaxing sprit—'half banter, half satire'" (124).[16] He specifically doubts whether "'Metzengerstein' is to be taken with complete seriousness" and claims that the story's use of "the metempsychosis motif is a fling at the subtleties of German philosophy" (124–25). Stuart and Susan Levine group "Metzengerstein" with other Poe tales that they call "slapstick gothic" and claim that "everything is so complicated and cockeyed that Poe must be joking" (295). Arthur Hobson Quinn, conversely, claims that the tale "is no mere burlesque" and reads it as an early example of Poe's "unity of construction and of tone, the masterly suggestion of the supernatural, the preservation of suspense, and the handling of the climax" (192). Mabbott also argues that "Metzengerstein" "is hardly a burlesque at all" ("Metzengerstein" 15), while Benjamin F. Fisher maintains that the tale "appears to be no more than an initial earnest, though somewhat amateurish, endeavor in the traditional type of Gothic or 'German' fiction then so popular" (489).

Critics have said little, however, about "Metzengerstein" as a revenge tale, which is surprising since the metempsychosis that occurs in the story not only creates terror but also brings about a supernatural revenge. Poe's nearly unapologetic use of the supernatural in "Metzengerstein" appears to overshadow the revenge theme in this tale to the point that critics focus almost entirely on the supernatural events—the animation of the Berlifitzing horse from the tapestry hanging on Baron Frederick Von Metzengerstein's wall and the apparent transfer of the soul of Wilhelm Von Berlifitzing into this demonic steed—and on the fear these events cause Metzengerstein rather than on the just revenge that the horse takes on the young Baron. Poe's depictions of the supernatural in "Metzengerstein" approach the mode of the fantastic, and reading "Metzengerstein" as a fantastic tale brings the Berlifitzing family's revenge on Metzengerstein to the forefront of the story.

"Metzengerstein" opens with a brief paragraph that couples the concept of horror with the story's principal supernatural theme—metempsychosis. The tale's third-person narrator states: "Horror and fatality have been stalking abroad in all ages. Why then give a date to the story I have to tell? Let it suffice to say, that at the period of which I speak, there existed, in the interior of Hungary, a settled although hidden belief in the doctrines of the Metempsychosis" (18). From the story's inception, then, the reader knows that the story's characters accept metempsychosis as a real possibility. The supernatural first enters the story as Metzengerstein sits in "a vast and desolate" chamber in his palace contemplating the destruction of his rival's stables by a fire that

Metzengerstein has apparently set (21–22). Metzengerstein's meditations are interrupted by the animation of a Berlifitzing horse in one of the room's many tapestries. The animal "alter[s] its position" and glares at the young baron with "eyes" that "now wore an energetic and human expression, while they gleamed with a fiery and unusual red," and "a flash of red light" casts the young Metzengerstein's shadow into the exact position of the ancient Metzengerstein in the tapestry who has just killed a member of the Berlifitzing family (23). The Baron leaves the palace in terror, only to find his servants struggling with a real "gigantic and fiery-colored horse" that resembles the horse from the tapestry (23). He notices the initials "W. V. B." on the horse's head and is then informed by a different servant that "a small portion of the tapestry" has strangely vanished (24). Almost immediately, the servants fighting with the horse relay to him that the patriarch of the Berlifitzing family—Wilhelm Von Berlifitzing—has died while trying to save his horses from the flames that destroyed his family's stables (24–25).

The news of the tapestry leaves Metzengerstein momentarily "agitated by a variety of emotions" that he quickly overcomes with "an expression of determined malignancy" (24), but the details of Berlifitzing's death baffle him: "'I—n—d—e—e—d!' ejaculated the Baron, as if slowly and deliberately impressed with the truth of some exciting idea" (25). Without the story's introductory paragraph, Metzengerstein's agitation about the incarnation of the tapestry's horse and his shock that this horse appears to be the reincarnated Wilhelm Von Berlifitzing—both revelations that he accepts after a brief period of doubt—would pull the text toward what Todorov calls the fantastic-marvelous since the baron overcomes this doubt by accepting the supernatural event as real. However, the story's introduction obviates this reading since Metzengerstein and his fellow characters already hold a belief in metempsychosis, which effectively explains away the magic of the horse's sudden appearance at the very moment the Berlifitzing patriarch dies.[17] From Todorov's and Chanady's perspectives, this story, at most, contains a fantastic moment but quickly collapses into the uncanny—a typical move in much of the gothic fiction that influenced Poe's writing of the tale.[18] However, according to Rodríguez-Luis's conceptualization of the fantastic, this moment of doubt is sufficient to qualify the narrative as fantastic even though Metzengerstein very quickly places the sudden manifestation of the horse within a code that he understands.

The tale's early nod to metempsychosis and its gothic setting in general help create a mood of terror or "un ambiente propicio al miedo" ["an ambiance favorable to fear"] (Bioy Casares, "Prólogo" 8), which both Borges and Bioy Casares see as typical in early fantastic fiction. However, Frederick Metzengerstein's actual fear does not spring from either of these sources. Instead, Metzengerstein's own villainous acts—"for the space of three days, the behavior of the heir out-heroded Herod" (21)—cause his terror because what he truly dreads is retribution. Since the baron and his community already hold "a settled although hidden belief" in metempsychosis (18), the actual transformation of Wilhelm Von Berlifitzing into a living version of the tapestry's horse does not, indeed cannot, terrify Metzengerstein as evidenced in his final response to his servants' narrations about the tapestry, the horse, and old Berlifitzing's fiery death; Metzengerstein has synthesized the information and realized that the horse *is* his recently killed rival, and he states, "Shocking!," but he does so "calmly" before "turn[ing] quietly into the palace" (25).[19] Metzengerstein knows that he must attempt to dominate the horse just as he had dominated the man who now embodies the animal, but in knowing the horse's identity, he also understands that the steed has come to seek vengeance, not only for Wilhelm Von Berlifitzing's fiery death but for the generations of Metzengerstein atrocities toward the Berlifitzing family.[20]

The remainder of the tale depicts a one-on-one battle between the baron and the horse—between young Metzengerstein and old Berlifitzing—as Frederick seeks to crush the horse's will and erase his own fear of revenge. The baron's changed and solemn behavior, and his new tendency of "turn[ing] pale and shr[inking] away from the rapid and searching expression of [the horse's] earnest and human-looking eye" (28), could suggest a sense of guilt for his actions, but these actions are driven by hatred and fear rather than remorse. While the rest of his attendants see an "extraordinary affection" between the baron and his stallion, a "misshapen little page" notices "an unaccountable and almost imperceptible shudder" in his master each time Metzengerstein mounts the horse and "an expression of triumphant malignity distort[ing] every muscle in his countenance" each time he finishes his ride (28). Metzengerstein fears that every outing may be his last, but he returns with the malevolent satisfaction that he has kept his enemy in check for one more day.[21]

The Berlifitzing family finally enacts its revenge on the house of Metzengerstein on a turbulent night when the Metzengerstein palace catches fire and the possessed horse storms the burning castle with the terrorized Frederick practically bound to its back. This supernatural finale—which ends as a smoke cloud in the shape of a giant horse hovers over the burning edifice (29)—performs a just revenge on the baron. He, like Wilhelm Von Berlifitzing, suffers death by fire. At the same time, the finale fulfills, with a twist, the "ancient prophecy" that had brought the two families into conflict: "A lofty name shall have a fearful fall when, as the rider over his horse, the mortality of Metzengerstein shall triumph over the immortality of Berlifitzing" (19). As the narrator notes, "The prophecy seemed to imply" the victory of the Metzengerstein house over the Berlifitzing house (19), but through the story's portrayal of metempsychosis, the opposite effect occurs. Metzengerstein the man and the house "have a fearful fall" when the mortal Frederick rides the immortal Wilhelm into the flames.

The final destruction of the Metzengerstein house—both family and palace—is clearly an act of poetic justice since, like Frederick, the family appears to be murderous while the edifice celebrates the family's malevolent deeds in pomp and grandeur.[22] How the flames that engulf the palace start, however, is far less clear. The fire could be the natural outcome of lightning striking the palace on that "tempestuous night" (28), but since the text does not mention lightning, the flames could have a supernatural origin somehow connected to the fiery charger or reincarnated Wilhelm Von Berlifitzing. Poe leaves a small hint, however, to suggest that a more active agent might be involved in this fire of vengeance. Upon observing the repeated rejections that the young baron made to various invitations from his neighbors earlier in the story, Wilhelm Von Berlifitzing's widow "was even heard to express a hope 'that the Baron might be at home when he did not wish to be at home, since he disdained the company of his equals; and ride when he did not wish to ride, since he preferred the society of a horse'" (26). Metzengerstein's death so perfectly fulfills widow Berlifitzing's wish—the baron finds himself at home at a moment he could certainly not wish to be there due to a wild ride, which "[t]he agony of his countenance, the convulsive struggle of his frame" and "his lacerated lips, which were bitten through and through in the intensity of terror" (29) demonstrate that he does not wish to take—that the reader must question whether Countess Berlifitzing takes part in the action by starting the blaze that engulfs the palace, the horse, and the baron.

If the countess starts this fire, her actions appear warranted since the fire that killed her husband was allegedly started by Metzengerstein. However, if this is the case, then we must explain the coincidence that takes place in the story's finale. How does the horse know that the palace will be engulfed in flames on the very night that he finally overpowers the baron and takes Metzengerstein where he, Wilhelm Von Berlifitzing, desires? The easiest answer to this quandary simply connects the fiery horse to the fire in the palace, suggesting that the stallion/reincarnated count, who is already a supernatural presence, somehow starts the fire or knows that the fire is burning. Another answer suggests that if the charger is the count reincarnated, he could communicate with the countess and plan their revenge for his death/transformation by fire. A third, and a more exploratory, answer could suggest that the count and the countess, through some sort of witchcraft or magic, have developed a complex revenge plot for the entire Berlifitzing family line that requires the count's sacrifice (both the sacrifice of his human self to transform into the horse and the eventual destruction of the horse in the flames of the Metzengerstein mansion) but brings about the young baron's death, destroys the Metzengerstein family line, and fulfills the prophecy in the Berlifitzings' favor.[23] This is a speculative reading that cannot be overtly supported by textual evidence other than the Berlifitzings' belief in metempsychosis, their knowledge of the prophecy, their "bitter animosity" (20) about the divination, and Poe's own portrayals of witchcraft in later tales like "Morella" and "Ligeia."[24] Whether the story's finale is the outcome of a complicated revenge plot or the unwitting fulfillment of the prophecy through a realization of the local belief in metempsychosis, the tale's supernatural revenge suggests, in the end, that revenge cannot only be justified but that it can be exact—in the Old Testament tradition of an eye for an eye, one fiery death deserves another. The reader leaves the story, regardless of any doubt or fear created by Poe's portrayal of metempsychosis, satisfied that Frederick Metzengerstein has received his just desserts.

Eleven years after he first published "Metzengerstein," Poe released another tale of supernatural revenge—his masterful piece entitled "The Black Cat." As Mabbott notes, this story "combines several themes that fascinated Poe—reincarnation, perversity, and retribution" ("The Black Cat" 847), all themes that Poe first approached in "Metzengerstein." Poe creates in "The Black Cat," but this time with an eerie closeness absent from the earlier, distant tale of the Hungarian baron, a story whose supernatural events and horrific elements, especially when interpreted by literary critics, overshadow the delivery of a just revenge. Critics most often approach "The Black Cat" through a psychoanalytic lens that connects the story's strange happenings to the psyche(s) of Poe and/or his unnamed narrator. For example, Marie Bonaparte famously, and somewhat heavy-handedly, reads the cat, Pluto, as representative of the mother figure and suggests that the violent relationship between Pluto and the story's confessional narrator reveals Poe's fears of birth, separation, anxiety, castration, conscience, and death (481–82). Similarly, Daniel Hoffman interprets the cat as "a displacement of the wife" (233). In a very different mode, Susan Amper reads "The Black Cat" as "a first-rate detective story [. . .] Poe's best detective story" (485) and convincingly argues that the narrator "is lying" (475) about the death of Pluto to hide the fact that he has killed his wife, not in a rage when she tries to protect the second cat from the narrator's axe, but at the very moment that he claims to have killed Pluto (478–79). For Amper, "It is not merely that the wife was always the intended victim; she was the original, in fact the only victim" of the narrator's violent hand (479).[25]

Both psychoanalytic and ratiocinative readings of "The Black Cat," however, deflate and remove the story's supernatural elements in an attempt at clarity that the tale itself beautifully avoids. Without the tools of the psychoanalyst and/or the methods of the detective, the story leaves both the narrator and the reader in an ambiguous space where they cannot be sure if the second cat is Pluto's reincarnation, Pluto's double, Pluto's ghost, Pluto's memory, a disguised witch—as the narrator's wife alludes (850)—or simply a cat who coincidentally resembles Pluto down to his missing eye, with the only difference being a patch of white fur that becomes, in the view of the narrator, a gallows that both reminds him of his crime and foreshadows his doom. In short, "The Black Cat" functions as a fantastic tale, and the doubt that surrounds the narrator and the reader during the story and at its conclusion is an integral part of the pleasure the reader experiences when reading the tale.[26]

A psychoanalytic interpretation destroys this magic while a deductive approach simplifies the tale's complexity. Todorov suggests that "psychoanalysis has replaced (and thereby has made useless) the literature of the fantastic" (160), and we can see this replacement in the works of Bonaparte, Hoffman, and many others since in their readings the story's supernatural events no longer exist as such but, instead, represent the narrator's projections, his complexes, the return of what he seeks to repress, and a slew of other psychoanalytic concepts. Amper's interpretation, although it reads directly against the grain of the psychoanalytic tradition surrounding "The Black Cat," accomplishes the same end by explaining away the tale's supernatural elements. In essence, she performs an act on "The Black Cat" that Borges suggests Poe never attempts—she invites the ratiocination of Poe's detective Dupin into Poe's world of the supernatural and resolves the story's ambiguity as though she were solving a mystery. One clear advantage of this approach, she suggests, is that "the story gains an important virtue it otherwise lacks: intelligibility" (475). Yet this very asset can be read as a drawback for a reader who finds pleasure in the unresolved antinomy of a fantastic text.

Even more important than the negative effect this shift from ambiguity to explanation can have on a tale of the fantastic, both psychoanalytic and ratiocinative approaches to "The Black Cat" mask the story's powerful portrayal of supernatural revenge. If the cat represents Poe's anxieties about his mother figures, his bride Virginia, or any of his relationships with other women in his life, or if the story's narrator is a liar and the whole narrative is really about his attempts to hide or even deny the murder of his wife, then the possibility of Pluto's vengeful reincarnation, doubling, or reappearance disappears. Reading the text, instead, as a fantastic tale in which we interpret the supernatural events as paranormal—rather than as symptomatic or representative of something else—emphasizes the story's revenge theme and reveals how Poe refined his portrayal of supernatural revenge between the publishing of "Metzengerstein" and "The Black Cat."

Like "Metzengerstein," "The Black Cat" shows the supernatural revenge of an animal on a human tormentor, and in both cases, the animal takes on demonic traits in the eyes of the character who fears its vengeance. The animals in each tale might be transformed humans—the horse as old Berlifitzing and the cat as a disguised witch—but whether animal or human in disguise, both the charger and the feline form only one-third of two parallel revenge triangles—Countess Berlifitzing, Baron Metzengerstein, and the horse/Count Berlifitzing; the unnamed wife, the unnamed narrator, and the cat(s)/disguised witch. In each story, the animal or transformed human takes revenge on the story's violent central character, but the female characters play disparate roles. In "Metzengerstein," the countess might be a force in the revenge plot on the young baron or not, while in "The Black Cat" the narrator's unnamed wife is victim, prop, or both in the revenge that occurs—certainly the victim of her husband's violence and possibly the collateral damage of the cat's supernatural revenge plot—rather than an active agent who seeks vengeance. Another important difference between these two stories lies in their narration. Unlike the earlier tale in which an outside narrator details the Berlifitzings' revenge and young Metzengerstein's torment in the third person, Poe tells "The Black Cat" in the first person through the eyes of a confessional narrator who seeks to "unburthen [his] soul" before facing the gallows (849).[27] This shift in narration is significant when reading "The Black Cat" as a fantastic tale since this first-person perspective better allows the reader to see the doubt and hesitation the narrator experiences when confronted with the supernatural by allowing the reader to enter his head.

"The Black Cat" appears to begin as a realistic narrative, but the narrator's inability to understand how "a series of mere household events" (849) has led him to uxoricide and a hangman's noose foreshadows the fantastic mode the story exemplifies. He opens the tale stating: "For the most wild, yet most homely narrative which I am about to pen, I neither expect nor solicit belief. Mad indeed would I be to expect it, in a case where my very senses reject their own evidence. Yet, mad am I not—and very surely do I not dream" (849). The narrator's first words demonstrate the antinomy Chanady calls essential for a fantastic story by casting the tale as both "wild" and "homely," both unbelievable and mundane, and throughout the piece the narrator remains in a shroud of doubt caused by the lack of resolution between the story's realist and supernatural codes.[28] The narrator couples this hesitation—essential to Chanady, Rodríguez-Luis, and Todorov—with the fear that Borges and Bioy Casares find so important to early fantastic narratives. He claims that these events have given him "little but Horror," but he suggests that to others "they will seem less terrible than *baroques*" and proposes that in the future someone else might "perceive, in the circumstances [he] detail[s] with awe, nothing more than an ordinary succession of very natural causes and effects" (850). The narrator continually follows these patterns. Throughout the tale, he consistently hints toward the supernatural, attempts to explain it away, and then remains baffled when he fails to contain the supernatural within a natural code; he then describes this sense of bewilderment as fear, torment, or anguish.

The supernatural first manifestly enters the story on the night after the narrator brutally kills Pluto by hanging the cat from a tree in his garden. The narrator wakes from his slumber surrounded by flames that engulf his house and destroy his "entire worldly wealth" (852).[29] The next morning, he finds his neighbors gawking at the image of a giant cat with a noose around its neck that is burned into the only remaining wall of the house (853). This specter suggests that Pluto, from beyond the grave, has enacted his revenge and left his mark on the scene. The cat's image on the wall initially brings about the same fear and awe that the narrator has coupled throughout the text: "When I first beheld this apparition—for I could scarcely regard it as less—my wonder and my terror were extreme" (853). However, the narrator immediately claims that "at length reflection came to [his] aid," and he proceeds to explain, in pseudoscientific but rather ridiculous terms, that the image must have been left by Pluto's carcass (burnt into the wall's fresh plaster) after a bystander saw the fire, cut Pluto from the tree, and tossed his lifeless body through the bedroom window in order to wake the narrator (853). This unintentionally comic and quite famous passage from "The Black Cat" serves as a microcosm for how the supernatural functions within this story. Each time the narrator confronts a situation that challenges his rational code, he doubts or hesitates and then attempts to explain away the supernatural event. If his endeavors were successful, "The Black Cat" could fall into Todorov's subgenre of the fantastic-uncanny, but the narrator is unable to truly convince himself that the destruction of his house is disconnected from his heinous act against his cat. He calls his explanation a "startling fact" based on "reason," but he also claims that "[f]or months [he] could not rid [him]self of the phantasm of the cat" (853). The story remains fantastic, even in Todorov's and Chanady's terms, and the fiery destruction of the house is only the beginning of the cat's supernatural revenge. Pluto, or his charred image as apparition, haunts the narrator and drags this vengeance process—and the narrator's doubts and fears that accompany it—through the remainder of the tale.

The supernatural reenters the text when a second cat, in the flesh, replaces and exacerbates the haunting by the first cat's phantom image. This second cat is often read as the return of the repressed, as a figment of the tormented narrator's imagination, or as a real cat that coincidentally resembles Pluto but whose "indefinite splotch of white" hair (854) that eventually becomes "the GALLOWS" (855) exists only in the narrator's mind. Amper, contrastingly, reads the second cat as Pluto (482) since she claims that the narrator originally kills his wife rather than his cat. As I have already noted, each of these explanations forbids the reader from accepting the second cat at face value as a supernatural presence even though the text, from its very introduction, has prepared the reader for the ambiguity of the fantastic experience that doubts but cannot explain away supernatural happenings. The mystery around this second creature's *appearance*—both its arrival out of nowhere at a bar that the narrator frequents and its physical attributes, which mirror Pluto's size, color, and missing eye and only vary from the former in the color of hair on the chest—suggest that the cat is a supernatural presence in the story: a double, a ghost, or a reincarnation.[30]

Reading the second cat as a supernatural presence within a fantastic narrative highlights the story's revenge plot. This supernatural cat—this returned Pluto—takes vengeance on its killer, and depending on how the reader interprets the scene in which the narrator kills his wife, this revenge is either exaggerated one-upmanship or perfectly parallel to the crime.[31] The narrator notes that the new cat "became immediately a great favorite with [his] wife" (854) even though he slowly began to despise the animal to the point of "absolute *dread*" (855). This fear keeps the narrator from attacking the cat until a day when the cat trips him on the staircase. In a rage, he attempts to destroy the cat with an axe, but when his wife impedes him, he brutally murders her with this same weapon (856). Here, the reader must decide whether the cat intentionally provokes the narrator into killing his wife as part of its plan of revenge or whether the cat merely acts out its ultimate revenge after the narrator commits this heinous crime. If read in the tradition of revenge as one-upping that Irwin describes in his analysis of Poe and Borges in *The Mystery to a Solution*, then the cat's actions could be seen as intentional. Not only does the cat lead the narrator to the gallows (tit for tat), but he does so by provoking the narrator into murdering "the wife of [his] bosom" (Poe, "The Black Cat" 858): into committing a parricide worthy of ancient Greek tragedies (one-upping).[32] From this perspective, the cat destroys the narrator's entire world (his house, his peace of mind, his wife, and, perhaps, his sanity) before taking his life. This interpretation, however, assigns a malevolence to the second cat (and, thus, to Pluto) that the text never even implies. Indeed, both cats befriend and are befriended by the narrator's wife, and using her as a tool to get back at the narrator appears out of character. Finally, reading the wife's murder as a step in a plot to one-up the narrator rather than as an act of violence perpetrated by the narrator that then allows for the cat's definitive revenge requires the reader to believe that the narrator actually loves his wife. The story itself and several well-known interpretations of it suggest that the opposite is the case.[33]

Since the text does not suggest that the cat has any reason to destroy the narrator's wife, her murder must fall on the head of the narrator, and thus, it is an event that the second cat merely uses to its advantage in order to bring about a just revenge. Pluto does not take the narrator's eye for his eye, but like the fiery stallion in "Metzengerstein," the second cat takes a life for a life and requires the perpetrator's death to mirror his original crime. Just as the narrator hangs Pluto, so will the narrator die by hanging, and although the narrator is literally being punished for killing his wife (not for hanging his cat), his castigation becomes a reality through the cat's actions. The cat's scream not only allows the police to unearth the narrator's hidden crimes, but it also leaves him "motionless, through extremity of terror and of awe" (859). In short, the cat—whether "walled [. . .] up within the tomb" (859) as the narrator surmises or magically appearing at the perfect moment to enact its revenge—places the narrator in an ambiguous locale where he simultaneously cannot/must believe his own eyes and ears. This fantastic space leaves the reader both intrigued by the impossibility of pinning down the cat and satisfied that the narrator has received a punishment equal to his crimes. Again, Poe's supernatural revenge appears justified or even necessary since without it the narrator, like Metzengerstein, would escape any retribution besides that brought about by his own conscience, which appears all too capable of blocking out his hideous actions.[34]

Both "The Black Cat" and "Metzengerstein" appear to have little in common with Borges's "El Aleph," at least according to most critical readings of Borges's famous tale, which was first published in the pages of *Sur* in 1945. While "Metzengerstein" and "The Black Cat" can be read in conversation with the German horror tradition, critics often connect "El Aleph," as I mentioned in the previous chapter, back to Italy and Dante's *Divina Commedia* or forward to the poststructuralist anxieties the tale so aptly foretells.[35] Without disparaging these interpretations, I argue that Borges's portrayal of the supernatural in "El Aleph" creates a fantastic revenge narrative that, like Poe's "Metzengerstein" and "The Black Cat," needs to be unpacked in order to understand the hidden revenge plot. Several literary critics describe "El Aleph" as a fantastic narrative, fewer analyze the story's revenge plot (and most critics who do so only broach the subject briefly), and none, to my knowledge, interpret "El Aleph" specifically as a fantastic revenge story. Reading "El Aleph" as a tale of fantastic revenge brings the story's hidden plotline to the forefront and alters how Borges's readers understand revenge when they return to Poe.

Unlike Poe's two fantastic revenge tales, "El Aleph" does not mask the supernatural with horror. Indeed, the supernatural elements trump the two overt moments of terror in the text: when Borges-narrator thinks that Carlos Argentino Daneri has poisoned him and locked him in the basement to kill him (624; 282) and when he leaves Daneri's basement and fears that he will experience the rest of his life in a state of constant déjà vu (626; 284). The Aleph itself squelches this first idea of fear and creates the second; Borges-narrator's terror in the basement ends almost as quickly as it begins because "cerr[ó] los ojos, los abr[ió]. Entonces vi[o] El Aleph" (624) ["[he] closed [his] eyes, then opened them. It was then that [he] saw the Aleph"] (282). His fear of déjà vu comes directly upon leaving Carlos Argentino Daneri's house after having seen everything in the Aleph, but his anxiety disappears within a matter of days due to "el olvido" (626) ["forgetfulness"] (284). Instead of terror, the story's supernatural elements themselves (the very existence of the Aleph and, more importantly, Borges-narrator's continued musings and doubt about his experience in Carlos Argentino Daneri's basement) conceal what is otherwise one of the tale's primary subjects—vengeance.

The importance of revenge to the plot of "El Aleph" is most visible in Borges's original manuscript, which is held at the Biblioteca Nacional de España in Madrid and has been published in facsimile in 1989 and in 2001.[36] According to Estela Canto—Borges's love interest in 1945 and the woman to whom he dedicated "El Aleph"—Borges took this manuscript to her home, dictated it to her, and delivered her typed version of the story to *Sur* shortly thereafter (208). As Canto suggests and as the facsimile of the manuscript makes abundantly clear, the manuscript contains several revisions, crossed-out phrases, and variants throughout. Even more important for this study, the manuscript does not contain either the "Posdata" ["Postscript"] or the paragraph that precedes it in the published versions of "El Aleph."[37] These changes and omissions exist before and outside of the published and supposedly definitive text, but they do alter our understanding of the story. As Lisa Block de Behar argues when referring to "El Aleph," "Publication does not repeal the manuscript; it transforms it in the same way that it is transformed by it" ("Rereading" 181). In essence, the relationship between the manuscript and the published tale, like the relationship between a writer and a precursor, is reciprocal. The manuscript of "El Aleph" emphasizes both Borges-narrator's reasons for seeking revenge on Carlos Argentino Daneri and the actual act of vengeance. Comparing the story's manuscript with the published version reveals revenge as a principal theme of "El Aleph" and demonstrates how the story shifts from a revenge tale with supernatural elements (in its manuscript form) to a fantastic story whose supernatural events conceal its revenge plot (in its published form)—a story of fantastic revenge.[38]

Both the manuscript and the published story begin with Borges-narrator's concern about the world moving on after the death of Beatriz Viterbo, whom he has loved from afar. He laments, "Cambiará el universo pero yo no, [. . .] alguna vez, lo sé, mi vana devoción la había exasperado; muerta yo podía consagrarme a su memoria, sin esperanza, pero también sin humillación" (617) [*The universe may change, but I shall not*, [. . .] I knew that more than once my futile devotion had exasperated her; now that she was dead, I could consecrate myself to her memory—without hope, but also without humiliation"] (274). Borges-narrator's grief is less about the loss of Beatriz than it is about his fear of forgetting her. Indeed, now that Beatriz is dead, the narrator can better "love" her since, for him, loving Beatriz appears to signify worshiping her as an ideal rather than consummating a physical relationship or maintaining any sort of communication with her as a person. The memory of

Beatriz becomes Borges-narrator's idol, and he returns to her parents' home to venerate her image or her various photographs every year on April 30, her birthday, from 1929 to 1941.

Through these visits, which grow longer year by year, Borges-narrator "recib[ió] las graduales confidencias de Carlos Argentino Daneri" (618) ["came to receive the gradual confidences of Carlos Argentino Daneri"] (275), Beatriz's cousin. During this annual ordeal in 1941, the narrator learns that Daneri considers himself a poet and that he writes fairly bad poetry to which he voluntarily adds his own bombastic literary criticism (618–21; 275–78). Two weeks later, Daneri breaks the routine of Borges-narrator's annual visits, phones him, invites him to eat at a local restaurant, and asks him to get one of his friends to write a prologue for his poem (621–22; 278–79). Up until this point, neither the manuscript nor the published text suggests that Borges-narrator has any reason to take vengeance on Daneri, unless, of course, the narrator is so annoyed with Daneri's bad taste and arrogance that he wishes to harm him.

This changes five months and a few paragraphs later when Daneri again phones Borges-narrator and begs for his help in preserving the old house where he lives—Beatriz's former home and Borges-narrator's shrine to her. Daneri claims that the house's basement contains an Aleph, "uno de los puntos del espacio que contiene todos los puntos" (623) ["one of the points in space that contain all points"] (280), which allows him to see "todos los lugares del orbe, vistos desde todos los ángulos" (623) ["all the places of the world, seen from every angle"] (281), and he declares that he cannot finish his poem without access to this mystical orb (622–23; 281).[39] Borges-narrator promises to go to the house to see the Aleph, but the conversation convinces him that Daneri is mad (623; 281). His reaction to this revelation foreshadows the desire the narrator eventually adopts to avenge himself of Daneri. He states, "La locura de Carlos Argentino me colmó de maligna felicidad; íntimamente, siempre nos habíamos detestado" (623) ["Carlos Argentino's madness filled me with malign happiness; deep down, we had always detested one another"] (281). The manuscript originally reads "asombrosa felicidad" ["astonishing happiness"] with "asombrosa" crossed out and replaced with the "maligna" ["malign"] that appears in the published text ("Facsímil" 41).[40] Whether Borges-narrator's contentment with what he thinks is Daneri's madness is amazed or hateful, he takes joy in this new knowledge. The revision, however, foreshadows the spite that Borges-narrator will feel after having observed the universe in the Aleph, and it hints to the reader that the narrator goes to Daneri's house with negative intentions, which will only be magnified by what he sees in this magical space.

Borges-narrator's primary reason for revenge grows directly from his experience with the Aleph. In his attempt to deliver in writing the infinite amount of information he ingested simultaneously while gazing into the Aleph, the narrator creates a complex paragraph of images that Rodríguez Monegal has called "dazzling and chaotic enumeration" (*Jorge Luis Borges* 414). The list is not—indeed, inherently cannot be—infinite, but its inclusion of very specific singular items and of so many uncountable things—"todos los espejos del planeta [. . .] convexos desiertos ecuatoriales y cada uno de sus granos de arena [. . .] cada letra de cada página [. . .] todas las hormigas que hay en la tierra" (625) ["all the mirrors on the planet [. . .] convex equatorial deserts and their every grain of sand [. . .] every letter of every page [. . .] all the ants on earth"] (283)—together with the idea that "[c]ada cosa [. . .] era infinitas cosas, porque [él] claramente la veía desde todos los puntos del universo" (625) ["[e]ach thing [. . .] was infinite things, because [he] could clearly see it from every point in the cosmos"] (283)—artfully portrays the idea of infinity and suggests that the narrator has not only seen everything but that he has done so from every possible perspective. The overall experience—his viewing "el inconcebible universo" (626) ["the inconceivable universe"] (284)—causes the narrator to weep as he feels "vértigo [. . .] infinita veneración, infinita lástima" (626) ["dizzy [. . .] infinite veneration, infinite pity"] (284). However, out of the infinite amount of detailed images the narrator views, only one elicits a specific emotional response—a drawer of letters from Beatriz Viterbo to Carlos Argentino Daneri. Borges-narrator states, "vi en un cajón del escritorio (y la letra me hizo temblar), cartas obscenas, increíbles, precisas que Beatriz había dirigido a Carlos Argentino" (625) ["saw in a desk drawer (and the handwriting made me tremble) obscene, incredible, detailed letters that Beatriz had sent Carlos Argentino"] (283).

Borges-narrator's newfound knowledge of these letters effectively destroys his exalted image of Beatriz.[41] The evidence of Beatriz's love affair with Daneri highlights what the narrator already knows but continually denies—the fact that this Beatriz, the divorcée turned bachelorette, differs greatly from her idealized namesake in Dante. That the letters testify to an affair with Daneri rather than detailing Beatriz's relationship with her former husband or with any man other than Daneri particularly vexes the narrator, not due to the relationship's incestuous implications, but due to Borges-narrator's persistent low esteem for Daneri.[42] Throughout the story, Borges-narrator critiques Daneri's bad taste, his pompous attitude, and his lack of culture.[43] Beatriz's affair with Daneri reiterates their similarities—the narrator has, already, pointed out several, from their "grandes y afiladas manos hermosas" (618) ["large, beautiful, slender hands"] (275) to hints that they both stumble on the fine line that divides lucidity from madness (623; 281)—and suggests that Beatriz *was* also all the things that the narrator cannot stand about Daneri. Finally, the fact that Beatriz not only had an affair with Daneri but also wrote to him about it in base and clear-cut language adds insult to injury by desecrating Borges-narrator's other idol, the written word, which the simultaneous nature of the Aleph itself has also called into question.

The existence of these letters testifies to the relationship between Daneri and Beatriz while Borges-narrator's descriptions of everything else he sees in the Aleph underscore the fact that he has no meaningful relationships at all. Borges the narrator is almost completely absent in the all-encompassing views that he describes having seen in the Aleph. None of the mirrors on earth reflects his image, and his views of his bedroom reveal that it is empty (625; 283). He sees his own blood, his own face, and his own entrails (625–26; 283–84), but each of these images remains surrounded by the infinite images from the Aleph without being intertwined with any of them; they are images of solitude, an isolation implied by the so-called unrequited love between Borges-narrator and Beatriz while she was still alive. This love "la había exasperado" (617) ["had exasperated her"] (274), and the fact that she never even took the time to open the books which Borges-narrator had brought to her house as an excuse to be in her presence reveals her complete lack of reciprocation and the narrator's utter loneliness (617; 275).

The Aleph, then, reveals the truth about Daneri's and Beatriz's relationship to Borges-narrator, and this truth simultaneously destroys the narrator's cult of Beatriz while accentuating his sense of isolation. He has seen everything, and the vision has left him with nothing. This devastation itself could be reason enough for Borges-narrator to avenge himself of Daneri, but the verbal exchange between the poets immediately before the narrator enters the basement to see the Aleph now takes on new meaning and adds to the narrator's motives for seeking revenge. Upon entering Daneri's house to see the Aleph, Borges notices that he is alone with Beatriz's portrait and virtually prays to it: "Beatriz, Beatriz Elena, Beatriz Elena Viterbo, Beatriz querida, Beatriz perdida para siempre, soy yo, soy Borges" (623) ["Beatriz, Beatriz Elena, Beatriz Elena Viterbo, [. . .] Beloved Beatriz, Beatriz lost forever—it's me, it's me, Borges"] (281). Daneri enters the room soon after, and while Borges-narrator assumes that Daneri has overheard nothing, Daneri shows otherwise right before leading him into the basement and closing the trap door: "Baja; muy en breve podrás entablar un diálogo con *todas* las imágenes de Beatriz" (624) ["Go on down; within a very short while you will be able to begin a dialogue with *all* the images of Beatriz"] (282). In the context of the all-encompassing Aleph that Daneri wants to reveal to Borges, his emphasis on *all* Beatriz's images could simply be his reiteration of the idea that the Aleph lets its viewer see everything from every possible angle. However, the fact that Daneri introduces Borges-narrator to the Aleph with an invitation to start a *dialogue* with all images of Beatriz suggests that he has overheard the narrator's appeal to Beatriz's picture and that he takes this opportunity to both prove the Aleph's existence and humiliate Borges. His emphasis on *all* Beatriz's images can thus be read as a specific hope that Borges-narrator will both see and react to images of Beatriz that reveal her relationship with Daneri—for example, the very letters that cause Borges to tremble—and that reiterate the uselessness of the narrator's unrequited love. By showing Borges-narrator everything, Daneri mocks him, flaunting his relationship with Beatriz in Borges-narrator's face. Daneri's open mockery of Borges-narrator and his role as the iconoclast of the narrator's idolized version of Beatriz only exacerbate the tenuous relationship between the two characters—an association that was already marked by a sense of competition and a shared although unstated enmity—and create a compelling space/reason for revenge.

Borges-narrator's revenge is simple; he refuses to admit to Daneri that he has seen anything:

> "¡Qué observatorio formidable, che Borges!" [. . .] "—Formidable. Sí, formidable." La indiferencia de mi voz me extrañó. Ansioso, Carlos Argentino insistía: "—¿Lo viste todo bien, en colores?" En ese instante concebí mi venganza. Benévolo, manifiestamente apiadado, nervioso, evasivo, agradecí a Carlos Argentino Daneri la hospitalidad de su sótano y lo insté a aprovechar la demolición de la casa para alejarse de la perniciosa metrópoli, que a nadie ¡créame, que a nadie! perdona. Me negué, con suave energía, a discutir el Aleph; lo abracé, al despedirme, y le repetí que el campo y la serenidad son dos grandes médicos. (626)

> ["What a magnificent observatory, eh, Borges!" [. . .] "Magnificent . . . Yes, quite . . magnificent," I stammered. The indifference in my voice surprised me. "You did see it?" Carlos Argentino insisted anxiously. "See it clearly? In color and everything?" Instantly, I conceived my revenge. In the most kindly sort of way—manifestly pitying, nervous, evasive—I thanked Carlos Argentino Daneri for the hospitality of his cellar and urged him to take advantage of the demolition of his house to remove himself from the pernicious influences of the metropolis, which no one—believe me, no one!—can be immune to. I refused, with gentle firmness, to discuss the Aleph; I clasped him by both shoulders as I took my leave and told him again that the country—peace and quiet, you know—was the very best medicine one could take.] (284)

Borges-narrator's denial of the Aleph accomplishes a tripartite vengeance on Daneri that should lead to the literal demolition of Daneri's house, the obliteration of his infinite muse (and thus the truncation of his ridiculous poem), and the erasure (or, at least, the concealment) of his affair with Beatriz. When Borges-narrator denies the existence of the Aleph, he inherently negates having seen the letters that Daneri wants him to see, and this action erases the letters (not from his own mind but from the arsenal of experience with and information about Beatriz that Daneri can use against him) because

Daneri now has to assume that only he knows about their secret existence. Daneri cannot use this information against Borges unless he stoops even lower than his buffoonish characterization suggests and reveals the letters to Borges personally. However, destroying the house, the Aleph, and a shared knowledge of the letters is not enough for Borges because he has seen the letters and now knows, even though Daneri does not know that he knows, that Beatriz's affair with Daneri really happened.

Just as Daneri's reference to a dialogue with all Beatriz's images ridicules Borges-narrator above and beyond the actual letters he sees from Beatriz to Daneri, so too the narrator torments Daneri beyond his simple denial of the Aleph. He purposefully and ingenuously suggests to Daneri that he thinks that Daneri is going mad, an outcome that Núñez-Faraco suggests the narrator "wishes to see" (615). These "destructive thoughts" (615) could simply be in spite, an attempt to get even with Carlos Argentino by one-upping him. Or, they could be Borges-narrator's only way to protect himself from the painful revelation of the letters. If he can convince himself that Daneri is mad, then perhaps he can pass the entire experience with the Aleph off as a hallucination caused by the drink Daneri gave him, his initial fear that he was going to be killed, and the dark and cramped quarters of Daneri's basement.

Borges-narrator's and Daneri's verbal exchange in the basement, as cited above from the published text, reveals that the narrator did not begin to plan his revenge on Daneri until after he was through seeing the Aleph. The uninterested tone of the narrator's voice in response to Daneri's gleeful banter takes the narrator by surprise, and he does not begin to concoct his revenge until the very moment that he hears fear in Daneri's voice. The story's manuscript, however, allows the reader to infer that Borges-narrator begins to plan his vengeance at some point after seeing the letters. The manuscript contains the following crossed-out sentence as an alternative to the narrator's musings about his voice in the published version: "El sonido de mi propia voz me asombró" ["The sound of my own voice astonished me"] (46).[44] The subtle differences between the published "extrañó" ["surprised"] and the deleted "asombró" ["astonished"] signify little compared to the blatant differences between the published "indiferencia" ["indifference"] and the deleted "sonido" ["sound"]. The published version emphasizes the tone of the narrator's voice while the alternate wording in the manuscript allows for diverse interpretations. The sound of the narrator's voice could still refer to its tone, but it could also refer very literally to the idea of sound as Daneri's and the narrator's own voices jar the narrator back into the world of five senses from his immersion in the world of ocular overload that is the Aleph. If his voice is not indifferent and the narrator is shocked by his voice's sound rather than its tone, then the possibility exists that he could have begun to plot his revenge while still observing the Aleph—before hearing Daneri's worried response.

The manuscript supports this reasoning since it also contains a crossed-out "Entonces" ["Then"] along with the much more time-specific "En ese instante" ["In that instant"] (46). Finally, the manuscript also contains "venganza perfecta" ["perfect revenge"] replaced simply with "venganza" ["revenge"] (46). Both "Entonces" and "venganza perfecta" are marked with a subscript numeral 1 in Borges's hand while "En ese instante" and "venganza" both carry a subscript 2, so while Borges the author eliminates the former options by crossing them out, the manuscript reveals that they were the original options. In his earliest attempts with this section of "El Aleph," Borges the author considered his narrator's revenge perfect while leaving the moment the revenge plot hatches more open for interpretation.

The finality of this exchange between Borges-narrator and Daneri in the manuscript is even more significant than the word- and sentence-level revisions throughout the manuscript's concluding paragraphs. Unlike the published tale, the storyline in the manuscript ends here. The very paragraph in which Borges-narrator introduces the idea of revenge and sets out to avenge himself of Daneri by denying (and thus helping to destroy) the Aleph and by insinuating that Daneri has gone insane serves as the tale's conclusion and clearly qualifies "El Aleph" as a revenge tale. Ortega and del Río Parra point out that the manuscript's back cover includes notes that look like the seeds for the postscript—specifically, "¿Existe un A. en el centro de una piedra labrada?" ["Does an A. exist in the center of a cut stone?"] and "Paradójicamente me favorecen las limitaciones de la memoria; yo vi todas las cosas, pero no recuerdo t. l. c." ["Paradoxically, the limitations of memory favor me; I saw all things, but I do not remember a[ll]. t[hings]."] (47).[45] However, these notes do not disallow the manuscript version of the story to function as a full and completed tale. Menéndez and Panesi suggest that the story in the manuscript "podría perfectamente leerse como una historia cuya *diégesis* está concluida (coincide con el final de la trama: revelación mística del aleph, palabras de venganza del narrador a Carlos Argentino Daneri)" ["could perfectly be read as a story whose *diegesis* is complete (it coincides with the end of the plot: mystic revelation of the aleph, the narrator's words of vengeance to Carlos Argentino Daneri)"] (94). The manuscript's culmination in revenge emphasizes the banal in the very face of the extraordinary. The narrator reacts to a specific image of Beatriz and rejects anything and everything else that exists.

In manuscript form, this revenge tale contains the same supernatural event that the published story reveals to its reader—the narrator's viewing of the all-encompassing Aleph.[46] The manuscript version of the story, however, cannot be interpreted as fantastic because the narrator does not react to the event. Indeed, the narrator's unwillingness to approach the subject of the Aleph with Daneri in the manuscript's final paragraph makes it nearly impossible to interpret this version of "El Aleph" via any rubric that relies on

character/narrator/reader doubt or hesitation because the manuscript offers almost no reaction on the narrator's part.[47] The manuscript does reveal,
as does the published text, that the simultaneous clarity of the vision "[le]
asombró" ["astonished [him]"] (44), but Borges-narrator does not doubt the
existence of the Aleph itself. Instead, his only doubts rest in his own inability
to accomplish the impossible by portraying the simultaneous/infinite Aleph
in linear, finite language (43–44).[48] The task of writing the Aleph, not the
actual viewing of the Aleph, overwhelms the narrator, and the manuscript's
placement of doubt around the worldly task of writing rather than around
the otherworldly experience of seeing infinity in a finite space reinforces the
narrator's uncontested acceptance of the Aleph as real. Finally, casting the
Aleph as real doubly affects how we read the manuscript as a revenge tale
since accepting the Aleph at face value keeps the final emphasis of the manuscript on Borges-narrator's revenge, rather than creating epistemological or
ontological debates about the Aleph, and highlights the ultimate reason why
Borges-narrator wants to take revenge in the first place.

Borges the author's expansion of "El Aleph" in published form—the inclusion of another paragraph at the end of the text proper and of a multi-
paragraph postscript—dramatically alters how the supernatural functions in
"El Aleph" and both underemphasizes and undermines the role revenge plays
in the story. In the postscript, Borges-narrator muses about Daneri's usage of
the term Aleph—"la primera letra del alfabeto de la lengua sagrada" (627)
["the first letter of the alphabet of the sacred language"] (285)—to describe
the sphere in his basement, and he then attempts to explain away Daneri's
Aleph, stating, "Por increíble que parezca, yo creo que hay (o que hubo) otro
Aleph, yo creo que El Aleph de la calle Garay era un falso Aleph" (627) ["Incredible as it may seem, I believe that there is (or was) another Aleph; I believe that the Aleph of Calle Garay was a *false* Aleph"] (285). He supports
his assertion in true Borgesian—both author and character—fashion by citing a recently discovered manuscript from Captain Richard Burton in which
Burton debunks the existence of several Aleph-type objects and claims that
the universe is contained within a pillar in a mosque in Cairo (627; 285).
If the reader buys the narrator's erudite dismissal of Daneri's Aleph, then
the text successfully removes the magic from the Aleph itself and becomes
fantastic–explained away (or fantastic-uncanny, in Todorov's terms), just as
Poe's "Metzengerstein" removes the baron's brief doubts in the reappearance
of his enemy as a horse by emphasizing in its introduction that the entire society already believes in metempsychosis.

Another possible way of explaining away the supernatural in "El Aleph"
relies on the details of how Daneri introduces Borges-narrator to the Aleph.
Before leading the narrator into the basement, Daneri serves him "[u]na co-
pita del seudocoñac" (624) ["[a] glass of pseudocognac"] (281), which Borges

later fears might be poisoned. Estrella B. Ogden reads this moment and Borges-narrator's idea that Daneri is mad as evidence that Borges the author explains away the Aleph's magic "a la manera de Edgar Allan Poe, atribuyendo el prodigio bien a la locura de Carlos Argentino o al efecto del licor" ["in the manner of Edgar Allan Poe, attributing the wonder to Carlos Argentino's madness or to the effect of the liquor"] (119). Daneri's initial viewing of the Aleph as a child could support this reading since he first saw the Aleph after falling down the stairs (623; 281). However, the other countless times that Daneri claims to have seen the Aleph cannot be blamed on a concussion, and since the story ends up proving that he is not insane, the enigma of the Aleph remains even if Borges-narrator's one experience with the Aleph might be connected to the alcohol he drinks before descending the staircase.

Borges-narrator's suggestion that Daneri's Aleph is false fails to convince him that he did not see infinity in Daneri's basement; he wonders if he saw Burton's version of the Aleph in Daneri's: "¿Lo he visto cuando vi todas las cosas y lo he olvidado?" (627) ["Did I see it when I saw all things, and then forget it?"] (286). Borges-narrator remains in a space of doubt. He questions the existence of Daneri's Aleph while still affirming that he has seen everything (but forgotten most of it) in the very object he now calls false. This realm of doubt is the very territory of the fantastic, and Borges-narrator's hesitation brings about the same effect of doubt or hesitation on the reader of the story. As Block de Behar argues,

> Fascinated by the minute description of the Aleph and suddenly incredulous because of the break introduced by the postscript, the reader is left in doubt, not knowing if he should have any confidence in a tale that seems to demand it or in the bad faith that depletes such confidence. Despite his willing suspension of disbelief, the reader cannot forget what he already knows and vacillates between observing the rules of the game or flaunting them. ("Borges" 13)

The reader's indecision during the postscript may cause her to question whether Borges the author plays in good faith, but it does not destroy the tale's newfound fantastic effect. On the contrary, the reader's vacillation confirms that the postscript shifts the story from another type of supernatural narrative that creates or requires the suspension of disbelief toward the fantastic, which provokes the reader, like the character/narrator, to initially question the supernatural events. Indeed, the doubt that Borges-narrator expresses in the postscript to "El Aleph" resembles the disbelief of Poe's unnamed narrator in "The Black Cat" who cannot deny what he has seen/done but cannot completely grasp how a sequence of supernatural happenings—which he tries to downplay as "a series of mere household events" (849)—has ruined his life. Both narrators hesitate in the face of the supernatural, attempt to explain the supernatural away, and ultimately sit in limbo—feeling the effects of these supernatural events without being able to understand how these events can be real.

"El Aleph" becomes a fantastic text somewhere between the manuscript that Borges left in Canto's home and the typesetters at *Sur*, and this shift toward the fantastic almost completely masks the story's revenge plot. The narrator's doubt about the existence of the Aleph shifts the emphasis of the story away from revenge and toward larger and more philosophical questions of being and knowing. This shift in focus also changes how we interpret the body of the text, especially the list(s) of what Borges-narrator sees in the Aleph. The manuscript's conclusion in revenge makes the letters from Beatriz to Carlos appear to be of more importance to the narrator than anything else in the universe, while the postscript's introduction of doubt adds weight to the last few items on the list, particularly to the Aleph itself, which the narrator "vi[o] [. . .] desde todos los puntos, vi[o] en El Aleph la tierra, y en la tierra otra vez El Aleph y en El Aleph la tierra (625) ["saw [. . .] from everywhere at once, saw the earth in the Aleph, and the Aleph once more in the earth and the earth in the Aleph"] (283–84). These shifts bury Borges-narrator's revenge beneath his musings about "el inconcebible universe" (626) ["the inconceivable universe"] (284). The revenge theme does not completely disappear in the published tale, but now it is hidden beneath these theoretical questions and behind Borges-narrator's final expression of grief as he slowly begins to forget "bajo la trágica erosión de los años, los rasgos de Beatriz" (627) ["through the tragic erosion of the years, the features of Beatriz"] (286). That the published story ends with the narrator lamenting the slow erasure of his memories of Beatriz rather than passing any sort of negative judgment on Beatriz for her relationship with Daneri—or embracing the oblivion that could wash away his knowledge of the letters as seen in the Aleph—demonstrates the complete alteration the text undergoes between manuscript and publication. In contrast with Poe's fantastic revenge stories—"Metzengerstein" and "The Black Cat"—in which the supernatural happenings initially hide the revenge plots but eventually bring the theme of revenge to the surface when interpreted specifically as fantastic texts, Borges the author takes a supernatural manuscript with a palpable revenge plot and masks that plot by recasting the supernatural vision of the Aleph in terms of the fantastic.

The published version of "El Aleph" not only deemphasizes the theme of revenge in the story, but it also alters the outcome of this now-peripheral revenge plot. While the manuscript implies that Borges-narrator leaves Daneri's house with a sense of vengeful satisfaction, the postscript turns this narrative on its head. Only six months after the destruction of both his house and his muse, the Aleph, Daneri wins second prize in a national literary contest while Borges-narrator's entry receives zero support (626–27; 284–85). Instead of destroying Daneri, Borges-narrator unwittingly creates a literary rival. His vengeance frees Daneri's "afortunada pluma" (626–27) ["happy pen"] (285) from the spell of the Aleph and launches Daneri—whose work was previously unknown to anyone but the narrator—on what appears to be a profitable career. While Canto suggests that through this mock portrayal of a national literary award Borges the author "husmeaba los abismos en que habría de caer la literatura" ["sniffed out the abysses into which literature would eventually fall"] (207), the text shows Borges-narrator react with jealousy and disbelief: "¡Una vez más, triunfaron la incomprensión y la envidia!" (626) ["Once more, incomprehension and envy triumphed!"] (285).[49] The narrator's attempt to avenge himself of Daneri backfires, bringing Daneri literary success while simultaneously humiliating Borges-narrator.

The swing from successful and satisfactory vengeance in the manuscript of "El Aleph" to revenge as total failure in the published version of the story mirrors the shift between Poe's portrayals of a justified, parallel, and satisfactory revenge in "Metzengerstein" and "The Black Cat" to Borges the author's final depiction of revenge in "El Aleph" as both petty and counterproductive. In "Metzengerstein" and "The Black Cat," we see the horrific crimes of young Frederick Metzengerstein and the unnamed narrator of "The Black Cat," we empathize with their victims, and we enjoy the poetic justice that both tales deliver as they send their characters to the fire and the gallows, respectively. In "El Aleph," the question of justification is more open for interpretation. Destroying Daneri's house and the mystical portal it contains might seem like one-upping rather than getting even, but if we recall Daneri's invitation for Borges-narrator to converse with "all" Beatriz's images and consider how the narrator's view of the letters from Beatriz to Daneri demolishes his idol—Beatriz—then the narrator's annihilation of Daneri's idol—the Aleph itself—begins to appear parallel to the offense. The fact that Daneri's house is both the Aleph's temple and Borges-narrator's shrine to Beatriz reiterates this sense of parallelism since both characters lose something important to them when the house is destroyed. However, the postscript's emphasis on both Borges-narrator's and Daneri's trivial natures and the narrator's complete dissatisfaction with his attempted revenge contradict the message of a just revenge delivered in "The Black Cat" and "Metzengerstein" and alter how readers go back to Poe's fantastic revenge tales. The parallelism, justice, and, in a way, cleanliness of Poe's characters' revenge no longer satisfy us in the same way now that we have seen how Borges-narrator's revenge blows up in his face and brings about the exact opposite of what he desires. "El Aleph" makes us doubt the possibility of the type of successful revenge that Poe puts forth in "The Black Cat" and "Metzengerstein," thus embodying the very method of the fantastic by creating doubt and hesitation in the reader—not only doubt in the supernatural events themselves but also doubt in the seemingly natural desire for revenge.

I have limited my analysis of Poe's and Borges's revenge fiction in this chapter to three fantastic stories that mix revenge with the supernatural, but my final argument that Borges's revenge fiction changes how readers return to Poe's revenge fiction also applies to Poe's and Borges's more overt revenge tales: "The Cask of Amontillado," "Hop-Frog," and "Emma Zunz." Emma Zunz accomplishes her complex revenge plot by killing Aarón Loewenthal and getting away with the murder. However, the dissatisfaction she feels at the end of the story due to the awful ordeal she has put herself through, along with the fact that she was not able to extract a confession from Loewenthal nor reveal her plan to him as she had dreamed, undermine her otherwise successful revenge. Borges offers an alternate title for "Emma Zunz" in a short inscription on the back of the fifth page of the first draft of the story—a typescript held in the Jorge Luis Borges Collection at the Harry Ransom Center at the University of Texas at Austin—in which he claims that the tale "también pueda titularse El castigo" ["could also be titled The Punishment"].[50] The finale of "Emma Zunz" reveals that the punishment named in this alternative title is plural and that it applies to Emma Zunz as much as it applies to Aarón Loewenthal. At the end of the tale, Emma Zunz feels no triumph and not even a sense of relief. Instead, only her "pudor [. . .] odio [. . .] [y] el ultraje que había padecido" (568) ["shame [. . .] hatred [. . .] [and] [t]he outrage that had been done to her"] (219) are "verdadero[s]" (568) ["real"] (219) as she tells her "increíble" (568) ["unbelievable"] (219) but true tale to the police. Unlike the experience of the narrator in "El Aleph," Emma Zunz's vengeance does not completely fail—Loewenthal is dead—but it does completely fail to satisfy.

Emma Zunz's lack of satisfaction creates further doubt in the reader concerning the validity of revenge as strategy, and this uncertainty requires the reader to reinterpret the successes of Montresor and Hop-Frog when she returns to Poe's "The Cask of Amontillado" and "Hop-Frog." In "Emma Zunz," we know Loewenthal's supposed crime—embezzlement—and we see how this action leads to the Zunz's family's ruin, Emma Zunz's father's exile and eventual death, and her self-sacrificing attempt to take revenge for her father/self. In "The Cask of Amontillado," we do not know with any certainty how, exactly, Fortunato insulted Montresor's family. If the reader had previously read with the grain of "The Cask of Amontillado" and accepted Montresor's destruction of Fortunato as justified within the story's implied code of family honor, which requires "an eye for an eye," that reasoning now seems less defensible since we have seen in "Emma Zunz" that even with a specific, although still only purported, family justification, revenge leaves the vengeful unfulfilled. With "Emma Zunz" in mind, Mabbott's suggestion that Montresor cannot rest in peace even fifty years after killing Fortunato ("The Cask" 1252) begins to appear more viable than Vincent Price's delighted and gluttonous portrayal of Montresor in film.[51] Emma Zunz's bitter, costly, and incomplete "success" in challenging both patriarchy and the local class system can even cause us to reinterpret Hop-Frog's extremely violent yet justified uprising against a demeaning king, his court, and the horrific system of slavery they maintain.[52] Hop-Frog's escape with Trippetta still demonstrates the triumph of the oppressed over the oppressor, but Hop-Frog's revenge now becomes less satisfactory to the reader since Hop-Frog has to adopt an exaggerated form of the king's violence in order to defeat him; he has to make the king "perform" in an even more ghastly manner than the king had continually forced upon him. "Hop-Frog" does not show us what becomes of the title character and his friend when they return to their homeland. However, "Emma Zunz" suggests that taking vengeance by adopting the violence of one's oppressor—whether that oppression rests in patriarchy and twentieth-century class division as in "Emma Zunz" or in slavery and feudal despotism as in "Hop-Frog"—exacerbates the pain from the original violence rather than erasing it.

Borges's fiction on revenge converses with Poe's—creating a literary dialogue between two disparate portrayals of vengeance—and influences how Borges's readers react to this theme when they reread Poe. After reading Borges, Poe's revenge, and all revenge, appear, as Canto suggests while analyzing Borges-narrator's vengeance on Daneri in "El Aleph," "mezquina y pueril, como suelen ser las venganzas" ["mean and childish, as revenge usually is"] (212). From this perspective, perhaps the best strategy to deal with revenge as a literary theme is to bury it underneath a slew of supernatural happenings and subsequently explain them away in hopes that the magic, the eventual disillusion, and the conversation created between the two will hide the theme. However, "Metzengerstein," "The Black Cat," and "El Aleph" suggest that vengeance cannot be silenced by a hidden acceptance of metempsychosis, a pseudoscientific explanation about the effects of fire and plaster on a fresh corpse, or the discovery of an esoteric manuscript on special mirrors. Revenge bursts out into flames, screams from behind freshly plastered walls, and whispers from the rubble of demolished basements, but its voice fails to comfort just as its practitioners fail to forget.

Epilogue

Commemorative Reframing

Borges's altering of Poe's image from poet-prophet to fiction-writing genius prepared Argentina, Spanish America, and the Spanish-speaking world for the most significant collection of translations of Poe's prose into the Spanish language: Julio Cortázar's 1956 two-volume set, *Obras en prosa*. Borges's first fifteen years of literary engagement with Poe, from the early 1920s to 1937, coincided with a resurgence of translations of Poe's poetry in Argentina, and the next decade of his relationship with Poe's works included his own and Bioy Casares's translations of "The Facts in the Case of M. Valdemar" and "The Purloined Letter" and Armando Bazán's release of *Obras completas*, a volume of translations that contains thirty-six tales, three essays, *Pym*, *Eureka*, and twenty-three poems from a total of nine different translators. During the next decade, the release of Cortázar's tomes dwarfed any previous attempt at translating Poe's prose in Spanish America and on the Spanish peninsula. The two volumes of *Obras en prosa* include translations of all sixty-seven of Poe's tales, twenty-three essays and reviews, *Pym*, *Eureka*, and "Marginalia."[1] In the early 1970s, Cortázar revised these translations and split what had originally been *Obras en prosa* volume 1 into two volumes, with the new title *Cuentos*, and released revisions of selected materials from *Obras en prosa* volume 2 as *Ensayos y críticas*. The two-volume set from the 1950s and the revised versions from the 1970s both include more of Poe's prose than any other collection published previously in either Spanish America or Spain, and they provide all this material through the frame of a single translator—something unheard of in other sizable Poe translations in Spanish during this time period.

Cortázar's Poe is Borges's Poe, a fiction writer and a literary critic rather than a poet. Cortázar dedicates only eight pages to Poe's poetry in his lengthy introduction to *Obras en prosa*, and the majority of the subsection entitled "El poeta" ["The Poet"] focuses on Poe's poetic theory rather than on his actual poems.[2] More importantly, Cortázar does not include a translation of even one poem in the scores of works he translated for these volumes; he does not devote a single leaf out of almost 1,700 pages of translated work to any of

Poe's poems.[3] We can speculate about Cortázar's reasons for focusing so intently on Poe's prose—his own penchant for fiction as demonstrated in his literary corpus, which contains scores of short stories, several lengthy novels, and only a selected number of published poems; the visible gap in the translations of Poe's prose works into Spanish compared to the abundance of translated versions of Poe's poems available in Spanish by the 1950s; or the particulars of his contract with UNESCO—but the extremely limited attention Cortázar gives Poe's poetry in his introduction and the complete absence of poetry in his translations recall Borges's emphasis on where Poe's genius rests. Cortázar accomplished his momentous Poe translations in Paris, but his choice to give the Spanish-speaking world the vast majority of Poe's prose rather than any of his poetry reflects Cortázar's "coming of age" in a Buenos Aires that slowly saw Poe's reputation shift from poet to storyteller during the first half of the twentieth century via the critical, translational, and fictional work of Borges.

Borges's work on Poe and Cortázar's Poe translations all play, either intentionally or by chance, commemorative roles. In the case of Borges, at least one of his Poe pieces in each of the three categories in which he engaged Poe celebrates, or comes very near celebrating, important anniversaries in Poe's life or literary career. Borges wrote "Edgar Allan Poe"—the article in which he openly critiqued Poe's poetry, examined the power of his poetic image, and praised his fiction—in September 1949 and published the piece in early October of that same year, marking the centennial of Poe's death on October 7, 1849. Borges and Bioy Casares published their translation of "The Purloined Letter" as "La carta robada" in 1943—102 years after Poe began the Dupin series with "The Murders in the Rue Morgue" and 99 years after he finished the trilogy with "The Purloined Letter."[4] Borges published his first solo-authored detective story, "El jardín de senderos que se bifurcan" ["The Garden of Forking Paths"], in 1941, one hundred years after Poe inaugurated the detective genre. Finally, as Irwin notes, the first English translation of this story appeared in 1948 in *Ellery Queen's Mystery Magazine*—a publication that began in 1941 to commemorate the one-hundredth anniversary of detective fiction (37).[5] Each of these publications pays tribute to Poe, but none of them honors Poe's poetry nor his role as poet-prophet. Instead, Borges memorializes Poe's creation of the detective genre. This act of commemorative reframing venerates Poe while simultaneously refashioning his image.

Cortázar's *Obras en prosa* and *Cuentos* were not connected to any particular Poe anniversaries when originally published in 1956 and 1970, but the long-lasting influence of these translations carried them to the forefront of the most significant Poe anniversary to date, the bicentennial celebration of his birth. Alianza Editores republished the two volumes of *Cuentos* over thirty times between 1970 and 2012, and these editions were typically "libros de bolsillo" or "pocket books"—paperback editions whose price made Cortázar's translations affordable for most readers and whose macabre covers were especially attractive to adolescents. This approach paid literary dividends since a wide variety of Spanish American and Spanish peninsular writers who grew up in the 1970s, unlike their predecessors of the so-called Latin American Boom who typically read Poe in English, came to Poe via Cortázar's pocket editions. In 2008–09 the Madrid publishing house Páginas de Espuma released a critical edition of Cortázar's translations of Poe's tales in one volume under the title *Cuentos completos: Edición comentada*. This book contains all sixty-seven of Poe's stories from *Cuentos*, and each tale is introduced by a different Spanish or Spanish American writer from the post-Boom generation. The volume also includes prologues by two of Cortázar's contemporaries—Peruvian Nobel laureate Mario Vargas Llosa and acclaimed Mexican writer Carlos Fuentes—to create what the volume's editors, another Peruvian and Mexican pair in Fernando Iwasaki and Jorge Volpi, call both "un homenaje" ["a tribute"] and "una genealogía literaria" ["a literary genealogy"] ("Poe & cía" 14).

Both the publishing house and the editors of *Cuentos completos* describe this edition as a commemoration. Páginas de Espuma's website begins their advertisement for the book by stating that "[e]l Bicentenario del nacimiento del escritor norteamericano Edgard Allan Poe (1809–1849) lo quiere celebrar la editorial Páginas de Espuma publicando la edición definitiva, crítica y comentada de sus *Cuentos completos*" ["the publishing house Páginas de Espuma wants to celebrate the bicentennial of the birth of the North American writer Edgar Allan Poe (1809–1849) by publishing the definitive, critical, and annotated edition of his *Complete Stories*"]. The collection's title and its content demonstrate the publisher's preference for Poe's fiction over his poetry, but the ad emphasizes this predilection even further by claiming that "[l]a contribución más importante de Poe a la historia de la literatura la constituyen los relatos cortos de todo género" ["the short stories of every genre constitute the most important contribution of Poe to the history of literature"]. Volpi and Iwasaki commemorate both Poe's bicentennial and the staying power for Cortázar's Poe translations by arguing:

> Todos somos descendientes literarios de Poe, pues gracias a Poe existieron Chesterton y Baudelaire, Conan Doyle y Maupassant, Lovecraft y Saki, Cheever y Borges, y así hasta Julio Cortázar, ancestro de los cuentistas que nacimos a partir de 1960. Y como todos leímos en su momento la memorable edición de bolsillo de los cuentos completos de Edgar Allan Poe traducidos por Cortázar, no encontramos otra manera mejor de celebrar el bicentenario de Poe, que rescatando aquellos míticos tomitos azules.

> [We are all literary descendants of Poe. Thanks to Poe, Chesterton and Baudelaire, Conan Doyle and Maupassant, Lovecraft and Saki, Cheever and Borges

all existed, on down to Julio Cortázar, ancestor of those of us storywriters who were born after 1960. And since we all read in our time the memorable pocket edition of Poe's complete stories translated by Cortázar, we find no better way to celebrate the bicentennial of Poe than by recovering those mythic little blue volumes.] (13)[6]

Volpi's and Iwasaki's introduction, like the publisher's advertisement, memorializes Poe by reframing him as a writer of short fiction. The "literary genealogy" that Volpi and Iwasaki trace clearly highlights Poe's influence on Borges and Cortázar and the latter's influence, combined with Poe's, on contemporary Spanish-language fiction writers. Their specific praise for Poe as storyteller, however, reenacts Borges's reinterpretation of Poe, demonstrating not only Poe's influence on Borges (and on a long chain of important writers from various literary traditions) but also Borges's reciprocal influence on Poe. Through *Cuentos completos: Edición comentada*, Cortázar invites Borges to Poe's bicentennial, and the two Argentines posthumously celebrate the living works of a dead master whose reputation as a fiction writer their works continually resuscitate.

Borges's commemorative reframing of Poe was conscious; he chose to publish works in conversation with Poe's literary corpus on specific Poe anniversaries. The commemorative part of Cortázar's reimagining of Poe, the bicentennial release of *Cuentos completos*, was coincidental; it depended on the desires of Cortázar's successors and subsequent editors. Cortázar's decision to reproduce Borges's version of Poe as fiction writer, however, was not a mere coincidence. While Cortázar does not cite Borges in his bibliography at the end of the second volume of *Obras en prosa*, Borges's influence on Cortázar's version of Poe remains visible in at least three ways.

First, Cortázar's discussion of Poe in the second half of his introduction to *Obras en prosa* mirrors Borges's descriptions of the U.S. writer. His assertion that "la profunda presencia de Poe en la literatura es un hecho más importante que las flaquezas o deméritos de una parte de su obra" ["the profound presence of Poe in literature is a more important fact than the weaknesses or faults of a part of his work"] (lv) resonates with Borges's claim that the staying power of "nueve o diez cuentos indiscutibles" ["nine or ten indisputable stories"], Poe's creation of *Pym*, his invention of the detective genre, and his influence on Paul Valéry "basta para la justificación de su gloria, pese a las redundancias y languideces que sufre cada página" ["is enough to justify his glory, regardless of the redundancies and languishing suffered on each page"] (*"Edgar Allan Poe*, de Edward Shanks" 333).[7] His claim that "creemos que un balance de la obra de Poe y sus consecuencias, [. . .] no puede lograrse si se la reduce a un caso clínico, o a una serie de textos literarios. Hay más, hay siempre más. Hay en nosotros una presencia oscura de Poe, una latencia de Poe.

Todos, en algún sector de nuestra persona, somos él" ["we believe that an assessment of Poe's work and its consequences, [. . .] cannot be achieved if it is reduced to a clinical case, or to a series of literary texts. There is more, there is always more. There is in us a dark presence of Poe, a latency of Poe. All of us, in some part of our person, are him"] ("Introducción" lvi) recalls both Borges's claim that Poe's image "es más visible ahora que cualquiera de las páginas que compuso y aun más que la suma de esas páginas" ["is more visible now than any of the pages he wrote and even more than the sum of those pages"] ("Prólogo, *La carta*" 9), and his description of that image as a posthumous projection of a "sombra luminosa" ["shining shadow"] (Borges and Ferrari, "Sobre Edgar" 191). Finally, Cortázar's reminder that Poe wanted to dedicate his life to poetry but that "las circunstancias" ["the circumstances"] led him to write a few poems while his "época creadora más intensa estuvo casi íntegramente dedicada a las narraciones y a la crítica" ["most intense creative epoch was almost entirely dedicated to stories and criticism] ("Introducción" lxiv) repeats Borges's argument in "Edgar Allan Poe," his 1949 article for *La Nación*, that "Poe se creía poeta, sólo poeta, pero las circunstancias lo llevaron a escribir cuentos, y esos cuentos a cuya escritura se resignó y que debió encarar como tareas ocasionales son su inmortalidad" ["Poe believed himself a poet, a poet only, but his circumstances made him write stories, and these stories that he resigned himself to write and which he faced as occasional tasks are his immortality"] (1).

Second, Borges's literary criticism on Poe, his Poe translations, and his own fiction opened up the Argentine literary market for more Poe fiction. The prominence Cortázar's translations received over a previous collection like Bazán's edition of Poe's *Obras completas* did not occur simply because Cortázar was a famous writer of fiction in his own right. The continual *republication* of his translations certainly owes something to Cortázar's own fame, but when he released *Obras en prosa* in 1956, he was not yet a well-known author. Rather, Borges had praised Poe's prose, a large portion of Poe's fiction and critical writings were not yet available in Spanish, and the pieces of Poe's prose that were available were scattered throughout various newspapers and magazines or collected in editions that relied on the work of multiple translators. Cortázar's Poe translations took center stage in Argentina, the Río de la Plata region, and the Spanish-speaking world because they filled a gap, a gap that first became visible through Borges's critiques of Poe's poetry and admiration for his prose.

Third, Borges was a major influence on Cortázar's literary career. Cortázar's short fiction often reflects Borges's style (a fact that becomes readily apparent to any reader of Cortázar who has already read Borges), but more significant for my current line of argument, Borges was instrumental in publishing Cortázar's first short story. Borges opens the prologue he wrote for an edition of Cortázar's short stories that Hyspamérica published in 1985 by telling the story of how, on a nondescript afternoon, a tall, young writer brought him a short-story manuscript.[8] He continues: "Volvió a la semana. Le dije que su cuento me gustaba y que ya había sido entregado a la imprenta. Poco después, Julio Cortázar leyó en letras de molde 'Casa tomada' con dos ilustraciones a lápiz de Norah Borges. Pasaron los años y me confió una noche, en París, que ésa había sido su primera publicación. Me honra haber sido el instrumento" (551) ["He came back the next week. I told him that I liked his story very much and that it had already been sent to the printer. Soon after, Julio Cortázar read the printed letters of 'House Taken Over,' accompanied by two pencil drawings by Norah Borges. The years went by, and one night in Paris he mentioned that this was his first publication. I am honored to have been instrumental"] ("Julio Cortázar" 514). Borges published Cortázar's "Casa tomada" in 1946 in *Los Anales de Buenos Aires*, a journal that Borges founded that same year and directed until 1948. In reality, "Casa tomada" was Cortázar's third publication—he had already published, under the pseudonym Julio Denís, a collection of poems entitled *Presencia* in 1938 and an essay on Arthur Rimbaud in 1941 (Mundo Lo 271)—but he always remembered how Borges assisted him with his first acknowledged publication, his first printed piece of fiction. Borges's prologue to Cortázar's stories evokes a conversation between the two writers in Paris, and Borges's humble attitude in this piece suggests that he was simply grateful to have played an early role in Cortázar's literary career. An anecdote that María Kodama shared with me in 2009, however, not only shows that the two writers respected each other, regardless of their conflicting political views, but that Cortázar maintained a sense of gratitude toward Borges decades after the original publication of "Casa tomada." According to Kodama, she and Borges crossed paths with Cortázar while viewing Francisco Goya's painting *El perro* at a European museum. Cortázar noticed the couple from across the room, walked toward them, embraced Borges, called him "maestro" ["teacher" or "master"], and told him that he would never forget that Borges had helped him publish "Casa tomada" (Personal Interview).

Apart from this anecdote, the Jorge Luis Borges Collection at the University of Virginia contains a letter from Cortázar to Borges that also hints at Borges's influence on his fellow Argentine writer. After commenting on the Minotaur in André Gide's *Thésée*, Cortázar praises Borges's portrayal of the Minotaur's intelligence in "La casa de Asterión" ["The House of Asterion"]—a tale Borges originally published in May–June 1947 in the same journal in which he had placed Cortázar's "Casa tomada." Then, he offers Borges a gift in the form of his own literary version of the Minotaur: "He querido entonces hacerle llegar este Minotauro mío, que curiosamente profetiza al morir (murió en enero de este año) lo que hoy ocurre: su retorno incesante y repetido.

Acéptelo usted como testimonio de cariño hacia Asterión, de nostalgia por su voz tan ceñida, tan libre de lo innecesario" ["So I have wanted to deliver to you this Minotaur of mine, who curiously prophesies while dying (he died in January of this year) what happens today: his incessant and repeated return. Accept this as proof of affection toward Asterión, of nostalgia for his voice so cautious, so free from the unnecessary"]. In the Small Special Collections Library, this letter accompanies Borges's manuscript of "La casa de Asterión," but the letter must have originally been delivered to Borges with a copy of Cortázar's retelling of the Theseus-Minotaur myth—his drama entitled *Los reyes*. Cortázar published *Los reyes* in Buenos Aires in 1949, and like Borges's story, which describes the Minotaur's existence from the perspective of the Minotaur himself, Cortázar's rendition of the myth also gives the Minotaur a voice. Both Borges and Cortázar let the monster speak, and in each text the Minotaur's words alter the reader's preconceived notions—the beast becomes an empathetic being, a protagonist. While Cortázar's letter contains no date, he must have written it in 1949, the same year he published *Los reyes*, since the play ends with the Minotaur's death, an "event" that Cortázar suggests in the letter happened "en enero de este año" ["in January of this year"]. With a brilliant, anachronistic mix of literature and reality, Cortázar claims that his Minotaur's prophecy that he, the Minotaur, will inhabit "cada corazón de hombre" ["every heart of man"] (*Los reyes* 66) fulfills itself in twentieth-century literature as the Minotaur's image resurrects in the works of André Gide, Borges, Cortázar himself, and many others.

This exchange between Cortázar and Borges might appear to have little to do with Poe on the surface level, but it establishes a pattern of respect and repetition that Cortázar follows when he translates and interprets Poe. Cortázar enjoys Borges's reframing of the Minotaur myth—his giving Asterión a name and a voice "tan ceñida, tan libre de lo innecesario" ["so cautious, so free from the unnecessary"] rather than depicting the Minotaur as a monster. With *Los reyes*, Cortázar writes his own version of the Minotaur following the tone Borges had already created in his rewriting of the myth. Cortázar also appreciates Borges's reframing of Poe—his casting Poe as a timeless fiction writer rather than a poet-prophet—and he replicates this version of the Poe image or myth in his biographical treatment of Poe and in his choice of which Poe texts he translates. In each case, Cortázar takes Borges's core idea and both runs with and expands upon it. "La casa de Asterión" is a brief tale, under 1,500 words, while *Los reyes* is a five-scene drama; Borges's literary criticism on Poe, his Poe translations, and his approaches to Poe in his own fiction fill a few hundred sheets of paper while Cortázar's Poe translations alone, not even considering his own Poesque fiction, require almost two thousand pages. In short, Cortázar's Poe translations bring Borges's Poe to the mind of every Spanish-speaking Poe reader far more than Cortázar's, or any other writer's, work brings the Minotaur to the heart of every man.

The Borges/Cortázar combination commemoratively reframes Poe for the Spanish-speaking world at the major moments of Poe memorialization from 1941 to 2009—the bicentennial of his birth in 2009, the centennial of his death in 1949, and the centennial of his most fruitful creation, the detective genre, in 1941—but Borges's work also attempts to alter Poe's image closer to Poe's home and for an audience that reads in Poe's native language. I hinted at this possibility in chapters 5 and 6 by arguing that Borges's stories "Funes el memorioso" and "El Aleph" make Poe's "Loss of Breath" feel Borgesian via the first type of reciprocal influence Borges suggests in the Kafka essay. I also asserted that "El Aleph" changes how Poe's readers understand the supernatural revenge plots Poe offers in "Metzengerstein" and "The Black Cat" through the second type of two-way influence Borges describes in "Kafka y sus precursores." Neither of these claims applies only to Spanish-language readers. Any Poe reader who reads Borges (whether in Spanish or in translation) can experience these uncanny and anachronistic feelings when returning to Poe. However, I suggest that Borges makes a more explicit attempt to bring his Poe "home" in the late 1960s and early 1970s through his publication of *Introducción a la literatura norteamericana* [*An Introduction to American Literature*] with Esther Zemborain de Torres and his visit to the University of Virginia. With the textbook, Borges tells both Spanish- and English-language readers where he thinks Poe fits into the U.S. literary tradition, and with his visit to Charlottesville, he brings his Poe to one of the author's principal shrines. In the former case, the evidence rests right on the page, but in the latter, it resides, appropriately for a study on Borges, in the memory of a librarian.

Borges and Zemborain de Torres published *Introducción a la literatura norteamericana* in Buenos Aires in 1967 with the "finalidad fundamental [. . .] [de] estimular el conocimiento de la evolución literaria de una nación que forjó la primera constitución democrática de los tiempos modernos" (8) ["fundamental purpose [. . .] [of] encourag[ing] an acquaintance with the literary evolution of the nation which forged the first democratic constitution of modern times"] (4), and L. Clark Keating and Robert O. Evans translated this short primer into English in 1971 in order to bring Borges's version of U.S. literary history "to English-speaking students everywhere" (vii).[9] In the prologue, Borges claims that in U.S. literary history "los grupos y los cenáculos literarios son menos importantes que el individuo" (8) ["literary groups and coteries are less important than individuals"] (3), and he provides more coverage of Poe than of most of the other individual authors he approaches in this text.

Introducción a la literatura norteamericana delivers the same general message about Poe that Borges had been telling his Spanish-speaking audience for decades—that Poe was a talented writer of fiction whose poetic image outshines the quality of his actual poetry. In the short chapter entitled "Hawthorne y Poe," Borges treats Poe directly as a prose writer. He offers a long summary of "The Philosophy of Composition," cites a few of Poe's works of fiction, repeats Poe's claim about terror's connection to the soul rather than to Germany, and once again names Poe as the father of detective fiction (18–20; 21–23). Borges only mentions Poe's poetry twice in this chapter—he names "The Raven" while summarizing "The Philosophy of Composition," and he suggests that "Poe aplicó a sus cuentos la misma técnica que a sus versos; juzgó que todo debe redactarse en función de la última línea" (20) ["Poe applied to his tales the same technique that he used in his verse; he believed that everything should be written with the last line in mind"] (23)—and both of these comments cast Poe's poetry as subsidiary to his prose. The rest of the book reinforces Borges's overarching judgment on Poe. Although he discusses Poe in several other sections apart from the chapter dedicated to Poe and Hawthorne, he does not include Poe in the chapter "Tres poetas del siglo XIX" ["Three Poets of the Nineteenth Century"], and he names Whitman, not Poe, as the primary influence on twentieth-century U.S. poetry in the chapter "Los poetas" (45) ["Poets"] (63).

Borges aimed this text at Argentine and Spanish-American audiences—audiences less familiar with U.S. literary history—but through the book's translation only four years after its initial publication date, he delivered his message about Poe to an audience well-versed in U.S. literary history and quite familiar with Poe's place in it. For this English-reading audience, Borges's emphasis on Poe as storyteller rather than poet-prophet would not seem foreign, regardless of the nationality of the source. However, the importance Borges assigns to Poe in this book would have surprised a U.S. readership in the early 1970s. Borges opens the book by suggesting that U.S. literature affects world literature, not just other literature in English, and that the nation's two primary influences on the world are Poe and Whitman (9; 5). In his penultimate chapter, "Novela policial, 'science fiction' y el lejano oeste" ["The Detective Story, Science Fiction, and the Far West"], Borges begins his discussions of both detective fiction and sci-fi with Poe—the creator of the former genre and a forerunner of the latter. In short, Borges frames his entire appraisal of U.S. literature with Poe as his bookends. For Borges, Poe is one of the tradition's two major influences on highbrow literature—"Poe engendró a Baudelaire, que engendró a los simbolistas, que engendraron a Valéry" (9) ["Poe begat Baudelaire, who begat the symbolists, who begat Valéry"] (5)—and he is a principal catalyst for two of the tradition's three most popular genres. While this assessment of Poe reiterates the image of Poe that Borges had been crafting for over a quarter of a century for his local and

regional audiences, it creates a new Poe narrative in English that not only recognizes Poe's genius—as several works in English had already accomplished
by 1971—but also clearly links that genius to his prose and places Poe front
and center in a national tradition that had often refused to take him seriously.

To conclude this Poe homecoming, we need to return to a South—not to
the Buenos Aires that Borges frequently left during the 1960s and 1970s, but
to the U.S. South that he visited several times during that same period—and
to the ideas of commemoration and reframing. From late 1961 through early
1962, Borges taught as a visiting professor at the University of Texas at Austin, beginning what would become a fruitful mid- to late-life career as a visiting scholar at various U.S. and U.K. universities. Several of Borges's university
stops have been well documented (e.g., his delivery of the Norton Lectures
at Harvard in 1967–68 and his brief visit to Johns Hopkins in April 1983 to
deliver the Pouder Lecture).[10] However, many of his campus visits live on only
through brief lines in long-archived issues of university newspapers or in the
memories of former students who were lucky enough to attend the events.
One such visit occurred in early 1968 at the University of Virginia, a campus
that takes great pride in Poe's brief sojourn there as a student from February
through December 1826.

Poe the student spent less than a year in Charlottesville, but the University
of Virginia has spent over a century commemorating him.[11] The memorialization began as early as 1897 when an English professor named Charles W.
Kent printed an article in the university newspaper, "suggesting that No. 13
West Range be furnished as a 'Poe room,' with pictures, autographs, and all
the editions of Poe's works" (Gilliam 6). During that same year, a group of
university students organized the Poe Memorial Association, which "raised
money to commission a bronze bust of Poe" and set apart "an alcove of the
University Library [. . .] for a collection of works by and about Poe," all "to
commemorate the fiftieth anniversary of Poe's death on October 7, 1899"
(6). In 1904 another group of students organized the Raven Society, the first
and still longest-running honors society at UVA (7), and between 1906 and
1909, the society restored one of the two rooms thought to have been Poe's
dormitory—room no. 13 West Range—as the Poe room, just in time for the
centennial celebration of Poe's birth (8–9). The university widely celebrated
Poe's centennial as the Jefferson Society, the Raven Society, faculty, students,
and even a visiting preacher all held memorializing services in Poe's honor on
January 16–19, 1909 (Kent and Patton).

Poe commemorative activities remain alive and well at the University of
Virginia in the twenty-first century. To celebrate Poe's bicentennial, the Harrison Institute and the Small Special Collections Library at the University
of Virginia collaborated with the Harry Ransom Center at the University
of Texas at Austin to create "From Out That Shadow: The Life and Legacy

of Edgar Allan Poe," a massive exhibition that contained several Poe manuscripts, rare editions, and artifacts, along with famous art based on Poe's works. The Raven Society still "maintains No. 13 as a shrine to Poe" (Kelly 1) that can be visited by the public, and in 2011 the society renovated the room once more (Sampson 1). Finally, and in a more academic vein, the Small Special Collections Library has held John Henry Ingram's Poe Collection—one of the most extensive Poe collections in the world—since 1922. In short, the University of Virginia commemorates Poe far more than any other university, and their memorialization of Poe combines the academic sanctuary of an archive with the popularity of a tourist monument.[12]

Borges visited the University of Virginia in 1968, offering a pair of lectures on Poe to a student body and faculty whose campus serves as a primary Poe sanctum. Neither of these lectures was recorded nor transcribed, and only scant, and very recent, documentation of this visit remains—a short 2012 magazine article, "Borges in Charlottesville," and a brief documentary film by Eduardo Montes-Bradley entitled *Loewenstein*, also from 2012.[13] C. Jared Loewenstein, the founding curator of the Jorge Luis Borges Collection at the Small Special Collections Library, is both the subject matter of and the detail provider for both the article and the film, and it seems only fitting that the traces of Borges's visit to the University of Virginia rest in the memory of a fellow librarian. According to Loewenstein, Borges came to the university as a guest of the Spanish Department, but the only lectures he gave were lectures on Poe. The first lecture consisted of Borges "reading and commenting on Poe's poetry" while the second lecture focused on Poe as "the inventor of the detective story" ("Re: A Few"). Loewenstein does not recall the specifics of the first lecture, but he remembers that in the second lecture Borges described Poe's "The Murders in the Rue Morgue" as "an important precursor to Sir Arthur Conan Doyle's Sherlock Holmes," that he spoke passionately about the importance of "analytic thinking" in both Poe's and Conan Doyle's work, and that he "praised [. . .] the descriptive force both related to landscapes and persons" in Poe's "The Tale of the Ragged Mountains" ("Re: A Few"). Loewenstein also recalls that after the second lecture a member of the audience invited to take Borges to visit the Ragged Mountains, just southwest of the university; he declined this invitation, but he did visit the Poe room where he listened to an extensive lecture and touched or hefted several of the items in the room ("Telephone").[14]

Loewenstein's recollections of Borges's visit to the University of Virginia suggest that in his second lecture he offered the university the same Poe he had been touting for decades to his local and regional audiences—Poe the story writer, the inventor of the analytic detective genre. His memories of the first lecture, however, leave space for speculation about what Borges said about Poe the poet. We cannot know exactly how Borges analyzed Poe's poetry after he read selections aloud to the audience, but we can trace patterns from Borges's other speeches and lectures to offer an educated guess—we can play the part of Dupin and deduce how Borges pitched Poe the poet at the University of Virginia based on our previous experiences with Borges as lecturer.

Borges's available lectures suggest that when he began lecturing on a subject, he would, through time, expand and adjust his analysis but always to support his initial perspective about the topic at hand. For example, in the series of lectures on the fantastic that I examined in chapter 6, lectures he gave between 1949 and 1968 across Europe and the Americas, Borges slightly altered his lists of fantastic texts, themes, and methods, but he always followed the same general outline of describing the fantastic rather than theorizing the concept. In a similar vein, Borges was extremely consistent when he discussed Poe's poetry and his fiction in his lectures. Borges mentioned Poe in at least fourteen lectures between 1949 and 1982, and the patterns in these lectures echo what Borges said about Poe in print from the 1920s through the 1980s.[15] He usually focused on Poe as a fiction writer, and when he approached Poe as a poet, he either did so to hint that Poe's poetic theory trumped his actual poetry ("La obra y destino de Walt Whitman" 43) or to openly claim that Poe was "más extraordinario en prosa que en verso" ("El cuento policial" 230) ["better in prose than in poetry"] ("The Detective Story" 492). Borges's preference for Poe's fiction over his poetry in *Introducción a la literatura norteamericana*—the revised and published version of lectures he offered to his students at the University of Buenos Aires—confirms that the Poe who appeared in Borges's lectures wore the same garb as the Poe who frequented Borges's critical texts. Finally, the fact that Borges offered two different lectures on Poe at the University of Virginia, one that restated his thoughts on Poe's importance for the detective genre and another that included an oral reading of some of Poe's poems, reiterates Borges's long-held judgment about Poe's place in the canon of world literature. As early as 1937, he had claimed that Poe's fiction and literary criticism survived while only a handful of his poems—"The Raven," "The Bells," and "Annabel Lee"—remained visible and that these poems "han sido relegadas al submundo (sin duda menos infernal que molesto) de la declamación" ["have been relegated to the underworld (without a doubt less infernal than bothersome) of oral delivery"] ("*Edgar Allan Poe*, de Edward Shanks" 332–33). When analyzed alongside his other lectures on Poe, even the limited memories of Borges's Poe lectures at UVA suggest that Borges brought his Poe with him to Charlottesville, reframing Poe once more in a space that continually commemorates him.

Borges's brief visit to the University of Virginia might not have fundamentally changed how the entire university community understood Poe, but it did serve as the catalyst for a major change in the university's special collections—a space already inhabited by Poe. Upon meeting Borges for the first time at a post-lecture party held in his honor, Loewenstein thought "I've got to get to know this man better" (*Loewenstein*). Over the next two decades, Loewenstein did get to know Borges better, and from the late 1970s to the present, Loewenstein's creation and expansion of the Jorge Luis Borges Collection at the Small Special Collections Library has helped students and scholars from UVA and from around the globe become far better acquainted with the Argentine's work. The collection began in 1977 when Loewenstein was approached by a Buenos Aires book collector and offered over four hundred rare Borges items—first editions, early critical material, and journal appearances by Borges ("Telephone"). At Loewenstein's request, the university purchased the materials, and he created the Jorge Luis Borges Collection, which now contains over three thousand items—each purchased "one or two at a time during the following years" ("Telephone"). This collection contains the largest and most important assembly of Borges material available to scholars, and it is only rivaled by the private collections held by the Fundación Internacional Jorge Luis Borges and the Fundación San Telmo, both in Buenos Aires, and the Borges holdings in the Sala del Tesoro at Argentina's National Library. Among the thousands of pieces in the collection, Borges's manuscripts are probably the most astonishing. The collection holds over thirty manuscripts, and several of these include illustrations by Borges's sister, Norah, and drawings by Borges himself.[16]

Tellingly, at least for a project that explores the literary relationship between Poe and Borges, the Jorge Luis Borges Collection resides in the Small Special Collections Library—the same library that contains John Henry Ingram's Poe Collection. In another manifestation of reciprocal influence, Borges alters Poe's space by occupying the same special collections library that houses one of the most significant Poe collections in the world while "Poe's university" changes Borges's global reputation by offering singular public access to rare Borges materials.

Borges's lectures on Poe both reframed Poe in Poe's home space and laid the groundwork for Borges's own reframing. The University of Virginia memorializes both Poe and Borges, celebrating each writer through texts, artifacts, and/or memories. A research trip to the Small Special Collections Library to study either writer is far more highbrow than a tour of room No. 13 West Range, but both types of visits serve as pilgrimages. The latter pays homage to Poe by preserving the space where he supposedly lived while the former honors both Borges and Poe by housing their works and by allowing visitors to touch the same paper on which these writers originally placed their pens. The two-way influence between Poe's and Borges's literatures—initiated by Poe's literary influence on Borges and reciprocated through Borges's literary criticism, his Poe translations, and his own fiction—continues on this campus just as it continues through the frequent reprinting of Cortázar's Poe translations and the proliferation of Borges's own work. Borges's Poe is not only the Spanish-speaking world's Poe; his version of Poe as a fiction-writing genius who only wanted to be a poet competes with Poe's other reputations in English, and his placement of Poe at the forefront of the U.S. literary canon as a major world influence plays itself out in literary traditions across Europe, Asia, and the Americas.

Notes

Introduction. Recipricoal Influence

1. For an example of Borges's post-*ultraista* critiques of Lugones, see his biting essay "Leopoldo Lugones, *Romancero*" in *El tamaño de mi esperanza*. Borges did praise Lugones and the *modernistas* later in life in pieces such as *Leopoldo Lugones*, which he wrote in collaboration with Betina Edelberg, and "Sobre Lugones."

2. Quiroga wrote two earlier articles on how to become a so-called perfect storyteller: "El manual del perfecto cuentista" and "Los trucs del perfecto cuentista," both published in *El Hogar* in 1925. "Los trucs del perfecto cuentista" focuses on what Quiroga calls local color or folklore, but "El manual del perfecto cuentista" converses openly with Poe's idea of aiming each line of a story toward the desired final effect. Quiroga states, "Comenzaremos por el final. Me he convencido de que del mismo modo que en el soneto, el cuento empieza por el fin. Nada en el mundo parecería más fácil que hallar la frase final para una historia que, precisamente, acaba de concluir. Nada, sin embargo, es más difícil. [. . .] Para comenzar se necesita, en el noventa y nueve por ciento de los casos, saber adónde se va. 'La primera palabra de un cuento— se ha dicho—debe ya estar escrita con miras al final'" ["We will begin with the end. I have convinced myself that in the same manner as the sonnet, the story begins with the end. Nothing in the world would seem easier than finding the final phrase for a story that, precisely, just came to an end. Nothing, however, is more difficult. [. . .] To begin, it is necessary, 99 percent of the time, to know where you are going. 'The first word of a story—it has been said—should be written with the end already in mind'"] (7).

3. *Los arrecifes de coral* fits well within the *modernista* milieu in the Río de la Plata region at the turn of the century, although some of Quiroga's readership considered it too risqué. This volume also includes a short prose piece titled "El tonel del amontillado," Quiroga's first of several attempts to rewrite or revise Poe's famous tale of revenge.

4. Strangely, Borges was not one of the local fiction writers attracted to Poe by Quiroga's stories. Borges never coupled Poe and Quiroga in his literary criticism, and in pieces like "La poesía" (303), he specifically critiques Quiroga's description in "Decálogo del perfecto cuentista" of how language functions.

5. See Sophia McClennen's "Inter-American Studies or Imperial American Studies?" for a sophisticated discussion of the threats inter-American approaches to literature can pose to the study of Latin American literatures, histories, and cultures.

6. See Maurice Bennett's "The Infamy and the Ecstasy: Crime, Art, and Metaphysics in Edgar Allan Poe's 'William Wilson' and Jorge Luis Borges's 'Deutsches Re-

quiem,'" Julia A. Kushigian's "The Detective Story Genre in Poe and Borges," Verónica Cortínez's "De Poe a Borges: La creación del lector policial," Graciela E. Tissera's succinct "Jorge Luis Borges" in Lois Davis Vines's *Poe Abroad: Influence, Reputation, Affinities*, a section of Rolando Costa Picazo's book on Borges's affinities with literature in English—*Borges: Una forma de felicidad*—Santiago Rodríguez Guerrero-Strachan's "Idea de Edgar A. Poe en la obra crítica de Jorge Luis Borges," Christopher Rollason's "The Character of Phantasm: Edgar Allan Poe's 'The Fall of the House of Usher' and Jorge Luis Borges's 'Tlön, Uqbar, Orbis Tertius,'" and several articles by John T. Irwin (most of which appear as chapters in his *The Mystery to a Solution*).

7. Bennett's "The Infamy and the Ecstasy" and Rollason's "The Character of Phantasm" serve as exceptions to this emphasis on detective fiction. Irwin also analyzes several of Borges's other stories, but he always connects his analysis of these works back to his focus on the analytic detective story. Both Irwin and Bennett refer to some of Borges's important critical pieces on Poe. However, neither critic analyzes Borges's repeated readings of "The Philosophy of Composition," which I find essential to understanding how Borges shifts Poe's image from poet to story writer.

8. Even though Borges read Poe in English rather than through the many translations available in Argentina during his youth (e.g., Charles Baudelaire's French translations, Spanish translations of Baudelaire's French versions, and Spanish translations from Poe's English), he commented several times on the irony of Argentina's and Spanish America's reception of the Bostonian Poe through the translations of a French poet ("Sobre los clásicos" 231 and "Prólogo de prólogos" 13; "Diálogo sobre el Modernismo y Rubén Darío" with Osvaldo Ferrari 119).

9. There are, of course, exceptions to this generalization, including Irwin's *The Mystery to a Solution* and George Handley's *New World Poetics: Nature and the Adamic Imagination of Whitman, Neruda, and Walcott*.

10. Although Woodward specifically claims that the U.S. South shares these experiences with "nearly all the peoples of Europe and Asia," his argument that a history of "military defeat, occupation, and reconstruction" differentiates the U.S. South from the U.S. North (190) has provided clear and continued justification for scholars to compare U.S. southern literatures and histories with the literary and historical traditions of Latin America and the Caribbean.

11. Several literary critics offer readings of "El sur" that connect the story's protagonist, Juan Dahlmann, to Borges. For an intriguing reading of the tale that links Borges to Dahlmann, southernness, and Poe, see Irwin 171–75.

12. Torres García famously illustrated his focus on the South as North in two pieces in which he inverted the map of the South American continent—*South America's Inverted Map* from 1936 and *América invertida* (see book cover) from 1943.

13. In many ways, this project could be seen as a "literary history of literature" as described by Pascale Casanova in *La République mondiale des lettres* [*The World Republic of Letters*] (350). Borges's literary relationship with Poe supports Casanova's driving thesis "that there exists a 'literature-world,' a literary universe relatively independent of the everyday world and its political divisions, whose boundaries and operational laws are not reducible to those of ordinary political space" (xii). Casanova puts forth a "model of world literary space" that "makes it possible to compare writers who

are not contemporary in the usual sense with reference to a measure of literary time that is relatively independent of the political chronologies that for the most part still organize histories of literature" (101). This concept of a "world republic of letters," as Casanova calls it, shrinks the temporal and spatial distance between Poe's writings in the 1830s–1840s on the eastern seaboard of the United States and Borges's career in 1920s–1980s Buenos Aires. As Casanova notes, however, the existence of a parallel republic of letters does not deny that this space is "relatively *dependent*" on the politics and economics of "the ordinary world" (349, italics in original). Thus, as I argue in my introduction, Poe's, and especially Borges's, times and places in history also matter.

14. "Writing the history of literature," Casanova claims, "is a paradoxical activity that consists in placing it in historical time and then showing how literature gradually tears itself away from this temporality" (350). In my literary history of Borges and Poe, Borges acts as what Casanova would call an "'eccentric' cosmopolitan" and polyglot (100), with "eccentric" meaning peripheral rather than strange, who serves as a broker between various regions of the world republic of letters. My analysis of Borges's relationship with Poe differs from the majority of literary relations that Casanova describes in two important ways. First, I focus on a writer who changes a previous author's already well-known reputation. Borges responds to Poe, who had already been imported into Paris, the capital of Casanova's world republic of letters, and into a regional hub of this literary republic, Buenos Aires. Poe was already a famous, even a central, figure in both French and Río de la Plata literary traditions. Borges's response to Poe, then, does not introduce the latter to either space. Instead, it significantly alters Poe's image in what Casanova would call a peripheral capital. Second, my interpretation takes a hemispheric approach that requires an adjustment of what Casanova sees as central and eccentric, center and periphery. Poe's importance in France is indisputable, Argentina's fascination with things French is also well documented, and, as we shall see in chapter 2, Borges's eventual entrance into English via translation depends on his own success in France. However, Borges does not grant the same amount of cultural clout to Paris that his contemporary Argentine colleagues do, and Paris does not serve as his "Greenwich meridian" (Casanova 88–90) in the way that it does for almost all the authors Casanova examines in her treatise. Borges was an anglophile who preferred English, German, and eventually Old Norse literary canons, and he recognized, but found somewhat disturbing, the fact that both Poe's and his own global careers were launched in France. Unlike the authors whom Casanova argues seek "consecration" in the capital of the world republic of letters, and unlike the cosmopolitan polyglots who bring said writers to this particular center, Borges never longs for Paris. His re-creation of Poe takes Buenos Aires, not Paris, as the center and concerns itself with a national, then regional, then hemispheric reshaping of Poe's image that is not particularly concerned with the city of light / Casanova's city of letters.

15. Borges's father owned several works by English-speaking authors that Borges read in his youth, including volumes by Charles Dickens, H. G. Wells, Mark Twain, and Lewis Carroll and English translations of *Don Quijote* and *A Thousand Nights and a Night* (Borges and di Giovanni 42). Borges claims that he had to hide on the roof to read Burton's translation of *A Thousand Nights and a Night* because the text that "was then considered obscenity, was forbidden" (42), mirroring Julio Cortázar's

claim that he "stole" a copy of Poe as a nine-year-old because his mother thought that he was too young to read it (Weiss 73).

16. *Siete noches* contains seven lectures that Borges gave at the Coliseo theater in Buenos Aires from June through August of 1977, while *Borges, oral* includes five classes that he delivered to students at la Universidad de Belgrano in Buenos Aires in 1978.

17. Bloom does not deny Poe's worldwide influence: "That Poe is inescapable I concede: he dreamed universal nightmares" ("Introduction," *Bloom's Classic* xi), and "Whitman, except for the egregious Edgar Allan Poe, is the only American poet who has worldwide influence" (*The Anatomy of Influence* 9), but he cannot bring himself to see any of Poe's genius. He states, "Poe's verse (I will not call it poetry) is indefensible" and argues that Poe's prose is full of "ghastly diction and dubious syntax" ("Introduction," *Bloom's Classic* xi). Of Poe and Emerson, he states, "If you dislike Emerson, you probably will like Poe. Emerson fathered pragmatism; Poe fathered precisely nothing, which is the way he would have wanted it. [. . .] Emerson, for better and for worse, was and is the mind of America, but Poe was and is our hysteria, our uncanny unanimity in our repressions. I certainly do not intend to mean by this that Poe was deeper than Emerson in any way whatsoever" ("Introduction," *Bloom's Modern* 1). This statement reveals Bloom's strategy of criticizing one writer in order to praise another, a strategy Borges laments in a 1946 prologue—"Nota preliminar a Francis Bret Harte, *Bocetos californianos*"—in which he argues that Baudelaire does the same thing to Emerson that Bloom does years later to Poe: "La observación confirma esta melancólica ley: para rendir justicia a un escritor hay que ser injusto con otros. Baudelaire, para exaltar a Poe, rechaza perentoriamente a Emerson (que como artífice es harto superior a aquél)" ["The observation confirms this melancholy law: to bring justice to one writer you must be unjust with others. Baudelaire, to exalt Poe, peremptorily rejects Emerson (who, as a craftsman is far superior to the former)"] (92). Bloom's claim that Poe fathers nothing also demonstrates Bloom's highbrow bias since he willingly admits that "Poe did invent the analytic detective story" ("Introduction," *Bloom's Classic* xii). Although Borges also critiques Poe's language use and his poetry, he sees Poe's invention of analytic detective fiction as a fruitful endeavor "cuya progenie es innumerable" ["whose progeny is innumerable"] ("Prólogo a Edgar Allan Poe, *La carta robada*" 10).

18. Borges's thoughts on precursors are almost always cited from the 1951 Kafka essay that focuses specifically on this topic. However, Borges had already offered a shorter version of his theory of influence two years earlier in his article "Hawthorne"—a lecture he delivered at the Colegio Libre on March 23, 1949, that appeared in print in July of the same year in *Cursos y conferencias*. While analyzing Nathaniel Hawthorne's short story "Wakefield," Borges claims the following: "La circunstancia, la extraña circunstancia, de percibir en un cuento de Hawthorne, redactado a principios del siglo XIX, el sabor mismo de los cuentos de Kafka, que trabajó a principios del siglo XX, no debe hacernos olvidar que el sabor de Kafka ha sido creado, ha sido determinado, por Kafka. 'Wakefield' prefigura a Franz Kafka, pero éste modifica, y afina, la lectura de 'Wakefield.' La deuda es mutua; un gran escritor crea a sus precursores. Los crea y de algún modo los justifica" ["The circumstance, the strange circumstance, of perceiving in a tale of Hawthorne, composed at the beginning of nineteenth century,

the very flavor of the tales of Kafka, who worked at the beginning of the twentieth century, should not make us forget that the flavor of Kafka has been created, has been determined, by Kafka. 'Wakefield' foreshadows Franz Kafka, but the latter modifies, and refines, the reading of 'Wakefield.' The debt is mutual; a great writer creates his precursors. He creates them and in some manner justifies them"] (232).

19. Pierre Bayard has recently offered similar thoughts in even more provocative terms in his 2009 book *Le plagiat par anticipation*. Bayard argues that former writers actually plagiarize later writers through a process he dubs "anticipatory plagiarism," and he suggests that studying literature with this concept in mind will require a complete rewriting of literary history ("Anticipatory Plagiarism" 231).

20. Before Bloom's own *The Anatomy of Influence*, which admits in passing that Borges eschews rivalry but does not take the next step of pointing out how Bloom's theory revolves around the idea that Borges rejects, I know of only one other text that argues that Bloom's theory misreads Borges's Kafka essay. In a little-known piece, "Borges / de Man / Derrida / Bloom: La desconstrucción 'Avant et après la lettre," which Emir Rodríguez Monegal published in Uruguay in a collection on deconstruction, he calls out his fellow Yale professor by claiming that Borges's Kafka essay has nothing to do with rivalry between writers and that Bloom "confunde intertextualidad con parricidio" ["confuses intertextuality with parricide"] (123). In contrast to Bloom's portrayal of anxiety, Rodríguez Monegal suggested, decades earlier in one of his books on Quiroga, that "ningún escritor fuerte [. . .] teme" ["no strong writer . . . fears"] the authors who influence him/her (*La objectividad* 23).

21. Considering the inherent oedipal nature of the detective genre, Irwin offers several passages of analysis to suggest that Borges does view his rewriting of Poe's detective tales as a competition (163, 303–07). Borges, however, never suggests this in his own writings; instead, he defends Poe from the critiques of his twentieth-century readers by claiming that while we might see Poe's solutions—e.g., the orangutan killer of "The Murders in the Rue Morgue"—as transparent, we only do so because we are already trained in the very tradition that Poe began ("El cuento policial" 230, 235–36; "The Detective Story" 492, 496–97). He argues that "[n]osotros, al leer una novela policial, somos una invención de Edgar Allan Poe" ["we, when reading a detective novel, are an invention of Edgar Allan Poe"] (236).

22. In Casanova's terms, this first section reveals the literary world in which Borges responds to Poe above and beyond any political or economic connections between each author's nation, creating a "literary history of literature" rather than a "historical history of literature," a phrase that Casanova borrows from Lucien Febvre (350).

Chapter 1. Borges's Philosophy of Poe's Composition

1. Borges delivered this praise of Poe and Whitman in the following texts: "El cuento policial" (231), "Prólogo a Edgar Allan Poe, *La carta robada*" (9), "Prólogo a Edgar Allan Poe, *Cuentos*" (646), and "Sobre la llegada del hombre a la Luna" with Osvaldo Ferrari (40). His most famous rendition of Poe giving birth to Baudelaire and the French symbolists appears in "Pierre Menard, autor del Quijote" ["Pierre Menard, Author of the *Quixote*"] (447; 92), but Borges made the same claim in the Buenos Aires

daily *La Nación* in 1949 ("Edgar Allan Poe" 1), in his coauthored *Introducción a la literatura norteamericana* [*An Introduction to American Literature*] (9; 5), and in one of his many dialogues with Ferrari ("Sobre Edgar" 190).

2. In "Indagación de la palabra," Borges alludes to both "The Philosophy of Composition" and "The Poetic Principle" by mentioning Poe's famous claims that "no hay poemas largos" ["long poems do not exist"] (17–18). He makes a similar claim in a 1934 prologue for a book of poetry by Elvira de Alvear ("Prólogo a Elvira de Alvear, *Reposo*" 105).

3. Unless otherwise noted, all italics in passages from Poe are his own.

4. The translations of Poe's most famous advocate, Charles Baudelaire, reveal the fiction-like qualities of "The Raven." Baudelaire translated forty-four of Poe's stories and only four of his poems, including "The Raven," which he translated in prose rather than verse. Santiago Ferrari calls "The Raven" "un cuento en verso" ["a story in verse"] (27) and suggests that several of Poe's poems are stories (28).

5. In "La última invención de Hugh Walpole," which Borges published in *La Nación* in 1943, he demonstrates his own proclivity for short fiction over novels by applying Poe's ideas on poetry to fiction. He states, "Edgar Allan Poe, en *The Philosophy of Composition* (1846) y en *The poetic principle* (1850), arguye que los poemas largos no existen, ya que de hecho se resuelven en una sucesión de poemas breves, por imposibilidad de agotarlos en una sola lectura; ese argumento es trasladable a la prosa y cabría razonar que la novela no es un género literario sino un mero simulacro tipográfico" ["Edgar Allan Poe, in 'The Philosophy of Composition' (1846) and in 'The Poetic Principle' (1850), argues that long poems do not exist since they actually become a succession of brief poems due to the impossibility of exhausting them in a single reading; this argument is transferable to prose, and it would make sense to reason that the novel is not a literary genre but a mere typographical simulacrum"] (207–08).

6. Borges playfully emphasizes the importance of Poe's challenge to various schools of thought from the Romantics through the surrealists: "¡Del interlocutor de las musas, del poeta amanuense de un dios oscuro, pasar al mero devanador de razones! La lucidez en el lugar de la inspiración, la inteligencia comprensible y no el genio, ¡qué desencanto para los contemporáneos de Hugo y aun para los de Breton y Dalí!" ["From the speaker of the muses, from the amanuensis-poet of a dark god, to become a mere weaver of reason! Lucidity in the place of inspiration, understandable intelligence and not genius, what disillusionment for Hugo's contemporaries and even for those of Breton and Dalí!"] (2).

7. Borges takes the humble route in this article by following the previous sentence with the following parenthetical remark: "(Es la tarea vitalicia de Valéry)" ["(This is Valéry's life work)"] (2). Although he does not further the argument of the Romantic professing a theory of poetry based on the classical respect for reason in this article, Borges returns to this very point in several of his other pieces, including "Flaubert y su destino ejemplar" (263 n.1), "Juan Ramón Jiménez" (41), *Introducción a la literatura norteamericana* (18), the prologue to *El informe de Brodie* (457–58), and "Prólogo a Edgar Allan Poe, *Cuentos*" (647). Borges remains both puzzled and pleased with Plato's preference for the muse and Poe's preference for the intellect as the source of poetry. Throughout his career, Borges comments on this strange phenomenon with

statements like the following: "No deja de admirarme que los clásicos profesaron una tesis romántica, y un poeta romántico, una tesis clásica" ("Prólogo," *El informe* 458) ["I never cease to be amazed that the classics professed a Romantic theory while a Romantic poet espoused a classical one"] ("Foreword," *Brodie's Report* 346).

8. La Fundación Internacional Jorge Luis Borges, created and directed by María Kodama, maintains one of Borges's personal libraries. The other is held by Argentina's National Library and is a part of their Sala del Tesoro. The library held by the Fundación contains hundreds of books in several languages, and scores of the books contain Borges's personal notes—typically in the front or back covers of the texts rather than in the margins. Almost all the notes that Borges left in his copies of Poe are quotes with page numbers rather than commentary. The notes are in one of four hands—Borges's medium hand, Borges's small hand, the hand of Borges's mother—Leonor Acevedo de Borges—and María Kodama's hand. The collection of Borges's personal books held at the national library includes over five hundred books that also contain Borges's notes in the covers. In 2010 librarians Laura Rosato and Germán Álvarez published *Borges, libros y lecturas*, a book that catalogs the handwritten comments Borges left behind in 496 of these texts and offers extensive explanations for most of Borges's notes.

9. The size of Borges's handwriting and/or the inclusion of the notes that he dictated to Mrs. Borges and María Kodama reveal approximate dates for Borges's notes, even in texts that he did not date. Both Kodama and Loewenstein insist that Borges's writing decreased in size as his eyesight slowly deteriorated. Any notes in Borges's mother's hand range from the mid-1950s to her death in 1975, and the notes in Kodama's hand are from 1975 to Borges's death in 1986. Borges was famous for continually revising his own texts, and several of the manuscripts held in the Jorge Luis Borges Collection at the Albert and Shirley Small Special Collections Library at the University of Virginia show Borges's revisions. These manuscripts also confirm the shift in Borges's handwriting since the original texts—dated in the early 1920s—are written in Borges's medium handwriting while the revisions—dated in the early 1940s—are always in a smaller, tighter script.

10. In "El jardín de senderos que se bifurcan," Borges portrays time, rather than thought, as both fragmented and total. Stephen Albert relates to Yu Tsun that in Ts'ui Pên's conception of reality, time splits at every moment and that an infinite number of times coexist, collide, and contain every possible outcome: "Creía en infinitas series de tiempos, en una red creciente y vertiginosa de tiempos divergentes, convergentes y paralelos. Esa trama de tiempos que se aproximan, se bifurcan, se cortan o que secularmente se ignoran, abarca *todas* las posibilidades" (479) ["He believed in an infinite series of times, a growing, dizzying web of divergent, convergent, and parallel times. That fabric of times that approach one another, fork, are snipped off, or are simply unknown for centuries, contains *all* possibilities"] ("The Garden" 127). The story itself plays out this thesis as Yu Tsun, whom Albert considers a friend, ends up enacting some of Albert's hypothetical currents of time in which he is Albert's enemy or in which he finds Albert dead (479; 127).

11. In "El cuento policial," Borges emphasizes that Poe's choice of a raven as speaker is one option among many, and he suggests that this choice is easier to explain

in the essay than some of the other options might have been. "Poe pudo haber llegado a la idea del ser irracional usando, no un cuervo, sino un idiota, un borracho; entonces ya tendríamos un poema completamente distinto y menos explicable" (233) ["Poe could have reached the idea of an irrational being by using not a raven but an idiot, a drunkard; we would have then had a completely different and less explicable poem"] ("The Detective Story" 494). However, Poe's preference for the animal over the human in this case might not be based primarily on the supposed ease of analyzing the poem with the raven as the speaker of the refrain since the talking raven recalls Poe's usage of the orangutan in "The Murders in the Rue Morgue." In both the tale and the poem, an animal plays a significant and destructive role in human life by mimicking human behavior—shaving and speech—without the logic behind the action.

12. In "El cuento policial," Borges reiterates that it is Poe's personal preference and experience that lead him toward a raven as the speaker of the refrain. He states: "Pensó en un loro, pero un loro es indigno de la dignidad de la poesía; entonces pensó en un cuervo. O sea, que estaba leyendo en aquel momento la novela de Charles Dickens *Barnaby Rudge*, en la cual hay un cuervo. De modo que él tenía un cuervo que se llama *Never more* y que repite continuamente su nombre. Eso es todo lo que Poe tenía al principio" (232) ["He thought about making it a parrot, but a parrot is unworthy of the dignity of poetry; then he thought of a raven. Or rather, he was reading Charles Dickens' novel *Barnaby Rudge* at the time, in which a raven figures. So he had a raven which is named Nevermore and which continually repeats its name. That is all Poe started out with"] ("The Detective Story" 494). In *A Fable for Critics*, Poe's contemporary, James Russell Lowell, had both mocked Poe and suggested that his idea of a talking raven was not completely original by quipping: "There comes Poe with his raven, like Barnaby Rudge, / Three-fifths of him genius and two-fifths sheer fudge" (78).

13. These English translations of "El cuento policial" are Esther Allen's, and they are found in "The Detective Story" in Eliot Weinberger's edition of *Selected Non-Fictions*. In an interview with María Ester Gilio, Borges offers similar sentiments from a literary rather than a realist perspective: "Lo que me atraía de la novela policial era que de alguna manera estaba defendiendo lo clásico, el orden. Mientras que la literatura de cierta época y quizás también la de ahora tienden al caos" ["What attracted me to the detective novel was that in some manner it was defending the classical, order. While the literature of certain epochs and perhaps also the literature of today tends toward chaos"] (47).

14. Poe's original line in the 1843 serialized publication of the third section of "The Mystery of Marie Rogêt," published in *Ladies' Companion*, points only to murder and does not leave the possibility of a "fatal accident." Poe introduced the idea of an accident in subsequent versions in order to square the story with the news of Mary Rogers's botched abortion. In both cases, Dupin takes the same approach of "summing up" the analysis that makes up the bulk of the story.

15. Darío is not alone when equating the Greek and Roman concept of the muse with a Judeo-Christian version of the concept of faith. Even Borges suggests that the dichotomies muse vs. mind and inspiration vs. intellect can be described in spiritual terms. In the prologue to his book *La rosa profunda*, he states: "Por Musa debemos entender lo que los hebreos y Milton llamaron el Espíritu y lo que nuestra triste mi-

tología llama lo Subconsciente" (97) ["For Muse, we must read what the Hebrews and Milton called Spirit, and what our own woeful mythology refers to as the Subconscious"] ("Prologue," *The Unending Rose* 343), and in "El cuento policial" he claims that Poe's argument that poetry is born of the mind "se opone a toda la tradición anterior, donde la poesía era una operación del espíritu" (231) ["goes against the whole of prior tradition, for which poetry was an operation of the spirit"] ("The Detective Story" 493).

16. This is not to say that the *modernistas* despised all of Poe's literary criticism. Indeed, Poe's praise in "The Poetic Principle" for "the poem written solely for the poem's sake" (5) and his favoring of beauty in this later essay both allow for Darío's hyperbolic descriptions of Poe as an artist who creates art for art's sake in "Los raros."

17. Like Baudelaire before him, Darío reads Poe as an anomaly in, rather than a product of, the United States. Darío goes on to suggest that Poe inherits his "don mitológico" ["mythological gift"] (262) from his ancestors the Le Poer family, paraphrasing the words of Sarah Helen Whitman in *Edgar Poe and His Critics* (85–88). Borges, as I will demonstrate in my analysis of his 1949 article "Edgar Allan Poe," vehemently rejects any reading that divorces Poe from the United States.

18. While I cite Allen's translation of "El cuento policial"—"The Detective Story"—throughout this chapter, the translation in the sentence above is my own. Borges's friend and frequent cowriter Adolfo Bioy Casares also confirms Borges's lingering suspicions about "The Philosophy of Composition" in his recollections entitled *Borges*. Bioy Casares affirms that in 1959 Borges considered Poe's and Paul Valéry's attempts to cast poetry as the victory of reason as "inexacta e inadecuada" ["inexact and inadequate"] (551).

19. "La poesía" was the fifth of seven lectures that Borges gave at the Coliseo theater in Buenos Aires from June through August of 1977.

20. Borges's suggestion resonates well with his portrayals of predetermination in several short stories, essays, and interviews.

21. I include the extended passages here in the notes for comparison. From "Borges on Borges": "I think it is a rather passive process. I mean, I may be walking down the street and suddenly feel that something is about to happen. And then I glimpse something—let us say—I glimpse the end of a story, or I may glimpse the beginning, but generally both of them at the same time, then I try to find out what was in between. That, of course, is only revealed to me through patient work. I have to go in for writing, I have to imagine the setting[,] I have to invent the characters, and so on. And then if I am lucky I may write a story or a poem. But at first the thing is given to me and generally I'm given the end of a story, the end of a poem, and I have to work up to it. I try to interfere very little with my own work. That goes on, of course, and I try to reject it, and then, I sit patiently down. I write it in order to be rid of it, finally to publish it and forget it" (13). Borges's claim that he publishes his texts in order to forget them is less than genuine as his attempts to ignore or to physically destroy copies of his earliest books—*Inquisiciones* and *El tamaño de mi esperanza*—and his tendency to revise pieces time and time again for republication suggest. From "Cómo nace y se hace un texto de Borges": "Empieza por una suerte de revelación. Pero uso esa palabra de un modo modesto, no ambicioso. Es decir, de pronto sé que va a ocurrir algo y eso

que va a ocurrir puede ser, en el caso de un cuento, el principio y el fin. En el caso de un poema, no: es una idea más general, y a veces ha sido la primera línea. Es decir, algo me es dado, y luego ya intervengo yo, y quizá se echa todo a perder (*ríe*). En el caso de un cuento, por ejemplo, bueno, yo conozco el principio, el punto de partida, conozco el fin, conozco la meta. Pero luego tengo que descubrir, mediante mis muy limitados medios, qué sucede entre el principio y el fin" ["It begins with a type of revelation. But I use that word in a modest fashion, not ambitious. In other words, suddenly I know that something is going to occur and that thing which is going to occur can be, in the case of a story, the beginning and the end. In the case of a poem, no: it is a more general idea, and at times it has been the first line. In other words, something is given to me, and then I intervene, and perhaps the whole thing is ruined (*he laughs*). In the case of a story, for example, well, I know the beginning, the starting point, I know the end, I know the goal. But then I have to discover, through my very limited means, what happens between the beginning and the end"] (62). María Kodama also describes Borges's creative process as muse driven. She claims that Eduardo Comesaña's famous photograph that shows Borges with his face slightly tilted upward and his eyes shut tight is one of her favorites because it captures the look on Borges's face "cuando se le venía un poema" ["when a poem came to him"]. Kodama recalls that Borges would get a similar look on his face, stop whatever he was doing, and then ask her to transcribe the lines of the poem that inspiration had delivered (Personal Interview).

22. Borges pulls the opening line of this quote almost directly from a letter he wrote to Ramón Sopena in 1935 in response to this editor's question "¿QUÉ PIENSA USTED DE SÍ MISMO?" ["WHAT DO YOU THINK OF YOURSELF?"] in which Borges claimed "[v]aría la respuesta según la hora, la temperatura, régimen dietético, o las personas que no espero ver" ["[t]he answer would vary depending on the hour, the temperature, diet, or the people whom I hope not to see"] (["Letter to Ramón Sopena"] 1). In this letter, he claims, "No puedo no escribir sin ese peculiar sentimiento de miseria engendrado por la cobardía y la deslealtad [. . .] soy inteligente con las personas inteligentes; nulo con los estúpidos" ["I cannot not write without that peculiar feeling of misery bred by cowardice and disloyalty [. . .] I am intelligent with intelligent people; useless with stupid ones"] (1). This letter is written in Borges's medium hand on two postcards, and it is held in the Jorge Luis Borges Collection at the Small Special Collections Library at the University of Virginia.

23. My reference to the king and the prefect as blind characters plays off of Jacques Lacan's famous interpretation of "The Purloined Letter" that he offered in his "Seminar on 'The Purloined Letter'" in 1956. For a succinct critique of Lacan's analysis of "The Purloined Letter," Jacques Derrida's response, and how both thinkers' interpretations of the story link back to Borges, see pages 1–12 and 442–49 in Irwin's *The Mystery to a Solution*.

24. Borges published an early version of "Las *Kenningar*" in *Sur* in 1932 as "Noticia de las *kenningar*." This piece is significantly shorter than the 1933 version of *Las Kenningar*, which was published as a book from Francisco A. Colombo and the 1936 version "Las *Kenningar*" collected in *Historia de la eternidad*. The 1932 version does not contain any kennings for "el cuervo" while the 1933 version contains only two.

Neither of the earlier versions contains the kenning "primo del cuervo" nor the Poe footnote, which both appear in Borges's 1936 revision of the text.

25. Obligado's 1932 translation of Poe's poetry—*Los poemas de Edgar Poe: Traducción, prólogo y notas*—is one of the finest translations of Poe's poetry into the Spanish language. Obligado's version of "El cuervo" is particularly impressive. While Pérez Bonalde's earlier translation of "The Raven" is still the most popular version of the poem in Spanish America, it does not match the rigor of either the meter or the rhyme/assonance that Obligado offers in his translation of the poem.

26. Obligado repeated these sentiments in a reading of his translations at the Instituto Popular de Conferencias in Buenos Aires, arguing that "Poe no fue en manera alguna el semi-desequilibrado y el alcoholista impenitente que inventó cierta ojeriza puritana" ["Poe was not in any way the semi-unbalanced person and unrepentant alcoholic that a certain Puritanical grudge invented"] ("Los poemas" 68). Darío also "realized that [Poe] had long been the unfortunate victim of Puritanical bias and of selfish literary revenge" (Englekirk 180), but rather than challenging Griswold's portrayal of Poe, Darío identified with and sympathized with the Poe whom Griswold gave the world.

27. Over three decades later, Borges makes a move that was typical of nineteenth- and early twentieth-century studies of Poe in various languages—he links Poe's death to one of his literary works. In "Prólogo a Edgar Allan Poe, *Cuentos*," Borges describes Poe's deathbed as follows: "En el delirio repitió las palabras que había puesto en boca de un marinero que murió, en uno de sus primeros relatos, en el confín del Polo Sur. En 1849 el marinero y él murieron a un tiempo" ["In delirium he repeated the words that he had placed in the mouth of a sailor who died, in one of his first tales, in the confines of the South Pole. In 1849 the sailor and he died at the same time"] (646). This conflation of Poe's literary creations and his reality only further romanticizes his image, but, importantly, it romanticizes his image through his fiction rather than his poetry. Borges does not claim that the dying Poe repeats the word "Nevermore."

28. Borges makes a similar claim in his 1985 "Prólogo a Edgar Allan Poe, *La carta robada*": "A la obra escrita de un hombre debemos muchas veces agregar otra quizá más importante: la imagen que de ese hombre se proyecta en la memoria de las generaciones. Byron, por ejemplo, es más perdurable y más vívido que la obra de Byron. Edgar Allan Poe es más visible ahora que cualquiera de las páginas que compuso y aun más que la suma de esas páginas" ["To a man's written work we should, many times, add another, perhaps more important: the image of this man that is projected in the memory of the generations. Byron, for example, is more everlasting and vivid than the work of Byron. Edgar Allan Poe is more visible now than any of the pages he wrote and even more than the whole of those pages put together"] (9), suggesting that our contemporary image or construct of Poe supersedes not only Poe's poetry but his fiction and his complete written corpus as well.

29. Darío, too, sees the importance of Poe's image. Indeed, a large portion of "Los raros" focuses on Poe's physical features while the entire piece could be cataloged as a description of Poe's image rather than his actual work. Still, Darío's image of Poe as poet rests on Poe's poems, particularly on the lost lovers and female presences within

several poems. In "Los raros," Darío suggests that Poe's Irene, Eulalie, Lenore, Frances, Ulalume, Helen, Annie, Annabel Lee, and Ligeia bring Darío's own dead wife into his memory (260–61). Only one of these women exists in Poe's world of fiction; the remaining eight all occupy the melancholy world of his poetry.

30. Borges first published "El otro Whitman" in 1929 in the journal *La vida literaria*, an important venue for the Río de la Plata literati that consistently published articles by local writers such as Lugones, Quiroga, and Ezequiel Martínez Estrada and various well-known foreign writers including Peruvian José Carlos Mariátegui and U.S. traveler Waldo Frank. "El otro Whitman" was the only article Borges published in *La vida literaria;* however, this version of the article does not contain the Poe reference that Borges introduces in the 1932 version of the piece.

31. Bioy Casares's *Borges* also confirms that Borges favored Poe's prose over his poetry. Bioy Casares recalls Borges calling Poe a minor or poor poet several times (893, 1200, 1466).

32. While Von Schauenberg's collection does not rival those of Soto y Calvo and Obligado, various editors of Poe collections in the Southern Cone who piece Poe's poems together using multiple translators (including Soto y Calvo, Obligado, Pérez Bonalde, and several others) reprint Von Schauenberg's translations of several poems. Von Schauenberg nods to these other recent translations in his prologue and justifies the necessity of his translations by claiming that he hopes "lograr la reproducción de algún efecto no conseguido o alguna semejanza no alcanzada anteriormente" ["to achieve the reproduction of some effect not obtained or some similarity not reached before"] (14).

33. Englekirk demonstrates that Spain has always preferred Poe's stories over his poetry (34, 118), but Poe's poems, not his tales, created his iconic image in Spanish America in the late nineteenth and early twentieth centuries.

Chapter 2. Reading and Rereading

1. I cite Andrew Hurley's translation here although it would be more direct to translate the phrase as "reading does not matter but rereading does" or as "rereading is more important than reading."

2. Borges delivered "El libro" as the first of five lectures that he shared with la Universidad de Belgrano in Buenos Aires in 1978. The lecture was first published in 1979 in *Borges, oral* which now appears in the fourth volume of Borges's *Obras completas*.

3. "Prólogo a Wilkie Collins, *La piedra lunar*" serves as one of the many examples in which Borges calls Poe the creator of detective fiction. In this prologue, Borges describes "The Murders in the Rue Morgue" as "el primer cuento policial que registra la historia. Este relato fija las leyes esenciales del género: el crimen enigmático y, a primera vista, insoluble, el investigador sedentario que lo descifra por medio de la imaginación y de la lógica, el caso referido por un amigo impersonal, y un tanto borroso, del investigador" ["the first detective story recorded by history. This tale sets the essential laws of the genre: the enigmatic and, at first sight, insoluble crime, the sedentary investigator who figures it out through imagination and logic, the case related by an impersonal and slightly confused friend of the investigator"] (55).

4. Borges lists Poe's "MS. Found in a Bottle" as one of five stories to illustrate this point (365).

5. In *Invisible Work: Borges and Translation*, Efraín Kristal suggests that Borges also mixes the supernatural with the detective genre in his famous short story "La muerte y la brújula" ["Death and the Compass"] (xvii).

6. Caillois's use of "amor propio" could also be translated as "self-esteem" rather than the literal "self-love" I offer in text. However, I feel that the latter translation better matches the sarcastic tone of Caillois's concluding sentence in his response to Borges.

7. This essay is held in notebook number 2 of box 5 and folder 6 of the Julio Cortázar Literary Manuscripts at the Benson Latin American Collection at the University of Texas at Austin.

8. Borges repeatedly mentioned his debt to Caillois. For example, in a conversation with Roberto Alifano, Borges noted Caillois's "generosidad" ["generosity"] for forgetting their argument about detective fiction and supporting Borges's work in France ("La literatura policial—Poe y Chesterton" 15). At other times, Borges approached his relationship with Caillois in more ironic tones. For example, Alain Bosquet claims that upon being introduced to Borges by Caillois, "Borges me tendió una mano vacilante que enseguida se hizo más firme, y me dijo en un tono muy irónico, no desprovisto de calor: '—Ah, sin Roger Caillois, yo no existiría; él es mi inventor.' Luego añadió '—Soy un personaje de un libro de Caillois. Y ahora, dominado por la duda, es él quien cree ser un personaje creado por Borges'" ["Borges held out his shaky hand to me that at once became more steady, and he told me in an ironic tone, not devoid of warmth: 'Ah, without Roger Caillois, I would not exist; he is my inventor.' He quickly added, 'I am a character in a book by Caillois. And now, dominated by doubt, he is the one who believes he is a character created by Borges'"] (1).

9. Borges's career as a visiting scholar in the U.S. and the U.K. also began in the wake of the Formentor Prize. The award was announced in early May 1961, and he began his first stint as a visiting professor at the University of Texas at Austin during the fall semester of that same year.

10. These rejection slips are held as a part of the Alfred A. Knopf, Inc. records at the Harry Ransom Center at the University of Texas at Austin. They are filed under "Records. Series VI., Editorial Department Files, 1915–1984 (bulk 1948–1978)."

11. Casanova's claims that "[c]onsecration in Paris is indispensable for authors from all dominated literary spaces: translations, critical studies, tributes, and commentaries represent so many judgments and verdicts that confer value upon a text that until now has remained outside world literary space or otherwise gone unnoticed within" (127) and that "Paris has become the place where books—submitted to critical judgment and transmuted—can be denationalized and their authors made universal. By virtue of its status as the central bank of literature, to revert to the terms employed earlier, Paris is able to create literary value and extend terms of credit everywhere in the world" (127) seem very applicable in the case of Borges's translations into English. Ironically, Borges, who never looked to Paris for literary acceptance, reached the English-speaking world in a translated volume only after his work was consecrated in Paris.

12. For a fascinating read on how getting even functions as one-upping in Poe and Borges and how this concept is repeated in the relationship between Jacques Lacan and Jacques Derrida, see Irwin's *The Mystery to a Solution*, especially chapters 1, 3, and 45.

13. Apart from a few minor changes, the essays mirror each other until their conclusions. For the latter article, Borges deletes his original concluding paragraph, which I will refer to shortly, and replaces it with two paragraphs of analysis of Chesterton's detective fiction. "Los laberintos policiales y Chesterton" is available in English translation, and I cite Eliot Weinberger's translation of the text—"The Labyrinths of the Detective Story and Chesterton." In his discussion of detective stories that distance themselves from the crime, Borges also names Baroness Orczy's collection *Unravelled Knots* as a more contemporary example (127; 112).

14. In "Los laberintos policiales y Chesterton," Borges suggests that the rules apply more particularly to the "carácter problemático, estricto" (127) ["strict, problematic nature"] (113) of short fiction while he does not make this distinction in "Leyes de la narración policial."

15. This book also contains comments in Borges's small hand, but these two notations are in Kodama's hand, which reveals that Borges "took" these notes during one of his rereadings of "The Purloined Letter" sometime between 1975 and 1986. The former quote is missing the "a" between "is" and "little" from Poe's text.

16. I owe this observation to Ed Cutler, whose fascinating presentation at the Poe Studies Association's Third International Edgar Allan Poe Conference: The Bicentennial—"Coincidence and the Literary Absolute: Poe's German Romantic Inheritance"—stressed the point that the issue in Poe's second Dupin story is not murder but coincidence. Marie Rogêt herself—the coincidence of her existence and the coincidence of her death in circumstances so similar to those of the actual Mary Rogers—Cutler suggests, is the real mystery of the story.

17. Poe originally published "The Mystery of Marie Rogêt" serially in late 1842 through early 1843. However, he added the suggestion of an accident to the version of the story that appeared in the 1845 *Tales* edition.

18. Poe's murderous ape may seem ridiculous to some readers, but Thomas Ollive Mabbott notes in his scholarly edition of Poe's tales that Poe's idea of the criminal primate has historical antecedents ("The Murders" 522–24). Also, for twenty-first-century readers, the orangutan attack seems less outrageous than it might have appeared previously since the violent attack on Charla Nash by her friend's pet chimpanzee in February 2009 received prime-time news coverage for days.

19. Borges not only suggests that the creation of a quality detective plot requires more intellectual work than the writing of a sonnet, but he also suggests that it takes more mental rigor than "molestos diálogos entre desocupados de nombre griego o de poesías en forma de Carlos Marx o de ensayos siniestros sobre el centenario de Goethe, el problema de la mujer, Góngora precursor, la étnica sexual, Oriente y Occidente, el alma del tango, la deshumanización del arte, y otras inclinaciones de la ignominia" ["bothersome dialogues between idle men with Greek names; or of poems in the form of Karl Marx; or of sinister essays about the centennial of Goethe, the woman problem, Góngora as precursor, sexual ethnicity, East and West, the soul of

tango, the dehumanization of art, and other inclinations of ignominy"] (39). "[É]tnica sexual" appears to be a misprint in the reprinted version of the article since "ética sexual" or "sexual ethics" makes much more sense in context.

20. Borges ends this commentary on *Pym* by suggesting that Poe's image is more prevalent today than any of his works: "de hecho, su obra capital es la imagen trágica que ha legado a la posteridad" ["actually, his seminal work is the tragic image that he has passed on to posterity"] (353).

21. I cite Suzanne Jill Levine's translation as published in Eliot Weinberger's edited volume of Borges's *Selected Non-Fictions*.

22. This notation is in Borges's medium hand, so although it is not dated, Borges wrote it before the 1940s when his eyesight worsened and his script decreased in size. Thus, this copy of *Pym* could be the one Borges cites in "El arte narrativo y la magia" in 1932. See the previous chapter for further details about Borges's handwriting.

23. Poe's avoidance of a term that reveals the text's secret is not only Mallarmé-like; it is also very Borgesian. Nine years after writing "El arte narrativo y la magia," Borges published his famous short story "El jardín de senderos que se bifurcan," in which Stephen Albert explains to Yu Tsun that his ancestor's novel/labyrinth is "una enorme adivinanza, o parábola, cuyo tema es el tiempo; esa causa recóndita le prohíbe la mención de su nombre" (478–79) ["a huge riddle, or parable, whose subject is time; that secret purpose forbids Ts'ui Pen the merest mention of its name"] (126). Irwin provides a powerful interpretation of "El jardín de senderos que se bifurcan" alongside Poe's "The Mystery of Marie Rogêt" as a part of his reading of Borges's doubling of Poe's Dupin trilogy (420–21), but I am not aware of any literary critics who connect the riddle in Borges's story back to Poe's novel.

24. Borges's notations in his Poe texts also demonstrate how he perennially reread Poe. The notes in his medium hand, his small hand, his mother's hand, and Kodama's hand suggest that he was reading or having Poe read to him throughout the twentieth century.

Chapter 3. Theory, Practice, and *Pym*

1. Efraín Kristal's *Invisible Work: Borges and Translation* stands out as an exception to this rule. Kristal dedicates about ten pages to an engaging examination of Borges's version of "The Purloined Letter"—both as a translation and as an influence on Borges's own fiction. He does not, however, offer an extended analysis of Borges's translation of "Valdemar," nor does he approach Borges's *Pym* fragments.

2. Even-Zohar's description of what he means when he calls a translated literature central to a literary polysystem almost directly describes the place of Poe's work in the Argentine, Río de la Plata region, and Spanish American literary polysystems. He states: "To say that translated literature maintains a central position in the literary polysystem means that it participates actively in shaping the center of the polysystem. In such a situation it is by and large an integral part of innovatory forces, and as such likely to be identified with major events in literary history while these are taking place. This implies that in this situation no clear-cut distinction is maintained between 'original' and 'translated' writings, and that often it is the leading writers (or members

of the avant-garde who are about to become leading writers) who produce the most conspicuous or appreciated translations" (193).

3. My comparative analysis fits within Holmes's descriptions of "product-oriented DTS" while my examination of the place Borges's Poe translations creates for Poe within these literary polysystems would be described by Holmes as "function-based DTS" (176–77).

4. In claiming that Borges "domesticates" Poe's texts, I refer to the terminology of "domestication" and "foreignization" as examined by Lawrence Venuti in *The Translator's Invisibility: A History of Translation* and by several other translation studies scholars. Venuti focuses primarily on texts translated into English, and he consistently criticizes domestication as a form of ethnocentrism while favoring translations that emphasize rather than hide a translation's foreign origins. His disparaging views of domestication, however, appear less applicable to translations from English into less dominant languages. Sergio Waisman argues that for Borges and other Latin American writers, domestication of an English-language text through translation into Spanish or Portuguese can alter the power dynamics between the center and the periphery and "function as a form of resistance" (80–81).

5. One example of many in which Borges praises Poe's imagination but criticizes his language can be found in his review "*Edgar Allan Poe*, de Edward Shanks." Borges applauds Poe's accomplishments even while admitting that "cada página" ["each page"] is full of "redundancias y languideces" ["redundancies and weaknesses"] (333).

6. Esther Allen's translation of Borges's "The Translators of *The Thousand and One Nights*," for example, appears in Venuti's edited volume *The Translation Studies Reader*. In *Translation and Identity in the Americas: New Directions in Translation Theory*, Edwin Gentzler notes how Borges's ideas about translation foresee current translation studies. He states, "In many ways, Borges's theory precedes translation studies in dissecting basic concepts such as faithfulness and equivalence with his much more humane and ironic stance regarding fidelity" (111).

7. In *After Babel: Aspects of Language and Translation*, George Steiner states: "Arguably, 'Pierre Menard, Author of the *Quixote*' (1939) is the most acute, most concentrated commentary anyone has offered on the business of translation. What studies of translation there are, including this book, could, in Borges's style, be termed a commentary on his commentary" (73).

8. In his analysis of "Sobre el 'Vathek' de William Beckford," Waisman avers that through this piece "[t]he very concept [of fidelity] loses meaning as its prejudices are revealed. After Borges's inversion, it becomes as valid to ask if the original is faithful to the translation, as the other way around. The use of paradox serves to empty fidelity of its preconceptions. It shows it to be an unnecessary, biased judgment traditionally used to assert the power of the original over the translation by demanding its loyalty to it" (115).

9. "Los traductores de *Las 1001 noches*" is dated 1935, but it was not published until 1936 when it was included in Borges's *Historia de la eternidad*. Various pieces of this article were published earlier as "El puntual Mardrus" and "Las *1001* noches" in *Crítica: Revista multicolor de los sábados* in 1934. "Las dos maneras de traducir" first appeared in 1926 in *La Prensa* while "Las versiones homéricas" was first published

in *La Prensa* in 1932 and republished that same year in Borges's essay collection *Discusión*. Thus, Borges's ideas on translation, like his literary criticism and much of his fiction, were spread by both popular (daily) and highbrow publications.

10. "Las dos maneras de traducir" has not been translated into English. Here, I rely on Waisman's translation of the cited passage that he offers in his interpretation of Borges's essays on translation. Otherwise, translations from this essay are my own.

11. Most of Borges's important thoughts on translation include some reference to Poe. Poe appears in two of Borges's three early essays on translation, although Borges's reference to Poe in "Los traductores de *Las 1001 noches*" is much briefer than his discussion of Pérez Bonalde's translation of "The Raven" in "Las dos maneras de traducir." Borges also refers to Poe several times in his article on *Vathek*, and Poe plays a significant role in Borges's descriptions of Pierre Menard.

12. Carriego was an early twentieth-century street poet from Borges's neighborhood, Palermo, in the suburbs of Buenos Aires. Borges published a book on Carriego— *Evaristo Carriego*—in 1930.

13. By claiming that quality translations of poetry exist, Borges does not suggest that they are easy to produce. He goes on to discuss the difficulties of translating poetry compared to prose since in poetry "el sentido de una palabra no es lo que vale, sino su ambiente, su connotación, su ademán" ["the meaning of a word is not what matters, but rather its ambiance, its connotation, its expression"] (256–57).

14. Borges's division of the types of translation based on differences he sees between classicists and Romantics recalls his discussion I examined at length in chapter 1 of how Plato viewed poetry as muse driven while Poe saw it as a practice of the individual intellect. In both cases, Borges sees each stance as paradoxical.

15. The Spanish alphabet includes CH as its own letter following the letter C, making H the ninth letter in the system. The translation of "Las versiones homéricas" into English, then, loses this subtle hint at equality, at least for the English-only reader who will identify H as the eighth letter of the alphabet. The gist of Borges's example, however, is not lost in English translation since a comparison between 9 and H still resists the attempt to claim one as superior to the other.

16. Esther Allen translates Borges's phrase as "beautiful Newman-Arnold exchange" rather than "debate" in "The Translators of *The Thousand and One Nights*" (95).

17. The value of literal translations for Borges lies in their ability to juxtapose Homer's reality with "hábitos presentes" ["contemporary practices"] (243, 74). Borges elaborates on this idea in *This Craft of Verse* by suggesting that one positive element a literal translation can offer to its reader is a feeling of surprise and even beauty since certain literal phrases in the target language become strange in ways that they were not in the source text (65–68). He provides the English translation "song of songs" rather than "the best song" from the Bible (68) and Burton's title *Book of the Thousand Nights and a Night* rather than *Book of the Thousand and One Nights* (67) as examples of this phenomenon. Borges's thoughts on the type of surprise that can take place for the reader when reading a literal translation of an ancient or distant text prefigure the concept of foreignization in translation supported by Venuti and Antoine Berman.

18. Strategies 1, 2, and 4 all domesticate the source text in one form or fashion. Approach 3 can, but does not inherently, domesticate the source text since a specific addition may or may not be connected to the target culture and/or literary tradition. Approaches 1 through 4 also demonstrate several of the "deforming tendencies" that Antoine Berman examines in "Translation and the Trials of the Foreign."

19. I use italics here to mark the phrases that Borges cuts completely in his translation. Poe used italics to give emphasis to "limpidity" and "not." I have placed those words within quotation marks rather than in italics to maintain Poe's emphasis while avoiding confusion about which passages do not appear in Borges's translation.

20. The republications of this translation are almost verbatim. The version in Borges's and Bioy Casares's *Cuentos breves y extraordinarios* merely shifts the adjective/noun order of "perfecta separación" to "separación perfecta" in the last line (166). The versions in Borges's and Guerrero's *Manual de zoología fantástica* and *El libro de seres imaginarios* make that same minor change and also replace "[i]gnoro" ["I am unaware" or "I am ignorant"] with "[n]o sé" ["I do not know"], substitute "tornasolada" ["iridescent"] for "cambiante" ["changeable"], and drop "entera" ["entire"] from the phrase "entera masa" ["entire mass"] (24–25; 21–22).

21. Berman claims that rationalization "bears primarily on the syntactical structures of the original, starting with that most meaningful and changeable element in a prose text: *punctuation*. Rationalization recomposes sentences and the sequences of sentences, rearranging them according to a certain idea of discursive *order*" (288). Borges repeatedly changes Poe's word and phrase order, and these changes act as a form of domestication as he shifts Poe's English into Spanish. However, these changes seem minor compared to his complete elision of various phrases in this passage from *Pym*.

22. This elision also distorts the "scientific" style of *Pym*, which matched (or mocked) the verbosity of travel narratives and nature writing during the 1830s.

23. Both anthologies also include Borges's translation of the divisible water passage from *Pym*. The simple sentence that divides the two passages—"No menos singular era el agua de esas tierras australes" (24) ["no less singular was the water of these southern countries"]—demonstrates, once again, that Borges is interested in the strangeness of the water. The versions of the water passage in these anthologies contain minimal changes from the version Borges published in "El arte narrativo y la magia," which I list in note 20.

24. "Pata" in Spanish can be an animal's "paw/foot" or an animal's "leg." So while Poe's text talks about the animal's legs and its feet, Borges's refers to either one or the other.

25. "Drooping" would also work as a translation of these ears while "lop-eared" might serve as the best English translation if the text stated "orejas caídas" rather than "las orejas, que eran caídas."

Chapter 4. Facts and an Envelope

1. "La verdad sobre el caso de M. Valdemar" is typically described as being translated by Borges and Bioy Casares although nothing in the preliminary pages nor the

prologue to *Antología de la literatura fantástica* claims whether Ocampo was or was not involved in the translation process. The majority of my analysis of "Valdemar" and "La carta robada"—also a joint translation with Bioy Casares—will focus on Borges rather than on the pair. The similarities between the translation strategies in these two Poe stories and in the translations Borges offered on his own, along with Bioy Casares's fairly disparaging opinions on Poe (see Bioy Casares's *Borges*, pages 901–03), seem to justify this focus.

2. While Poe's tale was taken seriously by various readers involved in mesmerism in the early nineteenth century, the story itself continually casts doubt on the very events that the narrator tries to call "facts."

3. Olivera published his volume in Paris, but as his introductory "Al lector" notes, he did his work in Buenos Aires (vii). His volume was available in Argentina, and his translation of "Valdemar" appears to be the only Spanish-language version of the story translated directly from English, rather than from Baudelaire's French, during the nineteenth century. Neither Englekirk's, Heliodoro Valle's, nor Woodbridge's bibliographies contain Spanish American versions of "Valdemar" that predate Olivera's, and the two peninsular renditions of the tale that precede Olivera's translation were likely Spanish translations of Baudelaire's version of the story.

4. Bazán edited, but did not translate for, *Obras completas*. He cites R. Cansinos Assens, Carlos Olivera, Nicolás Estevanez, and Arturo Díaz Lorenzo as the four prose translators whose versions he uses in this edited volume, but he never clarifies which translator translated any given story. "El caso del señor Valdemar" is most likely from Estevanez or Díaz Lorenzo since it is not Olivera's version and since it did not appear in the volume that Cansinos Assens translated for a six-volume set from Ediciones Mateu in Madrid also entitled *Obras completas*. Due to this ambiguity, I will refer to this translation as "Bazán's edition" throughout my analysis. Bazán's collection was, by far, the most complete edition of Poe published in the Americas before Julio Cortázar's translations, and it was only rivaled by the six-volume set from Madrid mentioned above. I examine Cortázar's Poe translations in the epilogue.

5. Although Borges tries to not favor Arnold over Newman in his discussion of the Newman-Arnold debate on translation, reading him alongside Olivera, who makes claims such as "[h]acer una buena traducción, es hacer una buena copia. Cuanto menos subjetiva es una traducción, tanto mejor" ["Making a good translation is making a good copy. The less subjective a translation is, so much the better"] ("Al lector" iv), clearly places Borges on Arnold's side of the argument.

6. Bazán's edition follows Poe's source text and uses "o" ["or"] to divide degree from time period (211) while Olivera uses, instead, "extension" to describe the length of time: "tercero, la extensión del periodo por el que las vejaciones de la Muerte podían ser detenidas por este proceso" ["third, the extension of the period for which the humiliations of death could be detained by this process"] (246). Olivera's translation of this phrase, like Borges's, is less conditional than Poe's version or Bazán's edition; however, this is a unique moment in Olivera's translation, rather than a pattern, since the remainder of his text re-creates the doubt apparent in Poe's source text.

7. Both the Bazán edition and Olivera's translation follow Poe's source text in keeping the first-person singular. Bazán's edition states "cuando yo le dirigía una pregunta"

["when I directed a question to him"] (216), and Olivera's states "cuando dirigía á Mr. Valdemar alguna pregunta" ["when I directed to Mr. Valdemar a question"] (256).

8. Neither Olivera nor Bazán's translator writes the narrator out of this sentence. Olivera offers the following: "En todo ese tiempo el sonámbulo permaneció exactamente como lo he descrito la última ocasión" ["During that entire time the somnambulist remained exactly as I have described him on the last occasion"] (257), and Bazán's edition provides "Mientras tanto, el hipnotizado seguía en el mismo estado en que lo he descripto" ["Meanwhile, the hypnotized remained in the same state in which I have described him"] (217).

9. Olivera (250) and Bazán's translator (213) both label the narrator as the transcriber, following Poe's source text.

10. Once again, Olivera (247) and Bazán's translator (212) follow Poe's source text and call the narrator "P" rather than "Poe."

11. As I noted in chapter 2, Poe typically leaves a realistic path or escape valve in his tales that allows the skeptical reader to explain away any supernatural happenings. In these three stories, and in several others, Poe offers a realistic explanation for the bizarre events the narrators describe—in "The Black Cat" we have alcoholism, in "Ligeia" we have opium usage, and in "The Angel of the Odd" we have overeating. The reader, then, can suspend her disbelief if she chooses, but she can also simply chalk up the odd happenings to chemically induced hallucinations. While the strategy Poe uses in these tales differs somewhat from the one he adopts in "Valdemar," since the narrator of this story appears to be completely sober and awake, telling the reader that they are about to see something they will not believe creates the same type of safety hatch that comes from decreasing a narrator's reliability through substance abuse.

12. Both Bazán's translator and Olivera maintain the reader and the invitation to stop believing the narrative. Bazán's translator produces the following: "[m]i narración ha llegado a un punto en que los lectores se niegan ya a seguir creyendo" ["my narration has reached a point at which the readers refuse to continue believing"] (215). Olivera offers: "[c]omprendo que he alcanzado al punto de esta narración en que cada lector se verá solicitado por una positiva incredulidad" ["I understand that I have reached the point of this narration in which every reader will see themselves seized by a positive incredulity"] (254).

13. For more on these moments in Borges's stories where the narrator acknowledges his lack of ability to communicate his experience to his readers, see my extended analysis of "Funes" and "El Aleph" in chapter 5.

14. Poe's source text states: "Yes;—no;—I *have been* sleeping—and now—now— I *am dead*" (1240). Borges offers a literal translation: "Sí; no, *he estado* durmiendo, y ahora, ahora *estoy muerto*" ["Yes; no, *I have been* sleeping, and now, now *I am dead*"] (377). Olivera and Bazán's translator provide the exact same words but with minor changes in punctuation.

15. Both Olivera's translation (256) and Bazán's edition (216–17) follow Poe's source text closely, keeping the same verb construction and maintaining the temporal marker. Concerning Borges's use of "innegable" for "evident" rather than the Spanish cognate "evidente," it is important to note that Borges uses "evidente" in the next

sentence, offering "Nos pareció evidente que despertar a M. Valdemar [. . .]" ["It appeared evident to us that to wake M. Valdemar [. . .]"] (378) for Poe's "It seemed clear to us all that to awaken M. Valdemar [. . .]" (1241). His avoidance of "evidente" when describing mesmerism's power over death, then, could be simply to avoid repetition. However, as Olivera's translation and Bazán's edition make clear, various ways exist in Spanish to express "It seemed clear to us" without using the term "evidente," and both of those editions follow Poe's source text by offering the cognate "evidente" for "evident" in the prior sentence.

16. Once again, both Olivera (257) and Bazán (217) follow the source text more closely here, maintaining the idea of an experiment and commenting on the problematic nature of the narratives circulating from other sources.

17. Olivera (257–58) and Bazán's translator (217) each follow the source text by having Valdemar ask to be put asleep or awakened.

18. Both Olivera's translation of "La carta robada" and the translation of the story in Bazán's edition maintain the expression and offer the double negative as follows: "no estoy tan seguro de que respiro, como de que la carta no está en el hotel" ["I am not as sure that I breathe, as I am that the letter is not in the hotel"] (227; 94). While the translation of "Valdemar" that Bazán includes in his edition is clearly not Olivera's, the version of "La carta robada" that he publishes might be. The two are not identical, but they are close enough that it is possible that Bazán's version of the story is a slightly revised edition of Olivera's translation, especially since Bazán lists Olivera as one of the prose translators for his edition of Poe's *Obras completas*.

19. Both Olivera's and Bazán's editions offer a literal translation—"podría haber sucedido que no saliera vivo de la presencia del Ministro" ["it could have happened that I did not leave alive from the presence of the Minister"]—and both maintain the sentence about Dupin and the Parisian public (243; 103).

20. Unlike Poe's and Borges's versions, Olivera's translation and Bazán's edition both fail to mention the weather in the opening sentence. They both follow Poe's source text by not adding an adjective to describe "meditation," by translating "mentally discussing" literally as "discutiendo mentalmente," and by describing the particulars of Dupin's pipe. They tweak the source text's description of the "little back library, or book closet," however, and place the scene "en un pequeño cuarto detrás de su biblioteca" ["in a little room behind his library"] (217; 89).

21. Borges comments on Dupin's inaugural role as the first analytic detective of literature in several pieces of literary criticism, including a 1940 review he published in *Sur* entitled "Ellery Queen. *The New Adventures of Ellery Queen.*" In this piece, Borges juxtaposes Dupin with Sherlock Holmes, preferring the former who lacks human attributes and functions as a thinking machine.

22. Borges also lamented that Poe's work came to Argentina through French with Baudelaire as the intermediary. See his "Prólogo de prólogos" and his conversation with Osvaldo Ferrari entitled "Diálogo sobre el Modernismo y Rubén Darío."

23. Bazán's translator and Olivera follow the source text closely in both of these cases by offering "asunto de la calle Morgue" ["issue of Morgue Street"] and "el misterio respecto al asesino de María Rogêt" ["the mystery with respect to the murder of Marie Rogêt"] (89; 217) without introducing the concept of "double murder."

24. Olivera's and Bazán's editions both offer a nearly literal translation of this passage, including the second sentence that mentions the doubling of the reward (95; 228).

25. Olivera (228–29) and Bazán's translator (95) offer a fairly literal translation of this dialogue.

26. Dupin claims victory over the prefect to the narrator at the end of "The Murders in the Rue Morgue," stating: "Let him discourse; it will ease his conscience. I am satisfied with having defeated him in his own castle" (568).

27. Kristal mentions that Borges deletes these passages (66). He cites one of them, offering a one-sentence interpretation before moving on with his analysis (62).

28. Olivera and Bazán's translator both maintain the concept of a self-evident mystery throughout their translations.

29. Neither Olivera's edition nor the version in Bazán's collection place the letter inside an envelope.

30. Casanova also notes the power of translators and literary critics. She claims that "[t]ranslation is the foremost example of a particular type of consecration in the literary world" and that it "is the major prize and weapon in international literary competition" (133). She also argues that "[c]ritics, like translators, thus contribute to the growth of the literary heritage of nations that enjoy the power of consecration: critical recognition and translation are weapons in the struggle by and for literary capital" (23).

Chapter 5. Buried Connections

1. Borges rarely mentions Poe's poetry in his own fiction. In "Pierre Menard, autor del *Quijote*," Menard "[n]o pued[e] imaginar el universo sin la interjección de Poe: *Ah, bear in mind this garden was enchanted!*" (447) ["cannot imagine the universe without Poe's ejaculation 'Ah, bear in mind this garden was enchanted!'"] (92). The story's context and plot do cast Poe's "To Helen [Sarah Helen Whitman]" as slightly ridiculous, but Borges makes no argument for Poe the fiction writer in this piece. In "La otra muerte" ["The Other Death"], the narrator claims that Emerson is a superior poet to Poe (573; 226), and the name of one of Borges's protagonists in "Abenjacán el Bojarí, muerto en su laberinto" ["Ibn-Ḥakam al-Bokhari, Murdered in His Labyrinth"]—Dunraven (600; 255)—alludes to Poe's most famous poem. Borges's fictional references to Poe's fiction are also few, but as various critics have argued, several of his most famous stories converse with Poe's tales.

2. Mabbott's edition provides, in the text's footnotes, both the major and minor changes Poe and/or his editors made between various versions of his published texts and many of his manuscripts, while the Edgar Allan Poe Society of Baltimore offers full-text versions of the majority of the texts referenced by Mabbott.

3. Emecé released a three-volume collection entitled *Obras completas: Edición crítica* between 2009 and 2011. This edition contains extensive, yet very basic, notes, but Borges's texts appear in the same format in which Emecé had previously published them. This edition also lacks the fourth volume of *Obras completas* that was available in Emecé's 2007 printing.

4. Unfortunately, this approach is not possible for the majority of the Borges stories

I analyze in the following pages since the manuscripts for these tales no longer exist, are lost, are owned by private collectors who do not make them public for study, or are sold at exorbitant prices to wealthy collectors. In "Los manuscritos de Borges: 'Imaginar una realidad más compleja,'" Daniel Balderston calls Borges's manuscripts *"terra incognita"* since so few of them are available to the public (19). The manuscript for "Funes el memorioso," for example, exists but is not accessible. Balderston notes that Lame Duck Books has sold manuscripts of "Funes" and several other important Borges stories during the last few years but that "esos manuscritos no están a la disposición del estudioso, a menos que tenga en el bolsillo casi medio millón de dólares (el precio promedio de cada uno)" ["those manuscripts are not at the disposition of scholars, unless they have half a million dollars in their pocket (the average price of each one)"] (19).

5. Some translators offer the more literal "Funes the Memorious" as their translation of Borges's "Funes el memorioso." Hurley prefers "Funes, His Memory" in his collection of Borges translations.

6. In claiming that Borges buries an influential connection in a postscript, I am indebted to Irwin's word choice when he suggests that Lacan buries Borges's influence on his interpretation of "The Purloined Letter" in a footnote (442–49).

7. In "Poe and Magazine Writing on Premature Burial," J. Gerald Kennedy states: "From the early travesty 'Loss of Breath' (1832) to the late classic 'The Cask of Amontillado' (1846), living entombment remained a persistent and horrifying motif in Poe's fiction" (165).

8. Bonaparte even titles the section in which this chapter appears "The Confession of Impotence." The spelling of the primary character's name shifts in the various versions of the story from Lacko'breath, to Lack-o'Breath, to Lackobreath. Since my analysis focuses on the version published in *Tales of the Grotesque and Arabesque*, I use that rendition's version of the name—Lack-o'Breath.

9. The juxtaposition between Hoffman's book and the Levines' reader on Poe shows the vast but distinct influence of Bonaparte's Freudian interpretation of "Loss of Breath" since Hoffman's text is heavily psychoanalytical while the Levines' book is not. Bonaparte's analysis affects both literary critics who are directly invested in psychoanalysis and those who are not, but even after her work on "Loss of Breath," the story receives little emphasis in contemporary Poe scholarship. "Loss of Breath" remains a tale whose analysis occasionally requires a few pages, but usually takes up no more than a few lines, in book-length studies on Poe, and a story that elicits article-length studies only every decade or so in very disparate journals. The geographical distance between the publication sites of some of the articles that focus on "Loss of Breath"—Austria, Romania, South Africa, and the United States—demonstrates that, like most Poe texts, "Loss of Breath" has a global readership. However, the lapse of time between these articles reiterates the minor role this story plays in most Poe scholarship today.

10. In "The Great Chain of Memory: Borges, Funes, *De Viris Illustribus*," Robert Folger suggests that "'Funes el memorioso' has been given surprisingly little attention in literary criticism" (125). He goes on, however, to site over a dozen readings of the tale, and his list does not include several articles that have been published on "Funes

el memorioso" over the past decade since Folger published his piece. While "Funes el memorioso" is not as prevalent in Borges scholarship as "El Aleph," it is certainly not an understudied text.

11. Canto states: "Me repetía que él era Dante, que yo era Beatrice y que habría de liberarlo del infierno" ["He repeated that he was Dante, that I was Beatrice, and that I would have to liberate him from hell"] (95). Whether connecting "El Aleph's" allusions to Dante back to the biographies of Borges and/or Dante or analyzing the story's connections to Dante's work, numerous literary critics examine "El Aleph" with Dante in mind. For another example in English, see Jon Thiem's "Borges, Dante, and the Poetics of Total Vision."

12. The narrator in "El Aleph" is named Borges. Throughout my analysis, I will refer to this character as "Borges-narrator" (rather than "Borges's narrator") to differentiate between the literary creation and Borges the author.

13. For readings that discuss "El Aleph" in terms of Jewish mysticism and/or the Hebrew language, see, among others, Canto (210–12); Lisa Block de Behar's "Rereading Borges's 'The Aleph': On the Name of a Place, a Word, and a Letter"; and Mario Satz's "Borges, El Aleph y la Kabala." For scholarship that approaches the literary relationship between several of Borges's works and Jewish mysticism, see Jaime Alazraki's "Kabbalistic Traits in Borges' Narration" and "Borges and the Kabbalah" and Saúl Sosnowski's *Borges y la Cábala.* Also see Irwin's *The Mystery to a Solution* for connections between Borges's detective fiction and Kabbalah.

14. The following critics in one shape or form all comment on the debilitating effects of Funes's colossal memory, language's inability to capture reality, or both: Emir Rodríguez Monegal, Beatriz Sarlo, David E. Johnson, Clancy W. Martin, Edmond Wright, James D. Fernández, Ilán Stavans, Luis I. Prádanos, and Peter Standish. In contrast, Henry L. Shapiro offers a creative and refreshing reading of "Funes" against the grain provided by these scholars. In "Memory and Meaning: Borges and 'Funes el memorioso,'" he suggests that Borges's connection between the story and insomnia is a red herring (258), and he notes that Funes's physical disability "does not depress him" because the accident that left him paralyzed also gave him "immense gifts" (259). Shapiro openly claims that this story "is not what the critics have taken it to be. It is not, that is, the dark and gloomy tale of a piteous, tortured cripple whose condition demonstrates to us once again that objective reality is either unbearable, unattainable, or both" (258). Finally, he argues that "Funes' paralysis, his immobility, symbolize not his uselessness but the fixed stability and reliability of his mind. He cannot be moved or swayed. He is the sole guarantor of immutability—thus of knowledge, of meaning and of truth" (262).

15. The narrator in "Funes el memorioso" never identifies himself by name, but several Borges scholars call the narrator Borges—connecting Borges's own Argentine identification and childhood vacations to Fray Bentos, Uruguay, to those same details offered by the narrator. Since Borges continually writes himself as a character into his fiction, reading this particular Argentine narrator who visits his relatives in Fray Bentos as Borges might not seem like a stretch. The narrator's first encounter with Funes, however, occurs in 1884, fifteen years before Borges's birth. Thus, Borges, or at least Jorge Luis Borges, cannot be the narrator of "Funes el memorioso." Ilán Stavans notes

that the narrator's cousin "Bernardo Haedo" shares the last name of Borges's uncle on his mother's side of the family and suggests that Borges's father "en una especie de metempsicosis" ["in a sort of metempsychosis"] fulfills the role of narrator in this tale (99).

16. Fernández comments on the irony of finite thinkers attempting to capture Funes's infinite memory (242), but he does so in the vein of criticism that argues that Funes's powers paralyze him rather than arguing that the impossibility of the narrator's task also traps the narrator.

17. I do not make this claim as some sort of ontological game. I realize that one could argue that *any* experience is impossible to re-create through the synthetic system we call language. I am suggesting, however, that the extreme experiences of these three narrators make their narrations indescribable or impossible rather than arguing that these stories represent the impossibility of all communication via language.

18. As Mabbott's notes reveal, the differences between the 1835 version of "Loss of Breath" that appeared in *Southern Literary Messenger* and the 1840 version published in *Tales of the Grotesque and Arabesque* are minimal. Both publications include the deleted passages I analyze in the following paragraphs. I direct my comments toward the version from *Tales of the Grotesque and Arabesque* because of Borges's access to this book, which I analyze later in the chapter.

19. In "A Reconstruction of Poe's 1833 *Tales of the Folio Club*," Hammond argues that "The Quick Among the Dead" rather than "Loss of Breath" must have been the story Poe designed for his Folio Club character Mr. Blackwood Blackwood (29–30). However, in his later article—"Further Notes on Poe's Folio Club Tales"—he changes his line of argument to suggest that the 1835 version of "Loss of Breath," which includes both the later excised "The Quick Among the Dead" and the humorous, underground encounter between Lack-o'Breath and Windenough, which Poe did not edit out of the 1846 version of the tale, "probably did serve, [. . .] as Mr. Blackwood Blackwood's tale" (39).

20. One could argue that Lack-o'Breath's narration from the communal burial plot where he finds himself at the end of the story in all versions of "Loss of Breath" (although not in "A Decided Loss") is also a telling of the impossible. However, as Poe suggests in several tales in which he approaches the theme of premature burial—"The Fall of the House of Usher," "Berenice," "The Cask of Amontillado," and "The Premature Burial"—for those who suffer from disorders like catalepsy and for those who fall victim to brutal revenge plots, such a narration rests within the realm of possibility even if not within the realm of probability.

21. Various scholars point out possible influences on "Funes el memorioso." Robert Folger reads Saint Augustine as "one of the 'precursors' of Borges, the author of *Funes*" (126) while Ilán Stavans suggests that Borges might have "leído, o [. . .] escuchado del caso de algún 'memorioso' en tránsito por Buenos Aires. [. . .] O que haya leído un cuento de Ivan Turgueniev, traducido al inglés en la versión de Henry James como 'Living Holy Relics' (1852), sobre una sirvienta que tras un terrible accidente, no hace otra cosa que vegetar y recordar" ["read, or [. . .] heard of the case of some 'memorioso' in transit through Buenos Aires. [. . .] Or [he] might have read the story by Ivan Turgenev, translated to English in the version of Henry James as 'Living Holy

Relics' (1852), about a servant who, after a terrible accident, does nothing else than vegetate and remember"] (99). Stavans then goes on to compare Funes's memory with that of S. V. Shereshevsky—a Funes-like mnemonist studied by Soviet neuropsychologist Alexander Romanovich Luria.

22. Apart from the philosophical connections Martin makes between the two thinkers, he also reveals that Borges plays with important dates in Nietzsche's life in "Funes el memorioso." He states, "Funes is born in 1868, which Nietzsche later dates as the first great year of his life, when he met Richard Wagner; the narrator first meets Funes in 1884, when Nietzsche was in the middle of the composition of *Thus Spoke Zarathustra;* the narrator and Funes meet again in 1887, year of the publication of *Genealogy of Morals;* and Funes dies in 1889, the year Nietzsche collapsed into madness and silence" (268).

23. The narrator's description of Funes's memory of leaves once again recalls Nietzsche, who refers to the "leaf" in "On Truth and Lies in a Nonmoral Sense" as an example of "the formation of concepts" (83).

24. While the 1835 and 1840 versions of the story do not name the dramas, the earlier "A Decided Loss" lists them as *Metamora* and *Miantinimoh* (55) while the 1846 and 1856 versions drop *Miantinimoh* and suggest that Lack-o'Breath memorizes only *Metamora.*

25. The first publication of "El Aleph" in *Sur* in 1945 states that the copy of Pliny is "in" the house in Adrogué: "vi *en* una quinta de Adrogué un ejemplar de la primera versión inglesa de Plinio" (63, emphasis added).

26. In the following chapter, my reading of "El Aleph" relies heavily on Borges's manuscript. I save the case I make for the necessity of consulting the manuscript when reading "El Aleph" for that chapter rather than making it here. The reference to Silesius is found on page 45 of Julio Ortega's and Elena del Río Parra's facsimile/critical edition of "El Aleph." The manuscript page is marked by Borges as page 15.

27. Borges published a fairly negative review of Shanks's text in *El Hogar* entitled "*Edgar Allan Poe*, de Edward Shanks" in April 1937.

28. Borges attempts to elevate the prologue as genre in the "Prólogo de prólogos" that introduces his collection of prologues he wrote for other author's books, stating, "El prólogo, cuando son propicios los astros, no es una forma subalterna del brindis; es una especie lateral de la crítica" ["The prologue, when the stars are aligned, is not a subaltern form of praise; it is a lateral type of criticism"] (14). Even with this argument, however, Borges's prologues remain on the fringe of Borges scholarship when compared to his fiction, his poetry, and his critical essays.

29. Poe does deal with the concepts of infinity and/or eternity in other texts, including *Eureka: A Prose Poem*, "The Conversation of Eiros and Charmion," and "The Colloquy of Monos and Una." However, these texts suggest a postmortal comfort with these ideas rather than casting them as painful philosophical conundrums.

Chapter 6. Supernatural Revenge

1. J. Gerald Kennedy argues that "Poe forged his professional identity through hostile relations, and during his relatively brief career as a magazinist, he managed to

offend or antagonize an impressive segment of the American literati, either through slashing reviews, biting journalistic profiles, insulting letters, sober threats, or sodden incoherencies. [. . .] Poe had dozens of friends but scores of critics and foes" ("The Violence" 533).

2. Mabbott also suggests that "Poe longed for revenge" after being attacked repeatedly in print by Thomas Dunn English and Hiram Fuller ("The Cask" 1252), and he calls the tale "the working out of [Poe's] immediate emotions" toward this situation of enmity (1253). Silverman goes as far as to imply that "Cask" might also be a shot at Poe's pseudo–foster father, John Allan, since *Nemo me impune lacessit* is also the national motto of Scotland, one of whose sons, 'Scotch' John Allan, much resembled Fortunato in being a man 'rich, respected, admired, beloved,' interested in wines, and a member of the Masons. (His name is also contained in 'Amontillado.')" (316–17). However, the proximity of his disaccord with English, Fuller, and others appears to be a more likely catalyst for the revenge Poe depicts in "Cask," especially if we consider, as the Edgar Allan Poe Society of Baltimore points out in "Edgar Allan Poe's Works as Autobiography," that "[a]fter John Allan's death, far from nurturing the anger of his youth, Poe often conceded his own sad part in earning John Allan's displeasure and forgave his foster father for leaving him nothing in his will."

3. I am not suggesting here that critics agree that Poe always casts revenge in a positive light. The myriad of interpretations of Poe's "The Cask of Amontillado"— e.g., Mabbott's claim that "'The Cask,' on its surface completely amoral, is perhaps the most moral of his Tales. The murderer at the end remembers that his victim rests in peace. That is something the criminal had been unable to do for fifty years" ("The Cask" 1252); Kent Bales's suggestion that Montresor's narrative, although "'confessed' with relish," is "the confession of a dying man" to his priest (51); Shannon Burns's claim that the unseen "you" with whom Montrèsor converses are "the bones of his ancestors," and that to them, not to the bones of Fortunato, he wishes a peaceful rest (25); Kenneth Silverman's argument that Montresor "describes the event long after, in an afterglow of exaltation that has endured for fifty years" (316); and Vincent Price's gleeful and unrepentant portrayal of Montresor in his cinematic monologue of the tale—demonstrates that the theme of revenge in Poe is certainly open for debate. But, whether Montresor feels guilty or whether he boasts of his deed, his revenge *is* temporally successful. He literally gets away with murder, and his deed remains undiscovered "[f]or the half of a century" (Poe, "Cask" 1263).

4. All my citations of Todorov's text are found in Richard Howard's 1975 English translation—*The Fantastic: A Structural Approach to a Literary Genre*.

5. As my subsequent analysis reveals, I follow the line of critics who accept Todorov's argument that character/reader hesitation or doubt plays a critical role in the creation of the fantastic. For critics who fundamentally disagree with this description of the fantastic, see Irène Bessière's *Le récit fantastique* and Emir Rodríguez Monegal's "Borges: Una teoría de la literatura fantástica."

6. Apart from these lectures, several of which are now in print, Borges never set out to define the fantastic in print. Rodríguez Monegal suggests in "Borges: Una teoría de la literatura fantástica" that Borges's early essay "El arte narrativo y la magia" and his "Prólogo a Adolfo Bioy Casares, *La invención de Morel*" are key to understanding

Borges's conceptualization of the fantastic and that contemporary critics have misread Borges's use of the supernatural because they misread, ignore, or are unaware of these two pieces (177, 183). Neither of these essays, however, talks about the fantastic per se, and as Rodríguez-Luis notes, "Borges's arguments" in the former essay "are in fact difficult to follow, to some extent because the categories that he employs [. . .] lack sufficient critical definition" (29) while the latter text causes confusion because the stories Borges cites as fantastic do not contain the fantastic techniques he names in his lectures (31–33).

7. Until 2008, most sources that approached Borges's lectures on the fantastic referred almost exclusively to a talk he gave in Montevideo on September 2, 1949, that first appeared, in summary, the following day in the Montevideo newspaper *El País* as "Sobre 'La literature fantástica', disertó ayer Jorge Luis Borges," and which Rodríguez Monegal discusses in "Jorge Luis Borges y la literatura fantástica" and in "Borges: Una teoría de la literatura fantástica." The summary in *El País* carries no author name, but Rodríguez Monegal identifies the writer as Carlos A. Passos in both of his aforementioned articles. In 2008 Anna Svensson's piece "Borges en Gotemburgo: Sobre su conferencia 'La Literatura Fantástica' y sus contactos con el Instituto Iberoamericano" refers to several talks that Borges gave on the fantastic in Montevideo, Madrid, Toronto, Gothenburg, Buenos Aires, Rosario, and Tucumán and offers a comparison between the ways in which Borges explained the fantastic in Gothenburg in 1964, in Buenos Aires in 1967, and in Toronto in 1968.

8. As Svensson notes, Borges's terminology changes between lectures. Borges "[o]scila entre las palabras *tema, medio, procedimiento* y *esquema* como denominación de las categorías alrededor de las cuales desarrolla sus ejemplos" ["[o]scillates between the words *theme, means, method*, and *scheme* as the name of the categories around which he develops his examples"] in his lectures in Spanish, and he uses terms such as "*types, common source, common subject, idea, motif, pattern, elements*, [. . .] *field*" in his English lecture in Toronto (37, italics in original).

9. In both of his articles that refer to this talk, Rodríguez Monegal lists Borges's four methods as "la obra de arte dentro de la misma obra; la contaminación de realidad por el sueño; el viaje en el tiempo; el doble" ["the work of art inside the same work; the contamination of reality by dreams; time travel; the double"] ("Jorge" 449; "Borges" 186) thus making Borges's specific example of a dream's intrusion into reality—time travel—its own category while omitting invisibility. However, Rodríguez Monegal admits that his only sources for reconstructing Borges's talk in Montevideo are his own memory of the lecture and Passos's published summary. Although, as I explain in turn, Borges does add time travel as its own category in later versions of his lecture on the fantastic, Rodríguez Monegal's omission of invisibility is probably a slip of memory on his part since one of his pieces also reveals a date discrepancy. Borges gave this talk on September 2, 1949, and Passos's summary appeared the following day. But in "Borges: Una teoría de la literatura fantástica," Rodríguez Monegal claims that the talk included ideas Borges had *already* published in "Magias parciales del *Quijote*" (186) even though Borges did not publish this article until November 6, 1949, in *La Nación*. Rodríguez Monegal also cites "Magias parciales del *Quijote*" in "Jorge Luis Borges y la literatura fantástica" although he does not, in this piece, claim that the

later published article influenced the earlier lecture. Some confusion also exists concerning the publication date of Passos's summary. *El País* is not typically available via interlibrary loan, and few libraries hold hard copies of this Montevideo daily. The full text of the summary is available online at EspacioLatino.com, but this electronic version claims the article was published on December 3, rather than September 3, 1949. However, the newspaper archives at La Biblioteca Nacional de Uruguay confirm that Passos's summary did indeed appear on September 3, 1949, and that Borges's talk was delivered the day before.

10. "La literatura fantástica" is the published title of both the lecture Borges delivered on the fantastic in Gothenburg in 1964 and the published title of his 1967 lecture on the fantastic at the Escuela Camillo y Adriano Olivetti in Buenos Aires. Borges demonstrated the shifts, refinements, and additions I mention in text in the 1964 Gothenburg lecture, in the 1967 Buenos Aires lecture, and in his 1968 Toronto lecture published as "Tales of the Fantastic." Borges did not mention self-referential art in any of these three lectures, he only mentioned invisibility again in his Buenos Aires lecture, and he dropped the theme of the double from the Gothenburg lecture.

11. Patrick Quinn suggests that the narrator of "The Man of the Crowd" encounters "his future double" (230), which also brings the concept of time travel into this story.

12. In his lectures, Borges does give "William Wilson" as an example of his "procedimiento" of the double ("La literatura fantástica," *Los laberintos* 27; "Tales" 14).

13. Borges's emphasis on fear in the fantastic cuts against the readings of the genre or mode offered by Todorov and, even more so, by Chanady. Indeed, Chanady specifically approaches "The Facts in the Case of M. Valdemar" to differentiate between horror and the fantastic, claiming that the story "inspires repugnance rather than dread of the unknown, and the emphasis is more on the loathsome disintegration of the hypnotized body than on the question of whether mesmerism exists. The 'unplumbed space' soon becomes known territory, and no doubt remains in the mind of the reader that the extraordinary experiment described in the story is presented as true. The description of Mr. Valdemar's body at the end arouses disgust rather than speculation about the possibility of such an occurrence" (142). Todorov claims that "[i]t is surprising to find such judgments [that connect the fantastic to fear] offered by serious critics. [. . .] Fear is often linked to the fantastic, but it is not a necessary condition of the genre" (35), while Chanady "reject[s] fear and horror as a criterion in the case of the fantastic" in favor of "the concept of bidimensionality" (9) and suggests that "[u]nlike horror fiction, the fantastic does not present the object of horror or terror in such an unambiguous way" (142).

14. Bioy Casares includes his discussion of fear in his "observaciones generales" ["general observations"] (8) on the fantastic. He then provides a list of "argumentos fantásticos" ["fantastic arguments"] (10) that includes several of the methods Borges mentions in his lectures. In his posthumously published journal entitled *Borges*, Bioy Casares also comments, somewhat disparagingly, on Borges's proclivity for the macabre in "The Facts in the Case of M. Valdemar." On June 10, 1963, Bioy Casares writes: "Aunque este cuento tiene un final bastante repugnante, Borges no lo evita. Es curioso: las osadías en circunstancias físicas del amor lo ofenden; las más repugnantes

circunstancias macabras, no. Tiene una admiración un poco infantil por esta suerte de audacias. Admira el final de 'Mr. Valdemar'" ["Even though this story has a fairly repugnant ending, Borges does not avoid it. It is curious: boldness in the physical circumstances of lovemaking offends him; the most repugnant circumstances of the macabre do not. He has a slightly infantile admiration for this type of audacity. He admires the end of 'M. Valdemar'"] (903).

15. Valdemar's supernatural experience creates more horror than doubt, especially in Borges's and Bioy Casares's translated version of the text, while the narrative Poe creates in "A Descent into the Maelström" shows the horrors of nature at its extreme. The only doubt expressed in the latter tale appears in its concluding sentences as the survivor of the whirlpool claims, "I told them my story. They did not believe it. I now tell it to *you*—and I can scarcely expect you to put more faith in it than did the merry fishermen of Lofoden" (594). His suggestion that the story's narrator, like the fishermen, will not believe his ordeal does not change how he relates the tale as reality. His acceptance of the experience coupled with the fact that the maelstrom is a part of nature itself disqualify this adventure tale with horror elements from the fantastic when theorized around doubt. "The Pit and the Pendulum" also fails to qualify as fantastic since none of the horrendous experiences in the torture chamber are supernatural.

16. As Benjamin F. Fisher notes, "There is no solid agreement about just which of Poe's early tales were to figure among the 'Tales of the Folio Club'" (487 n.1).

17. Another possible escape from the supernatural that Poe provides in this text is the subtle suggestion that Metzengerstein dreams the entire experience. As he first contemplated the tapestry with the horse "[i]t was with difficulty that he reconciled his dreamy and incoherent feelings with the certainty of being awake. The longer he gazed, the more absorbing became the spell—the more impossible did it appear that he could ever withdraw his glance from the fascination of that tapestry" (22). However, this story differs greatly from a story like Poe's "The Angel of the Odd," which suggests a dream in the beginning and ends with the narrator sprawled out on the floor among the remnants of his previous night's food and drink (1110). Since "Metzengerstein" does not end with any suggestion that the baron "wakes up" from his experiences, his dream must end shortly after it started with the "tumult" (22) of the Berlifitzing's burning stables and the horror of the tapestry horse's gaze. Still, this subtle hint could qualify "Metzengerstein" as a story of the fantastic for Borges since he lists reality infiltrated by dreams as one of his methods for creating a fantastic text.

18. The introductory paragraph almost makes this story fit within Chanady's definition of the magical real since the narrative suggests a strange reality—the concept of metempsychosis—alongside the typical reality from the onset of the text. The overt nature of this paragraph, however, differs from much magical-realist fiction since it "tells" rather than "shows" the magical reality. If the story began with an example of metempsychosis rather than a discourse on the topic, it could possibly be read as a type of proto–magical realism. This reading, however, would also require different reactions on the part of Metzengerstein who both doubts (although only momentarily) and fears the metamorphosis that his actions bring about.

19. Some debate does exist between scholars about whether Metzengerstein un-

derstands who the horse is or not. Mabbott argues that the baron left the horse un-named because he "knew the horse was Wilhelm von Berlifitzing, and dared use no other name" ("Metzengerstein" 31 n.11), while Leonardo Valencia—who introduces the story in the recent *Edición comentada* of Julio Cortázar's translations of Poe's complete tales—claims that "no sabemos a ciencia cierta quién media en la figura del endemoniado caballo que atraviesa el cuento" ["we do not know for sure who mediates in the figure of the possessed horse that goes through the story"] (224). My reading of Metzengerstein's fear of retribution suggests that he knew all too well who the horse was and, for that very reason, feared it.

20. Poe makes this latter connection in the tapestry scene when the young baron's shadow "precisely fill[s] up the contour, of the relentless and triumphant murderer of the Saracen Berlifitzing" (23).

21. Metzengerstein's subjects interpret his strange behavior in varied ways. Some think he is grieving the death of his parents, the family doctor "speak[s] of morbid melancholy, and hereditary ill-health," and "the multitude" holds "dark hints, of a more equivocal nature" (26). Mabbott suggests that Metzengerstein goes mad ("Metzengerstein" 30 n.8), and although the "dark hints" from "the multitude" could suggest that reading, the only passage that directly approaches madness is the description of the baron "descend[ing] like a maniac from his chamber, and, mounting in hot haste" the horse on the night of the fire (28). Whether the stallion has driven Metzengerstein insane or not, the story's revenge theme remains. In fact, Metzengerstein's possible madness merely adds another level of revenge to the plot before the baron meets his fiery end.

22. The simultaneous destruction of Metzengerstein the palace and Metzengerstein the family line by fire foreshadows Poe's later masterpiece "The Fall of the House of Usher."

23. Poe's epigraph for "Metzengerstein"—"Pestis eram vivus—moriens tua mors ero"—which Mabbott notes "is part of a hexameter, addressed by Martin Luther to the Pope, meaning, 'Living I have been your plague, dying I shall be your death'" ("Metzengerstein" 30 n.1), foreshadows the idea of the count's death bringing about the death of the more powerful baron. However, the text suggests that it is the Metzengerstein house that has plagued the Berlifitzing line during life rather than the other way around.

24. The Hungarian and German references in "Morella" and "Ligeia" also create connections between these tales, witchcraft, and "Metzengerstein"—a story cast in ancient Hungary and, as the subtitle to its second and third printings suggests, "A Tale in Imitation of the German." Morella has a "Presburg education" and teaches her husband German philosophy (229) while Ligeia meets her husband "in some large, old, decaying city near the Rhine" (310). Poe casts both women as sorceresses who use their craft in an attempt to overcome death.

25. Amper's interpretation of "The Black Cat" is both original and powerful, and she provides ample textual evidence to support her argument that the narrator kills his wife rather than his cat and that his claim "that he has only killed his cat serves both to ease his own sense of guilt, and to shield him from prosecution for murder" (479). However, Amper's suggestion that the narrator's sorrow in the scene in which he de-

scribes Pluto's death is extreme "if applied merely to the killing of a cat" (479) ignores Poe's well-known affinity for felines. Mabbott refers to the work of Arthur Hobson Quinn to suggest that "Poe was from his earliest youth very fond of cats" ("The Black Cat" 848), and he argues that "[i]n 1840 [Poe] seems to conclude that [cats] think. The killing of a cat was for him the slaughter of a reasonable creature. The protagonist of 'The Black Cat' was already morally a murderer when his ultimate act of cruelty made him legally one" (848).

26. In his brief discussion of Poe's tales, Todorov suggests that "The Black Cat" is Poe's only tale that might be called fantastic "in the strict sense" rather than being connected to the uncanny or the marvelous (48).

27. Poe wrote some of his fiction in the first person from a very early point in his career, but he first adopted this confessional style with "Berenice" in 1835. Several of his most famous tales follow this style, including "Morella," "Ligeia," "William Wilson," "The Tell-Tale Heart," and "The Cask of Amontillado."

28. In "Poe's 'The Black Cat' and Freud's 'The Uncanny,'" Fred Madden plays with the meanings of the German terms *heimlich* and *unheimlich* to demonstrate how the homely or "familiar becomes strange and supernatural" in "The Black Cat" (58).

29. Mabbott notes that the earlier scene in which the narrator claims that "[t]he fury of the demon instantly possessed [him]" (851) contains "the hint of the supernatural" ("The Black Cat" 859 n.4). However, the narrator's inebriated state during this scene leaves the supernatural at the level of hint or suggestion—much like the story's introduction and its early foreshadowing—until the destruction of the house and the ominous image of the strangled cat that accompanies it.

30. While the story does not overtly state that the second cat magically appears, both the narrator's surprise upon discovering the cat on the top of a hogshead he "had been looking steadily at [. . .] for some minutes" (854) and the proprietor's claim to "ha[ve] never seen [the cat] before" (854) hint that the cat is an apparition.

31. Another supernatural interpretation of the cat(s) in the story would be to read them as witches in disguise, as the narrator's wife suggests. In such a reading, the witch could be taking revenge on the narrator for trying to kill the witch (and this revenge could include "making" the narrator murder his wife); the witch could be taking revenge on the wife for seeing through the cat disguise; or the witch could simply want to destroy both individuals. Reading the cat(s) as witch(es), although supernatural, is highly problematic since it lets the murderous narrator off the hook by placing the blame on someone else rather than on the man who admits his crimes before facing his own death.

32. This certainly coincides with the narrator's stated opinion about his situation. He finishes his tale by describing the second cat as "the hideous beast whose craft had seduced [him] into murder, and whose informing voice had consigned [him] to the hangman" (859).

33. For example, Hoffman's and Amper's very different approaches to "The Black Cat" both agree that the narrator despises his wife.

34. Although "The Black Cat," like Poe's earlier "The Tell-Tale Heart," suggests that murder will out, only "The Tell-Tale Heart" depicts the murderer's guilty conscience as his downfall. In "The Tell-Tale Heart," the narrator's overconfidence com-

bines with his feelings of guilt until *he* screams out a confession, while in "The Black Cat" the narrator's arrogance lures him into a situation in which one of his victims cries out.

35. Poe openly placed "Metzengerstein" in the German tradition when he republished the tale in 1936 with the subtitle "A Tale in Imitation of the German" ("Metzengerstein," *Southern Literary Messenger* 97) although he later resented connections between his work and German horror as evidenced in his 1840 preface to *Tales of the Grotesque and Arabesque,* in which he claimed "that terror is not of Germany, but of the soul" (6). "The Black Cat" was published over a decade after "Metzengerstein" and three years after *Tales of the Grotesque and Arabesque,* and Poe's penchant for terror—whether German- or soul-influenced—was as strong as ever.

36. Copies of the 1989 facsimile edition published by la Universidad de Alcalá de Henares are quite rare, and while I have seen this edition cited in the work of Salvio Martín Menéndez and Jorge Panesi and briefly mentioned in Julio Ortega's and Elena del Río Parra's 2001 facsimile/critical edition of "El Aleph," I have not been able to consult this facsimile. I cite Ortega's and del Río Parra's edition, which is more widely available. Ortega and del Río Parra note that Estela Canto sold the manuscript to Sotheby's in 1985, which then sold the manuscript to its current owner—the Biblioteca Nacional de España (23).

37. Since no text nor record of a text exists between the manuscript and Canto's typed version of Borges's dictation that he delivered to *Sur*, Menéndez and Panesi suggest that Borges made these significant revisions—e.g., the specific variants that appear in the published version, the last paragraph in the body of the story, and the entire postscript—either while dictating the story to Canto or on her typed version of "El Aleph" (95). Ortega and del Río Parra note that while the manuscript ends before the postscript, the back cover of the manuscript contains notes that "reaparecen en la posdata" ["reappear in the postscript"] (15), which suggests that Borges was thinking about adding to "El Aleph" before he sat down to dictate the manuscript to Canto.

38. Menéndez and Panesi compare the manuscript with the first published version of "El Aleph"—the 1945 version in *Sur* number 131. Ortega and del Río Parra compare the manuscript with the first book version of the story—the 1949 version in *El Aleph* published by Losada—because this version contains various revisions of the *Sur* text (23). I compare the manuscript with what is currently considered the definitive version of the text, the version that appeared in Borges's *Obras completas* in 1974 and that is continually republished in every new version of the *Obras completas* by Emecé.

39. Borges's manuscript of "El Aleph" shows that he originally used the Arabic word "mihrab" rather than the Hebrew word "Aleph" to describe the mystical space in Carlos Argentino Daneri's basement. See Menéndez's and Panesi's "El manuscrito de 'El Aleph' de Jorge Luis Borges" (97) and Block de Behar's "Rereading Borges's 'The Aleph': On the Name of a Place, a Word, and a Letter" (184–86) for analysis on this shift in wording.

40. This passage is found on page 41 of Ortega's and del Río Parra's facsimile/critical edition. The manuscript page is marked by Borges as page 11.

41. María Luján Tubio suggests that Beatriz "aparece entonces desacralizada mediante la multiplicidad de imágenes que deja entrever el aleph" ["thus appears des-

ecrated through the multiplicity of images that the Aleph allows to be glimpsed"] (3), but the narrator does not react to other images of Beatriz, not even to her "reliquia atroz" (Borges, "El Aleph" 625) ["horrendous remains"] (283). Only the letters elicit a response.

42. The manuscript of "El Aleph" reveals that Borges originally wrote Beatriz and Carlos as siblings rather than cousins—"hermanos" rather than "primo hermanos"—and that at some time in the writing process he substituted Carlos Argentino *Daneri* for Carlos Argentino *Viterbo*. Ortega and del Río Parra offer an interesting reading of this shift, which they openly admit confuses Borges author with Borges-narrator, by suggesting that Borges author takes vengeance on Carlos Argentino by denying him the sibling relationship with Beatriz that the manuscript suggests until the final page where Borges makes the change before going back to cross out Viterbo and insert Daneri in the story's other references to Carlos Argentino's full name (15).

43. Canto believes that "El Aleph" mocks Daneri with a "mordacidad [. . .] [que] ha perdido sus dientes" ["sharpness [. . .] [that] has lost its teeth"] (208). The bite in Borges's critique, she suggests, will be lost on readers who did not experience life in Buenos Aires of the 1940s (206–08).

44. All the passages I cite from the manuscript's conclusion appear on page 46 of Ortega's and del Río Parra's facsimile edition of "El Aleph," but the manuscript page is numbered 16 in Borges's hand.

45. The facsimile of this back cover, which Borges does not number, appears on page 47 of Ortega's and del Río Parra's edition of Borges's "El Aleph."

46. As Menéndez and Panesi point out and thoroughly examine, the manuscript contains three versions of the list of things that Borges-narrator saw in the Aleph. The list grows substantially in each new version. In the first version, Borges-narrator only repeats "vi" ["I saw"] four times; in the second he repeats the phrase seventeen times; and in the third he repeats it thirty-five times—one more time than in the published text (101–08).

47. In "El modelo de la literatura fantástica aplicado en 'El Aleph,'" Berta López Morales suggests that the hyperbole and repeated numeration within the narrator's description of the vision qualifies "El Aleph" as fantastic within Todorov's rubric (74–75). While this same vision exists in the manuscript, I argue that the lack of any reaction from the narrator *after* the experience distances the manuscript from the fantastic because the reader cannot really see how the narrator deals with the experience without the postscript in the published story.

48. Manuscript pages 43 and 44 in Ortega and del Río Parra are numbered 13 and 14 in Borges's hand. The manuscript offers several alternatives for the rhetorical question Borges poses about capturing the infinite via the finite, but each option shows that the doubt is in the narrator's linguistic ability to describe the Aleph, not in the Aleph's existence.

49. In "Lo absurdo somos nosotros: el humor en los personajes de Borges," Holly Cadena suggests that Borges-narrator's reaction in this scene demonstrates his shallow nature: "La superficialidad del personaje 'Borges' se delata en la importancia que él da al premio: acaba de ver en El Aleph una realidad que transciende las cosas mundanas; sin embargo, la pérdida de este premio le deja amargado y emotivo" ["Borges

the character's superficiality gives itself away through the importance that he gives to the prize: he has just seen, in the Aleph, a reality that transcends mundane things; nonetheless, the loss of this prize leaves him embittered and emotional"] (488).

50. This inscription is to Borges's friend Cecilia Ingenieros. In the epilogue to the collection *El Aleph* and in various texts and interviews, Borges claims that she provided him with the plot for "Emma Zunz" ("Epílogo" 629; "Afterword" 287).

51. See note 3 in this chapter for differing perspectives on Montresor's feelings of guilt or glee in "The Cask of Amontillado."

52. Mabbott claims that "in 'Hop-Frog' the motive [for revenge] is made all too clear. The reader is expected to sympathize with the murderous dwarf, but the vengeance is too much for poetic justice" ("Hop-Frog" 1343). My post-Borges interpretation of "Hop-Frog" also suggests that the story's depiction of revenge does not satisfy the reader, but for completely different reasons than those that Mabbott suggests. Mabbott disconnects Hop-Frog's immediate motive—the king's abuse of Trippetta— from the context of the story—the kingdom's violent and degrading system of slavery. While Hop-Frog's burning of the king and his advisors alive is certainly too strong of a reaction for the king's insult of Trippetta, it is no more violent than the system of slavery that the king maintains—a system that kidnaps Hop-Frog and Trippetta, forces them to labor for the king's pleasure, and strips them of their dignity. Hop-Frog's reaction is horrific and brutal, but from a twenty-first-century perspective it seems much more justified than the defense of family honor that Montresor maintains. The tragedy in Hop-Frog's revenge that becomes even clearer after reading "Emma Zunz" is that he has to become his enemy in order to escape from him, which suggests that his revenge cannot completely disconnect him from the king even though he escapes to his homeland.

Epilogue. Commemorative Reframing

1. Cortázar rereleased the two-volume version of *Obras en prosa* in 1969. He also published separate translations of *Pym* in 1968 and *Eureka* in 1972.

2. Cortázar opens volume 1 of *Obras en prosa* with an eighty-six-page introduction that he splits into two long essays—"Vida de Edgar Poe" and "El poeta, el narrador y el crítico." All of the republications of volume 1 as *Cuentos* in two volumes include the biographical essay but do not republish "El poeta, el narrador y el crítico" while *Ensayos y críticas* presents the latter essay as its introduction.

3. I realize that the subtitle of Poe's *Eureka* is "A Prose Poem," but while the idea of oneness presented in this scientific treatise might sound poetic, the work is a piece of prose. I also realize that the titles of Cortázar's major Poe translations—*Obras en prosa* and *Cuentos*—limit the contents of these volumes to prose, but while he also published individual translations of *Pym* and *Eureka*, Cortázar never saw fit to translate a collection of Poe's poetry nor a single poem.

4. A year before their translation of "The Purloined Letter" and a hundred years after Poe published the most sedentary of his detective stories, "The Mystery of Marie Rogêt," Borges and Bioy Casares published their collection of detective parodies—*Seis problemas para don Isidro Parodi*—under the pseudonym H. Bustos Domecq. The

collection's protagonist is the ultimate armchair detective in that he solves cases from a prison cell. Also in 1942, Borges released his now famous rewriting of "The Purloined Letter"—his masterful piece "La muerte y la brújula" ["Death and the Compass"].

5. See chapters 5 and 44 of Irwin's *The Mystery to a Solution* for a detailed analysis of how Borges's three solo-authored detective stories both commemorate the centennial of the Dupin trilogy and rewrite Poe's tales of ratiocination.

6. The "mythic little blue volumes" refer to one of the famous covers of the Alianza paperback versions of *Cuentos,* which consisted of a blue background and a skull with a splotch of red blood covering the right eye socket.

7. Cortázar also suggests, while defending *Eureka* from the attacks of another literary critic, that Paul Valéry's fascination with this text should change our perceptions of its worth ("Introducción" lvi).

8. This version of Cortázar's *Cuentos* is one of sixty-four books that formed a Hyspamérica collection entitled "Biblioteca Personal" ["Personal Library"]. Borges chose the titles and wrote prologues for each of the books. The series was going to contain one hundred titles, but Borges's death cut the series short (*Biblioteca personal: Prólogos* 547). The collection also includes a volume of Poe's stories.

9. This textbook grows out of Borges's work as a professor at the University of Buenos Aires, and as the title page notes, Zemborain de Torres "collaborates" with Borges in the creation of this book. Thus, my analysis approaches the ideas shared in *Introducción a la literatura norteamericana* as Borges's rather than Borges's and Zemborain de Torres's.

10. Borges's Norton Lectures at Harvard are available in print in *This Craft of Verse* and in audio online via UbuWeb. In the preface to *The Mystery to a Solution,* Irwin discusses Borges's 1983 visit to Baltimore.

11. In 1991 the Raven Society published a brief pamphlet by Professor Irby B. Cauthen Jr., *Edgar Poe at the University—1826,* which details Poe's short stay in Charlottesville.

12. Poe certainly does not lack groups and organizations that memorialize him and archive his works—e.g., the Edgar Allan Poe Society of Baltimore. The University of Virginia, however, remains the most visible academic/popular Poe site in the U.S. system of higher education although other universities, societies, and museums also hold important Poe collections.

13. When Loewenstein began to prepare what is now the Jorge Luis Borges Collection at the Small Special Collections Library at the University of Virginia in 1977, he searched the local and university newspapers for articles that recalled Borges's earlier visit to UVA but was unable to find any print sources that documented Borges's visit, his itinerary, or the specifics of his lectures on Poe ("Telephone"). From our twenty-first-century perspective, it seems mindboggling that no transcription or recording of these lectures was made. However, we must recall, "that in 1966 [. . .] Jorge Luis Borges was not yet considered the indisputable genius he is today" (Arias xi), as the editors of a recent book on Borges's 1966 lectures on British literature at the University of Buenos Aires—*Professor Borges*—remind us in their attempt to explain how the tapes that contained those classes "have been lost" (xi). Borges's six Norton Lectures that he delivered at Harvard in 1967 and 1968 were lost for almost three de-

cades before they were found, published as *This Craft of Verse*, and made available in an audio version online. The Special Collections at the Milton S. Eisenhower Library at Johns Hopkins claims to hold a sound recording of Borges's 1983 Pouder Lecture on Walt Whitman, but as of December 2013, this recording is lost. In short, the lack of a recording or transcription of Borges's lectures at UVA is not atypical.

14. Loewenstein's memories of Borges's visit to the Poe room at UVA recall the enthusiasm Borges showed when John T. Irwin took him to the Poe house and to Poe's grave, both in Baltimore (Irwin xx).

15. Most of these lectures were not lectures focused primarily on Poe, but we do know that Borges offered lectures specifically on Poe as early as 1946. In his "Autobiographical Notes" with Norman Thomas di Giovanni, Borges notes that Poe provided the material for one of the nine lectures he gave at the Asociación Argentina de Cultura Inglesa, his first teaching job (85).

16. Loewenstein notes that the Jorge Luis Borges Collection "began while Borges was still alive and before" too many people "were interested in collecting [his works]. Now his manuscripts sell for ridiculous amounts of money" ("Telephone"). In the twenty-first century, individual Borges manuscripts are advertised for $100,000 to $500,000 at auction and when sold by rare-book collectors.

Works Cited

Archives, Resources, and Special Collections

The Edgar Allan Poe Society of Baltimore. Web. < http://www.eapoe.org>.

La Fundación Internacional Jorge Luis Borges. Buenos Aires, Argentina.

John Henry Ingram's Poe Collection. Albert and Shirley Small Special Collections Library, University of Virginia, Charlottesville.

The Jorge Luis Borges Collection. Albert and Shirley Small Special Collections Library, University of Virginia, Charlottesville.

Jorge Luis Borges Collection. The Harry Ransom Center, University of Texas at Austin.

Julio Cortázar Literary Manuscripts. The Nettie Lee Benson Latin American Collection, University of Texas at Austin.

La Sala del Tesoro. Biblioteca Nacional Argentina. Buenos Aires, Argentina.

Published Sources

Alazraki, Jaime. "Borges and the Kabbalah." *TriQuarterly* 25 (1972): 240–67. Print.

———. "Kabbalistic Traits in Borges' Narration." *Studies in Short Fiction* 8.1 (1971): 78–92. Print.

Allen, Hervey. *Israfel: The Life and Times of Edgar Allan Poe.* 1926. New York: Rinehart, 1934. Print.

Álvarez, Germán. Personal interview. 26 Aug. 2011.

Amper, Susan. "Untold Story: The Lying Narrator in 'The Black Cat.'" *Studies in Short Fiction* 29.4 (1992): 475–85. Print.

Arias, Martín, and Marín Hadis, eds. *Professor Borges: A Course on English Literature.* Trans. Katherine Silver. New York: New Directions, 2013. Print.

Balderston, Daniel. "Los manuscritos de Borges; 'Imaginar una realidad más compleja.'" *Variaciones Borges* 28 (2009): 15–26. Print.

Bales, Kent. "Poetic Justice in 'The Cask of Amontillado.'" *Poe Studies* 5.2 (1972): 51. *The Edgar Allan Poe Society of Baltimore.* Web. 23 Sept. 2010.

Baudelaire, Charles, trans. "Double Assassinat dans la rue Morgue." By Edgar Allan Poe. *Histoires Extraordinaires.* 1856. Project Gutenberg, 2007. Web. 16 April 2013.

———. "La Lettre volée." By Edgar Allan Poe. *Histoires Extraordinaires.* 1856. Project Gutenberg, 2007. Web. 16 April 2013.

Bayard, Pierre. "Anticipatory Plagiarism." Trans. Jeffrey Mehlman. *New Literary History* 44.2 (2013): 231–50. Print.

———. *Le plagiat par anticipation.* Paris: Les Éditions de Minuit, 2009. Print.

Bazán, Armando, ed. "La carta robada." By Edgar Allan Poe. *Obras completas*. Buenos Aires: Claridad, 1944. 89–103. Print.

———. "El caso del señor Valdemar." By Edgar Allan Poe. *Obras completas*. Buenos Aires: Claridad, 1944. 211–17. Print.

———. *Obras completas*. By Edgar Allan Poe. Buenos Aires: Claridad, 1944. Print.

Benjamin, Walter. "The Task of the Translator." 1923. Trans. Harry Zohn. *The Translation Studies Reader*. Ed. Lawrence Venuti. New York: Routledge, 2000. 15–25. Print.

Bennett, Maurice J. "The Detective Fiction of Poe and Borges." *Comparative Literature* 35.3 (1983): 262–75. Print.

———. "The Infamy and the Ecstasy: Crime, Art, and Metaphysics in Edgar Allan Poe's 'William Wilson' and Jorge Luis Borges's 'Deutsches Requiem.'" *Poe and Our Times: Influences and Affinities*. Ed. Benjamin Franklin Fisher IV. Baltimore: The Edgar Allan Poe Society, 1986. 107–23. Print.

Berman, Antoine. "Translation and the Trials of the Foreign." 1985. Trans. Lawrence Venuti. *The Translation Studies Reader*. Ed. Lawrence Venuti. New York: Routledge, 2000. 284–97. Print.

Bessière, Irène. *Le récit fantastique*. Paris: Larousse, 1974. Print.

Bioy Casares, Adolfo. *Borges*. Buenos Aires: Ediciones Destino, 2006. Print.

———. "Prólogo." *Antología de la literatura fantástica*. Ed. Adolfo Bioy Casares, Jorge Luis Borges, and Silvina Ocampo. 1940. Buenos Aires: Sudamericana, 1971. 7–14. Print.

Block de Behar, Lisa. "Borges, the Aleph, and Other Cardinal Points." Trans. Alfred MacAdam. *Review: Literature and Arts of the Americas* 38.1 (2005): 7–16. Print.

———. "Rereading Borges's 'The Aleph': On the Name of a Place, a Word, and a Letter." Trans. William Egginton. *New Centennial Review* 4.1 (2004): 169–87. Print.

Bloom, Harold. *The Anatomy of Influence: Literature as a Way of Life*. New Haven: Yale University Press, 2011. Print.

———. *The Anxiety of Influence: A Theory of Poetry*. 2nd ed. New York: Oxford University Press, 1997. Print.

———. "Introduction." *Bloom's Classic Critical Views: Edgar Allan Poe*. Ed. Harold Bloom. New York: Infobase, 2008. xi–xii. Print.

———. "Introduction." *Bloom's Modern Critical Views: Edgar Allan Poe, Updated Edition*. Ed. Harold Bloom. New York: Infobase, 2006. 1–11. Print.

Bonaparte, Marie. *Edgar Poe: Étude psychanalytique*. Paris: Denoël et Steele, 1933. Print.

———. *The Life and Works of Edgar Allan Poe: A Psycho-Analytic Interpretation*. Trans. John Rodker. 1949. New York: Humanities Press, 1971. Print.

Borges, Jorge Luis. "Abenjacán el Bojarí, muerto en su laberinto." 1951. *Obras completas*. Vol. 1. Buenos Aires: Emecé, 2004. 600–06. Print.

———. "Afterword." *The Aleph*. Trans. Andrew Hurley. *Collected Fictions*. New York: Penguin, 1998. 287–88. Print.

———. "El Aleph." *Sur* 131 (1945): 52–66. Print.

———. *El Aleph*. 1949. *Obras completas*. Vol. 1. Buenos Aires: Emecé, 2004. 531–630. Print.

———. "El Aleph." *El Aleph*. Buenos Aires: Losada, 1949. 125–44. Print.

———. "El Aleph." 1974. *Obras completas*. Vol. 1. Buenos Aires: Emecé, 2004. 617–27. Print.

———. "The Aleph." Trans. Andrew Hurley. *Collected Fictions*. New York: Penguin, 1998. 274–86. Print.

———. "El arte narrativo y la magia." 1932. *Obras completas*. Vol. 1. Buenos Aires: Emecé, 2004. 226–32. Print.

———. *Artificios*. 1944. *Obras completas*. Vol. 1. Buenos Aires: Emecé, 2004. 481–529. Print.

———. "La biblioteca de Babel." 1941. *Obras completas*. Vol. 1. Buenos Aires: Emecé, 2004. 465–71. Print.

———. *Biblioteca personal: Prólogos*. 1988. *Obras completas*. Vol. 4. Buenos Aires: Emecé, 2007. 545–658. Print.

———. "Borges and I." Trans. Andrew Hurley. *Collected Fictions*. New York: Penguin, 1998. 324. Print.

———. "Borges on Borges." *Foco* 1.1 (1976): 1, 12–13. Print.

———. *Borges, oral*. 1979. *Obras completas*. Vol. 4. Buenos Aires: Emecé, 2007. 193–251. Print.

———. "Borges y yo." 1957. *Obras completas*. Vol. 2. Buenos Aires: Emecé, 2007. 221. Print.

———. "La casa de Asterión." 1947. *Obras completas*. Vol. 1. Buenos Aires: Emecé, 2004. 569–70. Print.

———. "The Circular Ruins." Trans. Andrew Hurley. *Collected Fictions*. New York: Penguin, 1998. 96–100. Print.

———. "El cuento policial." 1978. *Obras completas*. Vol. 4. Buenos Aires: Emecé, 2007. 229–40. Print.

———. "Death and the Compass." Trans. Andrew Hurley. *Collected Fictions*. New York: Penguin, 1998. 147–56. Print.

———. "The Detective Story." Trans. Esther Allen. *Selected Non-Fictions*. Ed. Eliot Weinberger. New York: Penguin, 1999. 491–99. Print.

———. "Las dos maneras de traducir." 1926. *Textos recobrados, 1919–1929*. Buenos Aires: Emecé, 1997. 256–59. Print.

———. "Edgar Allan Poe." *La Nación* [Buenos Aires]. 2 Oct. 1949, sec. 2: 1. Print.

———. "*Edgar Allan Poe*, de Edward Shanks." 1937. *Obras completas*. Vol. 4. Buenos Aires: Emecé, 2007. 332–33. Print.

———. "Ellery Queen. *The New Adventures of Ellery Queen*." 1940. *Jorge Luis Borges en Sur: 1931–1980*. Buenos Aires: Emecé, 1999. 231–32. Print.

———. "Emma Zunz." Typescript. Jorge Luis Borges Collection. The Harry Ransom Center, University of Texas at Austin.

———. "Emma Zunz." 1948. *Obras completas*. Vol. 1. Buenos Aires: Emecé, 2004. 564–68. Print.

———. "Emma Zunz." Trans. Andrew Hurley. *Collected Fictions*. New York: Penguin, 1998. 215–19. Print.

———. "Epílogo." *El Aleph*. 1949. *Obras completas*. Vol. 1. Buenos Aires: Emecé, 2004. 629–30. Print.

———. "La eternidad y T. S. Eliot." 1933. *Textos recobrados, 1931–1955*. Buenos Aires: Emecé, 2001. 49–52. Print.

———. *Evaristo Carriego*. Buenos Aires: Manuel Gleizer, 1930. Print.

———. "Facsímil." *"El Aleph" de Jorge Luis Borges: Edición crítica y facsimilar de Julio Ortega y Elena del Río Parra*. Ed. Julio Ortega and Elena del Río Parra. México: El Colegio de México, Centro de Estudios Lingüísticos y Literarios, 2001. 25–49. Print.

———. *Ficciones*. 1944. *Obras completas*. Vol. 1. Buenos Aires: Emecé, 2004. 425–529. Print.

———. *Ficciones*. Ed. Anthony Kerrigan. New York: Grove Press, 1962. Print.

———. "Flaubert y su destino ejemplar." 1954. *Obras completas*. Vol. 1. Buenos Aires: Emecé, 2004. 263–66. Print.

———. "Foreword." *Artifices*. Trans. Andrew Hurley. *Collected Fictions*. New York: Penguin, 1998. 129–30. Print.

———. "Foreword." *Brodie's Report*. Trans. Andrew Hurley. *Collected Fictions*. New York: Penguin, 1998. 345–47. Print.

———. "Funes el memorioso." 1942. *Obras completas*. Vol. 1. Buenos Aires: Emecé, 2004. 485–90. Print.

———. "Funes, His Memory." Trans. Andrew Hurley. *Collected Fictions*. New York: Penguin, 1998. 131–37. Print.

———. "The Garden of Forking Paths." Trans. Andrew Hurley. *Collected Fictions*. New York: Penguin, 1998. 119–28. Print.

———. "The Garden of Forking Paths." Trans. Anthony Boucher. *Ellery Queen's Mystery Magazine* 12.57 (1948): 101–10. Print.

———. "La génesis de 'El cuervo' de Poe." *La Prensa* [Buenos Aires]. 25 Aug. 1935. Print.

———. *"Half-Way House*, de Ellery Queen." 1936. *Obras completas*. Vol. 4. Buenos Aires: Emecé, 2007. 263–64. Print.

———. *"The Haunted Omnibus*, de Alexander Laing." 1937. *Obras completas*. Vol. 4. Buenos Aires. Emecé, 2007. 365–66. Print.

———. "Hawthorne." *Cursos y conferencias*. 35.208–10 (1949): 221–40. Print.

———. *Historia universal de la infamia*. 1935. *Obras completas*. Vol. 1. Buenos Aires: Emecé, 2004. 287–345. Print.

———. "The Homeric Versions." Trans. Eliot Weinberger. *Selected Non-Fictions*. Ed. Eliot Weinberger. New York: Penguin, 1999. 69–74. Print.

———. "Ibn-Ḥakam al-Bokhari, Murdered in His Labyrinth." Trans. Andrew Hurley. *Collected Fictions*. New York: Penguin, 1998. 255–62. Print.

———. "Indagación de la palabra." 1927. *El idioma de los argentinos*. 1928. Madrid: Alianza, 1999. 11–27. Print.

———. *El jardín de senderos que se bifurcan*. 1941. *Obras completas*. Vol. 1. Buenos Aires: Emecé, 2004. 427–80. Print.

———. "El jardín de senderos que se bifurcan." 1941. *Obras completas*. Vol. 1. Buenos Aires: Emecé, 2004. 472–80. Print.

———. "Juan Ramón Jiménez." 1957. *Textos recobrados, 1956–1986*. Buenos Aires: Emecé, 2003. 41–42. Print.

———. "Julio Cortázar, *Stories*." Trans. Eliot Weinberger. *Selected Non-Fictions*. Ed. Eliot Weinberger. New York: Penguin, 1999. 514–15. Print.

———. "Kafka and His Precursors." Trans. Eliot Weinberger. *Selected Non-Fictions*. Ed. Eliot Weinberger. New York: Penguin, 1999. 363–65. Print.

———. "Kafka y sus precursores." 1951. *Obras completas*. Vol. 2. Buenos Aires: Emecé, 2007. 107–09. Print.

———. *Las Kenningar*. Buenos Aires: Francisco A. Colombo, 1933. Print.

———. "Las *Kenningar*." 1936. *Obras completas*. Vol. 1. Buenos Aires: Emecé, 2004. 368–81. Print.

———. "Los laberintos policiales y Chesterton." 1935. *Jorge Luis Borges en Sur: 1931–1980*. Buenos Aires: Emecé, 1999. 126–29. Print.

———. *Labyrinths: Selected Stories & Other Writings*. Ed. Donald A. Yates and James E. Irby. New York: New Directions, 1962. Print.

———. "The Labyrinths of the Detective Story and Chesterton." Trans. Eliot Weinberger. *Selected Non-Fictions*. Ed. Eliot Weinberger. New York: Penguin, 1999. 112–14. Print.

———. "Leopoldo Lugones, *Romancero*." *El tamaño de mi esperanza*. 1926. Madrid: Alianza, 2002. 105–08. Print.

———. "[Letter to Ramón Sopena]." MSS 10155-af. The Jorge Luis Borges Collection, Albert and Shirley Small Special Collections Library, University of Virginia.

———. "Leyes de la narración policial." 1933. *Textos recobradas, 1931–1955*. Buenos Aires: Emecé, 2001. 36–39. Print.

———. "The Library of Babel." Trans. Andrew Hurley. *Collected Fictions*. New York: Penguin, 1998. 112–18. Print.

———. "El libro." 1979. *Obras completas*. Vol. 4. Buenos Aires: Emecé, 2007. 197–205. Print.

———. "La literatura fantástica." 1964. *Anales Nueva Época* 11 (2008): 11–24. Print.

———. "La literatura fantástica." 1967. *Los laberintos del signo: Homenaje a J. L. Borges*. Ed. Graciela N. Ricci. Milano: Dott. A. Giuffrè Editore, 1999. 19–28. Print.

———. "La lotería en Babilonia." 1941. *Obras completas*. Vol. 1. Buenos Aires: Emecé, 2004. 456–60. Print.

———. "The Lottery in Babylon." Trans. Andrew Hurley. *Collected Fictions*. New York: Penguin, 1998. 101–06. Print.

———. "Magias parciales del *Quijote*. 1949. *Obras completas*. Vol. 2. Buenos Aires: Emecé, 2007. 54–57. Print.

———. "*Las 1001 noches*." *Crítica: Revista multicolor de los sábados*. Year 1, number 31 (10 Mar. 1934): 5. Print.

———. "Modos de G. K. Chesterton." 1936. *Jorge Luis Borges en Sur: 1931–1980*. Buenos Aires: Emecé, 1999. 18–23. Print.

———. "La muerte y la brújula." 1942. *Obras completas*. Vol. 1. Buenos Aires: Emecé, 2004. 499–507. Print.

———. "Narrative Art and Magic." Trans. Suzanne Jill Levine. *Selected Non-Fictions*. Ed. Eliot Weinberger. New York: Penguin, 1999. 75–82. Print.

———. "1983 G. Harry Pouder Lecture." 19 Apr. 1983. Shriver Hall Auditorium, Homewood Campus, Johns Hopkins University. Audiocassette.

————. "Nota preliminar a Francis Bret Harte, *Bocetos californianos.*" 1946. *Obras completas.* Vol. 4. Buenos Aires: Emecé, 2007. 92–94. Print.

————. [Notations in *The Works of Edgar Allan Poe (1).*] *The Works of Edgar Allan Poe (1): Memoir-Tales.* La Fundación Internacional Jorge Luis Borges, Buenos Aires.

————. [Notations in *The Works of Edgar Allan Poe: The Poems.*] *The Works of Edgar Allan Poe: The Poems and Three Essays on Poetry, Narrative of Arthur Gordon Pym, Miscellanies.* La Fundación Internacional Jorge Luis Borges, Buenos Aires.

————. "Noticia de las *kenningar.*" *Sur* 6 (1932): 202–08. Print.

————. "La obra y destino de Walt Whitman." 1959. *Textos recobrados, 1956–1986.* Buenos Aires: Emecé, 2003. 43–47. Print.

————. *Obras completas.* 4 vols. Buenos Aires: Emecé, 2004–07. Print.

————. *Obras completas: Edición crítica.* 3 vols. Ed. Rolando Costa Picazo and Irma Zangara. Buenos Aires: Emecé, 2009–11. Print.

————. "Observación final." 1942. *Jorge Luis Borges en Sur: 1931–1980.* Buenos Aires: Emecé, 1999. 252–53. Print.

————. "On William Beckford's *Vathek.*" Trans. Eliot Weinberger. *Selected Non-Fictions.* Ed. Eliot Weinberger. New York: Penguin, 1999. 236–39.

————. "The Other Death." Trans. Andrew Hurley. *Collected Fictions.* New York: Penguin, 1998. 223–28. Print.

————. "La otra muerte." 1949. *Obras completas.* Vol. 1. Buenos Aires: Emecé, 2004. 571–75. Print.

————. "El otro Whitman." *La vida literaria* 2.14 (1929): 3. Print.

————. "El otro Whitman." *Discusión.* Buenos Aires: M. Gleizer, 1932. 65–70. Print.

————. "El otro Whitman." 1932. *Obras completas.* Vol. 1. Buenos Aires: Emecé, 2004. 206–08. Print.

————. "Pierre Menard, Author of the *Quixote.*" Trans. Andrew Hurley. *Collected Fictions.* New York: Penguin, 1998. 88–95. Print.

————. "Pierre Menard, autor del Quijote." 1939. *Obras completas.* Vol. 1. Buenos Aires: Emecé, 2004. 444–50. Print.

————. "La poesía." 1980. *Obras completes.* Vol. 3. Buenos Aires: Emecé, 2007. 301–17. Print.

————. "Prólogo." *Artificios.* 1944. Obras completas. Vol. 1. Buenos Aires: Emecé, 2004. 483. Print.

————. "Prólogo." *El informe de Brodie.* 1970. *Obras completas.* Vol. 2. Buenos Aires: Emecé, 2007. 457–59. Print.

————. "Prólogo." *La rosa profunda.* 1975. *Obras completas.* Vol. 3. Buenos Aires: Emecé, 2007. 97–98. Print.

————. "Prólogo a Adolfo Bioy Casares, *La invención de Morel.*" 1940. *Obras completas.* Vol. 4. Buenos Aires: Emecé, 2007. 29–31. Print.

————. "Prólogo a Edgar Allan Poe, *La carta robada.*" *La carta robada.* Madrid: Siruela, 1985. 9–13. Print.

————. "Prólogo a Edgar Allan Poe, *Cuentos.*" 1986. *Obras completas.* Vol. 4. Buenos Aires: Emecé, 2007. 646–47. Print.

————. "Prólogo a Elvira de Alvear, *Reposo.*" 1934. *Textos recobrados, 1931–1955.* Buenos Aires: Emecé, 2001. 104–07. Print.

———. "Prólogo a Julio Cortázar, *Cuentos.*" 1985. *Obras completas.* Vol. 4. Buenos Aires: Emecé, 2007. 551–52. Print.

———. "Prólogo a Ray Bradbury, *Crónicas marcianas.*" *Crónicas marcianas.* Buenos Aires: Minotauro, 1955. Print.

———. "Prólogo a Ray Bradbury, *Crónicas marcianas.*" *Crónicas marcianas.* Buenos Aires: Minotauro, 1974. Print.

———. "Prólogo a Ray Bradbury, *Crónicas marcianas.*" 1975. *Obras completas.* Vol. 4. Buenos Aires: Emecé, 2007. 32–34.

———. "Prólogo a Wilkie Collins, *La piedra lunar.*" 1946. *Obras completas.* Vol. 4. Buenos Aires: Emecé, 2007. 55–56. Print.

———. "Prólogo de prólogos." 1975. *Obras completas.* Vol. 4. Buenos Aires: Emecé, 2007. 13–15.

———. *Prólogos, con un prólogo de prólogos.* 1975. *Obras completas.* Vol. 4. Buenos Aires: Emecé, 2007. 11–192. Print.

———. "Prologue." *The Unending Rose.* Trans. Alastair Reid. *Selected Poems.* Ed. Alexander Coleman. New York: Penguin, 1999. 343, 345. Print.

———. "El puntual Mardrus." *Crítica: Revista multicolor de los sábados* 1.26 (3 Feb. 1934): 8. Print.

———. "Roger Caillois: *Le roman policier.*" 1942. *Jorge Luis Borges en Sur: 1931–1980.* Buenos Aires: Emecé, 1999. 248–51. Print.

———. "Las ruinas circulares." 1940. *Obras completas.* Vol. 1. Buenos Aires: Emecé, 2004. 451–55. Print.

———. "Una sentencia del *Quijote.*" 1933. *Textos recobrados, 1931–1955.* Buenos Aires: Emecé, 2001. 62–65. Print.

———. *Siete noches.* 1980. *Obras completas.* Vol. 3. Buenos Aires: Emecé, 2007. 237–343. Print.

———. "Sobre el 'Vathek' de William Beckford." 1943. *Obras completas.* Vol. 2. Buenos Aires, Emecé, 2007. 130–33. Print.

———. "Sobre los clásicos." 1941. *Páginas de Jorge Luis Borges: Seleccionadas por el autor.* Buenos Aires: Celtia, 1982. 228–31. Print.

———. "Sobre Lugones." 1974. *Textos recobrados, 1956–1986.* Buenos Aires: Emecé, 2003. 173–74. Print.

———. "The South." Trans. Andrew Hurley. *Collected Fictions.* New York: Penguin, 1998. 174–79. Print.

———. "El sur." 1953. *Obras completas.* Vol. 1. Buenos Aires, Emecé, 2004. 524–29. Print.

———. "Tales of the Fantastic." *Prism International* 8.1 (1968): 5–16. Print.

———. "El taller del escritor." 1979. *Textos recobrados, 1956–1986.* Buenos Aires: Emecé, 2003. 353–58. Print.

———. *This Craft of Verse.* Ed. Călin-Andrei Mihăilescu. Cambridge: Harvard University Press, 2000. Print.

———. *This Craft of Verse: The Norton Lectures, 1967–68.* UbuWeb. Web. 5 Nov. 2013. <http://ubu.com/sound/borges.html>.

———. "Los traductores de *Las 1001 noches.*" 1936. *Obras completas.* Vol. 1. Buenos Aires: Emecé, 2004. 397–413. Print.

———. "The Translators of *The Thousand and One Nights*." Trans. Esther Allen. *Selected Non-Fictions*. Ed. Eliot Weinberger. New York: Penguin, 1999. 92–109. Print.

———. "The Translators of *The Thousand and One Nights*." Trans. Esther Allen. *The Translation Studies Reader*. Ed. Lawrence Venuti. New York: Routledge, 2000. 34–48. Print.

———. "La última invención de Hugh Walpole." 1943. *Textos recobrados, 1931–1955*. Buenos Aires: Emecé, 2001. 207–10. Print.

———. "Utopía de un hombre que está cansado." 1975. *Obras completas*. Vol. 3. Buenos Aires: Emecé, 2007. 66–72. Print.

———. "Las versiones homéricas." 1932. *Obras completas*. Vol. 1. Buenos Aires, Emecé, 2004. 239–43. Print.

———. "Una vindicación de Mark Twain." 1935. *Jorge Luis Borges en Sur: 1931–1980*. Buenos Aires: Emecé, 1999. 13–17. Print.

———. "A Weary Man's Utopia." Trans. Andrew Hurley. *Collected Fictions*. New York: Penguin, 1998. 460–65. Print.

Borges, Jorge Luis, trans. "El Príncipe feliz." By Oscar Wilde. *El País* [Buenos Aires]. 25 June 1910. Print.

Borges, Jorge Luis, and Roberto Alifano. "La literatura policial—Poe y Chesterton." *Conversaciones con Jorge Luis Borges*. Buenos Aires: Atlántida, 1984. 11–18. Print.

Borges, Jorge Luis, and Adolfo Bioy Casares. "Del agua de la isla." *Cuentos breves y extraordinarios*. Buenos Aires: Raigal, 1955. 165–66. Print.

———. "Prólogo a *Los mejores cuentos policiales*." 1981. *Los mejores cuentos policiales*. 1943. Buenos Aires: Emecé, 1997. 7–8. Print.

———. *Seis problemas para don Isidro Parodi*. 1942. *Obras completas en colaboración*. Buenos Aires: Emecé, 1979. 11–121. Print.

Borges, Jorge Luis, and Adolfo Bioy Casares, eds. *Cuentos breves y extraordinarios*. Buenos Aires: Raigal, 1955. Print.

———. *Los mejores cuentos policiales*. 1943. Buenos Aires: Emecé, 1997. Print.

Borges, Jorge Luis, and Adolfo Bioy Casares, trans. "La carta robada." By Edgar Allan Poe. *Los mejores cuentos policiales*. 1943. Buenos Aires: Emecé, 1997. 23–38. Print.

———. "La verdad sobre el caso de M. Valdemar." By Edgar Allan Poe. *Antología de la literatura fantástica*. 1940. Buenos Aires: Sudamericana, 1971. 371–79. Print.

Borges, Jorge Luis, Adolfo Bioy Casares, and Silvina Ocampo, eds. *Antología de la literatura fantástica*. 1940. Buenos Aires: Sudamericana, 1971. Print.

Borges, Jorge Luis, and Norman Thomas di Giovanni. "Autobiographical Notes." *New Yorker*. 19 Sept. 1970: 40–99. Print.

Borges, Jorge Luis, and Betina Edelberg. *Leopoldo Lugones*. 1955. *Obras completas en colaboración*. Buenos Aires: Emecé, 1979. 455–508. Print.

Borges, Jorge Luis, and Osvaldo Ferrari. *Borges en diálogo: Conversaciones de Jorge Luis Borges con Osvaldo Ferrari*. Buenos Aires: Grijalbo, 1985. Print.

———. "Cómo nace y se hace un texto de Borges." *Borges en diálogo: Conversaciones de Jorge Luis Borges con Osvaldo Ferrari*. Buenos Aires: Grijalbo, 1985. 61–69. Print.

————. "Diálogo sobre el Modernismo y Rubén Darío." *Libro de diálogos*. Buenos Aires: Sudamericana, 1986. 112–19. Print.

————. *Diálogos últimos*. Buenos Aires: Sudamericana, 1987. Print.

————. "La ética y la cultura." *Borges en diálogo: Conversaciones de Jorge Luis Borges con Osvaldo Ferrari*. Buenos Aires: Grijalbo, 1985. 265–71. Print.

————. "Silvina Ocampo, Bioy Casares y Juan R. Wilcock." *Borges en diálogo: Conversaciones de Jorge Luis Borges con Osvaldo Ferrari*. Buenos Aires: Grijalbo, 1985. 81–92. Print.

————. "Sobre Edgar Allan Poe." *Diálogos últimos*. Buenos Aires: Sudamericana, 1987. 189–94. Print.

————. "Sobre la llegada del hombre a la Luna." *Diálogos últimos*. Buenos Aires: Sudamericana, 1987. 37–44. Print.

————. "Sobre la personalidad y el Buda." *Diálogos últimos*. Buenos Aires: Sudamericana, 1987. 156–62. Print.

————. "Sobre los poetas de New England." *Diálogos últimos*. Buenos Aires: Sudamericana, 1987. 176–82. Print.

Borges, Jorge Luis, and María Ester Gilio. "Jorge Luis Borges: 'Yo quería ser el hombre invisible.'" *Crisis* 13 (1974): 40–47.

Borges, Jorge Luis, and Margarita Guerrero. "El animal soñado por Poe." *El libro de los seres imaginarios*. Buenos Aires: Kier, 1967. 21–22. Print.

————. "El animal soñado por Poe." *Manual de zoología fantástica*. México: Fondo de Cultura Económica, 1957. 24–25. Print.

Borges, Jorge Luis, and Margarita Guerrero, eds. *El libro de los seres imaginarios*. Buenos Aires: Kier, 1967.

————. *Manual de zoología fantástica*. México: Fondo de Cultura Económica, 1957.

Borges, Jorge Luis, and Esther Zemborain de Torres. *Introducción a la literatura norteamericana*. Buenos Aires: Columba, 1967. Print.

————. *An Introduction to American Literature*. Trans. L. Clark Keating and Robert O. Evans. Lexington: University Press of Kentucky, 1971. Print.

Bosquet, Alain. "Borges o la dimensión imprevista." *La Nación* [Buenos Aires]. 20 Oct. 1974, sec. 3: 1. Print.

Burgin, Richard. *Conversations with Jorge Luis Borges*. New York: Holt, Rinehart and Winston, 1969. Print.

Burns, Shannon. "'The Cask of Amontillado': Montresor's Revenge." *Poe Studies* 7.1 (1974): 25. *The Edgar Allan Poe Society of Baltimore*. Web. 23 Sept. 2010.

Cadena, Holly. "Lo absurdo somos nosotros: el humor en los personajes de Borges." *Bulletin of Hispanic Studies* 82 (2005): 481–89. Print.

Caillois, Roger. "Rectificación a una nota de Jorge Luis Borges." *Sur* 91 (1942): 71–72. Print.

Cansinos Assens, Rafael, trans. *Obras completas*. Vol. 6. By Edgar Allan Poe. Madrid: Ediciones Mateu, 1918–21. Print.

Canto, Estela. *Borges a contraluz*. Madrid: Espasa Calpe, 1989. Print.

Casanova, Pascale. *The World Republic of Letters*. Trans. M. B. DeBevoise. Cambridge, Mass.: Harvard University Press, 2004. Print.

Castro, Andrea. "Edgar A. Poe en castellano y sus reescritores: El caso de 'The Oval

Portrait.'" *Anales Nueva Época* 11 (2008): 97–125. University of Gothenburg. Web. 11 Feb. 2011. <http://hdl.handle.net/2077/10436>.

Cauthen, Irby B., Jr. *Edgar Poe at the University—1826*. Charlottesville: The Raven Society, 1991. Print.

Chanady, Amaryll Beatrice. *Magical Realism and the Fantastic: Resolved Versus Unresolved Antinomy*. New York: Garland, 1985. Print.

Cohn, Deborah N. *History and Memory in the Two Souths: Recent Southern and Spanish American Fiction*. Nashville: Vanderbilt University Press, 1999. Print.

Cortázar, Julio. "Casa tomada." *Los anales de Buenos Aires* 1.11 (1946): 13–18. Print.

———. "Introducción." *Obras en prosa*. By Edgar Allan Poe. 2 vols. Madrid: Revista de Occidente, 1956. xi–xcvii. Print.

———. *Los reyes*. Buenos Aires: Gulab y Aldabahor, 1949. Print.

———. "[Untitled Essay About Roger Caillois.]" Notebook 2, Box 5, Folder 6. Julio Cortázar Literary Manuscripts, The Nettie Lee Benson Latin American Collection, University of Texas at Austin.

———. "[Untitled Letter to Jorge Luis Borges.]" MSS 10155-k. The Jorge Luis Borges Collection, Albert and Shirley Small Special Collections Library, University of Virginia.

———. "La vida de Edgar Allan Poe." 1956. *Cuentos completos: Edición comentada*. By Edgar Allan Poe. Ed. Fernando Iwasaki and Jorge Volpi. Madrid: Páginas de Espuma, 2008. 21–52. Print.

Cortázar, Julio, trans. *Aventuras de Arthur Gordon Pym*. By Edgar Allan Poe. La Habana: Instituto del Libro, 1968. Print.

———. *Cuentos*. By Edgar Allan Poe. 2 vols. Madrid: Alianza, 1970. Print.

———. *Cuentos completos: Edición comentada*. By Edgar Allan Poe. Ed. Fernando Iwasaki and Jorge Volpi. Madrid: Páginas de Espuma, 2008. Print.

———. *Ensayos y críticas*. By Edgar Allan Poe. Madrid: Alianza, 1973. Print.

———. *Eureka*. By Edgar Allan Poe. Madrid: Alianza, 1972. Print.

———. *Obras en prosa*. By Edgar Allan Poe. 2 vols. Madrid: Revista de Occidente, 1956. Print.

———. *Obras en prosa*. By Edgar Allan Poe. 2 vols. Río Piedras: Editorial Universitaria de la Universidad de Puerto Rico, 1956. Print.

———. *Obras en prosa*. By Edgar Allan Poe. 2 vols. Barcelona: Editorial Universitaria de la Universidad de Puerto Rico, 1969. Print.

Cortínez, Verónica. "De Poe a Borges: La creación del lector policial." *Revista Hispánica Moderna* 48.1 (1995): 127–36. Print.

Costa Picazo, Rolando. *Borges: Una forma de felicidad*. Buenos Aires: Fundación Internacional Jorge Luis Borges, 2001. Print.

"Cuentos de Edgar A. Poe." *El instructor peruano*. 21 Apr. 1847. Print.

"Cuentos de Edgar A. Poe." *El instructor peruano*. 24 Apr. 1847. Print.

"Cuentos de Edgar A. Poe: El gato negro." *El instructor peruano*. 28 Apr. 1847. Print.

Cutler, Edward S. "Coincidence and the Literary Absolute: Poe's German Romantic Inheritance." Presented at the Poe Studies Association's Third International Edgar Allan Poe Conference: The Bicentennial, 2009.

Darío, Rubén. *Azul*. 1888. Buenos Aires: Espasa-Calpe, 1945. Print.

———. "Los raros." 1893. *Obras completas*. Vol. 2. Madrid: Afrodisio Aguado, 1950. 245–518. Print.

"Edgar Allan Poe's Works as Autobiography." *The Edgar Allan Poe Society of Baltimore*. Web. 28 Sept. 2010.

Englekirk, John Eugene. *Edgar Allan Poe in Hispanic Literature*. New York: Instituto de las Españas en los Estados Unidos, 1934. Print.

Enguídanos, Miguel, et al. "Now I Am More or Less Who I Am." 1976. *Jorge Luis Borges: Conversations*. Ed. Richard Burgin. Jackson: University of Mississippi Press, 1998. 164–75. Print.

Even-Zohar, Itamar. "The Position of Translated Literature within the Literary Polysystem." 1978. *The Translation Studies Reader*. Ed. Lawrence Venuti. New York: Routledge, 2000. 192–97. Print.

Fernández, James D. "Artículo de reseña." *Revista de Estudios Hispánicos* 36.1 (2002): 241–45. Print.

Ferrari, Santiago. *Edgar Allan Poe: Genio narrador*. Buenos Aires: Poseidón, 1946. Print.

Fisher, Benjamin F. "Poe's 'Metzengerstein': Not a Hoax." *American Literature* 42.4 (1971): 487–94. Print.

Folger, Roger. "The Great Chain of Memory: Borges, Funes, *De Viris Illustribus*." *Hispanófila* 135 (2002): 125–36. Print.

"From Out That Shadow: The Life and Legacy of Edgar Allan Poe." The Harrison Institute and Special Collections, University of Virginia Library, Mar.–Aug. 2009. The Harry Ransom Center, University of Texas at Austin, Sept. 2009–Jan. 2010. Exhibit.

"Genio." *Real Academia Española*. Web. 4 Mar. 2010.

Gentzler, Edwin. *Translation and Identity in the Americas: New Directions in Translation Theory*. London: Routledge, 2008. Print.

Gilliam, Alexander G., Jr. "The Founding and Early Days of the Raven Society." [The Raven Society Centennial Dinner Keepsake.] TS. The Raven Society, Charlottesville, Virginia. 6–9.

Griswold, Rufus Wilmot, ed. *The Works of the Late Edgar Allan Poe*. Vol. 4. New York: Redfield, 1856. *The Edgar Allan Poe Society of Baltimore*. Web. 21 Oct. 2011.

Hammond, Alexander. "Further Notes on Poe's Folio Club." *Poe Studies* 8.2 (1975): 38–42. *The Edgar Allan Poe Society of Baltimore*. Web. 17 Oct. 2011.

———. "A Reconstruction of Poe's 1833 *Tales of the Folio Club*: Preliminary Notes." *Poe Studies* 5.2 (1972): 25–32. *The Edgar Allan Poe Society of Baltimore*. Web. 17 Oct. 2011.

Handley, George B. *New World Poetics: Nature and the Adamic Imagination of Whitman, Neruda, and Walcott*. Athens: University of Georgia Press, 2007. Print.

———. *Postslavery Literatures in the Americas: Family Portraits in Black and White*. Charlottesville: University Press of Virginia, 2000. Print.

Heliodoro Valle, Rafael. "Fichas para la bibliografía de Poe en Hispanoamérica." *Revista Iberoamericana* 16 (1950): 199–214. Print.

Hoffman, Daniel. *Poe Poe Poe Poe Poe Poe Poe*. New York: Anchor Press, 1973. Print.

Holmes, James S. "The Name and Nature of Translation Studies." 1972. *The Translation Studies Reader*. Ed. Lawrence Venuti. New York: Routledge, 2000. 172–85. Print.

"International Poe Bibliography (1969–2002)." *Poe Studies* 35.

Irby, James E. Introduction. *Labyrinths: Selected Stories and Other Writings*. Ed. Donald A. Yates and James E. Irby. New York: New Directions, 1962. xv–xxiii. Print.

Irwin, John T. *The Mystery to a Solution: Poe, Borges, and the Analytic Detective Story*. Baltimore: Johns Hopkins University Press, 1994. Print.

Johnson, David E. "Kant's Dog." *diacritics* 34.1 (2004): 19–39. Print.

Kelly, Matt. "At the University of Virginia, the Spirit of Poe Resides Evermore." *UVA Today*. 14 July 2011. Web. 19 Sept. 2013.

Kennedy, J. Gerald. "Poe and Magazine Writing on Premature Burial." *Studies in the American Renaissance* 1 (1977): 165–78. Print.

———. "The Violence of Melancholy: Poe Against Himself." *American Literary History* 8.3 (1996): 533–51. Print.

Kent, Charles W., and John S. Patton. *The Book of the Poe Centenary*. 1909. Charlottesville: Folcroft Library Editions, 1972. Print.

Kodama, María. Personal interview. 6 Aug. 2009.

Kristal, Efraín. *Invisible Work: Borges and Translation*. Nashville: Vanderbilt University Press, 2002. Print.

Kushigian, Julia A. "The Detective Story Genre in Poe and Borges." *Latin American Literary Review* 11.22 (1983): 27–39. Print.

Lacan, Jacques. "Seminar on 'The Purloined Letter.'" 1972. Trans. Jeffrey Mehlman. *The Purloined Poe: Lacan, Derrida, and Psychoanalytic Reading*. Ed. John P. Muller and William J. Richardson. Baltimore: Johns Hopkins University Press, 1988. 28–54. Print. Trans. of "Le séminaire sur 'La lettre volée.'" 1956. Print.

Lefevere, André. *Translating Literature: Practice and Theory in a Comparative Literature Context*. New York: Modern Language Association of America, 1992. Print.

Levine, Stuart, and Susan Levine. "Multiple Intention." *The Short Fiction of Edgar Allan Poe*. Ed. Stuart Levine and Susan Levine. Indianapolis: Bobbs-Merrill, 1976. 471–72. Print.

———. "Slapstick Gothic." *The Short Fiction of Edgar Allan Poe*. Ed. Stuart Levine and Susan Levine. Indianapolis: Bobbs-Merrill, 1976. 294–95. Print.

Lira, René. "Borges y Twain: Un caso de intertextualidad." *Crítica semiológica de textos literarios hispánicos*. Ed. Miguel Ángel Garrido Gallardo. Madrid: Consejo Superior de Investigaciones Científicas, 1986. 509–26. Print.

Loewenstein, C. Jared. Personal interview. 11 Mar. 2010.

———. "Re: A Few More Borges/Poe Questions." Message to the author. 8 Nov. 2013. E-mail.

———. Telephone interview. 19 Sept. 2013.

Loewenstein. Dir. Eduardo Montes-Bradley. Heritage Film Project, 2012. *Vimeo*. Web. 6 Nov. 2013.

López Morales, Berta. "El modelo de la literatura fantástica aplicado en 'El Aleph.'" *Estudios Filológicos* 15 (1980): 73–80. Print.

Lowell, James Russell. *A Fable for Critics*. 1848. Freeport, N.Y.: Books for Libraries Press, 1972. Print.

Luján Tubio, María. "'El Aleph' y la hiperrealidad mística." *Espéculo: Revista de estudios literarios* 32 (2006): NP. Web. 7 Dec. 2010.

Mabbott, Thomas Ollive. "The Black Cat." By Edgar Allan Poe. *Tales and Sketches Volume 2: 1843–1849*. Ed. Thomas Ollive Mabbott. Urbana: University of Illinois Press, 2000. 847–49. Print.

———. "The Cask of Amontillado." By Edgar Allan Poe. *Tales and Sketches Volume 2: 1843–1849*. Ed. Thomas Ollive Mabbott. Urbana: University of Illinois Press, 2000. 1252–56. Print.

———. "'A Decided Loss' and 'Loss of Breath.'" By Edgar Allan Poe. *Tales and Sketches Volume 1: 1831–1842*. Ed. Thomas Ollive Mabbott. Urbana: University of Illinois Press, 2000. 51–52. Print.

———. "Hop-Frog." By Edgar Allan Poe. *Tales and Sketches Volume 2: 1843–1849*. Ed. Thomas Ollive Mabbott. Urbana: University of Illinois Press, 2000. 1343–44. Print.

———. "Metzengerstein." By Edgar Allan Poe. *Tales and Sketches Volume 1: 1831–1842*. Ed. Thomas Ollive Mabbott. Urbana: University of Illinois Press, 2000. 15–18. Print.

———. "MS. Found in a Bottle." By Edgar Allan Poe. *Tales and Sketches Volume 1: 1831–1842*. Ed. Thomas Ollive Mabbott. Urbana: University of Illinois Press, 2000. 130–34. Print.

———. "The Murders in the Rue Morgue." By Edgar Allan Poe. *Tales and Sketches Volume 1: 1831–1842*. Ed. Thomas Ollive Mabbott. Urbana: University of Illinois Press, 2000. 521–27. Print.

———, ed. *Edgar Allan Poe: Tales and Sketches Volume 1: 1831–1842*. 1978. Urbana: University of Illinois Press, 2000. Print.

———, ed. *Edgar Allan Poe: Tales and Sketches Volume 2: 1843–1849*. 1978. Urbana: University of Illinois Press, 2000. Print.

Madden, Fred. "Poe's 'The Black Cat' and Freud's 'The Uncanny.'" *Literature and Psychology* 39.1–2 (1993): 52–62. Print.

Martin, Clancy W. "Borges Forgets Nietzsche." *Philosophy and Literature* 30.1 (2006): 265–76. Print.

Mazurek, Ray. "Art, Ambiguity, and the Artist in Poe's 'The Man of the Crowd.'" *Poe Studies* 12.2 (1979): 25–28. *The Edgar Allan Poe Society of Baltimore*. Web. 18 Feb. 2011.

McBride, Mary. "Jorge Luis Borges, Existentialist: 'The Aleph' and the Relativity of Human Perception." *Studies in Short Fiction* 14 (1977): 401–03. Print.

McClennen, Sophia A. "Inter-American Studies or Imperial American Studies?" *Comparative American Studies* 3.4 (2005): 393–413. Print.

Menéndez, Salvio Martín, and Jorge Panesi. "El manuscrito de 'El Aleph' de Jorge Luis Borges." *Filología* 27.1–2 (1994): 91–119. Print.

Mundo Lo, Sara de. *Julio Cortázar: His Works and His Critics: A Bibliography*. Urbana, Ill.: Albatross, 1985. Print.

Nietzsche, Friedrich. "On Truth and Lies in a Nonmoral Sense." *Philosophy and Truth: Selections from Nietzsche's Notebooks of the Early 1870s*. Ed. and trans. Daniel Breazeale. Atlantic Highlands, N.J.: Humanities Press International, 1979. 79–97. Print.

Núñez-Faraco, Humberto. "In Search of the Aleph: Memory, Truth, and Falsehood in Borges's Poetics." *Modern Language Review* 92.3 (1997): 613–29. Print.

Obligado, Carlos. "Los poemas de Edgar Poe." *Anales del Instituto Popular de Conferencias* 18 (1932): 67–85. Print.

———. *Los poemas de Edgar Poe: Traducción, prólogo y notas*. Buenos Aires: Viau, 1932. Print.

———. "Prólogo." *Los poemas de Edgar Poe: Traducción, prólogo y notas*. Buenos Aires: Viau, 1932. 9–37. Print.

"Obtuvo un premio literario el escritor Jorge Luis Borges." *La Prensa* [Buenos Aires]. 3 May 1961. Print.

Ogden, Estrella B. "Borges en la poesía de Gonzalo Rojas: 'Aleph, Aleph.'" *Borges: Nuevas lecturas*. Ed. Juana Alcira Arancibia. Buenos Aires: Instituto Literario y Cultural Hispánico/Corregidor, 2001. 115–23. Print.

O'Hare, Mary Kate. *Constructive Spirit: Abstract Art in South and North America, 1920s–50s*. Petaluma, Calif.: Pomegranate, 2010. 11. Print.

Olivera, Carlos. "Al lector." *Novelas y cuentos*. Paris: Garnier Frères, 1884. 1–7. Print.

———, trans. "La carta robada." By Edgar Allan Poe. *Novelas y cuentos*. Paris: Garnier Frères, 1884. 217–44. Print.

———, trans. "Mr. Valdemar." By Edgar Allan Poe. *Novelas y cuentos*. Paris: Garnier Frères, 1884. 245–58. Print.

Ortega, Julio, and Elena del Río Parra. "Nuestra Edición." *"El Aleph" de Jorge Luis Borges: Edición crítica y facsimilar de Julio Ortega y Elena del Río Parra*. Ed. Julio Ortega and Elena del Río Parra. México: El Colegio de México, Centro de Estudios Lingüísticos y Literarios, 2001. 23–24. Print.

———, eds. *"El Aleph" de Jorge Luis Borges: Edición crítica y facsimilar de Julio Ortega y Elena del Río Parra*. México: El Colegio de México, Centro de Estudios Lingüísticos y Literarios, 2001. Print.

Páginas de Espuma. *Cuentos completos: Edición comentada*. By Edgar Allan Poe. Trans. Julio Cortázar. Web. 22 Oct. 2013. <http://paginasdeespuma.com/catalogo/cuentos-completos>.

Passos, Carlos A. "Sobre 'La literatura fantástica,' disertó ayer Jorge Luis Borges." *El País* [Montevideo]. 3 Sept. 1949: 4. Print.

———. "Sobre 'La literatura fantástica,' disertó ayer Jorge Luis Borges." *EspacioLatino.com*. Web. 1 Feb. 2011. <http://letras-uruguay.espaciolatino.com/aaa/Borges/sobre.htm>.

Pattee, Fred Lewis. *The Development of the American Short Story: An Historical Survey*. 1923. New York: Biblo and Tannen, 1966. Print.

Peeples, Scott. *The Afterlife of Edgar Allan Poe*. Rochester, N.Y.: Camden House, 2004. Print.

Pérez Bonalde, Juan Antonio, trans. "El cuervo." 1887. *J. A. Pérez Bonalde: Estudio* preliminar de Pedro Pablo Paredes. Ed. Pedro Pablo Paredes. 2 vols. Caracas: Academia Venezolana, 1964. 151–57. Print.

Pérez Firmat, Gustavo. "Introduction: Cheek to Cheek." *Do the Americas Have a Common Literature?* Ed. Gustavo Pérez Firmat. Durham, N.C.: Duke University Press, 1990. 1–5. Print.

Piñeyro, Enrique. "Notas críticas." *Revista cubana* 8 (1888): 563–68. Print.

Poe, Edgar Allan. "The Angel of the Odd." 1844. *Tales and Sketches Volume 2: 1843–1849.* Ed. Thomas Ollive Mabbott. Urbana: University of Illinois Press, 2000. 1100–12. Print.

———. "Berenice." 1835. *Tales and Sketches Volume 1: 1831–1842.* Ed. Thomas Ollive Mabbott. Urbana: University of Illinois Press, 2000. 209–21. Print.

———. "The Black Cat." 1843. *Tales and Sketches Volume 2: 1843–1849.* Ed. Thomas Ollive Mabbott. Urbana: University of Illinois Press, 2000. 849–60. Print.

———. "The Cask of Amontillado." 1846. *Tales and Sketches Volume 2: 1843–1849.* Ed. Thomas Ollive Mabbott. Urbana: University of Illinois Press, 2000. 1256–66. Print.

———. *The Centenary Poe: Tales, Poems, Criticism, Marginalia and Eureka.* London: The Bodley Head, 1949. Print.

———. "The Colloquy of Monos and Una." 1841. *Tales and Sketches Volume 1: 1831–1842.* Ed. Thomas Ollive Mabbott. Urbana: University of Illinois Press, 2000. 608–19. Print.

———. *The Complete Tales and Poems of Edgar Allan Poe.* New York: Vintage, 1975.

———. "The Conversation of Eiros and Charmion." 1839. *Tales and Sketches Volume 1: 1831–1842.* Ed. Thomas Ollive Mabbott. Urbana: University of Illinois Press, 2000. 455–62. Print.

———. "A Decided Loss." 1832. *Tales and Sketches Volume 1: 1831–1842.* Ed. Thomas Ollive Mabbott. Urbana: University of Illinois Press, 2000. 52–61. Print.

———. "A Descent into the Maelström." 1841. *Tales and Sketches Volume 1: 1831–1842.* Ed. Thomas Ollive Mabbott. Urbana: University of Illinois Press, 2000. 577–97. Print.

———. *Eureka: A Prose Poem.* New York: Geo. P. Putnam, 1848. *The Edgar Allan Poe Society of Baltimore.* Web. 6 Nov. 2009.

———. "The Facts in the Case of M. Valdemar." 1845. *Tales and Sketches Volume 2: 1843–1849.* Ed. Thomas Ollive Mabbott. Urbana: University of Illinois Press, 2000. 1233–44. Print.

———. "The Fall of the House of Usher." 1839. *Tales and Sketches Volume 1: 1831–1842.* Ed. Thomas Ollive Mabbott. Urbana: University of Illinois Press, 2000. 397–422. Print.

———. "Hop-Frog." 1849. *Tales and Sketches Volume 2: 1843–1849.* Ed. Thomas Ollive Mabbott. Urbana: University of Illinois Press, 2000. 1345–55. Print.

———. *The Letters of Edgar Allan Poe.* Ed. John Ward Ostrom. 2 vols. Cambridge: Harvard University Press, 1948. Print.

———. "Ligeia." 1838. *Tales and Sketches Volume 1: 1831–1842.* Ed. Thomas Ollive Mabbott. Urbana: University of Illinois Press, 2000. 310–34. Print.

———. "Loss of Breath." *Southern Literary Messenger* 1 (1835): 735–40. *The Edgar Allan Poe Society of Baltimore.* Web. 3 Dec. 2013.

———. "Loss of Breath." 1846. *Tales and Sketches Volume 1: 1831–1842.* Ed. Thomas Ollive Mabbott. Urbana: University of Illinois Press, 2000. 61–77. Print.

———. "Loss of Breath." *Tales of the Grotesque and Arabesque.* Vol. 1. Philadelphia: Lea and Blanchard, 1840. 123–49. *The Edgar Allan Poe Society of Baltimore.* Web. 10 Oct. 2011.

———. "The Man of the Crowd." 1840. *Tales and Sketches Volume 1: 1831–1842.* Ed. Thomas Ollive Mabbott. Urbana: University of Illinois Press, 2000. 506–18. Print.

———. "Metzengerstein." 1832. *Southern Literary Magazine* 2 (1836): 97–100. *The Edgar Allan Poe Society of Baltimore.* Web. 2 Mar. 2011.

———. "Metzengerstein." 1832. *Tales and Sketches Volume 1: 1831–1842.* Ed. Thomas Ollive Mabbott. Urbana: University of Illinois Press, 2000. 18–31. Print.

———. "Morella." 1835. *Tales and Sketches Volume 1: 1831–1842.* Ed. Thomas Ollive Mabbott. Urbana: University of Illinois Press, 2000. 229–37. Print.

———. "MS. Found in a Bottle." 1833. *Tales and Sketches Volume 1: 1831–1842.* Ed. Thomas Ollive Mabbott. Urbana: University of Illinois Press, 2000. 135–48. Print.

———. "The Murders in the Rue Morgue." 1841. *Tales and Sketches Volume 1: 1831–1842.* Ed. Thomas Ollive Mabbott. Urbana: University of Illinois Press, 2000. 527–74. Print.

———. "The Mystery of Marie Rogêt." 1842–43. *Tales and Sketches Volume 2: 1843–1849.* Ed. Thomas Ollive Mabbott. Urbana: University of Illinois Press, 2000. 723–88. Print.

———. "The Mystery of Marie Rogêt—Part III." *Ladies' Companion,* Feb. 1843: 162–67. *The Edgar Allan Poe Society of Baltimore.* Web. 18 Mar. 2010.

———. *The Narrative of Arthur Gordon Pym of Nantucket.* New York: Harper & Brothers, 1838. *The Edgar Allan Poe Society of Baltimore.* Web. 23 Sept. 2009.

———. "Nathaniel Hawthorne." 1850. *The Works of the Late Edgar Allan Poe.* Vol. 3. New York: J. S. Redfield, 1850. 188–202. *The Edgar Allan Poe Society of Baltimore.* Web. 9 Mar. 2010.

———. "The Philosophy of Composition." *Graham's Magazine* 28.4 (1846): 163–67. *The Edgar Allan Poe Society of Baltimore.* Web. 28 Sept. 2009.

———. "Philosophy of Furniture." 1840. *Tales and Sketches Volume 1: 1831–1842.* Ed. Thomas Ollive Mabbott. Urbana: University of Illinois Press, 2000. 495–504. Print.

———. "The Pit and the Pendulum." 1842. *Tales and Sketches Volume 1: 1831–1842.* Ed. Thomas Ollive Mabbott. Urbana: University of Illinois Press, 2000. 681–700. Print.

———. "The Poetic Principle." *The Works of the Late Edgar Allan Poe.* Vol. 3. New York: J. S. Redfield. 1850. 1–20. *The Edgar Allan Poe Society of Baltimore.* Web. 30 Oct. 2009.

———. "Preface." *Tales of the Grotesque and Arabesque.* Vol. 1. Philadelphia: Lea and Blanchard, 1840. 5–6. *The Edgar Allan Poe Society of Baltimore.* Web. 2 Mar. 2011.

———. "The Premature Burial." 1844. *Tales and Sketches Volume 2: 1843–1849*. Ed. Thomas Ollive Mabbott. Urbana: University of Illinois Press, 2000. 954–72. Print.

———. "The Purloined Letter." 1844. *Tales and Sketches Volume 2: 1843–1849*. Ed. Thomas Ollive Mabbott. Urbana: University of Illinois Press, 2000. 974–97. Print.

———. "The Raven." 1845. *Complete Poems*. 1969. Ed. Thomas Ollive Mabbott. Urbana: University of Illinois Press, 2000. 364–74. Print.

———. "Some Words with a Mummy." 1845. *Tales and Sketches Volume 2: 1843–1849*. Ed. Thomas Ollive Mabbott. Urbana: University of Illinois Press, 2000. 1177–1201. Print.

———. "A Tale of the Ragged Mountains. 1844. *Tales and Sketches Volume 2: 1843–1849*. Ed. Thomas Ollive Mabbott. Urbana: University of Illinois Press, 2000. 939–53. Print.

———. *Tales of the Grotesque and Arabesque*. 2 vols. Philadelphia: Lea and Blanchard, 1840. *The Edgar Allan Poe Society of Baltimore*. Web. 10 Oct. 2011.

———. "The Tell-Tale Heart." 1843. *Tales and Sketches Volume 2: 1843–1849*. Ed. Thomas Ollive Mabbott. Urbana: University of Illinois Press, 2000. 792–99. Print.

———. "William Wilson." 1839. *Tales and Sketches Volume 1: 1831–1842*. Ed. Thomas Ollive Mabbott. Urbana: University of Illinois Press, 2000. 426–51. Print.

———. *The Works of Edgar Allan Poe: The Poems and Three Essays on Poetry, Narrative of Arthur Gordon Pym, Miscellanies*. Ed. R. Brimley Johnson. London: Oxford University Press, 1927. Print.

———. *The Works of Edgar Allan Poe (I): Memoir-Tales*. Ed. John H. Ingram. 3rd ed. Edinburgh: Adam and Charles Black, 1883. Print.

———. *The Works of Edgar Allan Poe (II): Tales—Continued*. Ed. John H. Ingram. 3rd ed. Edinburgh: Adam and Charles Black, 1883. Print.

Prádanos, Luis I. "Disfunciones de la memoria en 'Funes el Memorioso' y *Memento*: Una lectura neurocultural." *Ometeca: Journal on Science and Humanities in Hispanic Literature* 13 (2009): 174–85. Print.

Price, Vincent, perf. "The Cask of Amontillado." *An Evening of Edgar Allan Poe*. Dir. Kenneth Johnson. 1970. MGM, 2003. DVD.

Quinn, Arthur Hobson. *Edgar Allan Poe: A Critical Biography*. 1941. Baltimore: Johns Hopkins University Press, 1998. Print.

Quinn, Patrick F. *The French Face of Edgar Poe*. 1954. Carbondale: Southern Illinois University Press, 1971. Print.

Quiroga, Horacio. *Los arrecifes de coral*. Montevideo: Imprenta el siglo ilustrado, 1901. Print.

———. "Decálogo del perfecto cuentista." 1927. *Sobre literatura*. Montevideo: Arca, 1970. 86–88. Print.

———. "El manual del perfecto cuentista." *El Hogar* 21.808 (10 Apr. 1925): 7. Print.

———. "Los trucs del perfecto cuentista." *El Hogar* 21.814 (22 May 1925): 11. Print.

Rathbone, Emma. "Borges in Charlottesville." *The University of Virginia Magazine*. Summer 2012. Web. 5 Nov. 2013.

"Recompensó un jurado literario a J. L. Borges." *La Nación* [Buenos Aires]. 3 May 1961. Print.

Rodríguez Guerrero-Strachan, Santiago. "Idea de Edgar A. Poe en la obra crítica de Jorge Luis Borges." *Borges Studies Online*. J. L. Borges Center for Studies & Documentation. Web. 23 Feb. 2010.

Rodríguez-Luis, Julio. *The Contemporary Praxis of the Fantastic: Borges and Cortázar*. New York: Garland, 1991. Print.

Rodríguez Monegal, Emir. "Borges: Una teoría de la literatura fantástica." *Revista Iberoamericana* 42.95 (1976): 177–89. Print.

———. "Borges / de Man / Derrida / Bloom: La desconstrucción 'Avant et après la lettre.'" *Diseminario: La desconstrucción - otro descubrimiento de América*. Ed. Lisa Block de Behar. Montevideo: XYZ Editores, 1987. 119–23. Print.

———. *Jorge Luis Borges: A Literary Biography*. New York: E. P. Dutton, 1978. Print.

———. "Jorge Luis Borges y la literatura fantástica." *Número* 1.5 (1949): 448–54. Print.

———. *La objetividad de Horacio Quiroga*. Montevideo: Número, 1950. Print.

Rojas, Armando. "Edgar Allan Poe en la América Hispana." *Revista nacional de la cultura* 142–43 (1960): 152–61. Print.

Rollason, Christopher. "The Character of Phantasm: Edgar Allan Poe's 'The Fall of the House of Usher' and Jorge Luis Borges's 'Tlön, Uqbar, Orbis Tertius.'" *Atlantis* 31.1 (2009): 9–22. Web. 23 Feb. 2010.

Rosato, Laura, and Germán Álvarez, eds. *Borges, libros y lecturas: Catálogo de la colección Jorge Luis Borges en la Biblioteca Nacional*. Buenos Aires: Ediciones Biblioteca Nacional, 2010. Print.

Russ, Elizabeth Christine. *The Plantation in the Postslavery Imagination*. New York: Oxford University Press, 2009. Print.

Sampson, Zinie Chen. "Edgar Allan Poe's University of Virginia Room to Undergo Renovation." *Huffington Post*. 28 Apr. 2011. Web. 19 Sept. 2013.

Sarlo, Beatriz. *Jorge Luis Borges: A Writer on the Edge*. London: Verso, 1993. Print.

Satz, Mario. "Borges, el Aleph y la Kabala." *Borges y la literatura: Textos para un homenaje*. Ed. Victorino Polo García. Murcia: Universidad de Murcia, 1989. 73–83. Print.

Shanks, Edward. *Edgar Allan Poe*. London: Macmillan, 1937. Print.

Shapiro, Henry L. "Memory and Meaning: Borges and 'Funes el memorioso.'" *Revista Canadiense de Estudios Hispánicos* 9.2 (1985): 257–65. Print.

Silverman, Kenneth. *Edgar A. Poe: Mournful and Never-ending Remembrance*. New York: HarperCollins, 1991. Print.

Smith, Jon, and Deborah Cohn, eds. *Look Away! The U.S. South in New World Studies*. Durham, N.C.: Duke University Press, 2004. Print.

Sosnowski, Saúl. *Borges y la Cábala: La búsqueda del verbo*. Buenos Aires: Hispamérica, 1976. Print.

Soto y Calvo, Francisco, trans. *Joyario de Poe*. Buenos Aires: El Inca, 1927. Print.

Standish, Peter. "Borges and the Limits of Language." *Revista Canadiense de Estudios Hispánicos* 16.1 (1991): 136–42. Print.

Stavans, Ilán. "El arte de la memoria." *Mester* 19.2 (1990): 97–108. Print.

Steiner, George. *After Babel: Aspects of Language and Translation*. 2nd ed. New York: Oxford University Press, 1992. Print.

Svensson, Anna. "Borges en Gotemburgo: Sobre su conferencia 'La Literatura Fantástica' y sus contactos con el Instituto Iberoamericano." *Anales* Nueva Época 11 (2008): 25–47. *University of Gothenburg*. Web. 11 Feb. 2011. <http://hdl.handle.net/2077/10436>.

Thiem, Jon. "Borges, Dante, and the Poetics of Total Vision." *Comparative Literature* 40.2 (1988): 97–121. *JSTOR*. Web. 1 Mar. 2011.

Tissera, Graciela E. "Jorge Luis Borges." *Poe Abroad: Influence, Reputation, Affinities*. Ed. Lois Davis Vines. Iowa City: University of Iowa Press, 1999. 221–26. Print.

Todorov, Tzvetan. *The Fantastic: A Structural Approach to a Literary Genre*. Trans. Richard Howard. Ithaca, N.Y.: Cornell University Press, 1975. Print.

———. *Introduction à la littérature fantastique*. Paris: Éditions du Seuil, 1970. Print.

Torres García, Joaquín. *América invertida*. Montevideo: Museo Torres García, 1943.

———. "La escuela del sur." 1935. *Universalismo constructivo*. Madrid: Alianza, 1984. 193–98. Print.

———. *South America's Inverted Map*. New York: Cecilia de Torres, 1936.

———. *Universalismo constructivo*. Madrid: Alianza, 1984. Print.

Twain, Mark. *Life on the Mississippi*. 1883. New York: Harper & Row, 1951. Print.

Valencia, Leonardo. "Metzengerstein: Comentario de Leonardo Valencia." *Cuentos completos: Edición comentada*. By Edgar Allan Poe. Trans. Julio Cortázar. Ed. Fernando Iwasaki and Jorge Volpi. Madrid: Páginas de Espuma, 2008. 223–24. Print.

Vázquez, María Esther. "El encuentro con Borges." *La Nación* [Buenos Aires]. 28 Jan. 1979, sec. 3: 1. Print.

Venuti, Lawrence. *The Translator's Invisibility: A History of Translation*. 1995. 2nd ed. New York: Routledge, 2008. Print.

———, ed. *The Translation Studies Reader*. New York: Routledge, 2000. Print.

Vines, Lois Davis, ed. *Poe Abroad: Influence, Reputation, Affinities*. Iowa City: University of Iowa Press, 1999. Print.

Volpi, Jorge, and Fernando Iwasaki. "Poe & Cía." *Cuentos completos: Edición comentada*. By Edgar Allan Poe. Trans. Julio Cortázar. Ed. Fernando Iwasaki and Jorge Volpi. Madrid: Páginas de Espuma, 2008. 13–14. Print.

Von Schauenberg, Alberto L., trans. *Edgar Poe: Traducción de sus poemas*. Buenos Aires: Orientación, 1937. Print.

Waisman, Sergio. *Borges and Translation: The Irreverence of the Periphery*. Lewisburg, Penn.: Bucknell University Press, 2005. Print.

Weinstock, Herbert. ["Rejection Slip."] Alfred A. Knopf, Inc., "Records. Series VI, Editorial Department Files, 1915–1984 (bulk 1948–1978)." The Harry Ransom Center, University of Texas at Austin. 1949.

———. ["Rejection Slip."] Alfred A. Knopf, Inc., "Records. Series VI, Editorial Department Files, 1915–1984 (bulk 1948–1978)." The Harry Ransom Center, University of Texas at Austin. 1952.

———. ["Rejection Slip."] Alfred A. Knopf, Inc., "Records. Series VI, Editorial Department Files, 1915–1984 (bulk 1948–1978)." The Harry Ransom Center, University of Texas at Austin. 1955.

———. ["Rejection Slip."] Alfred A. Knopf, Inc., "Records. Series VI, Editorial Department Files, 1915–1984 (bulk 1948–1978)." The Harry Ransom Center, University of Texas at Austin. 1957.

Weiss, Jason. "Writing at Risk: Interview with Julio Cortázar." *Critical Essays on Julio Cortázar*. Ed. Jaime Alazraki. New York: G. K. Hall, 1999. 70–82. Print.

Whitman, Sarah Helen. *Edgar Poe and His Critics*. 1860. New York: Gordian Press, 1981. Print.

Williamson, Edwin. *Borges: A Life*. New York: Viking, 2004. Print.

Woodbridge, Hensley C. "Poe in Spanish America: A Bibliographical Supplement." *Poe Newsletter* 2 (1969): 18–19.

Woodward, C. Vann. *The Burden of Southern History*. 3rd ed. Baton Rouge: Louisiana State University Press, 1993. Print.

Wright, Edmond. "Jorge Luis Borges's 'Funes the Memorious': A Philosophical Narrative." *Partial Answers: Journal of Literature and the History of Ideas* 5.1 (2007): 33–49. Print.

Yates, Donald A. "Borges: Philosopher? Poet? Revolutionary?" 1982. *Jorge Luis Borges: Conversations*. Ed. Richard Burgin. Jackson: University Press of Mississippi, 1998. 192–98. Print.

Zia, Lizardo. "Agenda." *Clarín*. 15 May 1955: 9. Print.

Zoltowaska, Evelina. "La literatura argentina en París." *La Nación* [Buenos Aires]. 4 Oct. 1959, sec. 2: 6. Print.

Index

Bayard, Pierre, 171n19

Bazán, Armando, 81–83, 185n4; "El caso del señor Valdemar" (ed.), 81–83, 185n4, 185–87nn6–18; *Obras completas* (ed.), 81, 152, 156, 185n4, 187n18. *See also* "Purloined Letter, The"

Beckford, William, 182n8; *Vathek*, 16, 69

"Bells, The" (Poe), 44, 163

Benjamin, Walter, 69

Bennett, Maurice J., 168n7; "The Detective Fiction of Poe and Borges," 4

"Berenice" (Poe), 191n20, 198n27

Berman, Antoine, 183n17; "Translation and the Trials of the Foreign," 77

Bessière, Irène, 193n5

"biblioteca de Babel, La" ["The Library of Babel"] (Borges), 119

"Biblioteca Personal" ["Personal Library"] (Hyspamérica collection), 202n8

Bioy Casares, Adolfo: on Borges's preference for Poe's prose over his poetry, 178n31; on Borges's reaction to Poe's characterization of poetry, 175n18; the fantastic, understanding of, 124–28, 130, 135, 195n14; on fear and the macabre, 195n14; opinions on Poe, 185n1; on Valdemar's supernatural experience, 195–96nn14–15

—works of: *Antología de la literatura fantástica* (ed., with Borges and Ocampo), 81, 89, 99, 184n1; *Borges*, 178n31, 195n14; *Cuentos breves y extraordinarios* (ed., with Borges), 67, 77, 184n20; detective parodies with Borges, 201n4; *Los mejores cuentos policiales* (trans. with Borges), 9, 67, 99; prologue to *Antología de la literatura fantástica*, 127; *Seis problemas para don Isidro Parodi* (with Borges), 9, 201–02n4. *See also specific titles, in English, of Poe's works*

"Black Cat, The" (Poe): "El Aleph," relationship with, 18–19, 120, 147–51, 159; Amper on, 197–98n25, 198n33; in Borges-Poe dynamic of reciprocal influence, 13–14, 17, 151; as detective story, 133; as fantastic revenge tale, 121, 122, 124, 128, 133–38; Hoffman

on, 198n33; Mabbott on, 133, 198n25, 198n29; Madden on, 198n28; "Metzengerstein" compared with, 134–35, 137–38, 199n35; supernatural and, 18, 50–51, 86, 133, 186n11; Todorov on, 198n26

Block de Behar, Lisa, 139, 147

Bloom, Harold, 44, 170n17; *The Anatomy of Influence*, 11, 171n20; *The Anxiety of Influence*, 9–12

Bonaparte, Marie, 133, 134, 189nn8–9; *Edgar Poe: Étude psychanalytique*, 105

Borges (Bioy Casares), 178n31, 195n14

Borges, Jorge Luis: as anglophile, 7, 169n14; anthologies collecting Poe translations by, 99; versus Baudelaire's view of Poe, 6–7, 45; blindness of, 27, 37, 173n9; Caillois, relationship with, 51–53, 121, 179n8; career of, 2, 9, 161, 179n9; discovery of Poe, 8–9; English authors and, 67, 169n15; the fantastic, Borges's understanding of, 124, 126–28, 130, 163, 193–94nn6–7; as Formentor Prize winner (1961), 15, 53, 179n9; handwritten notes of, in personal copies of Poe's works, 5, 14–15, 27, 57, 95, 117, 173n8, 180n15, 181n22, 181n24; on Hawthorne, 170n18; insomnia of, 106; as literary critic on Poe, 2, 5, 14, 15, 48, 63, 171n21; literary critics coupling Borges with Poe, 4, 188n1; love relationships of, 106; personal libraries, preservation of, 116–17, 173n8; on Poe's deathbed, 177n27; Poe's influence on writing of, 1–2, 5, 8–10, 14, 155; reading Poe in English, 168n8; as southern writer, 6–7; theory of influence and, 13–14; theory of translation and, 69–75; as translator of Poe, 1–2, 3, 5, 67, 68–69, 75, 99; two-way influence and, 8, 118–19, 151, 155, 159; visit to Baltimore, 202n10, 203nn13–14; writing process of, 35–37, 175–76n21, 180n19. *See also specific titles, in English, of Poe's works, and specific titles, in Spanish, of Borges's works*

—fiction of, compared with Poe's: "El Aleph" versus Poe's "Metzengerstein"

Kabbalah, 106, 190n13
"Kafka y sus precursores" ["Kafka and His
    Precursors"] (Borges): Bloom's theory
    and, 171n20; on reciprocal influence
    between earlier and later writers,
    10–11, 13, 118, 122, 159; on reciprocal
    influence between Hawthorne
    and Kafka, 170–71n18; reciprocal
    relationship between Borges and Poe
    and, 19, 103
kenning, 37–38, 177n24
"Kenningar, Las" (Borges), 37–38,
    176–77n24
Kerrigan, Anthony, 54
Knopf publishing house, 15, 54–55,
    179n10
Kodama, María: on Borges's creative
    process, 176n21; Borges's handwriting
    and, 27, 173nn8–9; Borges's notes
    on Poe and, 95, 180n15, 181n24; on
    Borges's relationship with Cortázar,
    157
Kristal, Efraín. See Invisible Work

"laberintos policiales y Chesterton, Los"
    ["The Labyrinths of the Detective Story
    and Chesterton"] (Borges), 55, 58–59,
    180nn13–14
Labyrinths (ed. Yates and Irby), 54, 55
Lacan, Jacques, 12, 176n23, 180n12, 189n6
Latin American Boom, 1, 154
Lefevere, André, 1, 98–99
Leopoldo Lugones (Borges and Edelberg),
    121
"Leopoldo Lugones, Romancero"
    (Borges), 121, 167n1
Levine, Stuart and Susan, 129; The Short
    Fiction of Edgar Allan Poe, 105, 189n9
"Leyes de la narración policial" (Borges),
    55, 58, 59, 180n14
"libro, El" (Borges), 48, 178n2
"Ligeia" (Poe): confessional style of,
    198n27; Hungarian and German
    references in, 197n24; lost female
    presence lamented in, 178n29;
    supernatural and, 50, 86, 186n11;
    theme of doubling and, 127; witchcraft
    in, 133

literary history, 159–60, 171n22, 188n30
"literatura argentina en París, La"
    (Zoltowaska), 52
"literatura fantástica, La" (Borges), 125,
    195n10
Littmann, Enno, 73
Loewenstein, C. Jared, 27, 162, 164, 173n9,
    202–03nn13–14, 203n16
logic and order in creative writing, 29–31
"Loss of Breath" (Poe): in Borges-Poe
    dynamic of reciprocal influence, 13,
    17; Freudian interpretation of, 189n9;
    hanging scene in and deletion from,
    18, 105, 110–12, 118; likelihood
    Borges read lengthy version of, 118;
    literary critics on, 105; Mr. Blackwood
    Blackwood's tale and, 191n19;
    premature burial in, 189n7, 191n19;
    publication history of, 104–05, 191n18;
    relationship to Borges's "Funes el
    memorioso" and "El Aleph," 18,
    103–19, 159
"lotería en Babilonia, La" ["The Lottery in
    Babylon"] (Borges), 119
Lowell, James Russell, 174n12
Lugones, Leopoldo: Borges's reaction to,
    2, 11–12, 121, 167n1; as modernista
    writer, 2; Quiroga and, 3; in La vida
    literaria (journal), 178n30

Mabbott, Thomas Ollive: on "The Black
    Cat," 133, 198n25, 198n29; on "The
    Cask of Amontillado," 150, 193nn2–3;
    on criminal primate, 180n18; on Flying
    Dutchman legend in Poe's writing,
    128; on "Hop-Frog," 201n52; on "Loss
    of Breath" in multiple versions, 105;
    on "Metzengerstein," 129, 197n19,
    197n21, 197n23; noting changes
    in Poe's editions and manuscripts,
    188n2, 191n18; on Poe's fondness
    for cats, 198n25; on Poe's revenge on
    critics, 193n2; two-volume scholarly
    edition of Poe's tales and sketches
    compiled by, 103
Madden, Fred, 198n28
Magical Realism and the Fantastic
    (Chanady), 123

Plato, 32, 34, 35, 59, 172n7
Pluto (cat character). *See* "Black Cat, The"
Poe, Edgar Allan: commemorations of,
154, 159; compared with Emerson,
170n17; confessional style, use of,
198n27; death of, 177n27; deceased
wife of, 178n29; education at University
of Virginia, 161, 202n11; fondness for
cats, 198n25; as genius, 42–43, 170n17;
grudges and literary fights of, 120,
193n2; on Hawthorne, 25; mirrors,
fear of, 47; neurosis and alcoholism of,
40; reliance on intellect, 32, 172n7; as
romantic classicist, 32; as southerner, 6.
See also Borges, Jorge Luis: fiction of,
compared with Poe's; *and specific titles*
—influence of: on Borges, 1–2, 5,
8–10, 14, 155; Borges's ranking of
Poe's works, 44, 159, 163; Buenos
Aires translation frenzy, 44, 152;
contemporary literature's debt to, 23,
154–55; on French literary tradition,
23; on *modernistas*, 2, 11–12, 23, 38,
68; during Poe's lifetime, 1; reframing
Poe's image in Spanish America,
12–15, 19, 40, 45, 98–99, 152, 153,
155, 159, 169n14, 177–78nn28–29,
181n20; in U.S. literary history, Borges's
assessment of, 159–61; visibility of Poe
as person exceeding any of his writing,
156, 177n28; worldwide, 160, 170n17,
189n9
Poe Abroad (Vines), 45
"Poe in Spanish America" (Woodbridge), 45
poemas de Edgar Poe, Los (Obligado), 40,
44–45, 177n25
Poe Poe Poe Poe Poe Poe Poe (Hoffman),
105, 189n9
"poesía, La" (Borges), 34–35, 47, 119,
167n4, 175n19
"Poetic Principle, The" (Poe), 172n2,
172n5, 175n16
poetry: Borges's preference for Poe's prose
over his poetry, 23–24, 38–39, 41–42,
45–46, 47, 59, 153, 160, 163, 178n31;
effect, use in, 25, 35, 167n2; "long
poems do not exist," 172n2, 172n5;
Poe's description of creating, 25–26,

34, 175n15; Whitman compared with
Poe, 62, 160
premature burial. *See* burial
"Premature Burial, The" (Poe), 191n20
Prensa, La (Buenos Aires newspaper), 5,
27, 48, 53
Price, Vincent, 150–51, 193n3
"príncipe feliz, El" ["The Happy Prince"
by Wilde] (trans. Borges), 67
"Prólogo a Adolfo Bioy Casares, *La
invención de Morel*" (Borges),
193–94n6
"Prólogo a Edgar Allan Poe, *Cuentos*"
(Borges), 126, 127–28, 177n27
"Prólogo a Edgar Allan Poe, *La carta
robada*" (Borges), 127, 177n28
"Prólogo a Wilkie Collins, *La piedra
lunar*" (Borges), 178n3
"Prólogo de prólogos" (Borges), 48,
192n28
Prólogos, con un prólogo de prólogos
(Borges), 117
prologue as genre, 192n28
psychoanalytic approach to Poe, 105,
133–34, 189n9
"Purloined Letter, The" (Poe): Baudelaire's
French translation of, Borges's
familiarity with, 92, 187n22; blindness
in, 37; Borges's notes on, 95, 180n15;
Borges's opinion of, 44; Borges's
prologue to, 62; Borges's translation
of (with Bioy Casares) ["La carta
robada"], 2, 9, 17, 67, 75–76, 81,
89–99, 152, 153, 185n1, 202n4; "La
carta robada" (ed. Bazán), 187nn18–
20, 187–88nn23–25, 188nn28–29;
"La carta robada" (trans. Olivera),
187nn18–20, 187–88nn23–25,
188nn28–29; Derrida's interpretation
of, 12; Dupin portrayal in, 32, 89–99;
envelope introduced into Borges's
translation, 89, 96–98, 188n29; focus
on *how* over *whom* in, 57; influence on
Borges's own writing, 25; Kristal
on Borges's translation of, 181n1;
Lacan's interpretation of, 176n23,
189n6; monetary reward, treatment
in translations of, 93–94, 188n24;

nature of crimes in, 58; plot changes in translation of, 89, 97–98; relationship to "The Raven," 38; suspects in, 56

Works of Edgar Allan Poe (II), The (ed. Ingram), 117

The New Southern Studies

The Nation's Region: Southern Modernism, Segregation, and U.S. Nationalism
by Leigh Anne Duck

Black Masculinity and the U.S. South: From Uncle Tom to Gangsta
by Riché Richardson

Grounded Globalism: How the U.S. South Embraces the World
by James L. Peacock

*Disturbing Calculations: The Economics of Identity in Postcolonial
Southern Literature, 1912–2002*
by Melanie R. Benson

American Cinema and the Southern Imaginary
edited by Deborah E. Barker and Kathryn McKee

*Southern Civil Religions: Imagining the Good Society in the
Post-Reconstruction Era*
by Arthur Remillard

Reconstructing the Native South: American Indian Literature and the Lost Cause
by Melanie Benson Taylor

Apples and Ashes: Literature, Nationalism, and the Confederate States of America
by Coleman Hutchison

Reading for the Body: The Recalcitrant Materiality of Southern Fiction, 1893–1985
by Jay Watson

Latining America: Black-Brown Passages and the Coloring of Latino/a Studies
by Claudia Milian

Finding Purple America: The South and the Future of American Cultural Studies
by Jon Smith

The Signifying Eye: Seeing Faulkner's Art
by Candace Waid

*Sacral Grooves, Limbo Gateways: Travels in Deep Southern Time,
Circum-Caribbean Space, Afro-creole Authority*
by Keith Cartwright

Jim Crow, Literature, and the Legacy of Sutton E. Griggs
edited by Tess Chakkalakal and Kenneth W. Warren

Sounding the Color Line: Music and Race in the Southern Imagination
by Erich Nunn

Borges's Poe: The Influence and Reinvention of Edgar Allan Poe in Spanish America
by Emron Esplin

Eudora Welty's Fiction and Photography: The Body of the Other Woman
by Harriet Pollack

Keywords for Southern Studies
edited by Scott Romine and Jennifer Rae Greeson